European Military Riv:
1500–1750

European Military Rivalry, 1500–1750: Fierce Pageant examines more than 200 years of international rivalry across Western, Central, and Eastern Europe and the Mediterranean rim.

The book charts the increasing scale, expenditure and duration of early modern wars; the impact of modern fortification on strategy and the movement of armies; the incidence of guerrilla war and localized conflict typical of the French wars of religion; the recourse by warlords to private financing of troops and supplies; and the creation of disciplined standing armies and navies in the age of Absolutism, made possible by larger bureaucracies. In addition to discussing key events and personalities of military rivalry during this period, the book describes the operational mechanics of early modern warfare and the crucial role of taxation and state borrowing. The relationship between the Christian West and the Ottoman Empire is also extensively analysed.

Drawing heavily upon international scholarship over the past half-century, *European Military Rivalry, 1500–1750: Fierce Pageant* will be of great use to undergraduate students studying military history and early modern Europe.

Gregory Hanlon is a French-trained behavioural historian. His books include *The Hero of Italy* (2014), *Italy 1636: Cemetery of Armies* (2016), and *Twilight of a Military Tradition: Italian aristocrats and European conflicts 1560–1800* (1998), winner of the Marraro Prize for Italian history.

European Military Rivalry, 1500–1750

Fierce Pageant

Gregory Hanlon

Routledge
Taylor & Francis Group

LONDON AND NEW YORK

First published 2020
by Routledge
2 Park Square, Milton Park, Abingdon, Oxon OX14 4RN

and by Routledge
52 Vanderbilt Avenue, New York, NY 10017

Routledge is an imprint of the Taylor & Francis Group, an informa business

British Library Cataloguing-in-Publication Data
A catalogue record for this book is available from the British Library

Library of Congress Cataloging-in-Publication Data
Names: Hanlon, Gregory, 1953- author.
Title: European military rivalry, 1500-1750 : fierce pageant / Gregory Hanlon.
Description: Abingdon, Oxon : Routledge, 2020. | Includes bibliographical references and index.
Identifiers: LCCN 2019058834 (print) | LCCN 2019058835 (ebook) | ISBN 9781138368972 (hbk) | ISBN 9781138368989 (pbk) | ISBN 9780429428913 (ebk)
Subjects: LCSH: Europe–History, Military–1492-1648. | Europe–History, Military–1648-1789.
Classification: LCC D214 .H35 2020 (print) | LCC D214 (ebook) | DDC 355.0094/0903–dc23
LC record available at https://lccn.loc.gov/2019058834
LC ebook record available at https://lccn.loc.gov/2019058835

ISBN: 978-1-138-36897-2 (hbk)
ISBN: 978-1-138-36898-9 (pbk)
ISBN: 978-0-429-42891-3 (ebk)

Typeset in Galliard
by Swales & Willis, Exeter, Devon, UK

To three generations of Italian military historians: Virgilio Ilari (Rome), Mario Zannoni (Parma), Giovanni Cerino Badone (Milan), and to their posterity.

Contents

Maps, charts, and table

Maps

Charts

Table

Images

Preface

It has been almost 30 years since a proper textbook in English on European warfare in the early modern period has appeared. The works commissioned by John Keegan and including the book by John Childs have been out of print for years. Textbooks are not merely works of synthesis: they pose their own special challenges for the author. The first problem is to choose the best altitude, like a drone hovering overhead. Too high up, much of the important detail is absent or illegible to the novice reader. Too low, and there is no way to fit essential information to the length of the book. The period of analysis selected here, roughly 1500 to 1750, precludes in-depth analysis, but it allows us to begin with the Renaissance innovations resulting from mobile artillery and hand-held firearms, and conclude with the period of relative stasis after the early eighteenth century. We must identify a place to study, too. European ways of warfare must include the greater part of the continent by population, and, above all, include the Ottoman world and North African periphery that constituted a real menace. A book dealing with Europeans around the world has its own virtues, but to study it here would make the project unwieldy.

Another set of choices revolves around two opposing strategies: to recount the story of European conflicts as they unfolded over a quarter-millennium, or else adopt a thematic approach that glosses over specific events. The second has been the strategy adopted by many previous authors, particularly when constrained by space. In the number of pages allotted here, I will attempt to do both: three or four large chapters deal as comprehensively as possible with periods of military history that seem to have their own coherence, each followed by chapters dealing with important themes. This allows me to encapsulate the great majority of the international contests taking place over the period, with the exception of internecine warfare in the Baltic zone. Russia made its entry on to the European stage only in the eighteenth century. The book also brings maritime history into the picture, both in the form of national fleets and navies as long-term institutions, and the important aspect of privatized naval warfare in the form of corsairs.

New syntheses have the duty of updating the literature by introducing the revisions brought by scholars in the field. This entails challenging received ideas that are difficult to dismiss, but that constitute the very rationale of original detailed research following rules of evidence and empirical knowledge. There are degrees of certainty and the laws of empirical demonstration assist immensely in separating what we can know with a reasonable level of confidence from mere speculation or patriotic cant. I also stress the importance of scholarly works based on archival research, which introduces its own flavour. The book is not overly concerned with historiography and will probably betray deep misgivings about the importance of intellectual history. It posits that the thesis of the Military Revolution has been argued to an inconclusive end, and so needs no further elaboration here. Historiographies are often steeped in national traditions, which this book eschews. On the other hand it will exhort students and scholars to focus new research in specific areas where this is crucially wanting. On some topics and some conflicts there already exists a rich and abundant literature. In other important areas, we still lack good scholarly studies. Finally, I would like to plead the reader's indulgence whenever a useful and perhaps important book has not been cited. The potential bibliography of works pertinent to military history over a quarter-millennium is huge and growing daily, and far surpasses the ability of a single scholar to be familiar with them all. This overview draws on a wide-ranging literature in four languages, listed in the ample bibliography. Instructors who use the book as a reference text are indeed invited to add readings of their choice to the corpus cited here.

Military history has been identified with tribalism from the outset of its long existence. This is a particularly difficult challenge to overcome, even for someone not belonging to a country with a long military tradition. Care has been taken to consult authors who have taken the trouble to examine conflicts from the point of view of both belligerents, without sorting them into camps of good and bad. The best antidote to tribalism and historiographical provincialism is to read works in several languages and to exhort ambitious students to do so also, as much as possible.

Today, military history has returned to the academic mainstream from the relative wilderness. For this to continue, historians must balance their specialized knowledge with information drawn from other disciplines, such as anthropology, psychology and demography. I find much important inspiration in neo-Darwinian theory, as manifested in human and animal ethology. Humans are social animals born with evolved instincts and behavioural predispositions that are common to societies throughout time and across space. Social environments – or historical contexts – change considerably but the human behavioural repertoire is impressively stable over time, notwithstanding myriad attempts to break free of it. Violent conflict is one of these, and understanding its evolution over time is an important intellectual project.

A number of colleagues have provided answers to my questions, sounding boards for my ideas, and sources of suggestions for further research; in no particular order they are Fadi el-Hage, Philippe Hamon, Denis Crouzet, Jean-Philippe Cénat, Hervé Drévillon, Serge Brunet, Bertrand Fonck, Thierry Sarmant, Roberto Barazzutti, Jean-Marie Le Gall, Frédéric Chauviré, Stéphane Gal, Giuliano Ferretti, Lucien Bély and Clément Oury in France, Mario Zannoni, Mario Rizzo,

Luciano Pezzolo, Stefano Condorelli, Vigilio Ilari and Giovanni Cerino Badone in Italy, Guy Rowlands, David Parrott, Mark Greengrass, Steve Murdoch and Padraig Lenihan in the United Kingdom and Ireland, Raymond Fagel in the Netherlands, Zoltan Peter Bagi in Hungary, and Yoko Kitada in Japan. The base maps provided here are courtesy of my geographer Dalhousie colleague, James Baxall, and especially his research assistant, Lama Farhat. To all, my fulsome thanks.

1 Renaissance innovations

The logic of conquest

Medieval life was resolutely local for the vast majority of the population, reliant on autarchy for the maintenance of justice and for defence against predators. European kings might reign over large political entities, but their power rested on a host of local mediators whose allegiance could not be taken for granted. Most medieval conflicts unfolded within large states – and the actors included bishops and monasteries, knights and towns, guarding a multitude of defensive structures, such as castles, mills, bridges and churches, against a wide array of threats, from bandit gangs to rebellious lords, as well as armies invading from abroad. Medieval campaigns were conceived to inflict as much damage as possible to the enemy's resources, without stopping to besiege towns and castles in a systematic manner. This *chevauchée* war rewarded its participants with animals, captives for ransom, the arms and armour of vanquished opponents, and punished the enemy warlord by setting fire to his farms and fields. 'War without fire is like sausages without mustard: it has no value!' King Henry V of England once exclaimed. Defence against predation of this sort was, above all, self-defence; villagers assembled to defend their hearths and their livestock, under the direction of their lords. Monarchs without charisma found themselves hamstrung for resources, and their great subjects might ally themselves with foreign rulers. Most of the earlier medieval kings were umpires rather than autocrats, who arbitrated the competing interests of the elites under their wardship. In Western Europe, the advent of rulers who were able to emerge stronger than any coalition of their subjects dates largely from the late fourteenth or the fifteenth centuries.[1] For a long time after, a coalition of warlords seeking vindication of their rights could make large states limit their ambitions.

When they finally emerged, European states engaged in an ongoing 'tournament' of war against each other, a series of contests with a constantly-changing array of participants who sought to achieve their goals of expansion.[2] The ambitions of kings to dominate their neighbours were often a prime mover in the genesis of wars, fed by concepts of honour and glory, but this could lead to a sort of social Darwinism of international competition using war as its process.[3] Honour and glory are sometimes thought to be motives in themselves, but behind the ideological reasons, one should seek more tangible underpinnings for armed conflict. For monarchs, war and expansion appeared not merely possible, but *necessary* if the realm were to survive in the longer term. Size mattered: opting out of territorial expansion would not be sensible in the long run, for a peaceful state would eventually become the target of an ambitious neighbour. Rulers sought simultaneously to gain territory and to consolidate their authority within it, both of which increased their profile among princes.[4] Rulers of smaller states had every interest in broadcasting their readiness to defend their lands and interests by force or arms, in order to dissuade all but the mightiest of foes. They were careful to erect powerful castles, make strategic alliances (usually through marriage) and to have on hand a war-chest of ready cash to hire soldiers.

When laying out the chronology of war for the six principal powers of Europe between 1494 and 1750, the sobering conclusion is that war dominated the history of states. If one were to combine the years of international conflict with those of major rebellions, and to consider only those of some considerable scale (that is, not counting small-scale colonial operations), not a single 'country' was at peace for half the 257 years under consideration. Great Britain stood largely free of continental entanglements from the end of the Hundred Years' War in 1453 until the Dutch *coup d'état* in 1688, but it was still at war 52% of the time. French kings managed wars against myriad adversaries for 57% of the years encompassed here. Measuring 185 years, beginning with the first rebellion against Spain, the Netherlands was at war for 62% of the time until 1750. The German Habsburgs waged wars almost two years out of three, at 64%, against the Ottomans, against the French, the Swedes and Hungarian insurgents. The Ottoman Empire fought major wars against its neighbours, both Christian and Islamic, for almost three-quarters of this quarter-millennium, at 72%. Spain's rulers fought primarily defensive wars, but these spanned 72% of the years also (see Chart 1).

No state was more ambitious than France, Europe's most populous single state until the unification of Germany in 1870. After ejecting the English from the continent in 1453 (English monarchs claimed the French crown until the nineteenth century), French kings recovered breakaway Burgundy in 1477, brought Provence into the realm in 1480 and forcibly subdued Brittany in 1488, with singular consistency of policy aimed at reducing feudal autonomy. They then turned their attention to expanding the kingdom abroad, with the ultimate aim of restoring Christian rule to Constantinople and the Middle East.[5] The dukes of Milan and Ferrara actively solicited King Charles VIII to intervene in Italy, confident that they could manipulate the French monarch to their advantage against their local rivals. The Kingdom of Naples was disputed for most of the fourteenth century and much of the fifteenth between a French royal house (the Angevins, descending from the ducal Anjou branch of the reigning Valois dynasty) and the Aragonese of Spain, who recovered the kingdom in 1442 and held it until the death of King Ferrante in 1494. Charles saw the opportunity to make good on his legal claim to the kingdom and gathered a great army to take possession of it.

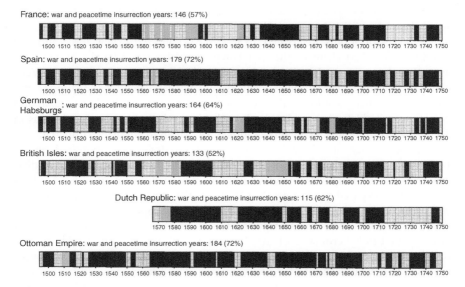

France: war and peacetime insurrection years: 146 (57%)

Spain: war and peacetime insurrection years: 179 (72%)

Gernman Habsburgs: war and peacetime insurrection years: 164 (64%)

British Isles: war and peacetime insurrection years: 133 (52%)

Dutch Republic: war and peacetime insurrection years: 115 (62%)

Ottoman Empire: war and peacetime insurrection years: 184 (72%)

Chart 1 Military chronology of European powers 1494–1750

The invasion of Italy by Charles VIII and the march of the French to Naples in 1494 triggered a period of momentous conflict lasting over two generations. By their duration and their scale, these Italian Wars (1494–1559) inaugurated a new period in European military history and spurred a number of innovations whose effects would play out over the entire world for centuries. Until then, Italian states competed with each other in short armed contests punctuated by modest battles that did not alter the balance of power. In the absence of any overall monarch protecting the rights of the weaker states against the strong, northern and central Italy experienced a rapid reduction in the number of autonomous city-states, numbering circa 100 in 1300, but only a handful of larger territorial states survived two centuries later. By the late fifteenth century, the five largest powers (Milan, Venice, Florence, the Papacy and Naples) could each maintain an army of 10,000 men without excessive strain. King Charles, with an army of 30,000 men and a collection of 40 siege cannon overwhelmed them all 'in a kind of blitzkrieg', accompanied by an excess of terroristic violence to which they were not accustomed.[6] Most Italian states submitted temporarily to an army they could not stop with their own resources. Charles then treated the kingdom of Naples as conquered territory – that is, he ruled without recognizing pre-existing institutions and power relations – but, since he never intended to take up residence there, he returned home after a few short months. In the interval, several Italian states, including Mantua and the Republic of Venice, coalesced with the intention of destroying his army on its return home. They were bested at the River Taro fording of Fornovo, near Parma; Charles was lucky to escape, and he quickly lost control of Naples to several weak claimants of the Aragonese dynasty.

His successor, Louis XII (ruled 1498–1515), collected a new force and, for good measure, laid claim to the rich Duchy of Milan ruled by the Sforza dynasty. French armies in Lombardy also asserted claims on Genoa and the Venetian Terraferma (the Republic's territory on solid land behind the lagoon) and troops based there would be able to reach Naples more easily. Both Milan and Naples were held for a time by the French king, whose territorial ambitions in 1501 seemed limitless. The Sforza dukes of Milan recognized Imperial, not French, suzerainty, and Louis's claims to northern Italy were contested by the Habsburg Holy Roman Emperor, Maximilian I. The heir to the Aragonese dynasty in southern Italy, Ferdinand of Aragon (whose domains included Sardinia and Sicily), prepared to recover Naples from the invaders. Ferdinand and his wife, Queen Isabella of Castile, united the various Spanish realms following their marriage in 1469 and conquered the last remaining Muslim kingdom of Granada in 1492. Ferdinand's battle-hardened professional army quickly ejected the French from Naples in 1503 and restored the Spanish connection to southern Italy that would endure for two centuries. The French enjoyed a brief success against their Venetian adversaries for control over Lombardy, but the combination of Venice, the Pope Julius II, the Emperor Maximilian, the Spanish and the Swiss confederacy proved too strong. Despite winning the bloody battle of Ravenna in 1512, a defeat at Novara the next year precipitated a new French retreat from Italy.

In 1515, the young King François I led a new invasion of Lombardy that confronted the hostile Swiss just south of Milan at Melagnano (Marignan). The ponderous Swiss pike phalanxes were on the point of overwhelming the French foot and horse in their entrenchments on the second day of fighting when Venetian allies arrived on their flank and drove them off. Scores of French cannon had already inflicted grievous losses on the attackers. Newly ensconced in Lombardy, François dreamed of marching on Naples, too, but had to renounce the project for the time being in order to repel the German army of emperor Maximilian. Battles in Italy were on a much grander scale than before, with larger and more diverse armies, and thanks to the appearance of field artillery and musketry, they were much more bloody, too. Soldiers from Italy, France, Spain, Germany and Switzerland took the measure of each other in constantly shifting alliances. The wars were a proving-ground for modern weaponry and new tactical formations that combined polearms with musketeers.[7] Over the first two decades, commanders tried different combinations of weapons and tactics by trial and error. Swiss blocks consisting of thousands of disciplined pikemen marching in unison fought musket-wielding armoured cavalry, and confronted batteries of cannon aligned behind entrenchments.[8]

The struggle amplified still more after 1519 when young King Charles I of Spain inherited the Holy Roman Empire from his German Habsburg grandfather. Now the Habsburg monarch controlled three composite realms: 1: the

Germanic Imperial title and its Austrian heartland north of the Alps, 2: the Burgundian inheritance of the combined Low Countries from his father (modern Belgium, Netherlands, Luxembourg, northern France and the Franche-Comté of Burgundy), and 3: the united Spanish kingdoms acquired from his maternal grandparents, (Castile, Aragon, then Navarre in 1512) including Sardinia, Sicily and Naples. These combined possessions of the Emperor Charles V (German numbering) were now at least the equal of his French opponent. The wars then spread from Italy to theatres in the Pyrenees and Northern Europe, where the king of England, Henry VIII, was an intermittent Habsburg ally hoping to conquer France from his base in Calais.

French armies invaded Italy anew in 1521 under the Vicomte de Lautrec, and held Milan briefly before they were ejected from it again in 1522. King François I, unwilling to concede defeat, led a new army into Lombardy at the end of 1524. He was laying siege to Pavia in the winter of 1525 when an Imperial force under Charles de Lannoy attacked his army from the rear. Spanish arquebusiers fighting as skirmishers disorganized the French heavy cavalry and prevented it from deploying effectively. The French monarch was captured in the close fighting that followed, and was compelled in the ensuing negotiations to cede all his claims in Italy, and extensive lands in eastern France as well, to Charles V. After returning home, the king repudiated the treaty, and prepared a new Italian expedition. Pope Clement VII Medici, an important French ally, was unable to prevent the unfurling of Imperial troops over northern Italy. A German army swelled by Spanish and Italian deserters hungry for booty then seized and sacked Rome itself in 1527. A French army under Lautrec came very close to capturing Naples with a new invasion in 1528, but the Republic of Genoa, a key ally that ensured the French army's supply by sea, changed sides during the siege and Lautrec's force melted away due to disease and desertion. The advantage of war in Italy gradually passed to the Habsburg ruler. The Medici Pope and the emperor struck a bargain to replace the fractious Florentine republic with a Medici principality in 1530 that would be anchored in the Imperial alliance. As emperor, Charles V also enjoyed the right to designate the heir to any state in the Empire without a legal successor. The last Sforza Duke of Milan died childless in 1535, so Charles added the strategic duchy to his own territories and planted a permanent garrison of Spaniards there. After 1530, the monarch maintained about 3,000 to 4,000 Spaniards each in Lombardy, Naples and Sicily, strengthening the territories against a new French invasion. These troops also facilitated the mobilization of money, food and weapons from these rich territories for the Habsburg cause.[9]

After a brief pause in the fighting, a new French army overran the duchy of Savoy and Piedmont in an offensive towards Milan in 1536 but it could advance no farther. But the momentum was quickly lost as the king withdrew troops to defend his borders with the Habsburgs north of the Alps. Emperor Charles passed into southern France the same year but failed to capture Marseille. A counteroffensive the next year saw the French recover Savoy and most of Piedmont, which, by the peace of 1538, were annexed without much in the way of a legal claim. François I renewed the wars in 1542, this time assisted by a controversial formal alliance with the Ottoman Empire. The Moslem fleet wintered in Provence over 1543–1544, which enabled it to strike the coasts of Spain and Italy more easily. French troops (and their Swiss mercenaries) were by now engaged in multiple theatres from Roussillon in the eastern Pyrenees to Scotland, which was a reliable French ally against England. In 1542, the French king might have employed 100,000 soldiers, spread across several field armies and many far-flung garrisons.[10] French obstinacy compelled Emperor Charles, who similarly was an active field commander, to mobilize matching men and resources. The English King Henry VIII was a willing Habsburg ally in northern France but his improvised armies proved ineffectual. Charles was also compelled to confront the problem of German Protestant princes, who, from the 1520s, frequently allied themselves with the French. Turkish progress in Hungary also diverted Habsburg resources towards Central Europe, and Moslem corsairs in the Mediterranean tied down many thousands of men.

The next French king, Henri II (1547–1559), a *roi de guerre* (to use Joël Cornette's phrase) like his father, placed more emphasis on fighting the Habsburgs in eastern France and the Low Countries, although he did not entirely neglect his armies in Piedmont. By the 1540s, however, the progress in modern fortification slowed down the advance of field armies considerably. Battles were more frequent and decisive in the initial period of the Italian wars, when a victorious army could advance hundreds of kilometres towards the main objective. Now breakthroughs became rarer and were less likely to bring an end to the fighting when they did occur. Fortifications made it difficult for the Habsburgs to eject the French from Piedmont, from which they could attract Italian allies. During the 1550s, France obtained enough support from the upstart Farnese dynasty in Parma, from the rebellious Sienese Republic and from the Carafa Pope Paul IV to seriously distract the Habsburg dynasty. Charles was resolved to yield no ground to his French opponent.

Neither was the emperor ready to concede legal toleration to the Lutheran Protestants who had gained control over most of Germany. In 1547, Charles V personally led his Catholic army to victory over the Lutheran Schmalkaldic League at Mühlberg, but his triumph was short-lived. The defeated princes formed a new alliance with the French king in January 1552, and the diversion enabled French armies to occupy much of the duchy of Lorraine (part of the Holy Roman Empire) the same year. In 1555, Charles and his brother Ferdinand, who co-ordinated Habsburg policies in Germany, agreed to a compromise Peace of Augsburg, which recognized the right of each prince (or city-state) to determine the official religion of each of the hundreds of constituent territories of the Holy Roman Empire. Habsburg territories in Bohemia and Austria were to remain officially in the Catholic fold.

The difficulty in facing so many challengers finally induced an ageing Charles V to abdicate both the Imperial and Spanish thrones in 1556 and to divide his huge patrimony into two unequal parts. The Imperial title and the Habsburg hereditary patrimony in Central Europe (increased in 1526 by lands in Hungary and the rich kingdom of Bohemia) passed to his brother Ferdinand, who had spent his adult life in Germany as a faithful lieutenant. The larger segment of Habsburg territory (the Low Countries and the Franche Comté of eastern Burgundy, the Italian territories of Sicily, Sardinia, Naples and Milan, the kingdoms in Spain and the rapidly growing conquests in the Americas) passed to his son Philip II, who identified as a Castilian. Both branches of the Habsburg, in Germany and Spain, would remain natural allies, which they reinforced generation after generation through consanguine marriages.

The Imperial and Florentine siege of Siena prompted Pope Paul IV to join France in a new Italian war, but the Spanish general Alva overwhelmed him before he had the chance to mobilize his troops. By the time of the capitulation of Siena (1555) almost all the Italian princes rallied to the new king of Spain, Philip II, making French claims unrealistic for the time being. The shattering defeat of the French army at St Quentin in northern France in 1557 was the signal for a gradual de-escalation of hostilities. In the last campaign of 1558, France seized Calais, the sole English possession on the continent, and Henri II consolidated his hold over three small territories in French-speaking Lorraine, but he was forced to relinquish all his conquests in Italy save the Alpine fortress of Saluzzo, a convenient gateway. No one could foresee that the treaty of Câteau Cambrésis in 1559 was anything more than a truce, like the previous peace accords. Christian Europe remained a multi-polar system with no one power able to enjoy hegemony over the continent. The French Valois kings and the Habsburg dynasty were two superpowers still fairly evenly balanced. Of 100 significant military encounters over a half-century of fighting, the French won 47 (mostly in the early period) and lost 53.[11]

The advent of gunpowder warfare

As these wars became increasingly international, Italian forces fought outside the peninsula in expeditionary forces under their own commanders. The first mercenary companies were levied by independent contractors called *condottieri* (a *condotta* was a licence to recruit troops) who served employers whose strategic aims they shared. A successful *condottiere* could hope to rise socially in wealth and status, while one who already controlled a territory could enlarge it, and receive generous subsidies from patrons who required his services. The Marches, Romagna and Umbria in North-Central Italy gave birth to a great many of these warlords, who could supply veteran soldiers willing to fight away from home. Regional princes like the Montefeltro Dukes of Urbino who received such largesse could shower money on their feudal warriors.

The French armies employed a preponderance of heavy cavalry organized in small units called 'lances', whereby each armoured *gendarme* (man-at-arms) would bring several foot-soldiers who fought separately from them. Larger organizations of infantrymen, such as the Gascons from South-western France, also wore heavy armour, a legacy of medieval combat. Learning from their experience fighting the Burgundians, the French hired large contingents of Swiss pikemen, who were the most fearsome infantry of the era. Pikes were long poles over 5 metres in length, which were a big improvement over spears and halberds. Used individually, pikes were useless, but they were formidable weapons when wielded by troops who were taught to employ them in unison. These weapons required drill and a powerful social cohesion within the phalanx, achieved by recruiting men from specific cantons in Switzerland.[12] The *landsknecht* infantry emerged in Southern Germany in the 1480s as disciples of the Swiss, but as their quality was lower they were notably cheaper. As an association of professional soldiers, master craftsmen of combat, they were tightly organized and delegated power to committees negotiating working conditions with their commanders. Like the Swiss, they might lay down their weapons and go on strike if they were unhappy with their pay and conditions.[13] More so than other contingents, they were followed by large numbers of civilians, including women and children, who slowed down their movement. The French hired them periodically in Northern Europe, as well as contingents of Italians and Scots. Field armies employed a variety of ethnic contingents whose national pride constituted part of their *esprit de corps*. Militia organizations raised by cities and provincial peasant levies were no match for these professionals, even if they were well armed.

Spanish professional armies were founded by a series of royal decrees between 1492 and 1503 in the aftermath of the Granada war. These were typically recruited from Spain's central provinces of Castile, and up to 15% of them might have been of noble birth. Between 1520 and 1550, in the complete absence of conscription or impressment, 180,000 Spaniards joined the colours.[14] Relative to the French, Spanish forces comprised a larger proportion of foot soldiers, who carried a higher number of hand-held firearms called arquebuses.[15] The tallest men were handed pikes and were drilled like the Swiss. All the soldiers carried swords and daggers for close combat.[16] The progressive diffusion of personal firearms drove many other changes. One of the main advantages of an arquebus (apart from the noise and the unnerving effect of unseen bullets whizzing by the ears of men, which was debilitating) was that it required little muscular ability or long training to employ it effectively, unlike bows. Its muzzle velocity was high enough to penetrate plate armour within a hundred metres. Cerignola (1503) was the first in a series of battles when the various weapons systems encountered each other. The French, Spaniards, Germans and Italians quickly combined cannon, entrenchments, arquebuses and pikes on the battlefield. The Spaniards also favoured light cavalry (a Spanish and Neapolitan speciality, developed in the wars against the Moors) over heavy lancers. Light cavalry served to protect the army from surprise, collected intelligence and assured the food supply. Light cavalry gradually adopted firearms too, with the troopers becoming adept in skirmishing on foot and on horseback.

By the 1520s, the matchlock arquebus (detonated when a burning cord was lowered on to the priming pan) became the primary missile weapon everywhere.

Large-scale manufacturing of these firearms in Southern Germany and in Northern Italy reduced their cost and made these weapons more widely available.[17] These early arquebusiers were soon deployed with pikemen in new combined-arms tactics. The French are reported to have employed rotating volley fire at Marignan in 1515, imitated by the Spanish at Bicocca in 1522, although it was not a standard tactic in that era. The Spanish formations were smaller and more mobile than the great pike phalanxes, and their principal superiority over the Swiss lay in their ability to decompose and recompose the formations of shot and pike into separate contingents.

The late medieval companies of soldiers were no longer adequate battlefield formations, and so larger infantry contingents comprising a collection of about ten companies emerged that Charles V recognized as *tercios* in 1536, that is, permanent administrative entities under the command of a colonel.[18] François I similarly formed his medieval companies into 'legions' in the early 1540s; both constituted the ancestors of modern regiments.[19] The decline of expensive heavy cavalry and their substitution by infantry and light horse enabled states to increase army sizes, although field armies larger than 35,000 men were rare and could be fed only with great difficulty.[20] By the 1550s, we see the ancestors of three standing, or permanent, armies in Spain, France and the Venetian Republic, offering stable long-term careers to officers and soldiers serving in them.

Cannon were increasingly numerous in armies as well, both in the form of smaller battlefield weapons and as heavy siege guns, which existed in a wide variety of calibres. The former tended to be defensive weapons, placed along entrenchments. They were especially effective when firing at large formations of foot, for a cannonball could kill everything in its path. French siege cannon were redoubtable weapons at the outset of the wars, capable of smashing down high city walls in a single day. But, with the development of bastioned fortifications and artillery towers, ever more numerous after the 1530s, fortresses could fire back. The sieges became much more lengthy and required larger armies; states hired garrisons of professional troops to defend their own strongholds and raised field armies able to besiege the enemy's fortresses for weeks or months. The guns, which were served by private artisans hired independently of the soldiers, required a great deal of hardware and ammunition, plus the services of thousands of civilian *pioneers* and transporters with their expensive horses.[21] These great guns slowed down the movement of armies considerably and the logistics for their service could not be improvised. All of these innovations constituted a body of new knowledge, of tactics, of ballistics, of logistical organization and military architecture.

Constant war spurs financial innovation

Erecting palaces and maintaining opulent courts constituted only a modest fraction of the expenditures of states, as did the cost of justice and tax collection. War was by far the principal outlay of kings and republics, either in the active pursuit of it, or paying in peace-time the interest on loans undertaken to wage previous conflicts. Soldiers were expected to purchase their food and pay for lodgings from the pay they received. Well-paid soldiers lived a glamorous life-style, owning horses and employing servants to take care of them, and further employed prostitutes and female camp followers who tended them in their quarters. When overextended treasuries could no longer pay the soldiers, men resorted to foraging and stealing from civilians, or had recourse to mutiny.[22] Armies could quickly dissolve if they were not well maintained.

To finance war, European governments were compelled to extend their taxation authority over their respective populations. Almost all monarchs negotiated with bodies of notables (such as the English Parliament), who consented to subsidize them, but these assemblies typically controlled the administrative machinery permitting tax assessment and collection. French kings were the first to establish permanent direct taxation (the *taille*) designed to finance companies of *gendarmes* during the later period of the Hundred Years War. They continued these after 1453 and then increased them during the first half of the sixteenth century, given that France was at war for 42 years between 1494 and 1559.[23] Not just the *taille*, but the salt *gabelle* (a tax on salt, a royal monopoly) and the *aides* (a whole host of indirect taxes) were increased in 1515 to finance François I's invasion of Italy. French monarchs also began to sell judicial offices to eligible candidates, called venal office-holding, and used the windfall cash to hire troops. In the 1550s, Henri II created new appeal court jurisdictions across the kingdom with the principal aim of raising money for the army. King Henry VIII of England, like other Protestant princes, seized the lands and buildings of monasteries and hurriedly auctioned them off in order to pay for his wars. It was also customary to assign the financing of fortification to the cities themselves, whose magistrates carried out these works over years and decades.

Kings also greatly increased their borrowing, particularly François I, who sold royal bonds paying 8⅓% interest out of the City Hall of Paris beginning in 1522, in a period of moderate inflation of 3–4% annually. City administrators collected the funds and passed them on to the royal treasury, which then paid out the interest or rent to lenders. François made five such loans, but Henri II made 30 more during his shorter reign, totalling seven million *livres tournois*, about six months' tax revenue. The bonds were only part of the monarchy's borrowing.[24] Florentine and Lucchese bankers who operated from Lyon kept the king's armies operational in Italy by dint of their loans of good coin that mercenary soldiers demanded.

Emperor Charles V, in order to meet the challenge, did not hesitate to mobilize resources from all his kingdoms to finance campaigns in particular places. Charles viewed his patrimony as a single entity, sending resources from one state to another as they were needed.[25] Charles spent money far beyond his revenues, and, like the kings of France, he learned to squeeze his subjects more tightly. This irked the assemblies such as the Iberian Cortés or the German Diets that were ordered to raise large sums to be spent in faraway places. The Pope periodically authorized the king to raise significant sums from the Spanish clergy, which was transformed into a regular levy after 1561.[26] Given the extreme decentralization of the Holy Roman Empire, and the Emperor's inability to compel every state to contribute to the war, the Imperial Diet created a subsidiary jurisdiction called the *Circle* (Kreise), which divided the great territory into ten smaller areas (not including Italy or Bohemia) that were responsible for collecting military resources. In 1521, these set out an assessment schedule for each state, which was periodically modified. States refusing to follow the majority decision within the Circle could be penalized by the others, partly solving the 'free rider' problem of German political fragmentation.[27]

Charles, like King François, also borrowed heavily from bankers by leasing them the rights to raise future tax revenues themselves. Each of the emperor's key realms employed procedures for marketing bonds secured by annual receipts of crown revenue. In fact, the long wars were only possible by developing smooth credit transfers between great banking houses in Germany (the *Fugger*) and Italy (increasingly Genoese) who employed agents across Europe to mobilize local credit on the sovereign's behalf.[28] The emperor, like French kings, also drew heavily on the good will and the resources of ambitious elites who spent their own money on his projects. Many regimental commanders in Southern Germany were military entrepreneurs who raised men on their own credit and offered them to the emperor's cause in the expectation of later reward. The feudal nobles of southern Italy were drawn more tightly into the Emperor's projects when they moved to Naples and relied on royal patronage to increase their revenues. Naples began to contribute more to wars after the failed French siege of 1528 and it quickly became a pillar of the Spanish empire.[29] Genoa's allegiance shifted to the Habsburg cause the same year, and the republic's bankers moved to Spain, where they quickly became indispensable.

By the 1550s, however, both France and the combined Habsburg realms were financially exhausted and could only continue the war through financial expedients. The Peace of Câteau-Cambrésis inaugurated an era of peace in Italy that lasted almost undisturbed until the 1620s. This was a period of unprecedented commercial and industrial prosperity and cultural influence for that country, but it was a *Pax Hispanica*, under the protective shadow of the Catholic Habsburg monarchy. The military innovations forged in the struggle for control of the peninsula would then spread to other theatres in the half-century that followed.

Notes

1 Jan Glete, 2010.
2 Philip T Hoffman, 2015: 16.
3 Jeremy Black, 2006: 9–10.
4 Black, 2006 : 57.
5 Jean-Louis Fournel and Jean-Claude Zancarini, 2003: 14.
6 Marco Pellegrini, 2009: 27.
7 Michael Mallett and Christine Shaw, 2012: 31.
8 Maurizio Arfaioli, 2005: 5.
9 James D. Tracy, 2002: 132.

10 David Potter, 2008: 63.
11 Potter, 2008: 208.
12 Jeremy Black, 2011: 38.
13 Reinhard Baumann, 1996: 134.
14 Idan Sherer, 2017: 29.
15 Luis A. Ribot Garcia, 1998: 43–81.
16 Réné Quatrefages, 1992: 191–204.
17 Mallett and Shaw, 2012: 177.
18 Tracy, 2002: 31.
19 Potter, 2008: 107.
20 Lauro Martines, 2013: 154.
21 John R Hale, 1998: 156.
22 Sherer, *Warriors for a Living*, 75, 106.
23 Potter, 2008: 3.
24 Olivier Poncet, 1996: 1079–81.
25 Tracy, 2002:101.
26 Henry Kamen, 2005: 91.
27 Peter H. Wilson, 2004: 183; Joachim Whaley, 2012: 354.
28 Tracy, 2002: 308.
29 Mallett and Shaw, 2012: 214.

2   Clash of civilizations 1550–1610

The Ottoman threat from Eastern Europe

Even more than Christian feudal states, the Ottoman Empire was designed for almost permanent warfare. The Sharia law justified war when it was waged against enemies of the faith, because expanding the domain of Islam was a pious end in itself.[1] Originating in Western Anatolia and with the conscious intention of replacing the Roman Empire with an Islamic one, the first Ottoman armies crossed the Dardanelles and erected a capital at Adrianopolis (modern Edirne) in 1369. After extending control over Bulgaria, Serbia, Bosnia and much of Albania in Europe, the Turkish sultans pressed eastward across Central Anatolia in the fifteenth century. Sultan Mehmet II captured Constantinople in 1453, moved his capital there, and invited both Christians and Muslims to restore the city's greatness. The Ottomans occupied most of Greece in the aftermath, and reduced the Romanian princes in the lower Danube regions of Wallachia and Moldavia to the status of tributary princes: that is, they were left to govern themselves, in exchange for formal subjection, permanent alliance and payment of an annual tribute in money and in kind. Grain, livestock and timber from the lower Danube area enabled Istanbul (Constantinople renamed) to become Europe's largest city in the course of the sixteenth century. With 600,000 inhabitants in 1600, it was also far more populous than any other city in the empire.

The Ottoman military threat to Western Europe in 1500 was very real. Large raiding parties galloped north out of Bosnia to make sweeps of booty and slaves in north-eastern Italy under Venetian jurisdiction. In 1480, a large Ottoman army disembarked at Otranto (at the bottom of the 'heel' of the Italian boot, closest to Albania) and devastated the entire region. They were about to occupy Southern Italy when Sultan Mehmet II died and the army re-embarked. In Asia, Ottoman conquests then spread eastward to cover most of Anatolia, but, early in the sixteenth century, the Turks encountered a bitter rival in the form of Safavid Persia, which embraced the Shi'ite strain of Islam. Shi'ism spilled out of Iran and into Mesopotamia, quickly spreading as far west as Lebanon, and then began to trickle into Anatolia, too. Ottoman Sultan Selim I the Grim (r. 1512–1520) led his firearm-wielding armies east to roll back the Safavid armies, which relied principally on mounted archers. Profiting from success at

Chaldiran in 1514, he marched south against the Mameluk Arab state, seizing first Syria in 1516, and then Egypt the following year. The lightning Ottoman conquest of the Arab lands increased the Empire's population by about 70%, and made the sultan, who claimed to be caliph, or steward of Sunni Islam in its entirety, the guardian of the Holy Cities of Mecca and Medina. Conquest of Egypt subsequently extended Ottoman influence along the entire northern coast of Africa and throughout the Red Sea.

Selim's son, Suleiman I the Magnificent (r. 1520–1566) inaugurated his reign with a long and costly siege of Rhodes, seat of the Knights of Saint John, whose sole purpose was to harass Islamic shipping in the Aegean Sea. The powerful fortress port was a constant threat to the sea lanes connecting Istanbul with Egypt, the Levant, and the pilgrimage routes to Arabia. The knights' surrender in 1522 enabled the young ruler to turn his ambitions westward, towards the strong feudal kingdom of Hungary. The Ottoman Empire might have numbered 12–13 million inhabitants at the time, compared to Hungary's population of 3.5 million.[2] The fortress of Belgrade was the first to fall in 1521, removing the obstacle to invasion of the great Danubian plain. In 1526, a strong Ottoman army marched north along the western bank of the river towards the Hungarian capital of Buda. Young King Laszlo hurriedly added feudal contingents to his modern mercenary force, but he advanced to fight the Turks before his Bohemian vassals arrived. Suleiman's army is purported to have numbered 87,000 men, of whom 37,000 were mounted *sipahis*, or armoured cavalry (Agoston estimates 60–70,000) fighting 24,000 Hungarians.[3] The Ottoman triumph at Mohacs on 29 August 1526, where the childless king of Hungary was slain, enabled the Turks to occupy Buda. Hungarian and Bohemian nobles elected Ferdinand of Austria (younger brother of Emperor Charles V) to be their king and, they hoped, saviour. Sultan Suleiman then marched another army farther up the Danube to lay siege to Vienna in 1529. Only the lateness of the siege (begun in September) prevented the Ottomans from spreading their conquests into Germany itself. At first, Suleiman treated Hungary as a vassal state with a king he designated, while detaching the region of Transylvania to form another satellite dependency. Ferdinand of Austria launched several fruitless invasions to recover the lost kingdom, from 1540 to 1542. The Ottomans captured the Danube fortress of Esztergom north of Buda, preventing the descent of the river by German armies, and then, in 1541, Suleiman annexed the Hungarian kingdom to the Ottoman domain. The Habsburgs clung to a narrow western rim of the kingdom, dubbed Royal Hungary, consisting of part of modern Croatia and most of Slovakia, and moved the capital to Pressburg (modern Bratislava) on the Danube close to Vienna. The Ottomans incorporated the conquered zone into the direct domain in 1540 and stationed a large garrison there. By the Treaty of Edirne in 1547, Ferdinand consented to pay a tribute to the sultan, and presented himself as a 'dutiful son' to the Islamic monarch.

The disparity of forces was exacerbated by the different ways the adversaries mobilized their military resources. In this period, referred to as the Ottoman 'classical' era, the sultan was an autocrat, who theoretically enjoyed total control over the lands and persons under his rule. Only Muslims (in theory) were allowed to bear arms in the Ottoman system. Deserving *sipahis* were granted jurisdiction, called a timar, over a sliver of the empire, which enabled them to serve on campaign with a handful of retainers, while the residue of the income was passed on to the central treasury. These timars were not hereditary and individuals moved from one to another quite frequently. Those who failed to present themselves to the army or send someone in their stead would be deprived of this revenue. This was very different from the Western feudal nobility, which cultivated the loyalty of vassals over generations in the same locality. There were tens of thousands of timars across the Empire, although some regions, such as Egypt, were exempt. Each sipahi brought, on average, five additional warriors to the camp. Timar levies are estimated to number 60,000 men in 1520 but perhaps 80–100,000 in 1600, though they were never all collected in one place. The sipahis themselves were mounted troops, well-armoured archers for the most part, fighting in the oriental manner, which entailed advancing and retreating individually, looking for the weak point in an enemy formation.

Alongside the mounted troops was an original category of troops called *janissaries*, who were technically slaves of the sultan, and not originally Muslim. The chances of promotion of these troops to high rank meant that these were no ordinary slaves. Janissaries were never sold to private persons, neither were they used for menial tasks after the initial period of training. They were paid in good coin and received periodic bonuses. After a decade or two, they could marry, acquire property and leave it to their heirs.[4] They were a full-time professional force, loyal only to the sultan, trained with modern weapons and disciplined on the march and in camp.[5] They wore little armour and took heavy losses in battle, but their numbers were continually replenished through a levy on Christian boys, called the *devshirme*. The lads were collected like a tax on Christian households, converted to Islam, marched to Istanbul and then trained in barracks. The devshirme raised about 200,000 Balkan boys (mostly Slavs) over two centuries, although not all were destined to be soldiers.[6] Janissaries numbered only about 7–10,000 men over most of the sixteenth century, although their numbers increased thereafter.[7] They were among the first corps to carry arquebuses, and there is evidence that they employed volley fire at Mohacs in 1526.[8] Like the horsemen, janissaries were also trained to use the short and powerful composite bow, and never entirely abandoned that weapon. In battle, the Ottomans anchored their line at the centre with an array of cannons, sometimes chained together to form a great barrier, with janissaries deployed around them in nine ranks or lines to provide rolling musketry fire. The sipahi cavalry were aligned on both flanks in a great half-moon formation, while light infantry and cavalry formed an advance skirmish line.[9]

In addition to the 'regular' contingents of sipahis and janissaries, Ottoman armies employed a variety of auxiliary troops, such as local militia detachments guarding the Danube river corridor. Ottoman armies on the march were preceded by a swarm of light cavalry, the *akinjis*, Muslims who served primarily to collect booty. Tatar light cavalry bands originating on the Crimean steppe often assisted them, but they created havoc in Ottoman lands as well as those of their enemies. Light cavalry were not very useful in open battle, but they pinned down the enemy in castles and fortified points over a vast area, sometimes 100 kilometres ahead of the main army. Europeans had good reason to fear them.

Indeed, raiding in search of livestock and slaves became a way of life over the vast area of Eastern Europe until the early eighteenth century. The Tatars relied on slavery as the pillar of their economy (Images 2.1 and 2.2), collecting them in the Crimea for sale abroad. In 1578, the slaves exported from there numbered about 17,000, mostly Russians, Poles, Ukrainians and Circassians.[10] To deter the raiders, the Russians built a great wall of logs across the steppe in the late sixteenth century, putting Moscow out of reach after 1571. Colonies of freemen called *Cossacks* patrolled the frontier and launched their own raids towards the Black Sea. Slaving campaigns against Russia and Poland took place every year, but more rarely in Hungary, where the Tatars served only intermittently. The Ottomans took slaves of their own in Central and Eastern Europe, ransoming those who appeared to be wealthy, and selling the others in Sarajevo or Istanbul. Some 200,000 slaves were reputedly captured during the invasion of Hungary in 1526, but after they converted to Islam, many were freed.[11] Slaves might be attached to the retinue of an Ottoman dignitary if they were lucky, or sold to the navy as oarsmen. The sultans claimed the best captives, a fifth of the total, for themselves. All told, perhaps two million Christians – not including recruits of the devshirme – were forced into slavery in Central and Eastern Europe.[12] Ottoman subjects, prisoners of war, passed into slavery in Christian lands as well, but in far fewer numbers.[13]

Before the main contingents of the army left Istanbul at the end of April to begin the campaign, army commissioners stockpiled provisions in forward castles, drawing upon a vast hinterland in Bosnia, Serbia and Bulgaria. Thousands of *pioneers* were mobilized to repair roads and build bridges along the line of advance. Ottoman troops were always well supplied with bread, rice and yogurt; they consumed less meat than their Christian adversaries, and drank very little wine.[14] Christian observers usually exaggerated the numbers of Ottoman troops. Geza David evokes unspecified 'concrete evidence' from the 1540s that indicates that the Ottoman field army in Hungary numbered 50–60,000 combatants, that is, 40–45,000 'regulars' and 10–15,000 irregulars and auxiliaries. These last were volunteers who joined the host without pay in the hope of attracting attention by their bravery and being rewarded with a timar or a janissary post. Local pashas (military governors) collected their own retinues of such men. Christian militias, called 'martolos', or 'armatoles', garrisoned strategic passes and guarded bridges behind the main army. Satellite states such as Transylvania, Wallachia and Moldavia, under their Christian leaders, supplied additional contingents, which may not have been very combative. The Ottoman army did not travel with numerous

Image 2.1 Luigi Ferdinando Marsigli: Tatars herding captives across a river, Etat militaire de l'Empire Ottoman, Amsterdam 1732, BNF 41612558, page 48. Tatars moving captives across a river in Hungary, in which prisoners (at the top centre) are towed across the stream with their hands tied to the horses' tails. The author was himself subjected to this ordeal

Image 2.2 Jan Luiken?: Slave market in Constantinople, BNF C 17191; Vendors and captives stand in a circle near the waterfront as new prisoners are freshly disembarked (on the right). On the left, a mother is separated from her child

women and children like German armies, although there were probably some women in camp who were not captives. Large numbers of servants and grooms swelled the Ottoman camp, which grew daily as captives arrived. Hygiene was always a huge problem wherever large numbers of people were concentrated. The Turkish armies dug pits to serve as latrines and then filled them in and moved camp periodically in order to reduce the incidence of disease. Western armies (which were typically much smaller) generally ignored these precautions at the time.

Open warfare between the Habsburg ruler and the Ottomans punctuated the early 1550s, and in 1566 Sultan Suleiman took the field himself to expand his possessions in Hungary. He died of disease just as the Turks overwhelmed the single small fortress of Szigetvar, and his successor, Selim II, paused the hostilities to consolidate his rule. The ensuing Peace of Edirne in 1568 did not signify the end of war *per se*, for the Ottoman *ghazi* tradition meant that pious warriors, particularly from Bosnia, where the majority of the population was Muslim, could continue raiding across the border in order to inflict harm on unbelievers. During the 1570s' 'peace', the pasha of Bosnia periodically invaded Croatia with bands of up to 5,000 men, seizing cattle and slaves and overwhelming castles and forts insufficiently strong to resist him. The Ottoman Empire was never really at peace: when not at war with the Habsburgs they marched east to the Caucasus region to fight the Iranian Safavid dynasty in Georgia, Armenia, Azerbaijan and Mesopotamia. Smaller Ottoman armies struck north from the Caspian Sea against Russia, while others pushed south to Yemen and Ethiopia.

The Habsburg rulers, kings of Hungary and Bohemia after 1526, were not autocrats, since they were forced to negotiate with their subjects to extract subsidies to fight their wars. The king, and later Emperor Ferdinand, did not control the tax machinery of his realms: that apparatus belonged to regional assemblies called estates, or to town councils that protected doggedly every privilege. These regional estates were loath to spend local revenues on campaigns fought far away, although gradually Austrian and Bohemian provinces paid the military expenditures of the closest frontier.[15] Hungarian feudal lords in particular considered themselves to be kings in their own domains, and resisted every attempt of the Habsburgs to tax them. Even in peacetime, Hungarian taxes covered barely a third of necessary expenditure. The emperor therefore encouraged feudatories to spend their own money on defence, via tax exemptions. The principal magnate families in the kingdom's Diet (several dozen dynasties) decreed a general mobilization, or *insurrection*, in time of danger. This meant that each of the great lords fielded temporary private armies from their vassals numbering 300–500 men, called *haiduks*, who defended private fortifications, or followed them into the field.[16]

Emperor Maximilian II sought to harden the land frontier that extended for 1,000 kilometres between the Adriatic Sea and the Transylvanian Alps. Waves of Serbian refugees from the Ottoman interior, along with 'Vlachs', who were a Latin-speaking, warlike, semi-nomadic Balkan population, were settled under their native leaders in fortified villages in Habsburg territory. They were free to practise their Orthodox religion and exempt from most taxes as long as they served to protect the frontier. They were also free of Hungarian serfdom, which rankled the magnates considerably. In addition to these local forces, companies of mounted arquebusiers, professional soldiers, were paid by the Austrian Estates to operate in conjunction with local militias. This *Military Frontier* became a separate jurisdiction of the Kingdom of Hungary, which, in 1569, acquired a commissioner of fortresses whose task it was to erect defensive works to lengthen resistance beyond what the Ottomans could endure, given the short campaigning season at their disposal. Several dozen military architects, mostly Italians, erected scores of strongpoints, large and small. The Danube fortresses were the most important, at Komarom, and farther upstream at Raab (modern Györ in Hungary), for the Ottoman armies relied on river transport for supply. Kanisza, south of Lake Balaton, closed off the land route to Vienna. A new institution, the *Hofkriegsrat* (1556) was a board of German and Bohemian military and civilian officials at the court whose task was to plan and execute military projects. It supervised the fortification work and allocated resources from the centre.[17]

The Emperor wielded little direct control far from the largest fortresses where German garrisons patrolled. All told, Habsburgs and Hungarians employed about 22,500 soldiers in the 1570s and 1580s, dispersed across 120 forts and castles. The Hungarian and Croatian magnates were largely autonomous, but were expected to respond to Ottoman raids with forays of their own into enemy territory.[18] The Croatian Zrinyi dynasty, in particular, operated in a zone between Lake Balaton and the Adriatic Sea. His haiduks stepped up their attacks on Ottoman forts in Croatia over the 1580s. Raiding was so much part of daily life that peasants carried muskets into the fields. Feudal lords increased labour details on their peasants to build fortifications and to guard them. The problem for the Habsburgs, writes James Tracy, was that the Ottomans were stronger, both in small war and in full-blown invasions. Akinji light cavalry, numbering up to 10,000 men, increased their attacks along the Croatian frontier during every harvest season.[19]

This turbulent situation could not endure, especially as German and Hungarian raids increased in their ambition, which was to interdict the Ottoman Danube river supply corridor. In 1590, the Ottomans established a twelve-year truce with Persia, in order to prepare for a major land war in Europe.[20] In 1592, the Ottomans seized the Croatian stronghold of Bihac, forcing the Habsburgs to mobilize completely for what is called the Long Turkish War (1593–1606). The German–Hungarian army enjoyed some initial successes in 1593, by routing an invasion force at Sisak. The next year, a fully-mobilized Ottoman army under the Grand Vizir Sinan Pasha captured Raab and some smaller Hungarian forts, and placed heavy pressure on Komarom, too. The Turks kept up to 100,000 men in the field year after year. But it required six weeks to march 900 kilometres from Istanbul to Belgrade, and then march 200 kilometres farther to the border region.

The campaign of 1595 was marked by an extraordinary Habsburg effort, whose combined forces (on paper) in the theatre numbered 86,000 men, including sizeable detachments raised in Italy by the Pope. One of their armies captured the most important of the Ottoman fortresses at Esztergom, overlooking a Danube crossing north of Buda.[21] What made this success possible was an uprising in the Christian vassal state of Transylvania under Prince Sigmund Bathory, and of the Romanian principalities of Wallachia under their voivode, or leader, Michael the Brave. These Romanian and Magyar forces spread the war to the vital Lower Danube region, which interdicted normal Ottoman provisioning routes. A hundred Italian military experts sent by the Grand Duke of Tuscany assisted the insurgents as technical advisers.[22] This insurrection in his rear forced Sinan Pasha to concentrate Ottoman forces far from Hungary in order to reopen his lines of communication.

The Ottomans escalated their mobilization in 1596, with Sultan Mehmet III taking personal command of the army in Hungary. The Ottomans could not fight war by borrowing money like Western states, for lending at interest was un-Islamic. The sultan, or Grand Vizier, brought chests of gold and silver coins to pay his men, who might mutiny for lack of pay. The two million ducats carried by the Grand Vizier on campaign in Hungary were equivalent to the entire tax revenue of the Venetian republic. Leading Ottoman commanders willingly lent money to the sultan and Grand Vizier in order to gain favour and advancement, whenever there was a shortage. Coins paid soldiers and pioneers for their ordinary duties. There were bonuses for those who brought prisoners into camp, or the heads of enemies. The Ottomans laid siege to the Hungarian fortress of Eger and emerged victorious in the hard-fought battle of Mezokeresztes nearby – the only large field battle of the entire war. The serried ranks of German pikemen proved to be tactically superior to their adversaries. Christian soldiers wore heavier armour than the Ottomans and were better protected from arrows and lances. Turkish troops also advanced as a great crowd, and so were difficult to miss for the enemy musketeers. But the Ottomans offset these disadvantages by greater numbers and the better discipline of the janissaries.[23] At the end of the battle and during the chaotic retreat, the German army is thought to have lost 50,000 men killed and captured.[24] Ottoman military tactics and weapons in 1600 were almost equal to their European adversaries. The Turks possessed stronger and more reliable musket barrels, made from flat sheets of steel coiled into a spiral. Janissary musket fire was more accurate than that of their opponents, and their archery was still lethal to men and horses.[25] Ottoman artillery was produced in large quantity and principally in smaller calibre for field armies in Istanbul foundries (the largest), but also in Anatolia and the Balkans.[26] There was a sharp increase in the number of janissaries, to 35,000 men in 1598, but also of the trained household cavalry paid from the central treasury, only 2,000 at Mohacs but numbering 15,000 in the 1590s.[27]

In 1598, the Habsburg armies recaptured Raab, ending the threat of an Ottoman breakthrough on the Danube. In 1600, an Ottoman army threatened Vienna by another route, capturing Kanisza, south of Lake Balaton, by building artillery mounds higher than the town bastions. A Habsburg army with money and men from Italy laid siege the next year to take Kanisza back, but it failed with heavy losses, and the Ottomans slaughtered 6,000 sick and injured men they left behind. Unlike the Turks, the Christian armies were never able to establish a coherent system of logistics. They were supplied only with difficulty from distant Bohemia and Bavaria, and there was no central authority overseeing finance and supply. Shortages of cash and provisions were fatal to large armies. Mercenaries, who came from all walks of life, did not often receive their pay, so they stole what they needed from the peasants. The soldiers were gradually worn down by poor food and excessive drink, harsh climate, exposure, contagious disease, chafing and camp filth. European notions of hygiene were quite primitive, even by the standards of the time.[28]

The war intensified in nearby Transylvania in 1599, after Prince Zygmund Bathory abdicated for a third time in the face of the Diet's resistance. Michael the Brave stepped into the void in the name of Emperor Rudolph II but paid no heed to Imperial authority. The Habsburgs claimed that Transylvania was part of the Hungarian kingdom under their rule, and dispatched an army under the Italo–Albanian cavalry general, Giorgio Basta, with instructions to subdue the region and restore the Catholic Church to its monopoly status. Habsburg attempts to repress Protestantism in the region soon led to a rebellion against them. Basta's unpaid men ravaged the principality, but Ottoman and Tatar forces intervened to expel them. Habsburg officers murdered voivode Michael in 1601 in an attempt to retain their control. By 1605, Hungarian haiduk rebels and Ottoman forces expelled the Habsburgs from much of Royal Hungary and threatened Vienna, too, in a Calvinist uprising seeking to expel Catholic priests and missionaries. In the turmoil, Transylvania lost perhaps half its population to war and disease.[29] The same year, the Turks recovered Esztergom and the war ground to a halt due to the inability of either side to tip the balance. Peace talks desired ardently by both sides were concluded at Zsitvatorok (Map 1) in November 1606, since a great rebellion exploded in Anatolia itself, not far from Istanbul. The Emperor was no longer treated as a vassal of the sultan and ceased to pay tribute, but the Ottomans had won the only field battle, and they added two Hungarian towns, Kanisza and Eger, to their empire.

The peace restored the previous situation of unstable borders and periodic raiding. Outside the cities, the control of the Habsburg emperor or the Ottoman sultan was quite theoretical, the reality of power being in the hands of the local nobles in their stout castles. There were about 100 Ottoman forts in Hungary and Croatia, guarded by about 30,000 men, if one includes Sarajevo in Bosnia, a major city.[30] Only a few of these places possessed masonry ramparts designed to fire cannon from them, and the Ottomans never built bastions in the modern Italian style. The great majority of these strongholds were modest *palanka* forts built of earth and timber, designed to resist small cannon towed by raiding parties, but unable to withstand a longer siege by heavy guns. In the

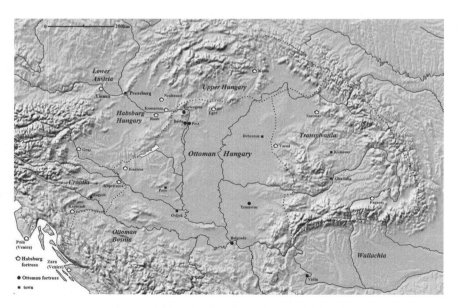

Map 1 The Danube frontier at the Peace of Zsitvatorok in 1606

aftermath of the war, Catholic powers exploited tensions in the Balkans, hoping to provoke a general rising of Orthodox Christians that they could exploit to their advantage.[31] With every local rising, the Ottomans forcibly removed populations and resettled them elsewhere in the Empire. Waves of Serbian refugees, in particular, reinforced those already settled along the Croatian frontier and organized resistance to the Turks from their new bases. The antagonism would continue for centuries.

Mediterranean menace

In 1500, the North African coast (known as the Barbary Coast, after the native Berber inhabitants) comprised a chain of autonomous city-states living from the plunder of Christian vessels, but each was vulnerable to attack from Spain and Portugal, whose best policy against corsairs was to occupy their bases piecemeal. The lead corsair chief in Algiers, Khair-ed-Din (nicknamed Barbarossa), decided to use the Ottoman conquest of Egypt as a pretext to submit the city to Ottoman sovereignty in 1519. In exchange for a janissary garrison, he pledged the service of the city's naval resources whenever the sultan called upon them. Not until 1533 did North Africa become part of Ottoman strategy, and the classical institutions of direct rule were never introduced there, but the corsairs enabled the Ottomans to double the size of their fleet and to carry the war on the Christians into the Western Mediterranean.[32] The combined Ottoman and Barbary Coast navies constituted a huge threat to European commerce and coastal populations from Cyprus and Crete in the Levant to Gibraltar and beyond.

Flotillas of oared vessels had been operating in the Mediterranean for millennia, because they were well suited to the geography of the theatre. Galleys, galeots and smaller oared barks were highly manoeuvrable and were not rendered immobile on frequent windless days. Second, with their shallow draft, they were designed to be beached, enabling the crews to disembark. War galleys measured about 40–45 metres long, but were only about six metres wide. They became still easier to row in the mid-sixteenth century by modifying the manner of propulsion: instead of placing each man to an oar on several levels, they employed three or four men on a bench pulling one very heavy oar of 100 kg. A typical war galley employed 200 oarsmen, on 25 benches, exclusive of other crew and soldiers. Corsair galleys and galeots (which had fewer benches and applied three men to an oar) more often employed free men, who were available to fight. As a warship, the galley displayed some important drawbacks. The centre of the vessel rode barely a metre above the waves, which made rowing easier but rendered it vulnerable to choppy seas (Image 2.3). Sometimes, whole flotillas were caught in squalls, with heavy losses in ships and men. Moreover, with a complement of 300–400 oarsmen, sailors and soldiers occupying 250 square metres, there was no room to store victuals or even water, which had to be replenished every few days.[33] Such crowding made basic hygiene difficult and disease spread quickly among the

Image 2.3 Stefano Della Bella, Galleys in a tempest ca. 1640, MET Museum. The vessel rode low in the water to facilitate rowing, but this made them vulnerable to storms and many were lost with all hands to unseasonable storms

oarsmen and soldiers indiscriminately. Sailing vessels, or roundships as they were called, accompanied most galley flotillas on longer missions. Although they could not match galleys in speed or manoeuvrability, they could carry cargo and operate in rougher weather. Space restrictions therefore limited the effective range of galleys to a few hundred kilometres and tethered their movement to the coastline (Image 2.4).[34]

With the advent of shipboard artillery, galleys mounted cannon on the prow in a battery of three or five guns, of which the centre piece fired heavy shot. It was, therefore, necessary to point the whole ship at the target. With their low profile, manoeuvrability and heavy cannon, galleys could sink the clumsy roundships with impunity.[35] Against other oared vessels the tactics were very different. Ideally, they would attack another galley from the side. Instead of a ram designed to sink the enemy, the prow was shaped as a spur, enabling the attacker to glide on to the deck of its prey and for troops aboard to fire on it from above (Image 2.5). In a set-piece battle (which was infrequent), fleets would align face to face with their adversary, bow against bow. Each side only had time to release a single cannon volley (the expert Venetians could manage two) before the vessels collided and boarding parties tried to force their way aboard their opposite number. Threatened or outnumbered galleys could slide on to a beach and point their bows seaward at an attacker. They could also assist sieges by transporting artillery and then dismounting it for use on land, or by firing from the sea in great batteries.[36] However, galley crews could not press a siege on land and defend themselves against a seaborne attack simultaneously. Men had to hastily abandon their earthworks and re-embark to defend their vessels from a threatening flotilla. This was not so much naval as amphibious warfare.

Image 2.4 Bruegel: A Galley and a Roundship in the Mediterranean 1560, Harvard
Fogg Museum. Early 'roundships' were unwieldy sailors and easy targets
for galleys in a calm sea, but improved Dutch and English models made
their entry into the Mediterranean after 1600

In the sixteenth century, the menace to southern Europe from roving fleets of
galleys from North Africa became extreme. After coming close to capturing the
Venetian base at Corfu in 1537, the Ottoman and Barbary fleet under Barbarossa
won a major naval victory off the north-western Greek coast at Prevesa (1538).

Image 2.5 Jacques Callot, Galley Battle, Harvard Fogg Museum. Maltese and Ottoman
galleys engaged in combat (ca. 1630). The Christian soldiers on the prow
were better armed and armoured than their adversaries in close fighting

This enabled the Ottomans and their Barbary Coast allies to make their presence
felt everywhere throughout the inland sea. From 1530 to 1560, the Ottomans frequently sailed in tandem with the French, sometimes in combined flotillas.
A Barbary fleet wintered in Toulon in 1543, courtesy of the king of France, who
considered them to be allies against the Habsburg enemy in Italy. The French and
Ottoman fleets came close to taking Corsica from its weak Genoese overlords in
1560. The corsairs fed a local insurrection there and multiple private wars, penning
the Genoese into a handful of fortified ports.[37] Between 1540 and 1574, Ottoman
and Barbary galley fleets moved entire armies across the Mediterranean with ease.
Barbary flotillas cruised the Christian shores seeking vulnerable targets, and whole
cities were seized and sacked in the 1540s and 1550s, such as Nice in Provence and
Reggio in Calabria. The islands were especially vulnerable, with the Lipari archipelago off northeast Sicily reputedly yielding 7,000 captives, Gozo, near Malta, which
lost 5,000, or Minorca in the Aragonese Balearic islands, which lost 6,000 inhabitants. Coastal towns without powerful fortifications and permanent garrisons were
everywhere vulnerable, such as Vieste in Puglia, from which 6,000 slaves were taken
in 1554. Corsair bases in North Africa sent a steady stream of slaves to Istanbul as
part of the price of Ottoman protection.

The corsairs were often led by *renegades*, Christians familiar with the European
coastline, who converted more or less voluntarily to Islam.[38] Many maintained

contact over the years with family members left behind. Renegades were an important part of the Ottoman universe, particularly in the Barbary ports. In Algiers, these were estimated at 9,000 people in 1600, and, of the 35 most important corsair captains, 24 of them had Christian origins, and half of those were Italian. One should not emphasize their 'ghazi' religious motivation. Corsairs were, first and foremost, entrepreneurs, who invested much capital in ships, provisions and crews, which they hoped to recover through successful expeditions. Ottoman governors forbade attacks on French, Venetian and, later on, Dutch and English ships, orders that the corsairs routinely ignored with impunity.[39] Each corsair ship was a private venture undertaken by partners who put up the capital, sometimes including slaves, who claimed a share of booty for their masters. Most small cargo ships were defenceless against privateers, so gave up without a fight. Corsairs often lingered for several days in enemy harbours so as to sell bulky goods they seized (such as cattle, or elderly persons) back to the inhabitants.[40] The galeots, which carried little or no artillery, were powered by as many as six free oarsmen per bench, which made them difficult to catch. Once they arrived home, the corsairs divided the booty among themselves according to rigid rules.

Slaves constituted the choicest prize. The number of them in Algiers, the most important base, oscillated from year to year, but probably averaged 25,000 in the later seventeenth century. All the Barbary ports combined might have held 35,000 slaves in that period, with an annual mortality of 20%, if they remained slaves. That meant that, in order to maintain stable numbers, it was necessary to acquire 8,500 new slaves every year. The phenomenon of Islamic raiding, which continued until the French conquered Algiers in 1830, led to the seizure of at least a million Christians over 300 years, in addition to the two million taken from Eastern Europe.[41] There were important slave markets in all the Barbary towns, but the primary aim was to exchange the wealthier captives, held in a pen called a *bagno*, for ransom. Europeans later employed consuls in the chief Barbary ports whose function was to negotiate and mediate the return of captives to Europe, and the Catholic church collected money in many parishes for this end. Slaves pulled the oars of Ottoman and Barbary vessels, and might participate in raids themselves to earn ransom money for their owners. Not all of them served on the oars. Many were skilled tradesmen who serviced galley hulls or helped navigate the craft.[42]

Sicily was the target most frequented by the Barbary corsairs, who attacked the island at least 136 times between 1570 and 1606, sometimes sending shore parties 15–30 kilometres into the interior in search of captives.[43] To close down the most active corsair bases, Charles V sent very expensive expeditions against Algiers and Tunis, with mixed success. He conquered Tunis at considerable cost with the aid of a Genoese fleet in 1535. An Imperial attempt to capture Algiers in 1541 was driven off with very heavy loss when a storm capsized many of the vessels. In 1559, Philip II undertook a large operation from Sicily against the North African coast, seizing the island of Djerba, where the soldiers disembarked and built a fort. The sultan reacted by dispatching his galley fleet from Istanbul unseasonably early (in May 1560) in order to catch the Hispano–Italian force by surprise. The unprepared Christians, whose ships were so overloaded with loot that they could neither fight nor flee, lost over half their galleys, half their roundships and 5,000 prisoners. The 15,000 soldiers remaining on the island, already weakened by typhus, capitulated from thirst not long after.[44]

To help combat this ongoing scourge, Catholic states expanded the role of medieval orders of Crusading knights. Emperor Charles V granted the islands of Malta and Gozo, off the southeast coast of Sicily, to the Knights of Saint John in 1530, after they lost their base in Rhodes. Malta's strategic location near the narrow passage separating the eastern from the western Mediterranean enabled the knights, with their own squadron of a half-dozen galleys, to carry the fight in several directions. These Knights of Saint John (soon called Knights of Malta) were a medieval religious order whose aristocratic members were celibate warrior-priests, who managed simultaneously a large hospital. Malta's deep harbour also sheltered a number of Christian corsairs who raided Muslim shipping in search of profit. They maintained a base at Tripoli on the Libyan coast until it was captured in 1551. The knights were obliged to undertake an annual 'caravan' cruise to fight the Islamic enemy: about 30 knights for each galley, plus the crew and 100–200 soldiers. The Knights of Malta often prowled among the Greek Aegean islands waiting for targets to cruise by on their way to or from Istanbul, Salonika or Alexandria in Egypt.[45] The Duke of Florence, Cosimo I (soon after, Grand Duke of Tuscany), established another crusader order based in Pisa, the Knights of Santo Stefano.

In 1565, Sultan Suleiman was tempted by Malta itself, whose knights barely had time to assemble reinforcements. The Ottoman–Barbary expedition numbered 140 galleys and 40,000 troops and sailors, but the knights' desperate resistance at fort St Elmo at the entrance to the harbour gave time to the king of Spain to react. The besiegers were on the verge of overwhelming the last defences of the city a month later, when a relief force of 11,000 Spanish and Italian soldiers disembarked on the island on 7 September, after 112 days of siege. The Ottomans could not finish the siege and protect their ships simultaneously and, much weakened by disease and combat, they withdrew. It was a defensive victory for Philip II and did nothing to diminish the Islamic threat. In the aftermath, the surviving Knights built a strong new city called Valletta and prepared for a fresh assault.

Ottoman men and weapons then assisted a rising of Islamic subjects of Philip II in southern Spain that developed into a vicious counter-insurgency conflict festering for two years. It had no sooner been quelled when the king was compelled to raise a new army to repress the rebellion in the Low Countries in 1568. With the king of Spain fully occupied, Sultan Selim II (r. 1566–1574) decided to attack a friendly state, the Republic of Venice, whose Greek empire in Cyprus and Crete lay astride Ottoman maritime communications. Selim ordered 116 galleys and 50,000 troops to Cyprus in early July 1570. Nicosia, whose expensive modern fortifications had just been completed, fell on 9 September and its garrison was massacred. Famagosta, a strongly held seaport, resisted for another 11 months until it surrendered when its ammunition was exhausted, and there, too, the survivors were butchered despite promises to the contrary. Venice dispatched ships and raised troops to defend the island in 1570, but its commander dared not attack the Ottomans with the forces at hand. The rich republic ruled barely two million inhabitants: finding enough infantry and oarsmen to outfit a large fleet was a daunting challenge, and some galleys had to be kept back in the Adriatic, as the Ottomans were attacking the Dalmatian ports from the Bosnian interior.[46]

To meet the threat, Pope Pius V brokered a Holy Alliance between Spain and the Venetian Republic, who were natural adversaries, while all the Italian states contributed men and money to the common cause. The Grand Duke of Tuscany supplied ships and soldiers to the Papacy. Genoese private contractors, called *asientistas*, provided dozens of galleys for the king of Spain. It took time and much trouble to assemble enough vessels to match the enemy numbers. Western galley fleets consisted of fewer ships than their Ottoman counterparts, but they were more heavily armed and their crews were more experienced. The convict oarsmen, in particular, were more robust, having been taught for years to row in unison. Ottoman crews were fresher, often consisting of militiamen and conscripts, but the harsh conditions wore them down over months at sea.[47] The Ottomans maintained such a great numerical advantage at the beginning of the season that Catholic commanders kept out of their way, but after August the attrition of their crews began to tell.

The combined fleet of the Holy League under the command of the Spanish prince Don Juan of Austria (King Philip's illegitimate half-brother) left the advanced naval base at Messina in Sicily and went hunting for the Ottoman navy. They found it on 7 October just inside the Gulf of Corinth in northeastern Greece, near a town the Venetians called Lepanto (modern Naupaktos). The ensuing battle was probably the largest single engagement since Ancient times, perhaps the largest in European history until Napoleon. The Catholic array numbered circa 25,000 soldiers (11,000 Italians, 8,000 Spaniards, 3,000 Germans and 3,000 noble volunteers, mostly Italians), in 206 galleys and six galleasses, propelled by 45,000 oarsmen, often freemen in the case of Venice.[48] The Ottomans aligned more galleys (circa 220, with an additional 58 smaller galeots) but disposed of fewer men per ship, bearing fewer firearms and wearing less armour. Spanish and Italian galleys mounted heavier cannon, augmented by many swivel guns along the side of the vessel firing small shot. One study evaluates the Catholic artillery advantage as 1,815 compared to just 750 guns for the Ottomans.[49] Venetian galleys consented to carry Spanish soldiers to offset their weakness in infantry. The Ottomans employed many proficient bowmen, who took years to train, but the Venetians attached removable wooden shutters to protect the crews from arrows and shot. The decisive Catholic weapon was the Venetian *galleass*, six of which preceded the line of battle by 700 metres, with the intention of breaking the cohesion of the Ottoman fleet. A galleass, a converted merchant galley 9 metres wide, propelled by 500 oarsmen, had four times the hull displacement of a normal galley, which enabled it to fire cannon from its sides. Sitting higher in the water, soldiers could fire from the decks down on the galleys around them as from a floating fortress.[50]

Both sides deployed their galleys in two long lines abreast, moving parallel close to one another, the front row of 65 ships articulated in three contingents perpendicular to the nearby shoreline. In the ensuing battle, the Ottomans attempted to outflank the Venetians along the shore in order to attack them from the side and the rear. The latter pressed them hard against the coast and did not let them through. The hand-to-hand fighting on the forecastles and the decks was especially fierce. Ottoman arrows rained down on the soldiers and oarsmen alike. The heavily armed Catholic galleys in the centre pushed their way into the Ottoman formation and boarded enemy vessels, killing before long the Ottoman admiral Muezzinzade Ali Pasha. After four hours' fighting, the Ottoman left (south) flank flotilla under command of the corsair Uluc Ali, a Calabrian renegade, found a gap in the Christian line and made its escape with 40 galleys, while the rest of the Muslim fleet was destroyed utterly. The Ottomans are reputed to have lost 113 galleys sunk and 130 more captured, to the loss of 12 galleys of the Holy League. The Ottomans lost 30,000 dead to 9,000 Christians (almost one third of their force, and a higher proportion among the Venetians), while 15,000 Christian slaves were liberated. The Venetians slaughtered Ottoman soldiers and seamen in the immediate aftermath of the fight, perhaps in retribution for the massacre of Nicosia's and Famagosta's defenders the year before.

Despite the resounding Catholic success, the battle was not decisive, given the ease of building new galleys. Within a year, Grand Vizier Mehmed Sokullu armed 250 new galleys and five galleasses (called mahones), although they wisely avoided combat with the enemy due to the lack of expert soldiers.[51] The unnatural alliance between Venetians and Hispano-Italians soon fell apart, for Venice wished to recover Cyprus or else occupy the Greek Peloponnesus astride its commercial routes. Spain preferred to strike the North African coast instead, and would not co-operate with the merchant republic. Venice made a separate peace with the Ottomans in March 1573 and ceded Cyprus and some small ports in Greece and Albania, in exchange for the right to trade freely in the Levant. A great Ottoman navy of 280 galleys and 15 mahones then pounced on Tunis and its port La Goletta in 1574, capturing both. Philip II was still supporting several flotillas in Spain, Genoa, Naples and Sicily, numbering 146 galleys, but the revolt in the Netherlands was becoming unmanageable and Spanish finances collapsed the next year.

In the aftermath of Lepanto, the Portuguese King Sebastian, only 24 years old, unmarried and without an heir, dreamed of continuing the Reconquista into North Africa. The Portuguese controlled a number of ports along the Moroccan coast, such as Tangier in the Mediterranean and Mogador on the Atlantic. The Moroccan monarchy was not hereditary like the Ottoman one and Sebastian tried to take advantage of a brief civil war among various factions to seize the interior of the kingdom. In 1578, Sebastian landed a mixed army of

20,000 men, predominantly infantry, of Germans, Walloons and Portuguese near Tangier, hoping to force his adversary Abd al-Malik to battle. The Moroccan force retreated instead into the interior and, despite the summer heat, Sebastian followed it. On 3 August, far from his base, the crusader king's army encountered the Moroccan host over twice its size at Alcazarquivir, with cannon and musket-bearing infantry, but composed predominantly of light cavalry. The Portuguese force was entirely surrounded and those who were not killed were captured and enslaved. King Sebastian, last of his house of Aviz, was never found. This opened a succession crisis for the throne of Portugal that was an unhoped-for benefit to Philip II of Spain, who enjoyed a respectable legal claim. To strengthen his argument, Philip advanced into Portugal with the Duke of Alva's army and defeated those who resisted him at Alcantara in 1580. Philip added Portugal and its far-flung maritime empire to the states he commanded, but it remained separate from Castile and he scrupulously respected its autonomy. By then, the Dutch problem took precedence over the war with Islam. Secret envoys to Istanbul produced a truce through various intermediaries in 1581, which was renewed in 1584 and again in 1587.[52]

Similarly, Sultan Murad III decided to direct his armies against the Safavid Persians in 1577. Since permanent peace with the Spanish empire and its Italian allies was not an option, the solution for both sides was to break up the great galley fleets into more manageable flotillas and to operate them as corsairs throughout the Mediterranean. This was the great age of Algiers, 100,000 inhabitants around 1600, of whom slaves numbered 20–50,000. Some of these were Europeans, the others African slaves from the Sahel. Something like 100 corsair vessels operated there in 1625, employing 25% of the active population.[53] Tunis kept perhaps 10,000 slaves in the same era.[54] We have a glimpse of their destinies through the extraordinary book by Bartolome and Lucile Bennassar, who encountered thousands of them in Inquisition records when they returned to Europe. The former captives hailed from all over Europe, but there was a plurality of Italians, mostly from the south and the islands, as well as escapees originally from Andalusia and the Algarve, alongside Provençaux and Languedocians, even Greeks. Many captives were taken primarily with ransom in mind, such as the priests and friars who were often redeemed by their orders. Most of the pressure on the captives to convert to Islam was aimed at children and adolescents, and most who converted did so freely.[55]

The anti-Christian animus of the North African coast received a further boost in 1609 when Spain expelled 2–300,000 Moriscos. At the end of the sixteenth century, Dutch and English ships attacked Catholic shipping in the area under pretext of waging war against Spain, using galleons and sailing vessels adapted for Atlantic waters. After 1610, the corsairs and their Mediterranean adversaries invested in similar vessels, since they could operate in winter.[56] Dutch and Flemish renegades operating out of Salé in Morocco, such as Simon Danser or Jan Janszoon, alias Murat Reis, became famous. Sailing vessels dramatically increased the range of daring corsairs, who struck the coast of Ireland, Iceland

(1627) and, most dramatically, Newfoundland (1625). English corsairs under Robert Dudley, self-styled Duke of Northumberland, operated out of Algiers until 1609, when Grand Duke Ferdinando of Tuscany convinced him to convert to Catholicism and to bring his flotilla of 12 vessels to Livorno. From there they continued to attack Christian ships as well as Muslim ones.[57]

The European response was to maintain galley squadrons for coastal defence, and to erect hundreds of coastal towers as early warning stations, many of which still stand today. Militia forces in Naples and Sicily were entrusted with coastal surveillance and to prevent corsair flotillas from landing to take on water.[58] In 1560, Spain maintained four squadrons totalling 60 galleys, half of which were leased from Italian allies such as Genoa and Tuscany, but after 1576 it could no longer maintain so many galleys in the face of rising commitments in Flanders (Map 2). It was better to lease galleys from private entrepreneurs, chiefly Genoese, who derived significant advantages from the pact, such as the right to export coin from Spain, or charging high interest on the unpaid balance. Genoese private galleys constituted over ten per cent of the Holy League fleet at Lepanto. A few were held back along the vulnerable Spanish coast, which had few convenient ports and extensive vulnerable beaches. Naples and Sicily supported modest flotillas whose vessels patrolled the coastal waters seeking out corsair vessels. The men they captured were then put to work rowing the royal galleys alongside criminals and some rare volunteers. Christian corsairs also operated out of Palermo, Messina and especially Trapani in Sicily, as well as Cagliari in Sardinia. Muslim or African slaves numbered about 12,000 in Sicily around 1600, equal to one per cent of the kingdom's population. Naples was a secondary corsair base, but it held perhaps 10,000 slaves.[59] Viceroy Osuna of Sicily operated his own corsair squadron, and later, in Naples, numbering four roundships and three galleys, manning it with soldiers from the garrisons and drawing stores from the King of Spain's warehouses.[60]

Italian states created their own galley flotillas. The Pope created a squadron of five galleys operating out of Civitavecchia, but he lost them all at Djerba in 1560 and had to start again. To meet his commitment of a dozen galleys for Lepanto he had to rent them from Tuscany. The Grand Duke of Tuscany, Cosimo I, established naval dockyards at Livorno, a deep-water seaport he developed as Pisa, on the River Arno, silted up. In 1561, he created a religious order of Knights of Santo Stefano, not unlike the knights of Malta, whose noble members were technically ecclesiastics but who could still marry. These were drawn from all of Italy and beyond, with headquarters in Pisa and dockyards and bagno in nearby Livorno. Tuscany's galley flotilla oscillated around six galleys and 100 knights on active caravan duty.[61] These frequently combined with the flotillas of Naples, Sicily and the Papacy for sweeps off the North African coast. The Tuscans made ambitious forays of galleys and corsair auxiliary vessels in the Aegean sea, looking for easy targets, and attacked Ottoman and Barbary ports, but they were not always successful. In 1607, a squadron of eight galleys of Santo Stefano and ten roundships carrying 1,800 soldiers attacked Bone (modern Annaba in Algeria), carrying off 2,000 men, women and children as

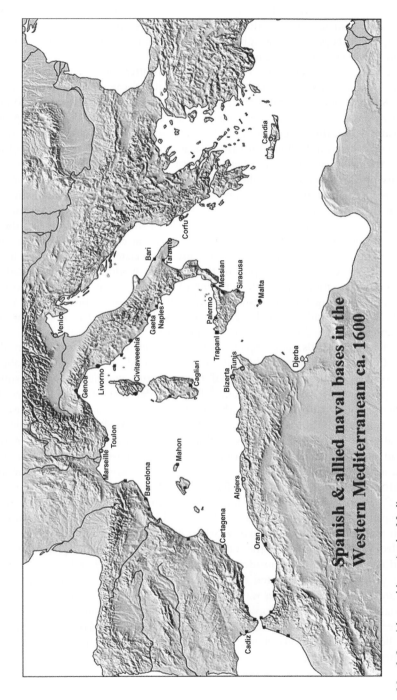

Spanish & allied naval bases in the
Western Mediterranean ca. 1600

Venice
Bari
Taranto
Corfu
Candia
Messian
Siracusa
Palermo
Malta
Gaeta
Naples
Trapani
Civitaveeehia
Genoa
Livorno
Cagliari
Bizerta
Tunis
Djerba
Toulon
Marseille
Barcelona
Mahon
Algiers
Cartagena
Oran
Cadiz

Map 2 Spanish naval bases in the Mediterranean

slaves. Slaves constituted 60% of Tuscan galley crews in 1617, while most of the others were convicts serving their terms for serious offences.[62] In addition to hosting the galleys of the Knights of Santo Stefano, heavily fortified Livorno became the main corsair base in Italy.

Malta quickly recovered as a base of operations after the siege of 1565, aided by the extensive assets the knights owned in the form of 500 farms located across Spain, France and Italy. The continental landed property they owned produced revenue equal to half the king of Spain's silver windfall from the Americas! After 1580, the knights attacked Venetian ships trading with Muslim states, too. People taken unlawfully with their cargos could theoretically sue the Order before the tribunal to obtain their freedom and recover their property. The Knights operated five or six galleys around 1600, and soon added one or two galleons to their strength. They patrolled, alone or with other flotillas, the seas off North Africa and the Levant coast, from Anatolia to Algeria, seeking to intercept enemy corsairs. Warships often avoided combat with vessels like themselves, and preferred to attack commercial vessels that could not resist. The best booty comprised slaves, but the knights also appreciated cargos of rice, linen, sugar and coffee that were staples of the Ottoman world. The galley squadron alone embarked more than ten per cent of Malta's active population around 1610, not counting the jobs ashore in the dockyards or in provisioning warehouses. With the addition of 10–20 corsair vessels also based in Malta, the war fleet represented 15–20% of the active population.[63]

By the later 1590s, both Spain and the Ottoman Empire had assembled larger flotillas with more ambitious targets in mind. A fleet of 223 galleys, fitted out by Istanbul at the end of the sixteenth century, cost the sultan three-quarters of his entire revenue.[64] In the quiet year of 1615, galleys still numbered about 200 throughout the Mediterranean. As the principal western power trading in the Muslim Levant, Venice was caught in the middle, its ships attacked by all and sundry. Chief among their tormentors were Christian Serbian corsairs, called Uskoks, operating out of coastal Croatia: they provoked a backlash so severe that it led to direct war between the Republic and the Holy Roman Empire in 1615, forcing the Emperor to hold them in check.[65] Faced with ruinous insurance fees, Venice tended to withdraw from the maritime carrying trade after 1610, by which time it could make use of Dutch and English vessels. In 1619, when it sought to intimidate the Neapolitan fleet of Viceroy Osuna, the Venetian navy consisted of 50 galleys and 50 rented roundships, still a considerable force.[66] It increasingly relied on convicts for its galley crews, and rented them from the Duke of Bavaria or nearby Italian states. The great *Arsenal* was able to furnish the Republic with up-to-date materials for its vessels. Corsair raiding, principally Muslim, continued for another two hundred years, but its intensity declined after 1620. The number of galleys declined everywhere, too, as improved Dutch-style roundships became more effective.

Crusade in Flanders 1568–1609

The Calvinist Reformation spread throughout Western Europe in the course of the 1550s, a doctrine much more international in its outlook than German Lutheranism or the Anglicanism of Henry VIII, and more radical, too. Based overwhelmingly on reading scripture in the vernacular language, Calvinism spread quickly through literate elites in Scotland and England, in Poland and Hungary, and throughout much of Calvin's native France and the Habsburg Low Countries in the course of the 1550s. Charles V and Philip II cracked down on them periodically, but without sustained persecution. Unlike other Reformation doctrines, which held Roman Catholic liturgy and tradition to be mere error, Calvinists considered Catholic doctrines to be blasphemous and diabolical, to be eradicated root and branch. Calvinist organizations multiplied among town elites in France and the Low Countries, and, since their assemblies had no buildings or recognized consecrated spaces, they gathered in the open air to hear sermons. Before long, armed spectators stood close by to keep hostile public officials at bay. Protestants in the Low Countries watched the growth of their movement in nearby France with a sense that their final triumph was imminent. Small crowds of enthusiastic evangelicals began methodically to smash the images and remove crosses from Catholic churches in 1566, which they then appropriated. Calvin himself approved of such measures. The regional grandees, who often shared Calvinist or Lutheran sympathies, began to organize resistance when they learned that Philip II planned to send an army to restore order. Philip was particularly angry that his leading dignitaries in the region, the Egmont, Horn and Orange, who assisted his stepsister Margaret of Austria's government in Brussels, did nothing to prevent the revolt. Armed Calvinist bands then moved to take over towns and suppress Catholic worship outright in 1566. A larger rebel force assembled near Antwerp in March 1567 but a small nucleus of professional soldiers destroyed it at Oosterweel and the active revolt was over by April.

Philip II planned to return to the region in person to reinforce his influence, but the Islamic uprising in Granada changed his mind. He tasked his ablest general, the Duke of Alva, to equip a modest army of Spanish and Italian troops, who marched over the Alps and arrived in the Low Countries late the same year. More German and Walloon (a generic term designating inhabitants of the Low Countries) soldiers were added to the force, and the arrests began. About 9,000 people were condemned and just over 1,000 were executed for their part in the troubles, but the political effect was enormous because most of the victims belonged to social elites. Alva then introduced two unpopular measures: he accelerated the reinforcement of the Catholic Church by creating new dioceses and establishing religious orders with the aid of public money. He next raised a tenth-penny tax to pay for his army of occupation, without the consent of the States (representative assembly) of the Seventeen Provinces that constituted the Low Countries. This was not an ancient body, for the various provinces had been united as a single entity only in 1549, but most of its members felt that Philip's kingship should be constitutionally limited.

The execution of major exponents of the high nobility left the German Lutheran William of Orange as the undisputed leader of the opposition. The Prince of Orange and Alva's other adversaries took refuge in Germany, England and France in order to organize armed resistance. Orange's first invasion in 1568, with a mercenary army levied in France and Germany, was easily defeated by what was now called the Spanish Army of Flanders. The Prince then delivered *letters of marque* to privateers in English ports known as the *Sea Beggars* in order to give them something to do, and to amass a war chest.[67] The foremost of these were French Huguenots based out of La Rochelle, not disgruntled subjects of the Habsburg king. Sea Beggars launched raids along the coast that created some havoc, and they preyed on commercial shipping of the region, including neutral vessels. Queen Elizabeth of England, who personally had no patience with Calvinists and who feared economic retaliation by Spain, expelled the Sea Beggars from England in the winter of 1572.

When Alva drew troops away from Antwerp to confront a Huguenot and French force attacking from France, a modest group of Sea Beggars disembarked nearby in the Scheldt estuary at Brill and Flushing on 1 April. A number of towns in Zeeland and Holland embraced the movement and armed their militias to join the rebels. Town councils seized and auctioned off the assets of the Catholic Church to finance the purchase of arms. The Provincial States of Holland and Zeeland rallied behind the movement and levied taxes on cargo vessels to raise professional soldiers. Although they constituted a minority of perhaps only ten per cent of the population, Calvinists prohibited Catholic worship everywhere they took power. They were hoping that a French attack led by Huguenots would come to their aid, but the St Bartholomew's massacre in Paris on 24 August 1572 made that impossible. The rebellion made tax collection difficult for Spain in the region, and so Alva begged for resources from Madrid at the height of the Ottoman threat in the Mediterranean.[68] Alva's first sieges over 18 months in 1572 and 1573 sought to restore order through terror, but this strategy produced the opposite result to what was intended: the rebels in cities like Haarlem and Leiden resisted to the utmost. He was unable to recover the coastal towns or regain Zeeland, because the rebel fleet moved reinforcements and supplies to threatened points.

Alva himself was recalled in 1573, for having antagonized almost everyone instead of restoring obedience. Even worse, the large army he hired on credit could not be paid. Philip II, who was financially overburdened in both the Low Countries and the Mediterranean, declared bankruptcy in 1575. Until that point, the rebellion was confined to Holland and Zeeland in the northern districts. Now Spanish troops began to mutiny for their pay and sacked towns in Flanders and Brabant. Alva's successor, Luis de Requesens, coped as best he could, but after his death in 1576 there was a vacuum of power in Brussels. Spanish mutineers then seized Antwerp, the economic capital of northern Europe on 3 November 1576, looted the city and killed several hundred people. This event was quickly magnified in a flurry of negative press that became a public relations disaster for the Spanish regime. Most of the States representatives, who had been at least halfway loyal to the king, coalesced to denounce royal policy and demanded the withdrawal of the army. The States raised troops of their own and amalgamated them with the rebels in Holland before November was over. Prince William of Orange and his Calvinist supporters further increased their control over the revolt in the course of 1577 (Image 2.6). Multiple provinces appointed William stadtholder, or captain general, of the armed forces, making him effectively commander-in-chief of the rebellion.

The king's half-brother and newly appointed representative, Don Juan of Austria, consented to a troop withdrawal to the loyal French-speaking provinces in the south, and the energetic counter-Reformation process shrivelled in their absence. Don Juan died on 1 October 1578, but his second-in-command, young Prince of Parma Alessandro Farnese, son of Margherita of Austria and hero of Lepanto, took the reins of the army of Flanders. He became Duke of Parma in Italy upon the death of his father in 1586 but, as ruler, he never set foot in his duchy. 'Parma', as he was called, destroyed

Image 2.6 Willem Baudartius: Entrance of William of Orange into Brussels 1577, British Museum (public domain). The collapse of Spanish authority in the aftermath of King Philip II's bankruptcy in 1575 enabled the rebels to occupy the Flemish-speaking cities almost unopposed

a large rebel army invading from France almost without Spanish losses at Gembloux. The southern Walloon provinces rallied to the Crown in the Union of Arras, while the northernmost provinces reacted with their own Calvinist Union of Utrecht in January 1579. City councils such as those of Ghent, Antwerp and Brussels were taken over by a minority of Calvinist zealots. By 1579 no official recognition was given to the king of Spain at all, and by 1581 the rebellious Netherlands formally declared itself a Republic of United Provinces.

The strategic context quickly shifted, however. After Spain and the Ottoman Empire reached a truce in 1581, Philip made the reconquest of the Protestant Low Countries his priority. A bonanza in silver remittances from Peru (Potosì in modern Bolivia) restored the king's finances. Farnese widened his base by taking control over the lower German Rhineland where supplies were easily obtained, and occupied some ports along the North Sea coast in order to facilitate communication with Spain. The arrival of strong contingents of Spanish and Italian troops from Milan in June 1582 (via the Alps, and marching through friendly Savoy and Lorraine, over what became known as the *Spanish Road*) enabled him to augment his army from 45,000 to 60,000 professional soldiers, who hailed from all of Europe. Indeed, when we speak of a Spanish army, it must be understood that ethnic Iberians, who were overwhelmingly Castilians, constituted at most 20% of the force. The remainder consisted of variable proportions of Walloons, Germans, Italians and whatever other forces were available.[69] Farnese first offered generous terms to towns that opened their gates to his army, restoring their privileges and authorizing the departure of anyone who refused the Spanish regime and Catholic primacy. If the town still resisted, he occasionally massacred the garrison to serve as an example. Unlike Alva, Farnese was a clever politician who understood that most of the inhabitants did not identify with Calvinist extremists. He was also aided by scores of Italian engineers who erected a chain of field fortifications and river barricades around selected targets of the army. In 1583, he occupied Dunkirk and Nieuwpoort on the North Sea, to facilitate maritime communication with Spain. In 1584, he captured towns in Brabant and Flanders, where the urban institutions were maintained or restored but Catholics took command. Antwerp submitted to Farnese in 1585 after a long blockade (Image 2.7). Then the counter-Reformation was applied afresh, as thousands of inhabitants reconciled themselves with Rome. Tens of thousands of steadfast Protestants migrated north to Holland and Zeeland. Between 1582 and 1589, Alessandro Farnese recovered over 80 towns for the king of Spain, with their considerable economic resources. The command centres of the revolt in the south disappeared and thereafter all the crucial decisions were made in Holland (Map 3).[70]

A Spanish contract killer assassinated Prince William of Orange in 1584. Until 1588 the rebels offered leadership of their movement to foreign princes, without success. Queen Elizabeth I of England, alarmed at the recovery of about three-quarters of the Low Countries by the army of Flanders, openly supported the rebels by the Treaty of Nonsuch in 1585. She had covertly financed the Dutch Revolt from its outset, and encouraged English subjects to join its ranks, while

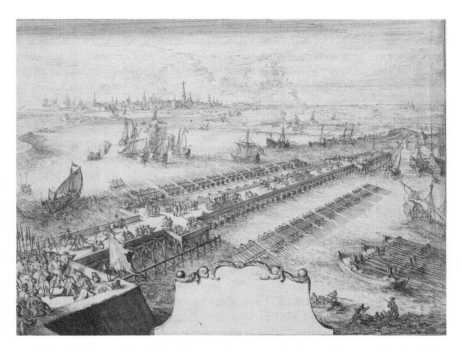

Image 2.7 Romeyn de Hooghe: Le Pont de Farnese, Harvard Fogg Museum M26581. The Duke of Parma's bridge spans the River Scheldt near its mouth and isolates Antwerp in 1585. Italian engineering prowess played a major role in the reconquest of the rebel cities between 1579 and 1588

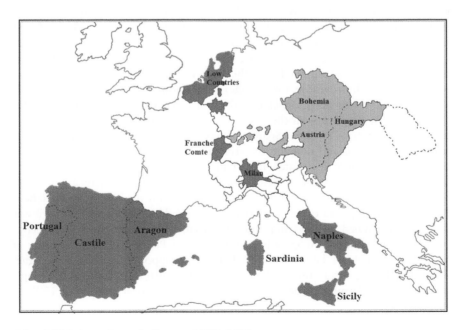

Map 3 Habsburg States in Europe 1580–1620

claiming friendship for her former brother-in-law, Philip II. Her ardent Calvinist commander, the Earl of Leicester, led a contingent of almost 10,000 men to the continent, and, together with the Scots, British soldiers constituted about a third of the soldiers fighting the Spanish. Probably the majority of the troops fighting Spain were foreigners by this time, including French and German contingents.[71] They were not nearly enough. Unpaid English troops turned several key towns over to the Spanish army in the late 1580s. The end of the revolt was in sight and the Duke of Parma proposed a plan to end the rebellion of Holland and Zeeland by granting limited toleration to the Calvinists there, but the king rejected it.

Spanish progress was halted due to events unfolding elsewhere. Queen Elizabeth removed by judicial murder her Catholic heir and successor, Mary Queen of Scots, early in 1587. King Philip reacted by assembling a fleet of 130 ships large and small, the Spanish Armada, and instructed Farnese to move troops to the Channel for an invasion of England. Parma protested that the Dutch revolt was on the verge of collapsing and that it was the wrong time to change targets. Philip insisted on obedience, and the naval force sailed up the Channel in 1588, skirmishing with the English navy. Almost intact, it put into the French Catholic town of Calais to repair its damage, where English and Dutch ships harassed it. Despite losing only five ships, the Admiral Duke of Medina Sidonia decided to take the Armada home by sailing north around Scotland, and it was largely wrecked by storms off Ireland, a 'Protestant wind'. Philip II lost 40 ships and circa 15,000 men that might have quelled the Dutch Revolt completely. It has been claimed that this marked the decline of Spanish sea power, but this is certainly not true.[72]

In 1589 Elizabeth and the Dutch launched an 'English Armada' of circa 200 vessels commanded by Sir Francis Drake to attack Portugal, and to invite the population to rise up against Philip II around a pretender to the throne. It attempted several landings in northwest Spain and Portugal, and occupied Lisbon for little more than a day but the expected rising never took place. Discipline among the soldiers and sailors, who were largely adventurers and volunteers, could not be maintained, and the army commander, Sir John Norris, did not stock enough provisions for a longer expedition. Resistance by the Spanish and Portuguese was fierce on land and on sea, where galleys picked off ships that could not keep up with the fleet. The expedition was defeated with heavy loss of men, perhaps equal to Spanish losses the year before. Spain replaced its ocean-going vessels and retained the strategic initiative at sea, which enabled it to convoy its treasure fleets safely from Cuba to Seville year after year.[73]

The diplomatic situation worsened for Spain in 1589 after a religious zealot assassinated the Catholic king of France, Henri III, for it made his legitimate heir, Henri de Navarre, head of the Protestant party, the king of France. The civil war in France intensified, as Paris and other major cities like Rouen refused to recognize Henri IV as king. Philip ordered the Duke of Parma to march his army of Flanders hundreds of kilometres into France to support the Catholic League, which lifted the pressure off the Dutch. While he personally deplored the king's policy, Farnese skirmished successfully with the French royal army from 1590 to

1592. The Duke of Parma died of wounds at the end of 1592, when the king had already decided to replace him as the head of the army. Most Catholic League towns submitted to Henri after he converted to Catholicism in 1593, following which he declared open war on Spain. This meant that the army of Flanders had to fight on two fronts until peace with France was signed in 1598.

William of Orange's son and successor, Maurice of Orange-Nassau, used Spain's mounting troubles to stabilize the resistance along the wide Rhine and the Ijssel rivers, by erecting a series of earthen and timber field fortifications and fortifying nearby towns with the bastioned trace. The immobilization of the war along a 'front line' certainly improved the lot of the peasantry. Soldiers of both sides plundered villagers on a vast scale when the war was fought in a broad no-man's-land between walled towns. Both the Duke of Parma and the Dutch rebels extorted money from civilians in the 1580s and imposed expensive safe-conducts on the movement of people and goods. Armed peasants occasionally rebelled against the States' soldiers, and the soldiers retaliated with local reprisals. They also suffered periodic strategic flooding inflicted on them by Dutch (but not Spanish) leaders. In the late 1580s, large stretches of North Brabant, Friesland, Groningen, Overijssel and Gelderland were depopulated by war.[74] After 1590, however, garrisons of professional soldiers and local militias held a belt of fortified towns and outlying earthworks that denied Spanish access to the Republic's prosperous core. Maurice protected the heartland even more by conquering thirty Spanish-held fortresses between 1590 and 1609. Maurice first seized the city of Breda by surprise in 1590 and occupied much of North Brabant. When the army of Flanders marched into France in 1591, Maurice advanced towards Antwerp and the Scheldt river estuary with a proper field army of 26,000 professional soldiers, cutting the city off from the sea.[75] By 1594, the Dutch had reconquered the Catholic northeast province around Groningen, thereby shortening the border considerably. Maurice's army operated on interior lines, and he trained the troops in forced marches in order to acquire local superiority. Dutch troops and artillery moved quickly by river barges along a multitude of canals and rivers in the waterlogged plain. Maurice became a specialist of siege warfare, which he managed to the smallest detail. He expedited operations by hiring thousands of pioneers to dig trenches and saps, and made the artillery more efficient by reducing it to just four calibres.[76] The field armies were now of comparable size and the Spanish were on the strategic defensive.

The Low Countries were always considered the 'School of War', where technical innovations of all kinds transformed fighting. In the 1570s and 1580s, the Italians dominated the technical arms. In the 1590s, the Dutch reduced the disparity and introduced changes quickly adopted elsewhere. Maurice of Nassau, stadtholder, or military governor, of the five southern provinces, made an effort to improve the quality of his professional soldiers after 1594 by drilling them incessantly, to reduce their skills deficiency against the expert Spanish infantry.[77] The originator of these reforms was probably his elder cousin, William Ludwig of Nassau, stadtholder in the northeast provinces, who was inspired by the infantry tactics of the ancient Greeks and Romans. Another key reformer was the spokesman, or Pensionary, of the States of Holland, Jan van Oldenbarnevelt, who placed that key province's finances on firmer foundations. The States General committed to paying the soldiers on time and in full in weekly instalments and increased their pay from five to eight guilders a month, a good wage for a single man. Dutch soldiers were also given bonuses for moving earth, which could double the monthly wage. The provinces refused to establish a central treasury, so wages and other military expenditures were assigned to individual provinces, continually negotiated. French money began to flow after 1595 just as English subsidies to the Republic were scaled back.

Dutch civilians did not like professional soldiers and the States did not like to raise taxes to pay for them, especially given that the majority of them were foreigners. Most soldiers adhered to the German landsknecht tradition of tight corporate groups, with a penchant for riotous living.[78] Maurice reduced company sizes from 300 to 100 men, probably on the French Huguenot model, in an attempt to improve their discipline. This increased the control of officers over the men. Sergeants and civilian judicial auditors were entrusted with imposing discipline on them. The States of Holland appointed special muster masters to reduce fraudulent practices committed by captains and soldiers alike. In 1596, the weaponry was standardized in order to facilitate supply. Maurice and his cousins, William Louis and Frederick Henry, then increased their control over the appointment of captains and their junior officers.[79] All these reforms reduced the incidence of mutiny among the soldiery.

While the Dutch economy began to flourish, the flow of treasure from the Americas dropped simultaneously and the Army of Flanders lacked the cash to continue the war. Most of the English troops withdrew to defend their homeland in 1588, while others were deployed to quell a Spanish-supported Irish rebellion in Ulster. The Spanish monarchy's resources were hopelessly overextended at the end of the sixteenth century, committed to endless warfare both in the Mediterranean and the Atlantic. The king was forced to declare bankruptcy again in 1596. The lack of pay triggered a spate of mutinies in the regiments and tercios serving Spain in the Low Countries.[80] In 1600, Maurice of Nassau tried to close off Spain's access to the sea by a coastal offensive designed to trigger a new rising in Flanders. His army, with a fleet in support, broke the small Spanish army on the dunes outside Nieuwpoort on 2 July, the rebels' only significant victory in a field battle, but the Dutch soon found themselves deep in hostile territory with no supplies and were forced to retreat.

Spain's situation improved again when a Genoese banker, Ambrogio Spìnola, stepped forward to offer troops and money in exchange for the right to command them. In 1602, he brought 9,000 fresh troops to Flanders, paid for out of his own resources and those of a consortium of Genoese financiers in his sway. The next year, Spinola took charge of the principal military operation, the siege of Ostend, the last remaining rebel town in the southern Netherlands, garrisoned with British troops and regularly relieved by sea. The banker possessed no experience as a soldier, but he was a superb organizer and so the siege operations accelerated until the city surrendered in August 1604. The following year, Spinola's army, operating along the Rhine, broke through the great river's barrier with relative ease and captured several fortresses, opening up the Dutch interior to organized 'contributions'. The Dutch accelerated their efforts to build a reinforced line of earthworks and redoubts over 200 kilometres in length. Spinola penetrated these again in 1606, and captured the remaining Dutch outposts in the German Rhineland. The Dutch army swelled from 35,000 men to 51,000 in order to stem the tide.[81] Spinola was forced to suspend his operations after the Spanish crown declared a fresh bankruptcy in 1607.

The revolt only survived because the rebels never lost the initiative at sea. Small Dutch vessels navigated everywhere along the coast and along the larger rivers, too. The States of Holland and Zeeland soon set up five Admiralty boards that reflected the decentralized nature of the young republic, although Amsterdam quickly came to the fore. Navy boards hired out arms, ammunition and stores to private enterprisers, and shipbuilding flourished in the areas removed from the fighting. The States derived dues from licensed trade, but much covert smuggling took place, and, as time went on, Amsterdam merchants found it profitable to supply the Spanish army, too, to the great annoyance of Maurice of Nassau. Dutch ships and forts eliminated Antwerp as a maritime hub after its recapture by Spain in 1585, and the blockade of the River Scheldt accelerated the growth of Amsterdam, which soon surpassed Antwerp in importance. From the outset of the revolt, privateering flourished, especially in Zeeland. When King James I of England made peace with Spain in 1604, many English privateers moved to Zeeland to continue their business, and perhaps 60% of the prizes belonged to them. So many neutral ships fell victim to Protestant privateers that the Dutch Republic imposed a 20,000 guilder deposit on its corsairs to break this habit.[82] In addition to the Mediterranean, Dutch privateers hunted Spanish and Portuguese ships in the distant waters of the Americas and Asia, but they were successful only in the latter ventures. In retaliation, Catholic Flemish privateers operating out of Dunkirk inflicted considerable damage on Dutch and English commerce.

The surge in Dutch maritime trade made it easier to import raw materials and to export finished goods over much of the world. One hundred thousand refugees arriving from the more industrial southern Netherlands brought their skills and their international networks with them. Industries new to the region multiplied in Amsterdam and Leiden. Dutch engineering expertise and money financed mining and arms production in friendly Sweden. The increasing standardization of weapons and military hardware of all kinds made the Republic a major producer, and foreign powers could buy arms and gunpowder much more cheaply there than anywhere else. Before long, Dutch armaments exporters developed into general army purveyors for foreign states, and were able to arrange the financing of their sales for the purchasers.[83]

The emergency taxation and fitful foreign subsidies from England and France of the early years gave way to regular wartime taxation. The revolt's origins lay in Alva's unconstitutional tenth-penny tax. As an independent entity, Holland became the most heavily taxed place in Europe, and perhaps the world. Oldenbarnevelt, the Pensionary, or spokesman, for the States of Holland, regularized the ordinary budget in the 1590s. Excise taxes, which provided the majority of receipts, were farmed out to businessmen who collected it on their own. Regular wartime taxation increased the ability of the States of Holland to borrow money and repay the interest and the principal on schedule. Given the widespread trust in the system, people were willing to lend money on a large scale in the 1590s, at a modest eight per cent interest (inflation ran at four per cent), then at 6.25% after 1600. The contrast is striking between the stability of the Republic's finances and the repeated bankruptcies of the overextended King of Spain.[84]

Map 4 The Low Countries divided by the Twelve Years' Truce in 1609

Burgeoning seaborne commerce gradually softened the ardour of Dutch merchants, who became aware that if they were at peace with Spain, they would be able to trade with the vast Spanish and Portuguese empires in America and Asia, and trade from Iberian ports in the Mediterranean, too. The new luxury industries could only flourish if they could obtain raw materials from southern Europe and access stable markets there. England made peace with Spain in 1604 over just such considerations. Maurice of Orange and the Calvinist church leaders desired to fight on in order to recover the increasingly Catholic areas to the east and the south, but Amsterdam merchant groups led by Oldenbarnevelt led the movement to reach a cease-fire with Spain. The belligerents signed a 12-year truce in 1609, which opened Spanish ports to Dutch ships (Map 4). Fighting ceased entirely in Europe, although it continued sporadically over control of distant colonies. The assassination of Henri IV by an isolated fanatic in 1610 stopped cold French preparations for a new war with the Habsburgs of Spain, and Europe found itself suddenly at peace.

Notes

1   John F Guilmartin, 1988.
2   Gabor Agoston, 2015.
3   Agoston, 2015.
4   Gilles Veinstein, 2013.
5   Jeremy Black, 2011: 99–100.
6   Noel Malcolm, 1994: 45.
7   Geza David, 2013.
8   Gabor Agoston, 2014,.
9   Gilles Veinstein, 1989,.
10 Maria Ivanics, 2007.
11 Malcolm, 1994: 66; Pal Fodor, 2000.
12 Ivanics, 2007.
13 Geza Palffy, 2007.
14 Caroline Finkel, 1988: 122.
15 James D Tracy, 2015
16 Geza Palffy, 2009: 97.
17 Palffy, 2009: 90.
18 James D Tracy, 2013.
19 James D Tracy, 2016: 36.
20 Finkel, 1988: 9.
21 Agoston, 2014: 118.
22 Angelo Pernice, 1925.
23 Finkel, 2008: 203.
24 Tracy, 2016: 325.
25 Black, 2011: 193.
26 Agoston, 2014: 106.
27 Veinstein, 2013: 120.
28 Zoltan Peter Bagi, 2015.
29 Gabor Barta, 2002.
30 David, 2013: 297.
31 Angelo Tamborra, 1974.
32 Emrah Safa Gurkan, 2010.
33 Maurice Aymard, 1974.

34 John Francis Guilmartin, 1974: 221.
35 Louis Sicking, 2010.
36 Guilmartin, 1974: 76.
37 Réné Emmanuelli, 1963: 72, 190.
38 Salvatore Bono, 1993: 143.
39 Emrah Safa Gurkan, 2010.
40 Alberto Tenenti, 1967: 23.
41 Robert C Davis, 2003: 23.
42 Phillip Williams, 2014: 112.
43 Davis, 2003: 8.
44 Charles Monchicourt, 1913: 124.
45 Peter Earle, 1970: 144.
46 Kenneth Setton, 1984: 956.
47 Phillip Williams, 2014: 71–77.
48 Fra Bartolomeo Dal Pozzo, 1703: 12.
49 Gregory Hanlon, 1998: 23–5; for more detail, see Niccoló Capponi, 2006: 253–86; for a view from the Ottoman side, Michel Lesure, 1972.
50 Guilmartin, 1974: 200.
51 Setton, 1984: 1076.
52 Emrah Safa Gurkan, 2014.
53 Michel Fontenay, 1988.
54 Bono, *Corsari nel Mediterraneo*, 191–99.
55 Bartolomé Bennassar & Lucile Bennassar, 1989 : 203.
56 Earle, 1970: 136.
57 Bono, 1993: 61.
58 Francisco Felipe Olesa Muñido, 1968: 977.
59 Bono, 1993: 199.
60 Aymard, 1974: 88.
61 Camillo Manfroni, *La Marina militare del Granducato mediceo* (Rome, 1895) 117–138.
62 Bono, *Corsari nel Mediterraneo*, 110.
63 Fontenay, 'La place de la course'.
64 Williams, 2014: 141.
65 Fulvio Babudieri, 1981.
66 Tenenti, 1967: 138.
67 Ivo Van Loo, 1997.
68 Geoffrey Parker, 1977: 162.
69 Geoffrey Parker, 1972: 29–32.
70 Violet Soen, 2012.
71 Hugh Dunthorne, 2018: 67.
72 Felipe Fernandez-Armesto, 1988.
73 Luis Gorrochategui Santos, 2018; I.A.A. Thompson, 1976: 17–22.
74 Ibid., 102–108.
75 Jonathan Israel, 1995: 242.
76 H.L. Zwitzer, 1997.
77 J.A. de Moor, 1997.
78 Erik Swart, 2006,.
79 Marjolein 't Hart, 2014: 40–46.
80 Parker, 1972: 195.
81 Israel, 1995: 259–65.
82 Van Loo, 1997.
83 Hans Vogel, 1997.
84 't Hart, 2014:, 149–71.

3   Modern fortification and its impact

Cannon versus medieval walls

The Chinese invented not only gunpowder in the eleventh century AD, but the first cannon, too. Both appeared in the West in the early fourteenth century, and entered widespread usage by mid-century. They were of dubious efficacy at first: the smaller cannon in use on battlefields had, until the later fifteenth century, primarily a psychological impact. One limitation to their adoption was that saltpetre, a principal ingredient of gunpowder, was extremely expensive up until the 1380s, when governments began to organize its systematic collection. Early siege cannon, or bombards, fired a heavy ball, usually made of hand-carved stone, from a thick metal tube placed on the ground close to the wall. This placed the crew, composed of private entrepreneurs, in considerable peril. Once the siege was over, moving the gun from its emplacement was another engineering challenge. Rather than lift the heavy barrels on to wagons for transport, it was often preferable to break up the tube into pieces and then recast it at the site of the next siege. The increased availability of gunpowder in the fifteenth century resulted in the fabrication of larger guns that were more efficient as siege engines.[1] Treating the powder to form small grains (corning) accelerated its combustion and, consequently, increased the propulsion of the shot. A greater supply of saltpetre, collected from processed faecal matter and urine mixed with wood ash, gradually became available, but its consistency varied considerably from one batch to another. Sixteenth century artisans mixed powder in two or three sizes of grain, coarser for the artillery, finer for hand-held weapons. The gun tubes had to be designed to withstand the force of the detonation inside the powder chamber, and pieces firing larger projectiles using greater explosive charges needed to be especially thick. Even then, the heat generated by the conflagration limited the gun to a few shots per day. Instead of forging tubes in iron strips bound with rings like a barrel, founders began to cast them whole. The best ones were made of bronze, which was less brittle than iron, but it was much more expensive.[2]

The French efforts to expel the English invaders from the kingdom in the first half of the fifteenth century would prove to be a decisive laboratory in the evolution of gunpowder weapons. Subsequent wars against the Dukes of

Burgundy until 1477, and the repression of feudal rebellions, maintained continuity in development. Both French and Burgundian gun carriages made it easier to transport and deploy their artillery.[3] In addition to the heavy bombards, the French developed more mobile guns, firing in unison as 'batteries'. They were limited to slow rates of fire in order not to overheat the piece, and cannon barrels would have to be melted down and recast after prolonged usage, 600 rounds for an iron tube, 1,000 for a bronze piece.[4] A further important improvement was to substitute iron projectiles in place of carved stone balls, which tended to shatter against town walls. Until the eighteenth century, metal was expensive to produce and most tools were made of wood. Expensive cast-iron balls inflicted several times more damage than stone projectiles, and when recovered could be fired multiple times. This made it possible to reduce both the bore of the gun and the thickness of the tube. It reduced the piece's overall weight while retaining the same or better destructive effect, and the thinner barrels cooled more quickly, enabling them to be reloaded sooner. Craftsmen lengthened the barrels so that the gases produced in the conflagration could expand more completely inside them, adding range to the projectile and increasing its accuracy, too. By the sixteenth century, the period of experimentation had come to an end. Both the artillery and smaller firearms achieved forms they would retain for 300 years. These were the weapons that would overwhelm Italian city states in 1494, whose ramparts were not built to withstand saturation bombardment.[5]

Medieval fortifications of stone and brick were very effective before the advent of modern siege artillery. Trebuchets and catapults hurling stones were designed as much to wreck buildings inside the walled perimeter and to render the town uninhabitable. Town defences relied on their great height, so they could not be scaled with ladders. The base of the wall might be several metres thick, but the depth of masonry would have to taper off the higher it rose so as not to collapse under the weight. The catwalk could accommodate archers firing from crennelated positions but it was not possible to concentrate soldiers along the narrow walkway. Attackers at the base of the wall would have to be hit by archers and crossbowmen firing from towers projecting outward from the curtain wall. Early cannon firing sacks full of metal could help keep the base of the wall clear of assailants attempting to dig underneath it to collapse the structure but they would, of necessity, have to be small. Neither the curtain wall nor the tower would be able to accommodate larger cannon designed to knock out the siege artillery used in the fifteenth century. Their weight and recoil would collapse the wall or floor of the tower on which they were positioned. The tower's roof would prevent the evacuation of dense smoke. One solution was to pack earth behind the wall in order to place soldiers and cannon on top, but repeat firing would eventually weaken the structure, just as the packed earth would eventually collapse the wall outwards into the ditch.[6] A second solution was to build a second wall behind the one being bombarded, which remained largely invisible to the besiegers until the first one collapsed.

Advent of the bastioned trace

Modern artillery shifted the advantage from the defender to the attacker. To respond effectively to a battery of besieger guns, town and castle walls had to be designed to accommodate artillery of their own. An early improvement was to replace square towers by circular ones, which helped deflect the shot. Governments adapted by building semi-circular platforms flush with the curtain wall, projecting into the moat, with guns placed on top to fire at distant targets and others placed lower down in *casemates* to fire into the moat. Artillery castles multiplied in the late fifteenth and early sixteenth centuries. Guns placed in enclosed casemates were not an ideal solution, however, for the thick smoke generated by every shot soon suffocated and blinded the crews. The rapid progress of the French army under King Charles VIII in 1494, unstoppable with its horse-drawn heavy cannon, placed great urgency upon Italian princes and cities to adapt to the threat. In the last decades of the fifteenth century, a number of Italian architects designed angular projections from the walls, called *bastions*, designed to enable guns placed on top of them to both fire at distant targets and to provide supporting fire to its neighbouring bastion and eliminate any dead ground. Brick and stone casemates with vaulted ceilings provided shelter for men and materials underneath the platforms. Walls were flared outward at the base to facilitate hitting men lodged there. The ramparts were then set into a deep ditch, making it impossible for enemy gunners to see the lower part of the wall until they were right up at the edge of it. Redesigned fortifications were attempted for castles or citadels at first, because of the prohibitive expense of revamping the walls of towns. Geoffrey Parker labelled this low-profile, angular system of fortification, first applied to Sarzanello in Liguria, the 'trace italienne', although contemporaries never used the term in French or any other language.[7] We will speak of the bastioned trace, or modern-style, fortification. The bastions could be protected by detached triangular-shaped works sitting in the ditch and open to the rear, called *ravelins*. These outworks protected both the curtain wall and the face of neighbouring bastions, making it impossible to fire at the latter from a distance. The ravelins would have to be captured before the curtain wall and the bastions facing them could really be threatened (Image 3.1). Within a few decades, engineers suggested establishing a protected area on the outer rim of the moat, the *counterscarp*, where soldiers would be stationed behind a palisade to keep the enemy at bay. Earth was landscaped into a gentle slope (a *glacis*) that removed the base of the fortifications from the view of the attackers. Governments then prohibited the erection of any permanent structure within almost a kilometre outside the ramparts, in order to have a clear field of fire. In the event of a siege, any buildings erected outside close to the wall were immediately demolished, with no compensation to the landlords.

The new designs were not the product of any single architect, but in the competitive city-state system of Italy in 1500, a number of contemporaries of Leonardo da Vinci emerged with fresh solutions. Most of the first generation of engineer–architects originated from Central and Northern Italy. One of the earliest engineers

Image 3.1 Sarzanello (public domain). The late fifteenth-century castle, set into
    a ditch to reduce its profile, was the prototype for future artillery forts,
    with mutually supporting platforms for cannon and musket fire, and one
    side protected by a detached ravelin

who designed angular towers for artillery was the Sienese Francesco di Giorgio
Martini (1439–1501). He invented the procedure of slanting the fortress walls outward to help deflect cannonballs. One of his disciples was the Veronese Franciscan
scholar, Fra Giovanni Giocondo (1433–1515), who participated in French sieges in
Italy after 1500. The Florentine Giuliano di Francesco Giamberti da Sangallo
(1445–1516) erected the bastioned fort of Poggio Imperiale (1487– abandoned in
1513), overlooking the highway between Florence and its enemy, Siena. His
brother, Antonio da Sangallo the elder (1463?–1534), began a small pentagonal
fortress at Civita Castellana in Lazio in 1494. The Genoese reinforced the triangular artillery castle just outside the strategic town of Sarzana after 1493, adding
a freestanding ravelin in 1497 to protect the gate. Giuliano da Sangallo erected
another fort at the Roman beach town of Nettuno in 1501. By the 1520s, the new
style emerged in recognizable form.

Fortification projects based on the new designs began to multiply in the 1520s,
and especially the 1530s, no longer being restricted to citadels and isolated forts.
Small bastions began to appear along the town walls of Civitavecchia and Senigallia
(both of them ports) in the Papal States and at Urbino and Ferrara, both ducal capitals. These works were added piecemeal, in order to strengthen a gate or
a vulnerable approach to the city. Architects then erected bastions at regular intervals along the wall, so that they might support each other. Duke Guidobaldo of
Urbino, an active condottiere, fortified Pesaro, the Adriatic port town where he

resided, with five mutually supporting bastions in 1528.[8] The first great project of city refortification began in 1530 at Verona, designed by a native son, Michele di Sanmicheli. Verona sat at the exit of an Alpine valley leading from the Brenner Pass in Austria, the only one that could accommodate wheeled vehicles. The city's Venetian masters hoped thereby to lock the German Imperial troops out of Northern Italy. Sanmichieli later devoted himself to strengthening other large cities in the Venetian Terraferma, including Padua, Brescia and Bergamo, which had all suffered terribly during the early Italian wars. In 1543, he began a powerful artillery fortress on the Lido, the beach at the entrance to the Venetian lagoon, to protect the harbour. J.R. Hale has emphasized the strain such building imposed, not only on the Republic's finances, but also on the civilians living in the shadow of the new bastions, who were often conscripted into labour details (called *corvées*) without pay.[9] The number of professional soldiers guarding these towns in peacetime was usually very modest, typically under 200 men, assigned to sentinel duty and to guard the military stores on site.[10]

Italian princes often preferred just to enhance the strength of the citadel, which was a fort designed to control a city. Citadels erected along the outer wall of a city could be held against a town in revolt by a fairly small garrison, typically fewer than 100 men. Milan's great castle, built by the Visconti lords in the fourteenth century, served as the prototype: it was modernized with bastions in the sixteenth century. Its Spanish garrison of 500–600 men kept the great city of more than 100,000 inhabitants in the king's obedience, and the fortress served thereafter as the seat of Spanish influence in all of Northern Italy. The first Medici Dukes of Florence (after 1570, styled Grand Dukes of Tuscany) erected three bastioned citadels to keep the former republican city under its firm rule. The first of these, the Fortezza da Basso on the north bank of the Arno, was begun in 1534.[11] The governor was always an outsider in the prince's employment, and, for security reasons, it was forbidden for Florentines to serve in the garrison there. The Medici built similar bastioned strongholds in most of their subject towns, such as Pisa, Arezzo, Cortona, Grosseto, Portoferraio and, most importantly, Siena (conquered in 1555), and erected additional fortresses controlling all the roads leading into the duchy, like an early Maginot line.[12] The king of Spain erected strong citadels at the edge of major towns in his kingdom of Naples (L'Aquila, Bari, Barletta, Lecce), which enabled him to control these with garrisons of 100 or 150 men in normal times. The Pope transformed the monumental Roman Emperor Hadrian's tomb on the bank of the River Tiber into a citadel enhanced with small bastions in the 1560s. A discreet corridor enabled the pontiff to flee from the new Vatican palace to safety there in 1527. The Urbinese Francesco Paciotto erected a very strong citadel at the edge of Turin's city walls in 1564, which served as a model for Antwerp at the onset of the Dutch Revolt, and then for other towns.[13] To better dominate the restive Monferrato district on the upper River Po, the Dukes of Mantua raised an imposing citadel at Casale that excited the covetousness of other powers (Image 3.2). Nothing expressed a prince's power so much as a citadel, commanded by a foreigner (that is,

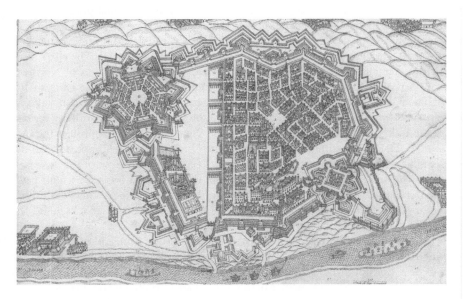

Image 3.2 Casale Monferrato ca. 1650, Biblioteca Palatina Parma 3711 fol.41. A mature example of Italian bastioned fortifications, the duke of Mantua's city on the Po river was enclosed by modern bastions, ravelins and outworks, its medieval castle enhanced by modern works (lower right) and a great citadel (1575) capable of resisting modern armies

someone not native to the city, and without kin living nearby) and a garrison that remained outside the jurisdiction of local magistrates. Citadels were places where plotters or recalcitrant feudal lords might be imprisoned for crimes, both real and imaginary. They were well stocked with weapons, powder and other stores that enabled princes to levy and equip an army in short order. Parrott sees the citadel as a tool of domination and intimidation, a symbolic declaration by the ruling dynasty that it was capable of imposing its will on any ambitious rival. It was comparable to the ducal palace as a symbol of dynastic power.[14]

The new techniques of fortification hurriedly applied in the Mediterranean enabled the Christian states to slow down the expansion of the Ottoman fleets and their Barbary Coast auxiliaries. Venetian Corfu held out long enough in 1537 to be relieved. The fortifications around the port of Malta in 1565 likewise withstood continuous assaults and bombardment long enough for the king of Spain to send help. After the siege, the Knights of Saint John designed a new city laid out on the peninsula inside the port, called Valletta, with massive ramparts designed to dissuade another attack. Elsewhere, European states erected bastioned traces around strategic port cities, some of which were huge by early modern standards. Spain authorized the levy of special surtaxes to finance these and paid for hundreds of coastal watchtowers in addition. Imagine the cost of erecting the city wall of Naples, eight kilometres in circumference, encircling close to a quarter of a million inhabitants in 1596 and bolted down with three distinct citadels![15] Palermo, home to a hundred thousand people, erected similar walls, as did Messina, main base of the king of Spain's galley squadron. Taranto and Gaeta, strategic ports with ample harbours in the kingdom of Naples, acquired similar defences designed by Italian architects. Italian engineers then designed and supervised dozens of fortification projects in Spain and Portugal and throughout their far-flung empires in Asia and America. After 1600, they hardened the Iberian ports enough so that Anglo–Dutch adventurers could no longer inflict great damage there.[16]

Venice's seaborne empire in Dalmatia and Greece relied upon a string of fortified harbours possessing very little hinterland. The Republic embarked on a programme of *fortificazione alla moderna* in order to strengthen these against amphibious attacks by the Ottomans, or by armies based in Bosnia.[17] The *Venetian Arsenal* (Europe's largest industrial complex) built galleys and stored them in sheds when they were not on patrol. It produced sails, rope and a variety of naval stores. Venice cast a great many bronze cannon in the Arsenal, and set up schools for gunnery there and in all the important cities.[18] The Republic of Saint Mark erected considerable modern ramparts, first around Famagusta in Cyprus, and then provided Nicosia with a circle of modern bastions, finished just shortly before the Ottomans captured it in 1570. Candia (modern Heraklion) was the strongest fortress on Crete, but smaller towns and isolated forts protecting strategic anchorages were all refortified in the late sixteenth century. The Papacy was compelled to fortify its Adriatic coast simultaneously, with bastioned fortifications around its principal port at Ancona. Even the Marian shrine at Loreto overlooking the Adriatic, filled with a fabulous treasure of ex-voto offerings, acquired bastioned fortifications during this period.

Three iconic fortress towns arose on empty sites. The first was on the island of Malta in the immediate aftermath of the siege of 1565. The walls of the port town Birgiu, which narrowly escaped capture, were overlooked by higher ground. A prestigious Tuscan engineer, Francesco Laparelli, an assistant to his countryman Michelangelo Buonarotti, was dispatched from Rome to erect a new city on the peninsula where Fort Sant'Elmo stood. With 3,000 pioneers working alongside soldiers and captives, Valetta gradually filled the skyline overlooking the deep harbour. The engineer calculated that it would require 345,000 man-days to build, which was an underestimate. Nevertheless, by 1569, most of basic work was complete and, in 1582, only a few lots stood empty. The new town was home to 4,000 people, while the old quarter of Birgiu gradually decayed. Valetta's fortifications later expanded outward to constitute one of the strongest cities in southern Europe.[19] Another major deepwater port to rise as a planned town was Livorno, only 15 kilometres away from Pisa, where the Medici intended to create an international trading hub, or free port. A very different town arose on the eastern extremity of the flat North Italian plain at Palmanova, within view of the Slovenian Alps. Ottoman raiding parties from Bosnia periodically ravaged this rich landscape in the fifteenth century, and the Venetian overlords also wished to keep out the German Habsburg emperors. Work on the perfectly regular (that is, symmetrical) fortress city began in 1593, under the direction of Venetian military overseers, who mobilized up to 7,500 pioneers.[20]

The engineers themselves, after 1550, hailed from all over Central and Northern Italy, and worked for a variety of Western employers.[21] Engineering quickly acquired high status as an intellectual pursuit, and urban aristocrats – even cardinals – felt no shame in pursuing it as a profession. Fortification, reduced to an abstract science built on mathematics and geometry, could be cultivated by educated people from all walks of life. Galileo himself taught a course on fortification at the university of Padua in 1592–1593. Over the entire period, Italians disseminated the principles of geometry, ballistics and fortification design in printed books, illustrated with engravings. The same people undertook ballistics studies and examined closely the effects of shot on different materials. Vannoccio Biringuccio's 'Pirotechnia' (1540) vulgarized specialist knowledge in mining, metallurgy and gun founding, while Nicolo Tartaglia's 'La nova scientia' (1537) explored the mathematics of gunnery. The same individuals also fostered an interest in cartography and surveying. Most of the early works, such as a great map of the kingdom of Hungary executed in 1570, were of Italian origin. Hélène Vérin notes that, of 32 published works on fortification between 1554 and 1600, 26 were penned by Italian authors, four were French, two Spanish, one was German and one was Dutch. Venice, the world's most important centre of the printing industry, was the place of publication of a third of these works.[22]

Italian engineers and their offspring in Northern and Central Europe

Proof of the engineers' prestige is found in the desire of kings to acquire their services. François I and Charles V employed them to prevent each other's success. In order to force France to weaken its grasp on Piedmont, the Emperor invaded the kingdom from the north and east, where there were no natural barriers between Imperial lands and Paris. The rich French heartlands of Picardy and Champagne were particularly vulnerable to attack. On several occasions the emperor Charles was able to enlist the help of King Henry VIII of England, still ensconced in Calais and advancing ancient claims to the French throne. King François I hired the Papal engineer Girolamo Marini in 1534 to buttress France's eastern defences. Another Italian, Antonio da Castello, fortified Saint Pol on the northern border.[23] Assisted by a new tax specially designed to finance fortification, these architects inaugurated a series of small fortress towns just north of the River Somme, thickening the old walls and erecting semi-circular artillery towers. Towns in Champagne along likely routes of invasion acquired bastions built not as an interlocking system, but erected individually to guard gates and exposed sections of wall. The Duke of Lorraine, caught between Habsburg and Valois armies, hired Italian engineers too, in order to protect his capital, Nancy.

In the course of the 1540s, both France and the Empire employed Italian engineers to modernize in earnest the fortifications of the principal frontier towns, and, in some cases, built fortress-towns *ex nihilo* to close off avenues of approach. As the wars dragged on in the northern theatre through the 1550s, King Henri II relied on the campaigning skill of the Duc de Guise, teamed with the engineering virtuosity of a Florentine exile, Piero Strozzi. On the Imperial side, in the single generation between 1530 and 1570, twelve towns and four citadels were newly fortified and another eighteen towns were largely modernized. Most of these were close to the French border, but the largest city, Antwerp, acquired new fortifications designed by Donato Buoni di Pellizuoli in 1542–1543.[24] By then, the term *ingénieur* was in common use in French to signify a specialist in military construction. In 1544, Henry of England and the Emperor Charles combined their efforts along the northern frontier, with the latter penetrating Champagne through Lorraine. The French had time to bolster the urban defences of Saint Dizier with earthworks, and held the Imperials at bay. Similar work proceeded on the Pyrenean frontier between the two dynasties. King Ferdinand of Aragon erected an important artillery castle at Salses in 1503, which blocked the advance of French armies into Catalonia along the malaria-infested coastal plain. Short of sporting angular bastions, it was a thoroughly modern and efficient fortress.

In 1544, Henry VIII of England hired, at great expense, an Italian engineer of his own, Girolamo Pennacchi, who was killed at the siege of Boulogne the same year. While the siege was successful, the town was handed back to France in the subsequent peace.[25] In order to shield his island kingdom from attack, Henry VIII commissioned a whole series of coastal artillery castles whose semi-circular gun platforms ignored advances in fortification design. Castles and coastal defence works were erected along the south coast and at Hull, a programme accelerated after 1538.[26] Another threat from France took the form of invasion from Scotland, a hereditary enemy. Queen Elizabeth began work on the northern fortress port of Berwick, begun by an English engineer Sir Richard Lee and then improved by the Florentine Giovanni Portinari.[27] More bastioned fortifications arose around the Thames estuary during the crisis of the Spanish Armada. The counter-insurgency war in Ireland also depended upon the multiplication of earthen strongpoints in the Huguenot manner, particularly in Ulster.

Compared with the cost of recruiting and maintaining soldiers in field armies, fortifications were a cheap means of defence, since the costs were spread out over decades. But even the best fortresses were unlikely to hold out for very long if the garrison lacked resolve, or if they knew that they could not be relieved.[28] One might imagine that fortresses not benefiting from redesign might be doomed to fall quickly. In fact, the siege of Saint Dizier in Champagne demonstrated that bastions were only one element governing the defence of strongholds. Castles and, above all, cities required garrisons comprising professional soldiers accustomed to fighting and oblivious to the damage to the local economy. (Bourgeois militias on their own quickly capitulated in order to avoid the sack of farms in the vicinity of towns, which they owned.) Garrisons also offered stiff resistance if they expected friendly troops to rescue them. In this regard, we might look at three emblematic sieges of the 1550s that reveal the difficulties of capturing fortresses willing to put up stiff resistance: Metz, Thérouanne and Siena.

In 1552, while the Emperor was distracted by German Protestant rebels, King Henri's army seized three (French-speaking) towns deep in Imperial Lorraine, Metz, Toul and Verdun. Charles retaliated with a risky siege of Metz begun in late October of 1552 with a huge army of 45,000 men and 150 cannon, including many heavy guns, an exceptional effort for the period. Metz was bereft of masonry fortifications in the bastioned style, but the Duke de Guise and his engineer, Camillo Marini, had time to build a second interior wall of packed earth whose very existence demoralized the attackers. Charles persisted in his siege until early January 1553, losing many more men to bad weather than to fighting, and then he withdrew with only the debris of his army. Only short months later, the Imperial army descended from the Low Countries towards the River Somme to lay siege to Thérouanne, a small town graced with one of the kingdom's largest cathedrals but with little in the way of modern fortification. The Imperial artillery, collected from all over the Low Countries, consisted of 135 guns of which at least 50 were heavy pieces. Some 4,000 pioneers assisted the Imperial field army of 30,000 men, but it took weeks to set up the cannon in battery. The defenders numbered about 2,000 men with about 20 heavy guns of their own. The Italian engineer, Girolamo Marini, who perished in the bombardment, oversaw the work of repair and retrenchment of the garrison. Imperial batteries pounded Thérouanne with 18,000 heavy balls, which consumed 145 tonnes of powder, a prodigious amount for the time. The rate of fire, about 2,000 shots a day and 80 shots per gun, was more than double the intensity at Metz. Thérouanne surrendered after two months' resistance; an irate Charles V ordered that the town and its cathedral, should be razed and the land sown with salt to prevent its resurgence.[29]

Henri II took advantage of the uprising of Siena against its Spanish citadel to send a relief force to Central Italy in 1553. Sensing an impending Imperial siege, the city authorities began to erect makeshift earth and brick fortifications along the medieval wall, and collected their own stock of artillery under the direction of the veteran French general, Blaise de Monluc. Duke Cosimo of Florence tried seizing the city by surprise with his own army of 5,000 men in January 1554, but it was far too small to be successful. An Imperial force of Spaniards and Germans then reinforced this nucleus and settled into a blockade, though without ever cutting the city off from its hinterland. The besieging army almost never rose above 10,000 men, barely enough to blockade a well-armed city of 25,000 inhabitants. The formal bombardment did not begin until January 1555 and even then, the few hundred shots did little damage. Cities could deploy thousands of workers to repair the walls or erect other barriers, demolishing houses in order to collect building materials. However, over the winter, the besiegers were joined by sizeable contingents of Tuscan militiamen who effectively cut the city off from its food supply. Siena capitulated to hunger, not to bombardment, in April 1555.[30]

A new Anglo-Imperial alliance seized the French fortress town of Saint Quentin in the late summer of 1557, destroying the French army in the field nearby on 10 August. The Duke de Guise responded with a surprise assault on the unprepared English fortress of Calais on 1 January 1558, which was quickly overrun. The Peace of Câteau-Cambrésis, signed in April 1559, left France in possession of the three Lorraine towns as well as Calais, but the kingdom lost almost all its territories in Italy to the benefit of Spain.

The Low Countries revolt against Spain was an engineers' war to an even greater degree. The rebel towns in Holland and Zeeland resisted to the utmost after 1572, although they had no engineers to help them in the beginning. The multiple sieges undertaken by Alva and Requesens, combined with Spanish commitments in the Mediterranean, quickly bankrupted the monarchy. William of Orange eventually imposed fortification commissioners on town councils after 1574. The great towns in the Southern Netherlands were quickly modified *à la huguenotte*, which entailed strengthening the medieval walls and planting ravelins in the ditch in front of them. They were not strong enough to resist the Italian engineers under Alva and Alessandro Farnese, although a few Italians assisted the rebels, such as Federigo Giambelli, who served Queen Elizabeth. Chiappino Vitelli, a Tuscan general, introduced the fortified siege camp, with an outer perimeter of circumvallation, which made it easier to repel relief forces. But the Dutch adapted quickly and by the time the Army of Flanders pressed its way into the Northern Netherlands, it encountered newly designed defences around all the major towns. The pre-eminent Dutch engineer from the period was Adriaan Anthoniszoon, who fashioned a system of earth embankments not clad with brick or stone, and bastions without casemates, set behind wide wet ditches. For years, town militias were the backbone of Dutch resistance, but they were not well trained and were reluctant to serve away from home. The rebellion would have collapsed had Philip II not decided to challenge England and Henri IV after 1587.

There was a noticeable improvement after 1590, once Prince Maurice of Orange took the offensive. About 50 engineers assisted the rebels between 1572 and 1604, but these were most effective as time went on. In 1592, Maurice imposed a controller, or director-general, of fortifications, and, after 1594, the engineers were directed by the States-General, instead of local authorities. This enabled the Dutch to call upon large numbers of pioneers to assist in trench-digging, and in erecting sconces, or earthen redoubts, in strategic locations.[31] The engineers required not only mathematics to design both fortifications and siege trenches, but also knowledge of soil and hydraulics and an understanding of the effects of erosion by wind and rain. They were often in the front line; at the siege of Ostend from 1601–1604, seven of the twelve Dutch engineers employed there were killed. Maurice of Orange emphasized sieges over battles and was a skilled mathematician. He also employed in his court the engineer Simon Stevin, who worked on only four or five projects after 1598,

but was an influential adviser. Maurice and Stevin introduced a course in mathematics for military engineers taught in Dutch at the University of Leiden in
1600. It is unclear whether any practising military engineers attended these lessons, however. By 1620, most Dutch fortification projects were complete, such
that the little Republic possessed a ring of powerful strongholds protecting its
inner core. Dutch engineers were, therefore, hired abroad in some numbers.
They were crucial in the fortification of Denmark and the Hanse towns in
Northern Germany, then at the great port of Danzig, and in Sweden. Dutch
engineers fortified the Rhine Palatinate after 1606, assisting the elector Frederick, who was Maurice's brother-in-law. Dutch engineers later served in the
English Civil War, where they enjoyed higher status than at home.[32] Indeed,
only Italy, the Netherlands and, later, France produced enough native engineers
to be able to found a distinctive national school before the eighteenth century.

Italian engineers and builders were called upon to strengthen the 1,000-
kilometre land frontier between Christians and Ottomans from the Adriatic Sea to
the eastern Carpathian Mountains, following the collapse of the Hungarian monarchy at Mohacs in 1526. Tatar auxiliaries, 20,000 or 30,000 horsemen, penetrated Habsburg territories far beyond the main army. Typically, they inflicted no
damage as they advanced, but then they turned about and looted methodically as
they moved to the rear. Most of them remained together to serve as a covering
force, while detachments were sent by regular rotation to scoop up captives and
booty and to bring them back to camp for later redistribution.[33] The poor inhabitants therefore streamed into any structure that might offer a defence against
lightly armed horsemen, such as stone churches, or small castles. Hungarian castles
offered no protection against Ottoman cannon, which in that period were just as
effective as their western counterparts.[34] Hungarian nobles built palanka forts, gar-
nished with light cannon in defence, but these could not be defended against
forces with siege guns.[35] The musket-bearing Hungarian haiduk militia's principal
purpose was to defend these fragile structures against superior forces.

In the subsequent decades, war in the Hungarian frontier focused around the
great liquid highway of the River Danube, from which large armies could not
stray for fear of outrunning their supplies. The Turks transported their heaviest
guns and their munitions upstream on the Danube, or along its navigable tributaries like the Tisza, the Drava and the Sava. The Habsburgs consolidated their
hold on the region north of Buda where the river bends to flow southwards.
Modern fortresses stocked with heavy artillery were erected at Komarom on the
Danube, at Eger nearby and in a few distant outposts to the north and east, at
Kassa, Szatmar and Varad. The Habsburg base of operations was the river town
of Raab (modern Györ in Hungary), whose fortifications, completed in 1564,
were designed by Pietro Ferrabosco and Bernardo Gaballio. Vienna was
reinforced with new bastions later in the century. The fortress town of Karlstadt
(modern Karlovac in Croatia) was erected in 1579 to block the Ottoman
advance towards Slovenia. It was besieged on seven different occasions, all of
them fruitless. Sultan Suleiman himself settled down to a stubborn six-week
siege at the small Croatian fortress of Szigetvar in 1566, dying the day before

the last defenders perished in September. The new defences seemed to end the era of rapid Ottoman advances.

Further east, in Transylvania, the first Italian engineers arrived in 1539, with or without Habsburg consent. The autonomous principality emerged in 1541 and from the outset its modest towns feared both the Ottomans and the Habsburg King of Hungary. The first modern defences were improved castles, built on a quadrangular base, but with bastions too small to carry much artillery, too widely separated to adequately defend the curtain wall, and with a complete absence of outer works beyond the moat. Bastions were erected around the walls of a few towns, but individually and without the ability to support one another. The most important project was the fortress town of Varad (Oradea), designed by Cesare Baldigara of Trieste, followed by the Genga brothers of Urbino. When it was finished the wall, 1.4 kilometres long, enclosed over 15 hectares. Over the course of 60 years, only eight strongholds were built, and four town walls were partly modernized. Italian architects in Transylvania were not supported by a dense civilian population possessing advanced machinery, as in Italy or the Low Countries. Work crews mostly comprised feudal corvée conscripts without specialized knowledge, who fled at every opportunity.[36]

The Ottomans built a number of artillery castles, with their round towers supporting scores of guns large and small, and posted about 20,000 professional soldiers in permanent garrison throughout the northern Balkans region. A good portion of the Ottoman garrisons comprised horsemen whose function was to conduct raids to seize cattle and captives across the frontier. Most forts were rudimentary *palanka* structures, made of earth and timber but designed for cannon.[37] The principal stone fortress and advanced base was at Esztergom, north of Buda, situated on a height overlooking the Danube and protecting a bridgehead across the river to facilitate the invasion of the northern bank. The other important forts were erected along the Danube waterway itself, in order to protect their military stores from raids.[38] These obeyed the fortification theory of the late fourteenth and fifteenth centuries once cannon had become more abundant. But the Ottomans, despite the presence of numerous German and Italian renegades in their ranks, did not adopt the Italian bastioned fortification style for the entire period under consideration here.

Modern militias

Even the strongest fortresses were merely envelopes, the hard outer shell of urban civilization. In medieval times, civilian males were, almost everywhere, liable to defend their towns and villages, under the leadership of city notables or district lords. Civilians were usually armed to the teeth with an array of blade weapons but they carried arquebuses, too, which were not very expensive and which were usually loaded with small shot for opportune poaching. Town walls and gates had to be guarded by sentinels, frequently compelled to take turns without pay. Local militias also embraced the quarrels of their masters and were liable to wage local wars resembling vendettas. Militiamen were compelled to defend their lord's castle as well as building or repairing it. This was not, in itself, a form of exploitation: the countryside was frequently targeted by bands of marauders, who could easily empty the contents of farms and carry people off for ransom. With every whiff of danger, peasants carried their most valuable goods inside the castle until the threat passed. The nobles themselves stored considerable quantities of ancient and modern weaponry in various states of repair, enough to outfit a small contingent of irregular soldiers. With the help of an armourer and a modest investment, these were refurbished and employed anew. Private wars were not yet a thing of the past in the sixteenth century but rulers were intent on stamping them out. Some monarchs decreed a monopoly over owning cannon, but this was not seriously enforced until the seventeenth century.

Sixteenth-century modern militias were a different organization altogether, although they did not entirely replace the older versions. Princes and republics created bands armed with muskets and pikes, which were periodically drilled in the ways of war, and assembled thousands of men in seasonal musters for counting and assessment. One key change was that the militia officers were the prince's men, not employees or clients of the feudal lord. Frequently enough, they were foreigners appointed because they had no property or relatives in the area where they served. They might have been elderly men or otherwise unfit for active duty, but they could defend a strongpoint. These militias were almost always defensive in nature, intended to defend the prince's domains from molestation by foreign bands or outlaws, and to defend the prince's jurisdiction from usurpation. It was not infrequent that they should seize for the prince a jurisdiction disputed with a feudal lord, and they seized the lord and his functionaries, too, who finished their existence in the prince's dungeons. Militia contingents might be assembled in large numbers to make a demonstration of force on the border of a neighbouring prince. Governments reinforced their armed bands whenever their interests clashed with those of a neighbour, like a cat's fur stands up to warn off a potential adversary. Occasionally, these militiamen were dispatched to assist a field army on campaign, but, even there, their tasks were confined to escorting munitions, guarding prisoners, intercepting deserters and digging earthen fortifications. Any task more dangerous usually led to disappointment.

Princes and republics promoted militias because they were virtually expenditure-free. The members volunteered to serve in exchange for honours and privileges, such as the right to carry weapons in public like noblemen, the right to hunt, freedom from the seizure of their goods in a lawsuit (very frequent) or freedom from imprisonment or torture for common offences. Tribunal sentences, both civil and criminal, imposed on militiamen were reviewed by the prince's functionaries, who reduced their fines and other punishments. Villages were very competitive places and the militia institution opened up new paths of social advancement. Typically, service in the countryside was limited to a fraction of village households or farmers, but it was important that they should be free men, not employees and dependents of powerful people. In exchange for rights and privileges, they were subject to a certain number of obligations, the first of which was to assemble at the sound of the drum or the church bell with their weapons and any armour they possessed. Cavalry militiamen had to provide their own horses, which limited the body to the rural elite. Militia musters entailed some marching in formation, target practice, wielding their weapons in unison and concluded with some wrestling matches.

These overarching militia organizations existed almost everywhere in Europe by the sixteenth century, from Portugal to the Ottoman Balkans. This kind of force was not, properly speaking, an army designed to challenge professional soldiers in the field, but it was a powerful tool in the hands of an ambitious ruler who intended to impose obedience on feudatories. The Republic of Venice relied heavily on both conscripted oarsmen for the navy in time of war and a substantial militia of peasants organized by a decree of 1507. Terraferma, or mainland rural, militiamen in the 1560s numbered about 20,000 men on paper, that is, about one per cent of the entire population or four per cent of adult males.[39] The proportion of men armed and enrolled might be much higher in zones close to a dangerous frontier. Republican Florence, on the suggestion of Nicolo Macchiavelli, enlisted a rural militia of 10,000 men early in the sixteenth century. Duke Cosimo I retained and expanded the institution after the Medici dynasty overthrew the republic. Its participation in the blockade of Siena was decisive in 1555. The Sienese peasantry then served in the same Tuscan militia, patrolling the homeland against bandits and Barbary Coast incursions. Duke Ottavio Farnese of Parma created a similar militia after 1550 that reached an impressive 30,000 men around 1600, for a duchy of only 300,000 inhabitants. County militiamen were very numerous in England under Henry VIII, but Queen Mary imposed Lord Lieutenants on them in order to tighten royal control. Elizabeth I then mustered formal 'Trained Bands' after 1573 for home defence.[40]

Urban, or bourgeois, militiamen also kept weapons at home and patrolled the streets at night to repress violent misbehaviour and thieving. Typically, they owned their houses and shops and paid taxes to the community. Authorities were wary of putting under arms men who had no property to lose. Most newly fortified towns in peacetime were garrisoned by very small numbers of professional soldiers, who resembled security guards. They resided in the citadel, where these existed, and left the city patrol to the urban guard. It was understood that militiamen would have no heart to withstand a siege by an enemy army; if a town was to be defended, it would require professional soldiers proportional to the extent of the fortifications, and stores to match their numbers. Thus, modern fortifications on their own were not sufficient to resist a hostile army. Geoffrey Parker argued, back in 1972, that a siege of a modern fortified town, well stocked with provisions and manned by a determined garrison, could only be undertaken by a large state with enough troops to blockade cities with large field armies and hammer them relentlessly with unprecedented numbers of heavy guns with abundant munitions, while defending its own fortresses against the enemy. Modern fortifications, therefore, pushed states into expanding the size of their infantry armies, and they made wars protracted, expensive affairs that could only end after lengthy negotiations.[41] Completely different from the fast-moving armies of 1494.

Notes

1   Bert Hall, 1997: 56–7.
2   Wayne Lee, 2016: 215.
3   Hall, 1997: 122.
4   Hall, 1997:, 154,
5   Simon Pepper, 1995.
6   Christopher Duffy, 1979: 2.
7   Philippe Bragard, 2014.
8   Luciana Miotto, 2002.
9   John R. Hale, 1986: 208.
10 Michael Mallett & John Hale, 1984: 381–90.
11 J.R. Hale, 1968.
12 Giorgio Spini, 1976.
13 Charles van den Heuvel, 1994.
14 David Parrott, 2007.
15 Antonio Calabria, 1991.
16 Phillip Williams, 2014: 240.
17 Dragos Cosmescu, 2015.
18 Mallett and Hale, 1984: 398.
19 Quentin Hughes, *Fortress: Architecture and military history in Malta* (London, 1969) 53, 78.
20 Mallett and Hale, 1984: 426.
21 Carlo Promis, 1874.
22 Hélène Vérin, 1993: 96 & 137.
23 David Buisseret, 2002 : 30.
24 Erik Swart, 2013.
25 Duffy, 1979: 48.
26 Brian Hugh St. John O'Neil, 1960: 41–64.
27 O'Neil, 1960: 67–71.
28 David Parrott, 1997.
29 Pieter Martens, 2011.
30 Simon Pepper & Nicholas Adams, 1986: 117–39.
31 Marjolein 't Hart, 2014: 101.
32 Swart, 2013.
33 Maria Ivanics, 2013.
34 Gabor Agoston, 2010.
35 Josef Kelenik, 2000.
36 Klara Kovacs, 2011.
37 Mark L. Stein, 2007: 48.
38 Klara Hegyi, 'The Ottoman network of fortresses in Hungary', *Ottomans, Hungarians and Habsburgs in Central Europe: The Military Confines in the era of Ottoman Conquest*, G David & P Fodor eds, Leiden & Boston, 2000, 163–93.
39 Peter January & Michael Knapton, 2007; Giulio Ongaro, 2017.
40 C.G. Cruickshank, 1966: 24–5.
41 Geoffrey Parker, 1972: 6.

4   French wars of religion 1561–1629

The French reformation

We cannot speak of a unitary Reformation process unfolding across sixteenth century Europe, for each country followed a different path depending upon the strength of the Roman Church and the attraction of opposing doctrines popularized by local leaders. The Reformation never succeeded when the government was set against it, but there was more than one level of government. The Habsburg emperor, Charles V, never embraced Martin Luther's anti-Roman doctrines, but German princes and city states were often enthusiastic promoters of the religious movement. They also happily despoiled the Church of its lands and buildings, and a good portion of the clergy embraced the Reformation, too. Luther and his followers did not take special aim at Catholic imagery and traditional religious spaces with ornate altars, conspicuous tombs, statues and altar paintings. In England, King Henry VIII seized control of the Church and its property, and auctioned much of it off to finance his wars in France, but he considered himself to be Catholic until his death. His adolescent son, Edward VI, embraced a more austere and Scripture-based Protestantism, inspired by the doctrines of the Frenchman Jean Calvin, and surrounded himself with a council of ardent Protestants.

Calvinist doctrines, based more closely upon Scriptures, were more radical than those of Luther, because they vehemently repudiated the Roman tradition. Calvin did not see the Roman liturgy, sacraments and saints as mere errors: for him they were diabolically inspired, to be stamped out in the same manner that early Christians destroyed pagan temples. He did not consider Catholicism to be a Christian doctrine at all. Instead of a pyramidal organization concentrating power among worldly prelates based in Rome, each congregation was equal to every other and managed its own affairs. A board (the consistory) of male notables, or elders, hired and dismissed the ministers. Ministers enjoyed no special sacramental status, like Catholic priests: their principal role was to explain the gospels to the congregation. The elders were a godly minority of men who were confident of their own salvation and who were held to be devout by their neighbours. Calvin also did not condone the separation of Church and State that was typical of European polities. Instead, each congregation was to promote to high office godly members from among its ranks, who would impose devout practices on the entire population for its own good. Calvin and his followers seized control and imposed a godly dictatorship on the city government of Geneva in 1541, not long after it seceded from the Duchy of Savoy and joined the Swiss Confederation. Wherever Calvinists seized control over local government, ministers, elders and judges directed local politics in tandem.[1]

All the Reformations grew out of dissatisfaction with the worldly organization and practices of the Catholic Church. Many French bishops promoted religious reforms in their dioceses, and a multitude of priests and friars (like Martin Luther in Germany) were ready to jettison Catholic tradition. The French monarchy nevertheless repressed heretics from their first appearance in the early 1520s, with capital executions averaging about ten annually under François I and Henri II. Each new crackdown triggered the flight of refugees to Geneva, where Calvin and his lieutenant Théodore de Bèze trained likely candidates for the ministry and sent them back into the kingdom to organize congregations. Henri II allied himself with German Protestant princes in order to fight the Habsburgs, and so the repression of French Reformers was fitful. He intended to crack down on Calvinists heavily in the aftermath of the Treaty of Câteau Cambrésis with Spain in 1559, but was accidentally killed in a joust soon after, leaving his widow, Catherine de'Medici, with four male children, the eldest of whom was only twelve years old.

At that precise moment, the number of Reformed congregations (the label these Protestants used to describe themselves) in France began to mushroom, from several dozen in 1559 to over a thousand in 1560. The movement was principally urban, led by defrocked priests and French-speaking magistrates, flanked by Latin teachers and students in universities and colleges. Protestants were exhorted to read the Scriptures in the vernacular language: it is not surprising that their adherents belonged disproportionately to the literate minority, who probably did not surpass 20 or 30% of adult males (with wide regional variations). Merchants and skilled artisans, who lacked formal Latin education, were disproportionately Calvinist, too. In Occitan-speaking southern France, where the movement was especially strong, merchants and magistrates dominated municipal assemblies. By 1560, notables who considered themselves the 'healthiest' part of the urban community closed down Catholic churches and monasteries and abolished the mass. The lower classes might still follow Catholic doctrines and attend church ceremonies, but they were compelled to practise these outside the town walls. Few peasants (the vast majority were illiterate) showed much enthusiasm for the new doctrines. In addition to the town elites, Calvinism appealed to much of the nobility, who established churches in their castles and hired ministers as their employees. Again, this was far more common in southern France, where, in several regions, a third or more of aristocrats joined the ranks of the Reformed church. Local lords chased away the Catholic clergy and compelled peasants to attend sermons by pastors of their choosing. On the other hand, the people rejoiced at no longer paying Catholic tithes, although they would have to contribute to the salary of the minister. No one could remain outside the ranks of one confession or the other, for baptism, marriage and burial were all religious ceremonies, and shunning the local clergy led to ostracism by neighbours and superiors. Belonging to the congregation did not necessarily entail believing the doctrines or approving the organization of either church, and individuals might change their minds as they matured and attached themselves to neighbours.

By 1561, there were more than 1,300 formally organized churches with their consistories, over two-thirds of which were located in southern France. (The geography of Calvinism did not coincide strongly with the medieval Cathar heresy, however: neither was there any doctrinal continuity between the medieval heresy and Protestant strictures.) There was a particular concentration of Reformed congregations in a vast crescent-shaped area from Dauphiné in the Alps, south to Mediterranean Languedoc, west across to Atlantic Aquitaine and north to Poitou in the west of France, a zone called the Huguenot crescent. (The term Huguenot was applied to French Protestants from its early years.) At its height in the 1560s, there might have been two million people in the sway of the Reformation, (about ten per cent of the total) although this does not mean they all believed the doctrines. They comprised about a quarter of the population of southern France, and, in some districts, the Catholic Church disappeared. They retained control of a number of mid-ranking cities such as La Rochelle, Montauban, Montpellier and Nîmes, but not the chief cities of the realm or the regional and administrative capitals like Bordeaux, Toulouse or Aix-en-Provence. Paris was always a bastion of Catholic loyalty, despite the presence of a tiny (relative to its population of 300,000 people) and influential Calvinist minority.

A godly insurgency 1560–1572

The great hope of the Calvinist political aristocrats at the court, where they became increasingly prominent after 1559, was that the young King Francis II might be separated from his entourage and convinced to impose the godly Reformation on the kingdom. This is what happened in England after the death of Henry VIII, whose adolescent son Edward VI took the lead in abolishing Catholicism. Only his death in 1553 at age 16 prevented the triumph of Calvinism in England. His sister Mary, a devout Catholic, wed Philip II of Spain and reversed the direction until her death in 1558. Had the union produced a child, English history would have been very different. The path the young Queen Elizabeth would take was still unclear in 1560. In France there was indeed a Calvinist plot, discovered in March 1560, to seize the person of the king at the court in Amboise, and scores of executions followed in the aftermath. The Italian Queen Mother tried to keep the polarizing factions communicating with each other, and there was talk of mixing elements of Calvinist doctrine with Catholicism, but the Reformed ministers rejected such proposals. When Calvinist ministers set up churches in towns, they would not accept the existence of Catholic clergy or any Roman ceremonies. Wherever they took control after

1561, a wave of iconoclasm followed, the smashing of images, altars and tombs, and the destruction of relics to which much of the population was deeply attached. Skirmishing broke out across Southwest France before the year was out, and on 1 March 1562, the Duke de Guise, a champion of Catholicism at the court, and his retainers massacred scores of Huguenots assembled for their sermon in a barn at Wassy, in Champagne.[2]

In the spring of 1562, after months of patient plotting, armed Protestant elites seized important cities across France, including Lyon, Orléans and Rouen; attempts to seize other major cities such as Toulouse were foiled only after days of bitter fighting.[3] The consistories then proceeded to appoint captains and hire troops with the proceeds of lands seized from the Church. The queen mother reluctantly authorized the mobilization of the royal army to recover the lost cities. Catholic or Protestant, French nobles were still very much a military class; thousands of veterans of the long wars against the Habsburgs raised men to follow them. Many soldiers were posted in distant border castles and uniting them into an army required months of preparation and marching.[4] Fearing a Huguenot victory, Philip II hastened Spanish troops to France and placed them under French royal commanders.[5] Calvinists invited an English expeditionary force to help them, and Queen Elizabeth sent a force to hold Le Havre in Normandy, which she hoped would replace Calais as a base for future conquests on the continent. Landgrave Philip of Hesse, one of the political leaders of the German Reformation, sent the Huguenots a large contingent of landsknecht troops, who caused havoc wherever they marched. A Protestant field army led by the Prince de Condé was defeated at Dreux in northern France on 19 December 1562 and a general peace followed in March 1563, but it resembled a truce rather than a general pacification and neither side disarmed. Calvinist churches continued to multiply and the movement used the pause in the fighting to organize. King François II died in 1561 and his successor, Charles IX, was still a boy under the direction of his mother, who was regent. The absence of an adult king meant that the monarchy lacked charisma and firm direction; Catholic nobles rallied instead behind the Guise dynasty, while Admiral Coligny led the Protestant party at the court.

Huguenot leaders planned another rising aimed to capture the adolescent king at Meaux, and to kill the Queen Mother and the leaders of the Catholic party across France. The plot was uncovered in September 1567 but its discovery accelerated Protestant operations in which a field army marched north from Languedoc to capture Paris. This episode triggered six months of large-scale clashes across France until Catherine de'Medici brokered a new truce in March 1568. Fighting soon broke out anew in western France, where Reformed churches were very numerous. The Pope sent Italian troops to assist the royal commander, Piero Strozzi (a Florentine, like the queen mother), and these participated in new Catholic victories at Jarnac and Moncontour in 1569. The subsequent Peace of Longjumeau was not applied everywhere and in Languedoc and elsewhere in south-western France the Reformation continued to gain ground. The Huguenot party was very strong in the south and west of France, especially around the port of La Rochelle, whose ramparts were modernized by Scipio Vergano from Friuli, beginning in 1569.[6] Huguenot leaders cultivated alliances with Queen Elizabeth I of England and with the Dutch Sea Beggars in revolt against Spain. The Calvinists in northern and eastern France also benefited from German Protestant infantry contingents that bolstered their strength.

The Queen Mother hoped to unite the factions by means of very ancient and universal mechanisms used to end feuding. One was to enhance solidarity by attacking an outsider, in this case an opportunistic war with Spain in the Low Countries, where the Duke of Alva was busy quelling the Dutch revolt. Philip II was simultaneously mired in the great galley wars against the Ottomans and could ill afford to send reinforcements. French Protestants tried inciting the population in Brabant to rise up against the Spanish army of Flanders, but their invasion force was routed at Gembloux. The second universal peace-making mechanism was to arrange high-level marriages between the two camps. Catherine de'Medici gave her daughter Marguerite in marriage to one of the rising stars of the Huguenot firmament, Prince Henri de Navarre, a great lord from the Occitan southwest, in order to enhance the fraternization of opposing leaders at the court. The 1572 wedding occasioned the arrival in Paris of a large portion of what we might call the Huguenot general staff, including its leading general, the Admiral Coligny. On 22 August, the admiral was wounded in an assassination attempt, which did not appear to have had royal backing. But after the Huguenot leaders threatened to go back to war, the Queen Mother and the adolescent king consented to order the Swiss Guards to assassinate Coligny and a handful of his supporters. On the night of 23–24 August, feast of Saint Bartholomew, the Guards went into action, killing scores of Huguenot leaders. The Guards compelled newly wed Henri de Navarre to abjure Protestantism at sword-point, and held him captive. Next, however, the population of Paris descended into the streets looking to kill other Protestants, while the city militia tried to stop the bloodshed. This event was never planned. The victims might have numbered 2,000–3,000 in the capital. Upon news of the massacre, similar bloodlettings occurred in a score of other cities, particularly those that had been seized by the Huguenots in the past and where their massacre was seen as justifiable retaliation. There is no way to calculate the exact number of victims of these massacres, but, including Paris, estimates fall into a range between 5,000 and 8,000.[7]

The Saint Bartholomew's Day massacre turned out to be a decisive event, because it reversed the rising tide of the Reformation in France, particularly in the economic and political heartland of the north of the kingdom. People who joined the movement for opportunistic reasons (and these were many) reconsidered their position and abandoned the Reformation in large numbers. The socially prominent Calvinist congregations in large cities such as Rouen and Lyon, quickly shrank by half or three-quarters. The French wars of religion have often been represented as an era of massacre, but these have only recently been subjected to greater scrutiny. A detailed study by David El Kenz notes that the majority of these incidents claimed fewer than ten lives, although they targeted social elites preferentially.[8] Most massacres were committed not by crowds, which were not good at making decisions, but by military units following political directives. They took place early in the war in order to seize power or to consolidate it. Military and political leaders ordered the massacres based on cold calculation: they were rational acts. And, in the case of the largest of these, the perpetrators obtained the desired outcome. In the aftermath of the Saint Bartholomew's Day bloodletting, however, massacres became quite rare.[9]

Accounts of the French Wars of Religion that place the emphasis on court intrigue and the clash of large armies obscure the fact that this civil war was fought locally between neighbouring towns and villages. This process came to the fore in the aftermath of the Paris massacre, as the remnants of the Huguenot command sought refuge in the regions where they were strongest. Since the Protestants could no longer trust the monarchy and its institutions, they would work through their own organizations. The autonomous churches quickly established regional assemblies called Colloquia, where delegations of military nobles, prominent elders and ministers discussed ways to collect money and prosecute the war. Fighting continued across France almost without interruption between 1572 and 1581. Royal tribunals fell into abeyance and normal tax collection became impossible in insurgent districts.

Both sides developed similar models of coping with crisis. Every town appointed a surveillance committee, focused on acquiring news of events and taking measures to prevent surprise attack. There was a flurry of new fortification, particularly in Protestant communities (Image 4.1). Huguenot towns acquired bastioned fortifications and collected artillery to defend them more than Catholic ones, especially in the 1570s and 1580s. La Rochelle raised massive defences, using rubble from demolished churches to erect new bastions, and dragooning peasants into hauling earth. Town craftsmen manufactured weapons and gunpowder in large quantities, and La Rochelle cast or purchased almost 200 cannon. Further south, at Montauban in Languedoc, the town council invested heavily in new bastions, financed by holding back royal taxes, by seizing the property of the church and by confiscating the lands of Catholic refugees. Emergency decrees authorized additional taxes in cash and in kind to purchase building supplies and to organize haulage to the worksite. Town councils supervised every stage of this process.[10] Smaller towns shored up decaying medieval ramparts *à la huguenotte* with earthworks reinforced with *fascines*. Strong Protestant towns designated military governors who periodically acted in unison with nearby leaders, and occasionally they lent troops to a larger force operating at the provincial level.

In Catholic Languedoc, the Parlement of Toulouse and the regional bishops authorized the levy of money to enable the military governors to enlist soldiers. These commanders and the lords in their allegiance then formed companies of 100–200 men, designating leaders without much outside interference.[11] Catholic militia units might be led by priests, who were often the targets of Calvinists. Nobles were already registered in the *arrière-ban*,

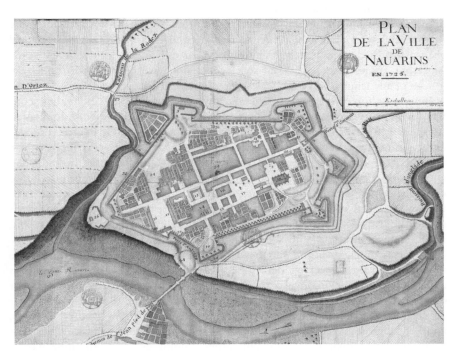

Image 4.1 Navarrens en 1725 BNF Registre C 20584. Hundreds of towns and villages raised modern fortifications during the course of the French Wars of Religion. Protestant Navarrenx in Bearn was close enough to Spain to escape demolition at war's end

a medieval feudal institution whereby the monarchy could order them to serve personally in an armed host at their own expense, or else make them pay for a replacement.[12] They also formed royal companies of mounted *gendarmes* (units of heavy cavalry) numbering 50–150 men, many of whom were noblemen, but these never comprised more than a nucleus of any operational force. These companies were often created by calling upon friends and relatives of the captain. Because of the strength of friendship and kinship, it was common to find Protestant gendarmes in a Catholic company, and vice versa. Many noblemen served as volunteers, without any commission, and were fed and housed by towns and villages where they stayed. Companies of foot numbering two or three hundred men would serve in the field for specific operations. Periodically, the regional officials could collect a makeshift army of 2,000–5,000 men, plus pioneers who dug entrenchments for them. A typical operation against a town or a castle would only rarely mobilize more than 1,000 men, who would not stay together beyond a few weeks. A large portion of the population would have served at some point, but not for very long. The turnover among the troops was very high: every camp saw the continual arrival and departure of men who disliked serving far from home. A large host of several thousand men would not have operated for more than several weeks, and their effectiveness depended largely upon the personal charisma of the leader. In consequence, these forces had very little strategic value. Makeshift armies in the medieval style would not have been able to undertake a siege of any length, and large-scale battles almost never occurred.

Protestant forces operated in the shadow of sizeable cities under their control, or in the wake of powerful feudal lords like the Turenne who dominated southern Limousin. In that remote province of south-central France, Protestant contingents roved the countryside destroying churches and monasteries, seeking to uproot the material existence of the Catholic faith. In the open countryside, peasants barricaded themselves and their possessions inside churches, which, from medieval times, were often fortified. Others sought protection in walled villages and towns, of which there were many. Armed bands seized the livestock in the fields, and often enough captured the peasants, too, holding them in castles and selling them back to their families and their villages for as much cash and supplies as they could command. Continuing the medieval *chevauchée*, roving detachments seized livestock, crops, grain stores and piles of hay belonging to their enemies, but also burned farms and cut down trees to inflict long-term damage and to undermine the tax base of their adversaries. Rural noblemen improved the defences of their medieval castles, and kept important stocks of weapons and supplies on the premises. They typically employed their farmhands and other employees to guard these works, and to join them on forays against the enemy. Social elites, unable to trust in the royal judicial system, took justice into their own hands, with the result that murders and vendettas multiplied.[13]

Huge France contained something like 4,000 walled towns, often numbering only a few hundred inhabitants. The captains and provincial governors pushed the local authorities to raise money to improve fortifications, and often compelled local inhabitants to work for free, a labour tax called a corvée. Royal and Reformed policy-makers placed the stronger towns under the direction of a military governor, who mobilized his personal clientèle and raised a company of soldiers. A bourgeois militia reinforced these, stocking military supplies either in private homes or in the town hall. Fortified villages typically mustered a garrison of 70 or 80 soldiers following a captain, noble or bourgeois, whose authority depended on local consensus. Local bourgeois were often compelled to take turn guarding the walls and the gates, which they did often reluctantly and fitfully. One danger came in the form of an explosive device called a 'petard', which could be wedged under a locked gate in order to blow it open. Towns and villages waged war against each other in the form of skirmishes, ambushes, hostage-taking and looting. They posted small garrisons in myriad makeshift forts along rivers and roads, whose primary function was to levy money from merchants supplying food and other goods to towns and cities.

The long civil war introduced a number of important transformations. As in the Middle Ages, warring towns established periodic truces in order to enable people to plough the land, to bring in the crops and harvest the grapes. Town authorities appointed intermediaries to shorten the captivity of hostages and to expedite their ransom. Massacre was no longer advisable, since the fortunes of war were fickle, and each atrocity called for reprisals. There were usually members of the opposite religion still living in each town. After 1572, there were no longer strenuous campaigns to convert them, and even mistreatment of local minorities became infrequent. Mixed marriage was not at all uncommon, with the result that the local religious minority dwindled over time without overt persecution. In the Estates-General of Blois in 1576, under the new King Henri III, the *Cahier de doléances* (lists of grievances) emanating from the rural population placed little emphasis on religious unity. The focus of complaints was, rather, on the high taxes placed on communities under royal control, and of the violence and impunity of soldiers.[14]

Henri of Navarre escaped from captivity in 1576 and returned to his native South-western France, where he exercised much influence through his high rank and his judicious use of patronage. Drawing from Protestant towns in Aquitaine and Languedoc, he could raise mobile armies of 3,000 to 4,000 men or even more. King Henri III's policy oscillated between offering peace and official toleration to French Protestants, and periodic repudiation of the same programme and promotion of zealous Catholicism. What undermined the unpopular king more than anything was his inability to sire a successor. His younger brother, François Duke of Alençon, died without an heir in 1584, making Henri de Navarre of the Bourbon dynasty next in line to the throne. By this time he was the undisputed military head of the Protestant party and a commander of proven talent. He maintained alliances with Protestant powers and occasionally levied German mercenaries. In reaction, the Duke de Guise and his two brothers served as the increasingly popular heads of the Catholic majority in France, and portrayed themselves as friends of the king of Spain. They helped forge a loose federation of towns into a Catholic League in 1585, which drifted largely outside of the unpopular king's control.

War of the League 1588–1598

The Catholic League quickly commanded allegiance in the richest and most densely populated parts of the kingdom, with widespread popular support in Paris, in particular. By 1587, Henri of Navarre decided to enter into an alliance with the king in order to counteract the threat. The discredited monarch resolved to take back control of his kingdom by having the Duke de Guise and his brother the Cardinal assassinated at Blois, where the court resided on 23 December 1588. A third brother, the Duke de Mayenne, escaped and took military direction of the dissident movement. The consequences of the assassination produced the opposite outcome to the one the king had hoped for. Paris rose in revolt against the Crown and a number of large cities likewise entered open rebellion. Henri III set up a blockade of Paris from his base at Chartres, where, with Henri de Navarre, he planned his return in force to the capital. On 1 August 1589, the monk Jacques Clément approached the king and stabbed him, before being killed by the guards. Catholic France cheered the demise of the last Valois monarch and the royal army quickly disbanded.

Henri of Navarre, now King Henri IV, made conciliatory gestures to the Catholic majority of France, but it had little effect at first. A number of Catholic noblemen and large Catholic cities remained loyal to the Crown, but without enthusiasm. Meanwhile, many other cities and regions passed into the sway of the Catholic League. It did not constitute a cohesive entity, however, or respond quickly to the command of national leaders. Many of its components, such as Marseille, functioned as autonomous republics. The crisis enticed the Duke of Savoy to invade Provence with the intention of annexing it to his states. In Northern France, Henri IV led a highly mobile but modest field army, weighted heavily with carbine-wielding light cavalry that could dismount and fight on foot. The royal army won some small-scale field battles against League forces, but Paris itself withstood a long blockade. King Philip II of Spain, on the cusp of quelling the great Dutch Revolt in 1587–1588, instructed the Duke of Parma to march into France with the Spanish army of Flanders to relieve the blockade, which he did in 1590, leaving 4,000 Spanish troops behind in garrison. Parma also lifted the royalist siege of Rouen the following year, something that Henri IV was unable to prevent. Most of all, the king's mobile army was unable to conduct large-scale sieges of fortified cities, whose number continued to grow.

Protestant nobles were pillars of the king's waning authority, and often operated in distant theatres with little supervision. In Alpine Dauphiné, the Duke de Lesdiguières hampered the ambitions of the League and the Duke of Savoy with an army of 5,000 or 6,000 men. To maintain them, he extracted an enormous amount of money and provisions from towns in the path of his army, some of which he employed to maintain his troops in the field, and some of which he kept back for future use. Lesdiguières patrolled his province continually, via long marches of 20–40 kilometres daily. In his castle at Vizilles, he stockpiled thousands of muskets and pikes, along with tonnes of gunpowder. He had a free hand to select his junior officers and maintained a large clientèle that fed him with resources and information. Like the king, he was able to seize towns and reinforce threatened strongpoints, but was unable on his own to undertake sieges of important cities.[15]

This kind of generalized and inconclusive warfare exhausted the towns and villages caught up in the fighting. Billeting was the chief burden on the population, whereby towns were forced to borrow large sums to lodge the soldiers, or pay present costs on future revenues. Should they close their gates to troops on the move, these last would devastate the farms and seize all the livestock in the vicinity. The war of the League took place against a background of pestilence (1585–1588) and of famine (1584–1591) that killed millions of people, far more than military operations did.[16] The Catholic League struggle spread the fighting across a much larger area of the kingdom, where the Catholic clergy helped mobilize the peasantry through impassioned sermons.[17] Improvised rural armies in Brittany, which included rural nobles and bourgeois militias as well as peasants, could never prevail against professional troops employing various stratagems. They were prone to falling into ambushes, or competed with each other for glory instead of coordinating their movements.[18]

Henri IV decided to resolve the crisis by converting to Catholicism, which he officially embraced on 25 July 1593 at Saint Denis, the royal basilica and mausoleum of French kings just outside Paris. He then decreed a suspension of hostilities in order to attract support to his cause. Leaguer towns, including Paris, began to capitulate the following year, and their resources started to fill the royalist coffers. The formal coronation, an elaborate Catholic liturgy that enhanced the legitimacy of his rule, took place at Chartres in February 1594. In many parts of France, rural populations were rebelling against soldiers of all stripes and refused to pay their taxes. Hostilities ceased in the southern Huguenot heartland in January 1596. War with Spain continued to 1598, after the Army of Flanders occupied towns in the north of France.

Henri then applied diplomacy to end his isolation, and delivered an amnesty covering most of the events in the previous decades. The Pope soon lifted his excommunication and annulled his childless marriage to Marguerite de Valois, while the Grand Duke Ferdinand I of Tuscany was happy to provide his niece, Maria de'Medici, as a suitable Catholic bride for the frisky alpha male. The monarch also used his considerable political acumen to grant the Protestants official toleration through the Edict of Nantes in 1598, while declaring Catholicism to be the sole religion of the French state. Secret clauses of the Edict promised to pay out of royal coffers the governors and garrisons of 70 Huguenot fortresses across France, in the event that war should break out afresh (Map 5). Protestants controlled some 200 towns, about half of which were well fortified. Their adherents had shrunk by about half, to 800,000 people in 1600, three quarters of whom lived in the Huguenot crescent in the south. And, finally, the king scaled back the royal army to a mere 10,000 soldiers (about equal to the Republic of Venice), scattered in castle garrisons when not serving as ornaments to the court. The tax pressure lifted immediately and the economy enjoyed a quarter-century of continuous growth. Future generations would look back on the reign of good King Henri as a kind of Golden Age.

End of the Protestant menace

While Henri IV encouraged his Huguenot friends and former comrades-in-arms to convert, like him, to Rome, he respected both the spirit and the letter of the Edict of Nantes. The French solution was utterly unlike that of any other European polity, where only members of the state religion enjoyed access to high positions of public authority (including the Dutch Republic and the Ottoman Empire, reputed to have been more tolerant). Huguenots continued to hold leading positions at the French court and in the army for 80 years after the king's conversion. Henri outwardly conformed to the official religion and gained the confidence of Catholic dignitaries. In 1610, he contemplated uniting

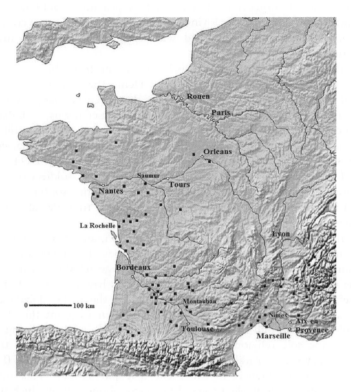

Map 5 Huguenot places of security at the time of the Edict of Nantes 1598

his kingdom still further through a new war against the Spanish Habsburgs with Protestant allies, and had already begun mobilization when an isolated assassin stabbed him in his coach in the streets of Paris. There was initial fear that this event would re-ignite hostilities between the two camps, but Queen Maria de'Medici quickly confirmed that she would continue to observe the articles of the Edict of Nantes.

Many Protestants thought that once they enjoyed public toleration, people would embrace the True Religion revealed in Scripture. However, it became clear after 1600 that the Catholic Church in France was gaining strength and confidence with each passing year. Henri's son and successor, Louis XIII, was a boy of eight in 1610, under the tutelage of his mother, but she had to endure the usual handicap of a regency in that royal authority suffered. The great lords (about 70 interrelated dynasties labelled collectively as the *Grands*), both Catholic and Protestant, jockeyed for influence over policy. Both were envious of the influence of the queen's Tuscan protégés. When Maria de'Medici married the adolescent king to the Spanish princess, Anne of Austria, in 1615, Protestant warlords under the leadership of the Duke de Rohan entered into a brief rebellion and had to be bought off. As he matured, the king increasingly resented his powerlessness and the overbearing influence of his mother. Finally, he resolved to restore the Catholic Church to the autonomous region of Béarn, in the South-west corner of France, where Calvinism was still the official religion but only 20% of the population adhered to it. His bloodless takeover of the region touched off a new Protestant rising in the West and South of France in late 1620, animated by the Duke de Rohan. This time, many of the Protestant military luminaries, like Lesdiguières, rallied to the king in the interest of national unity.

Louis XIII personally led the campaign of the royal army through the West and South in 1621, with mixed success. A timid man who felt awkward in public, he loved being a soldier and felt in his element accompanying the army, although he left the operational details to his generals. From Paris to Poitou, all the Huguenot towns surrendered to his army without a fight. Further south, modest fortified towns offered only feeble resistance and opened their gates after a few days' siege.[19] Many gave no thought to resisting at all, and meekly consented to demolish their ramparts. The strongest cities put up a spirited fight, however. The royal siege failed utterly at Montauban from July to November, where the king's army evaporated from fruitless assaults and disease, no doubt exacerbated by neglecting to bury dead men and horses (Image 4.2).[20] A siege of Montpellier in Languedoc the next year ended in negotiation. France's military aristocracy mobilized anew on both sides. In southern France these still constituted a military caste, residing in strong castles well stocked with weapons. They employed personal bodyguards and armed their employees for local expeditions. Nobles joined clientèles that were hierarchically organized but not confessionally homogeneous. The ranks they held in royal armies were not always well defined and they jockeyed for precedence and influence. Numerous noblemen were quick to join the armies as volunteers, if only temporarily, especially if the king was present in person.[21]

The formulation of royal policy after 1624 passed increasingly under the direction of the minister cardinal Richelieu, who was appointed head of the navy in 1626. He thought that France should replace the House of Austria as the pre-eminent power in Europe, but it must first eliminate the armed Protestant lobby at home, while maintaining their freedom of religion. Richelieu orientated French policy against Spain and the House of Austria, by launching repeated interventions in Italy and by encouraging French nobles to assist the Dutch Republic in its war against Spain. A fresh Protestant rising in 1625 convinced him that La Rochelle must become the priority target, for through that port the rebels received encouragement and supplies from England. In July, an English amphibious force occupied the nearby Ile de Ré and called upon La Rochelle to rise up. The king and the cardinal inaugurated in person the siege of the port city in 1627, with a strong royal army periodically numbering up to 30,000 men. Troops and pioneers erected a blockade 12 kilometres in circumference around the city, buttressed with 29 earthen forts and redoubts. The engineers Pompeo Targone and Clément Métezeau erected a huge barrier across

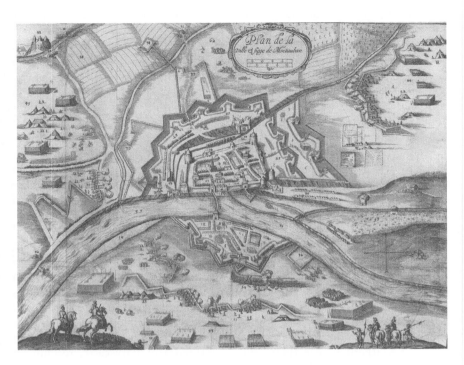

Image 4.2 Anonymous, Siege of Montauban 1621, BNF 41501129. The royal army was too small to effectively encircle the strongly fortified Huguenot stronghold, which resisted until the worsening weather made conditions in the siege camp unbearable

the entrance channel to the port, a kilometre and a half long. Two hundred boats loaded with rocks were sunk at the entrance in order to prevent larger ships from passing.[22] The English army sent to rescue the city was composed of only 7,000 pressed men, and, due in part to the lack of competent engineers, they were unable to capture the island fortress of Saint-Martin. In October, the French attacked them there and killed or captured two thirds of their army.[23] A new French fleet blockaded the city and they twice repelled an English relief force, in May and October 1628. After La Rochelle finally capitulated to hunger on 26 October 1628, its ramparts were razed and its surviving Protestant inhabitants relocated.

The Duke de Rohan animated Protestant resistance in Languedoc with mobile armies that lifted sieges or reinforced threatened towns, but they were never numerous enough to fight the royal army in the open field. Royal commanders such as the Duke de Montmorency sometimes burned farms and villages in order to provoke waves of refugees toward remaining Protestant cities. King Louis XIII laid siege to the small Languedoc town of Privas, executing its remaining defenders to serve as an example to the others. Louis and Richelieu finally imposed a definitive peace in the form of a pardon at Alais (or Alès) on 27 June 1629, which promised to maintain official toleration for Calvinism, but deprived the Huguenots of their means of resistance. During the 1620s, thousands of castles and town walls were razed to the ground around the kingdom, leaving only those that protected a frontier. The peace ended two generations of France's absence from the international rivalry that had characterized the era of the Italian wars. Habsburg Spain and Austria were thriving in the absence of a major challenger, but Richelieu and Louis XIII were now intent on bringing them down.

Notes

1 Janine Garrisson-Estèbe, 1980: 61.
2 Serge Brunet, 2015.
3 Mark Greengrass, 1983.
4 James Wood, 1984.
5 Bertrand Haan, 2013.
6 Michael Wolfe, 2000.
7 Nicolas Le Roux, 2009 : 138; Max P Holt, 1995: 85.
8 Jean-Marie Constant, 2002: 106.
9 Allan A. Tulchin, 2012.
10 Wolfe, 2000.
11 Pierre-Jean Souriac, 2008: 76.
12 Michel Cassan, 1996: 185.
13 Stuart Carroll, 2003,.
14 Constant, 2002: 190.
15 Stéphane Gal, 2007: 116.
16 Mark Greengrass, 1985.
17 Philippe Hamon, 2015.
18 Philippe Hamon, 2015.
19 Jack Alden Clarke, 1966: 70–93.
20 Clarke, 1966: 91.
21 Brian Sandberg, 2010: 35.
22 Jean-Christian Petitfils, 2008: 430–41.
23 Lawrence Spring, 2016: 186–205.

5   Europe's first great war 1618–1659

German civil war 1618–1648

The greatest conflagration of the early modern period ignited as a revolt against the Habsburg emperors by the German and Czech Protestants of Bohemia, the richest and most populous part of the dynasty's hereditary lands. The founding principle of the Peace of Augsburg of 1555 was *cuius regio, eius religio*, that subjects must adhere to the prince's faith. However, the direct subjects of Catholic Habsburg rulers converted in their great majority to Lutheran doctrines. Emperor Rudolf II (r. 1575–1612), who, in his later years, was psychologically unfit to rule, was reluctant to accept this state of affairs, but, as the Holy Roman Empire polarized into confessional camps after 1600, Protestant lords compelled him to grant freedom of public worship in Habsburg crown lands. His brother and successor, Matthias, cautiously tried to claw back these concessions in Austria and Bohemia but the effect was to alienate the noble and urban Estates who controlled the levers of tax assessment and collection. Matthias's nephew and successor, Ferdinand, a pupil of the Jesuits in Italy, made a solemn vow to the Virgin Mary to do all in his power to return both Habsburg states and the Empire in general to the Catholic fold. The Estates of Bohemia duly elected Ferdinand to be their king in 1618, but, after an order came to close down several Protestant churches, both the Germans and the Czechs rose in defiance. While heatedly discussing their concerns with the king's emissaries in the Bohemian Chancellery offices of Prague Castle, assembly members ejected three of them from a high window. ('Carried down by angels' in the Catholic account, they landed on a trash heap below and walked away unhurt.) The Estates proceeded with a new royal election in 1619 and designated the Palatine Elector Frederick, son-in-law of the king of England, brother-in-law of Maurice of Orange, to be their sovereign. A devout Calvinist from the central Rhineland, he was considered likely to attract the resources of England and the Netherlands to the Protestant cause. Over the preceding decade, German princes and Imperial cities gravitated into two confessional camps and the Empire's overarching institutions, such as the Supreme Court, broke down for lack of common ground. Protestant states like the Palatinate formed a Protestant Union in 1608 that was ready to join Henri IV of France in a general war against the Habsburgs in 1610. The king's assassination paused the preparations for war but the Protestants did not disarm.

Because of Emperor Rudolf's unfitness for his office, Duke Maximilian of Bavaria came to the fore as Germany's Catholic champion. He invited princes to join him in building up money and provisions to defend the Roman Church in a Catholic League (Image 5.1).

Before his death in March 1619, Emperor Matthias appealed to his cousin, King Philip III of Spain, for urgent assistance, and, in the summer of 1618, only Spanish silver saved Vienna from insolvency. Nevertheless, in 1619, the new Emperor Ferdinand II was forced to flee his capital, Vienna, as Protestant troops from Bohemia and Moravia advanced. The Estates of Upper and Lower Austria, dominated by Lutherans, joined the revolt as well. The Calvinist Prince of Transylvania, Gabor Bethlen, marched west with Hungarian nobles in aid of the revolt, in order to free that kingdom from Habsburg rule. To save the dynasty in Central Europe, Philip III earmarked a corps of 7,000 Spanish and Italian troops and ordered them to march from Naples to Austria, where they arrived in November 1619. Duke Maximilian of Bavaria raised an army of over 20,000 men, a considerable force for a state of just over a million inhabitants, under the command of Tilly Tserclaes, a Flemish general.[1] Money and men arrived from much of Catholic Europe, and from the Pope, too, to wage a new crusade against heretics.[2] In the course of 1620, the rebel territories withered under the weight of simultaneous assaults. A loyal Saxon army occupied Lusatia, north of Bohemia proper. Imperial troops liberated Moravia from the Hungarians, and Catholic League forces under Tilly and General Bucquoy (another 'Belgian', in charge of Imperial and Spanish Habsburg troops) occupied Upper and Lower Austria over the summer of 1620. No modern fortresses stood in the way of their advance.

Image 5.1 Della Bella Battery, MET Museum. Battery bombarding town ramparts, ca. 1640. Here, the guns have been quickly deployed without raising entrenchments around the pieces to protect the gunners. The target town, when bereft of bastioned fortifications, would quickly surrender

The Palatine Elector Frederick was not successful in coaxing resources from the English or the Dutch. His ardent Calvinism alienated Prague Lutherans and Catholics and the Bohemian Estates could not raise the money he needed for an effective army of his own. The States' army numbered about 21,000 men, part Czech, part German, and with a supporting contingent of Hungarian cavalry. On 8 November, the opposing armies met at a slope just southwest of Prague, called White Mountain (Cerna Gora) and formed up in array. The Protestant commander, Prince Christian of Anhalt, and his subordinates deployed their men in slender Dutch-style battalions ten men deep, in a line about two kilometres long, under the protection of ten cannon sited at the top of the slope. The Catholic League and Imperial troops numbered about 27,000 men; the infantry formed up in just five giant phalanxes of muskets and pikes. Then they advanced towards their adversaries into musket range. The exchange of fire was not very long or very lethal. The Polish Catholic cavalry under Tilly routed the Hungarian lighter cavalry on the Protestant left flank, who bolted in the direction of the camp. This success energized the Catholic troops, who surged forward seeing victory in their grasp. After two hours, the Protestant infantry broke up and a great number of them were slaughtered in the ensuing rout.[3]

White Mountain was an important date in Central European history, because it confirmed the hegemony of the Catholic Habsburg dynasty for three centuries. The Palatine Elector Frederick fled the region and was declared an outlaw by the victorious emperor in January 1621. Duke Maximilian of Bavaria seized the Elector's own lands north of the Danube, while the Spanish Army of Flanders under Ambrogio Spinola marched into the Rhineland Palatinate from the west and occupied it, too. Tilly advanced along the east bank of the Rhine and occupied the Elector's capital at Heidelberg, effectively depriving the rebel prince of all his lands and revenues.[4] Not one to neglect his advantage, Emperor Ferdinand II banned the Protestant religion in all his states, not just in his own direct royal jurisdiction: 150,000 Protestants, principally members of the social elite, left the Bohemian lands, and another 100,000 followed from Austria over the next several years. Twenty-seven leaders of the revolt were executed in a great ceremony in Prague on 21 June 1621, and their heads and hands were affixed to public monuments as a warning to rebels. The emperor confiscated the lands of a thousand families, equal to two thirds of the Bohemian nobility and half the land mass of the kingdom, and parcelled them out to Catholic army leaders from much of Europe. Missionaries from Catholic Germany and Italy then proceeded to mount a vigorous campaign of indoctrination that would make Bohemia Catholic once more.

Protestant states rallied around King Christian IV of Denmark, who, in addition to his rich kingdom outside Germany (modern Denmark, southern Sweden and Norway), possessed Holstein in the Empire and exercised a zone of influence in Lower Saxony. He hired new mercenary armies in North-central

Germany in 1625 to challenge the Catholic advance, and in the course of 1626 his general, Ernst von Mansfeld, fought several battles against Tilly and the Imperial army led by the Czech general, Albert von Wallenstein. Wallenstein campaigned in 1627 with an army of 100,000 men, led by capable officers.[5] Danish forces were no match in quantity or quality before the Catholic onslaught, and Christian sued for peace in 1628. Wallenstein's armies occupied part of the Baltic Sea coast, and he rushed troops to Poland to prevent a Protestant Swedish army from imposing its will on that Catholic kingdom.

In March 1629, a jubilant Emperor Ferdinand decreed the Edict of Restitution, whereby all Catholic lands confiscated by Protestant princes and cities since 1555 would have to be returned to the Church. By suppressing Protestant services in his own hereditary territories, such as Austria and Bohemia, Ferdinand was entirely within his legal rights. The Catholic Duke Maximilian of Bavaria acted likewise, as did the Lutheran and Calvinist princes in their own states. The Edict of Restitution, however, implied that the lands of bishoprics and some 500 monasteries would be restored to a Catholic administration that would use those revenues to finance a Counter-Reformation throughout the empire. In two years, five bishoprics and about 100 monasteries were restored, and wherever troops seconded the efforts of missionaries, those regions often remain Catholic to this day. The sixteenth century witnessed the advance of Protestantism throughout Central Europe (including Poland and Hungary) almost unimpeded. In the seventeenth century, the Catholic Church recovered much of the lost ground, in part by conversion, as in Poland or Croatia, in part by force of arms and the exile of Protestant leaders.

The emperor was then distracted by the problem of the Mantuan Succession in Northern Italy, where a French branch of the ruling Gonzaga dynasty seized control of the rich duchy and threatened Habsburg hegemony in Lombardy. In 1629, the emperor sent a large army across the Alps to besiege Mantua and thereby assist Spain in restoring control. It was a fatal distraction that diverted Imperial money and men away from Germany until 1631. The Lutheran bishopric of Magdeburg on the River Elbe rebelled against the Catholic settlement and General Tilly laid siege to the city in 1631. When it fell to storm in May, the city caught fire and thousands perished. This event was then lionized in Protestant propaganda and states rallied around the king of Sweden, who had just landed an army on the Baltic coast of Germany. This event would inaugurate the 'Swedish' phase of the war in Germany.

Gustavus Adolphus, since the start of his reign in 1611, aimed to impose Swedish hegemony over the entire Baltic Sea. He attacked Poland in the 1620s with the design of detaching coastal territories from it, and levying tolls and duties on goods exported from its ports. France brokered a peace between Sweden and Poland in September 1629 so that the former could devote its attention to the Holy Roman Empire. After January 1631, Cardinal Richelieu actively subsidized Gustavus Adophus to make war on the Habsburgs in Germany. The king wished to be the pre-eminent figure in Germany and the saviour of the Protestant cause. Swedish troops advanced from their Baltic base in the summer of 1631, too late to save Magdeburg, and, after compelling the Elector of Saxony to join his alliance, Gustavus Adolphus met Tilly's army at Breitenfeld on 17 September. The Saxon troops fled before the Catholic charge, but the Swedish cavalry swept around the left flank of the Imperials and attacked them from the rear, provoking the destruction of the army. More Protestant states rallied to Gustavus's cause, but, like Brandenburg, not always willingly. Swedish armies then roved across southern Germany as far as Alsace and the Central Rhine area, attracted by the abundant resources of food and forage. There they dug in and consolidated their contacts with the friendly but still neutral French. By this time, the Swedish forces had swelled almost to 100,000 men, of whom only a small percentage was ethnically Swedish or Finn.[6] Most were North German Protestants assisted by a strong component of Scots. In the face of the onslaught on Bavaria, Tilly was killed and both Bavarian and Imperial armies shrivelled for lack of resources.

Emperor Ferdinand decided to recall the brilliant but indocile General Albert von Wallenstein out of retirement. He raised another army of 100,000 men, in exchange for having untrammelled command over its operations. His field army alone numbered 40,000, which was very large for the period, while the remainder consisted of garrisons that sucked contributions from the population around them.[7] The Bohemian lord's career is worth examining in more detail. He was born a Czech Protestant but converted to Catholicism around 1609 and advanced at Matthias's court by virtue of his new religion. He became a regimental commander early in the war, and proved effective both on the battlefield and as a recruiter in his north Bohemian estates. Outside the Habsburg hereditary domains, he proved to be a prodigious extractor of resources, money and provisions from enemy lands via orderly '*contributions*'. He also organized his own estates in view of supplying his army with goods. In seven years, he is credited with having levied an annual average of four million gulden, equal to a quarter of the revenues the Habsburgs used to fight the war.[8] He had the emperor appoint him Duke of Mecklemburg, a large Protestant territorial state on the Baltic coast, in 1628 when his troops occupied it. But he was outspoken in his opposition to the Mantuan adventure, and Ferdinand considered him to be too accommodating towards Protestants. Wallenstein surrounded himself not only with Italian colonels and other foreigners, but with Protestant ones, too. The emperor was a 'hawk': he wanted to force German Protestant princes to convert to Catholicism. Wallenstein was more pragmatic and prone to taking initiatives without his master's approval. Ferdinand sidelined him in early 1630, provoking his bankruptcy.

In 1631, Wallenstein reorganized the Imperial army in a manner that increased his personal authority over it. Under him there were about 25 general officers and 130 proprietary colonels (as many as a third were not German) who made the army machine run. In 1632, Wallenstein fought two pitched battles against Gustavus Adolphus. He enticed the king of Sweden to attack him at Alte Veste near Nuremberg, where he created a fortified camp. In three days his army felled 13,000 trees and moved 80,000 tonnes of earth to create a perimeter of 15 kilometres. Gustavus Adolphus assaulted the position for two days, but then retired with heavy losses. In early November, Wallenstein began to break up his army for the winter, but the king of Sweden suddenly attacked his main force at Lützen, not far from Leipzig, on 16 November. Some 19,000 'Swedes' advanced resolutely against only 16,800 Imperials. Wallenstein recalled an important detachment of Imperial troops under General Pappenheim, which marched all night to reach the battle in time. Wallenstein's left flank was about to be crushed by Swedish cavalry when 2,500 cavalry troopers of this contingent finally appeared. Pappenheim was quickly killed but his Tuscan subordinate, Ottavio Piccolomini, saved the day with no fewer than seven charges. In one of those, his troops killed Gustavus Adolphus, who had ventured too close to the front lines. Swedes and Imperials contested the village of Lützen all day; the thick rectangular formations of Imperial soldiers proved more resistant in close combat than the Swedes, who took heavy casualties. After nightfall, Wallenstein withdrew undisturbed and so the battle is considered a tactical victory for the Swedes.[9]

The following year, Wallenstein ceased to act offensively against the Swedes and their Protestant allies, because he felt that it was time to make a general peace. His many enemies also thought that the contributions levied by his troops were enriching him personally – which was true. He was also believed to be corresponding covertly with enemy leaders without the emperor's permission. On the emperor's own initiative, a plot organized around the leading Italian generals, Galasso, Piccolomini and Colloredo, aimed to remove him from command. Feeling the ground slipping away, Wallenstein obliged all his colonels to swear an oath of loyalty to his person at Pilsen in January 1634, which enraged the emperor and convinced him to have the general assassinated. By having the general killed without trial as a traitor, the emperor could then confiscate all of Wallenstein's considerable property and use it to pay his debts.[10] British officers at Cheb in Bohemia carried out the deed on February 25 1634. Despite the fear that the troops loyal to the late field marshal would disband, most colonels and their troops transferred their loyalties to Emperor Ferdinand without qualms.

Swedish armies kept the field after the death of Gustavus Adolphus by means of generous French subsidies, as well as by imposing crippling contributions on the Rhine watershed from Alsace to Franconia. Swedish and German Protestant armies sparred with the Imperial and Spanish troops in Alsace and along the upper Danube. In 1634, the Imperial forces under Crown Prince Ferdinand, son of the emperor, and general Matteo Galasso laid siege to the modest town of Nördlingen in Franconia. The Swedish army under Count Gustav Horn and a German Protestant force under Bernhard of Saxe-Weimar advanced on the town to lift the siege. Before they could achieve this goal, Cardinal Ferdinand, Infante and younger brother of the king of Spain marched north from Milan with a sizeable reinforcement of Spanish and Italian troops, and joined the Imperial force just before the battle. A confident Protestant army of 25,700 men assailed 33,000 Catholics who were waiting for them in solid defensive positions outside the town. The Spanish troops on the critical southern flank were reinforced during the night. When the Swedes and Scots stormed them on the morning of 6 September with local superiority of numbers, the German Habsburg regiments broke and fled, but the Spanish and Neapolitan tercios held their ground. Repeat attacks on the thick Catholic formations wore the assailants down and shook their confidence, while the Habsburg cavalry prevented a Protestant outflanking movement. Then the armies engaged in the centre where Imperial superior numbers made the difference. The Protestant army collapsed and many thousands of them were massacred in the pursuit, while all their guns and baggage were captured.[11] The Cardinal Infante then proceeded with his victorious contingent to reinforce the Spanish Army of Flanders. Nördlingen seemed to be a more decisive battle than Breitenfeld, for German Protestant princes allied with the Swedes reconciled with the emperor in the Peace of Prague of May 1635. Ferdinand suspended the application of the Edict of Restitution to appease them. For a second time, the great war in Germany appeared to end with a resounding Habsburg triumph.

Much has been written about the tactical innovations of Gustavus Adolphus, but closer research shows that he was not so much a precursor as someone who consolidated contemporary practice into a system.[12] Maurice of Orange-Nassau was a more important tactical innovator but the Dutch shied away from field battles with the Spaniards, with good reason. At the start of the war, German Protestant states adopted the Dutch slender order of battalions numbering 500–600 men, six or seven deep, and drilled the musketeers intensively. The shock troops were still the pikemen, better armoured and essential in melee combat. Musketeers milled about the central corps of pikemen, and withdrew behind them when they were threatened. Muskets were powerful and more accurate than has been claimed, but they were clumsy weapons requiring almost two minutes to reload. Spanish-style tercios of thousands of men that won the battle of White Mountain were slow and ponderous, but they could still attack at a speed of about one metre per second, giving enemy musketeers little time to mow them down. Infantry formed up in great checkerboards, such that not all the foot was engaged simultaneously. Cavalry also came in several types; heavily armoured lancers all but disappeared from the field, replaced by a corps of pistol and carbine-wielding *reiters*, more manoeuvrable than heavy cavalry and more effective against the nimble Turks.[13] These reiters and light cavalry who fought in loose order were trained and equipped to fight on foot if required. A new arm of mounted infantry called 'dragoons', mounted on smaller, inexpensive horses emerged in the course of the war as a multipurpose unit. In battle, the cavalry often used the caracole tactic, similar to the infantry countermarch, which entailed unleashing fire at close range, then wheeling about to reload while the ranks behind them took their turn. Artillery was difficult to move once placed on the battlefield and its effective range was only about 500 metres. Usually the guns were placed ahead of the infantry and the battle began as an exchange of cannon fire aimed at large blocks of men.

Gustavus Adolphus increased the 'shock' aspect of infantry and cavalry tactics, first by drilling his men to advance within very short range of the enemy before unleashing a great volley of shot. (At Nördlingen, however, the Spanish had orders to crouch as soon as they heard the order to fire.) The king of Sweden distributed small parties of musketeers among his horse to increase the confidence of the troopers. Finding that the Dutch style of small, slender battalions lacked offensive punch, he combined several of them into 'brigades'. In addition, he multiplied small field cannons (three- and four-pound shot) that could be manhandled into position and loaded with grape-shot to spray the enemy at close range. After Breitenfeld, Wallenstein was quick to adapt some of these techniques, but Habsburg regiments remained larger and more solid formations of a thousand men arrayed eight or more deep, more effective at close quarters. Spanish tactics were still feared by their adversaries to 1640 at least; their foot were armed for two-thirds with muskets like the others, but, arrayed over ten deep, they were almost impossible to break open.[14] David Parrott argues convincingly that the effect of complicated tactics paled relative to the will of the men to fight and to win. The odds of victory were increased by a good run of continuous success and, over time, units would acquire a larger portion of veterans who knew what to expect in battle. Increasingly, battles were won by flanking movements of cavalry that chased off their mounted adversaries and then swung around to attack the foot from the rear or the flank, which demoralized them.[15] As field armies shrank in size, the cavalry contingent became even more important, consisting of a third or more of the soldiers.

The Swedish defeat at Nördlingen ushered in the 'French' phase of the Thirty Years' War. The strategy of defeating the Habsburgs by financing their enemies having failed, Cardinal Richelieu convinced Louis XIII to lead France into the war directly on multiple fronts. French armies tried to close off the Spanish Road across the Alps by occupying the Duchy of Lorraine, whose Catholic Duke Charles V was a sworn enemy of the cardinal. By 1634, French garrisons replaced Swedish ones in Alsace and the Rhine Palatinate, while a French army under the Duke de Rohan marched into Switzerland to strike Spanish Milan from the north weeks before Louis officially declared war. The German theatre of war was a minor front for the French after 1635, who hired the German army under Bernhard of Saxe-Weimar to achieve their aims. French money also kept the Swedish army in being, especially after it won an unexpected victory at Wittstock, near Berlin, in 1636, which kept the kingdom in the war.[16] In the following years, Swedish generals plundered resources and conscripted men from the Protestant states they occupied militarily, such as Brandenburg and Saxony.[17] The Swedes repeatedly attacked Habsburg territory from their base in Pomerania along the Baltic coast, inflicting heavy damage on the lands of the new Emperor Ferdinand III (r. 1637–1655). French armies advancing into Bavaria devastated the upper Danube region repeatedly, and replaced the Swedes in the Rhineland. But the size of field armies shrank to half the previous level, due to the increasing inability to feed them. Cavalry made up an increasingly large component of armies, due to the necessity of raising resources over a larger area. A number of states, such as Brandenburg and Saxony, began to make separate treaties with the belligerents around them. After 1645, even the emperor was determined to make a general peace, conceding to German princes a degree of sovereignty they had never hitherto enjoyed, and full autonomy in matters of religion.

The Peace of Westphalia in 1648 ended the German war with a general compromise. Habsburg dreams of a more centralized, Catholic monarchy had to be abandoned. The early conclusion that Germany experienced a population decline of about 40% has been borne out by more recent research.[18] The calculation of battlefield deaths is, in large part, guesswork, due to the lack of accurate sources. It had been calculated that some half-million soldiers perished during the conflict (some 16,000 annually) but battle losses made up only a third of that.[19] This was a modest proportion of the 200,000 soldiers on the move in the 1630s and 1640s (in multiple armies), and the figure does not include mortality among camp followers, who were more numerous in Germany than elsewhere. Historians have neglected to examine in detail the surviving parish registers, with their records of civilian burials. Most soldiers were not fighting for any ideals or principles, but were living off what they could obtain from the populations under their control. Soldiers saw everything in enemy territory as their property, or 'dowry'. In larger communities, officers negotiated the acquisition of food and money with local authorities, but soldiers in small detachments in winter quarters were difficult to supervise.[20] In the 1620s, soldiers' plundering was largely instrumental, designed and tolerated so as to keep the troops on the move. There is a persistent 'black legend' of wholesale violence unleashed upon civilians that was drawn from novels and pictures; people certainly believed that the soldiers would do their worst, but theft seems to have been much more widespread than murder.[21] Soldiers do not seem to have massacred civilian populations deliberately, unless they were provoked (Image 5.2). Bands of armed peasants indeed killed large numbers of straggling soldiers or set ambushes for raiding parties, or marauders.[22] During the Swedish phase of the war, there was certainly massive ransacking, arson and violence, particularly by the Protestants. Croat light horse in Imperial service was feared too: the term designated any Slavic light cavalry, and, typically, they were Poles or Cossacks rather than ethnic Croats or Serbs drawn from the Hungarian border.[23] Soldiers and refugees in cities upset the fragile sanitary conditions prevailing there, provoking terrible outbreaks of dysentery or e-coli. Even 'friendly' soldiers spread infectious diseases like the bubonic plague, as they marched from town to town. Probably worse was the soldiers' tendency to strip localities of their food supplies and the livestock needed to till the fields. Hunger reduced the normal immunity to common pathogens among civilians, such that they would succumb more readily to common fevers. Malnutrition and insecurity were not conducive to normal family life, and so losses were not quickly replaced. The population declined not because soldiers killed civilians, but because it could not reproduce itself over several decades.

A 30–40% population decline is only an average, however, and while some districts, such as Friesland and Westphalia in the northwest, escaped the worst

Image 5.2 Jacques Callot: Looting Village, Harvard Fogg Museum R4500. Sometimes soldiers killed civilians in their forays to lay waste to enemy territories, but the material damage and theft of property, livestock, and foodstuffs led to many more deaths from starvation and exposure. Note the armed men arrayed in a defensive enclosure around the church, who might be militia

effects of the war, a broad swath from Pomerania and Brandenburg in the northeast to Franconia and Alsace in the southwest lost about half its pre-war population. On the Francophone western fringe of the Empire, wholesale devastation reigned. The Franche-Comté was largely undefended and it could not easily withstand French invasion in 1635 and 1636, which coincided with the advent of the bubonic plague. Thirteen towns were destroyed by fire during military campaigns and in numerous raids, reducing the province's population by 55–60% in just eight years. Cardinal Richelieu instructed troops to destroy the region's mills, ovens, mines and forges. Destroying infrastructure and stripping the land of resources denied them to the enemy. Some people were killed in the fighting, but most died of starvation and disease, while many others fled to safer regions in France and Switzerland. Imperial forces eventually 'rescued' the province. Neighbouring Lorraine lost about 60% of its population between 1630 and 1660 for identical reasons. Most towns declined by 70–80%, as commerce collapsed. Armed bands roved the countryside using rural castles as bases of operations.[24] The scale of this destruction often led to the denigration or repudiation of rulers who could not protect the population, leading to a 'crisis of authority' directed towards ineffectual princes.[25]

The eighty years' war round two

In 1621, both Spain and the Low Countries both felt it was to their advantage to go back to war. Maurice of Orange-Nassau had gained the upper hand over the States of Holland but both felt that it was time to seize as much Spanish and Portuguese territory in the Indies as they could. Spain likewise felt that it could achieve a better peace through war, perhaps reopening the River Scheldt estuary to large ships so that Antwerp could recover its place as a leading port. In Madrid around 1620, it was freely admitted that Spain was on the decline, but the monarchy's ability to raise tax money and international loans was still considerable. Limited war in the Low Countries was feasible: the Army of Flanders cost Madrid 1.7 million ducats in peacetime, but only 2.5 million in the late 1620s (plus 500,000 ducats for the fleet), a modest increase.[26] The scattered Spanish Habsburg possessions around Europe totalled about 16 million inhabitants (nine million in Iberia, five million in Italy, two million in the Burgundian inheritance of the Low Countries and the Franche-Comté), fewer than in 1590, but still considerable. The Dutch Republic's population numbered just under two million.

The Army of Flanders under Ambrogio Spinola was still a very effective fighting force, its confidence enhanced after its victories in the Rhine Palatinate. The Genoese commander was unable to open up the Scheldt after failing to take the Dutch fortress of Bergen-op-Zoom in 1622, but he laid siege to Breda at the end of 1624 and repelled the attempts of the Dutch to relieve it. With Breda's fall in June 1625, the Spanish recovered almost a quarter of the land mass of the Dutch Republic. Flemish privateers operating out of Dunkirk inflicted grievous losses on Dutch North Sea commerce. Spinola then manoeuvred around the eastern border of the republic in Westphalia, in conjunction with Tilly, and imposed a commercial blockade on the Dutch to evaporate their financial resources. The Army of Flanders had already occupied the central Rhine and closed off many Dutch resources far upstream. Until 1625, the Catholic king's army was everywhere victorious, including in far-off Brazil, where it ejected a Dutch attempt at conquest.[27]

This success was accomplished by means of extraordinary spending and borrowing by Madrid. The new 'valido', or chief minister, of King Philip IV, Gaspar de Guzmàn, Count Duke Olivares conceived a great project, the *Union of Arms*, designed to draw taxes, men and ships from the entire Empire more equitably than before. Castile and Naples traditionally paid the lion's share of the fiscal burden; the Low Countries and Lombardy paid extra by virtue of being the principal battlefields. Other kingdoms, such as Aragon, Sicily, Portugal and the Franche-Comté, enjoyed ample privileges by which they escaped the full weight of Spain's commitments. The danger was that the taxpaying core of the empire would not be able to withstand the weight of a long war. Spinola went to the court in Madrid in 1628 to recover some of his own money he had lent over almost 30 years, and whose interest was rarely paid.[28] The general came to represent the 'peace' party, which gained the ascendancy after Castile went into bankruptcy in 1627. The financial situation worsened dramatically the next year when Dutch Admiral Piet Heyn seized the Spanish treasure fleet off Matanzas in Cuba. The crisis of the Mantuan Succession arrived simultaneously, requiring an army raised in Milan to eject the Gonzaga duke from Mantua and the Monferrato. Competing armies in Northern Italy unleashed a wave of bubonic plague that killed about a quarter of the population and crippled the country's manufactures.

Under Frederick Henry of Orange-Nassau, brother of Maurice (d. 1625), Dutch forces began to recover towns lost to Spinola, such as Hertogenbosch in 1629, Maastricht in 1632 and the crucial river fortress of Rheinberg in

1633. French subsidies enabled the Republic to hire mercenaries in numbers undreamed of for a state with only two million inhabitants, reaching 90,000 men (on paper). Olivares refused to make peace without establishing Spain's 'reputaciòn', which we would translate today as 'credible deterrence'. To cave in to one adversary was an invitation to other states to challenge and diminish the Spanish empire, and so Madrid had to fight on until it could make peace with honour. Olivares refused to make a compromise peace in Northern Italy, which proved elusive and cost much treasure until the settlement of Cherasco in 1631.[29]

After the battle of Nördlingen, Cardinal Richelieu forged an alliance with the Dutch Republic by which the two powers would split the Spanish Netherlands between them. The invasion from two directions in 1635 imperilled Brussels only briefly, as Spain was able to send enough troops and money to cope with the threat. The army in Flanders at the end of 1635 numbered 45 infantry tercios and regiments of diverse provenance (13 Spanish, 14 Italian, eight Walloon, four Irish, three German, two English and one Tyrolean), and 113 cavalry squadrons (39 Spanish, 12 Walloon, 12 Lorrainer, seven Italian, five Burgundian, 20 Polish and 18 Croatian).[30] This amounted to 60,400 infantry and 27,550 cavalry on paper, more like 70,000 effective men who threatened both the Republic and France.[31] The cavalry was mounted on smallish horses and proved unreliable, but the Spanish infantry still enjoyed an unmatched reputation in Europe for effectiveness on the battlefield. Spanish artillery was also very effective, and exploited a new weapon in the form of the exploding shell. In 1636, after meeting heavy resistance from the Dutch, the Cardinal Infante marched the army south into Picardy against the French. After quickly capturing fortresses along the River Somme frontier, he found an opening at Corbie and marched headlong for several days in the direction of Paris. The army was not prepared to advance very far, so it withdrew after exacting huge contributions over a wide swath of northern France.

Despite the entry of France into the war on their side, Dutch gains against the Spanish in northern Brabant were very modest and the sole field battle at Kallo, near Antwerp, in 1639 was a resounding Spanish victory. The only clear success for the Republic was a naval victory off the English coast near Dover in 1639 (Battle of the Downs), in which Admiral Tromp destroyed a Spanish fleet of almost a hundred vessels bringing supplies and 8,000 soldiers. The troops and the precious cash succeeded in reaching their destination notwithstanding, by marching through friendly England and crossing the Channel in English ships. By now, Olivares was prepared to make peace with the Republic, but the Dutch had high hopes of seizing distant Iberian colonies.

Franco-Spanish war 1635–1659

Cardinal Richelieu began preparing for a general confrontation against Spain from the very outset of his administration in 1624, the same year Olivares came to power. Louis XIII was seduced by the cardinal's project to make him 'the most powerful king in the world', and France harboured claims to large parts of the Spanish empire in Europe, including Lombardy and the kingdom of Naples in Italy, as well as the Low Countries and the Franche-Comté. France and Spain were involved in about ten conflicts between 1595 and 1689, and France initiated most of them. Olivares and Philip IV were deeply disturbed by what they considered French Machiavellianism (a general unscrupulousness) and by the French betrayal of the Catholic cause.[32] Pope Urban VIII was also grieved by French subsidies for Protestant states and military alliances with them just when the Habsburgs were on the cusp of complete success between 1625 and 1635. Richelieu launched a strike against Genoa in 1625 with the aid of the ambitious Duke Charles-Emmanuel of Savoy, but Spanish seaborne reinforcements from Naples and Sicily, along with a contingent of Imperial troops sent from Germany, forced it to retire. The French cardinal then assisted Duke Charles of Mantua to resist Olivares' efforts to eject him from Italy by sending French troops to garrison Casale Monferrato, and two epic sieges of the fortress in 1628 and 1630 were Habsburg failures. But there was a pro-Spanish party in Paris, too, assembled behind the Queen Mother Maria de'Medici and the king's brother and heir, Prince Gaston d'Orléans. Louis XIII could not make up his mind to support Richelieu's goal of a great war with the House of Austria until 10 November 1630. Even after the king's fateful decision to back the cardinal and war, Richelieu's preferred approach was to wear down the Habsburg monarchs indirectly by financing the Dutch and the Swedes. This was the policy that failed utterly at Nördlingen in September 1634.

In 1635, Cardinal Richelieu threw French armies against Flanders, Germany, Franche-Comté, Italy and Spain simultaneously. He had been increasing taxes relentlessly for years, to the point of provoking open rebellion in France in numerous towns and provinces. French infantry regiments numbered 72 in 1633, the year Richelieu overran Lorraine, then 135 in 1635, 174 in 1636; but the number of soldiers did not rise in similar proportions. All the French armies combined might have numbered 90,000 men in 1635, and with their Italian allies (who hired many French mercenaries) totalled perhaps 110,000. This was larger than any French force in the past, but it was not equal to the cardinal's ambitions.[33]

In Italy, Richelieu tried to whet the appetites for conquest of the Duke of Savoy, the Duke of Parma, the Duke of Mantua and the Swiss Grison League, but only Parma, with a limited capacity, was a willing ally. Duke Victor Amadeus I of Savoy attempted to retain the upper hand in the alliance, justifiably fearful that he would lose territory to his ally. Because of his lacklustre support for French plans, the campaign of 1635 in Lombardy was a complete failure. In 1636, Duke Victor-Amadeus prevented a complete rout of the French army under attack by the Spanish along the River Ticino at Tornavento, but it was a very close call. The intended conquest of Milan failed, too, and in the aftermath Spanish forces grew stronger than those of the confederates. Parma and Mantua were soon out of the war, and France's Swiss allies changed sides.[34] In the late 1630s and following the death of Victor Amadeus, Spain pressed the

Duchy of Savoy to the point of complete collapse and civil war. The independent duchy came close to disappearing as Cardinal Richelieu extended French garrisons there wherever he could.[35]

In other theatres, French successes were few and fleeting. In part this was due to Richelieu's inability to pay and supply armies in the field.[36] Desertion might reduce the men starting out by three-quarters in the course of a campaign. Reinforcements arrived continually to join the field army, but they were rarely enough to maintain its overall size. Grand master of the French navy from 1626, the cardinal could assemble large fleets of warships all owned and armed by the crown, as in the Mediterranean in 1636, but these never wrested control of the sea from Spain.[37] The French chief minister was loath to give much leeway to commanders in the field, and often divided the command, which led to infighting among the generals. Olivares was hoping that dissatisfaction at the French court would eventually lead to the cardinal's dismissal or, better, his assassination. It was not obvious before 1640 that his policy of an honourable peace and a return to the *status quo ante* was bound to fail.[38]

To fend off the French threat, Olivares raised taxes everywhere, leased royal jurisdictions to private interests (called alienation) and borrowed heavily at ever higher rates of interest. There was a localized outbreak of unrest at Evora in Portugal in 1637. Even in Madrid, plenty of people felt that Olivares' policy was too rigid. The Count Duke also undercut the bonds of loyalty between great lords of the realm and the person of the king by placing more emphasis on loyal functionaries without contacts in the areas they ruled.[39] Olivares challenged the claims of tax immunity by the Catalan elites of Barcelona by levying money and provisions by force. In 1640, the indiscipline of the soldiers led to armed rebellion against them by Catalan peasants, who occupied Barcelona and killed the viceroy. When Olivares sent troops to restore order, the Catalan assembly declared open secession from the Spanish realms, and recognized the sovereignty of Louis XIII in 1641. French armies penetrated Roussillon and captured Perpignan in 1642; however, Bourbon troops behaved with the same rough impunity towards civilians that had characterized the Castilians.[40] Olivares needed a new army to recover Catalonia and increased his pressure on the Portuguese aristocracy to provide more resources. These men assembled and designated one of their own to be king, John IV of the House of Braganza, at the end of 1640. Portugal (and its empire) seceded from the Habsburg monarchy, too. This opened a second theatre of war in Iberia, in order to recover the breakaway territories. Experienced troops had to be transferred from Milan and Naples to confront the French and their secessionist allies.

The year 1640 confirmed the decline of Spain, because excessive strain on the tax system led to paralysis and breakdown. Spanish troops were forced into a strategic defensive in the Low Countries, although the Dutch had lifted pressure on them considerably. French armies captured Arras after a long siege in 1640 and pushed north. A Spanish attack on the French camp at Honnecourt in 1642 marked the end of Bourbon progress, however. The next year, in order to relieve French pressure on Catalonia, the loyal Portuguese governor-general of the Low Countries, Francisco de Melo, collected a substantial force of 26,000 men from detached garrisons and launched a counterattack into Champagne via the small fortress of Rocroi. De Melo laid siege to the place for several days but, overconfident, he did nothing to stall the approach of a French relief force and did not even dig lines of circumvallation to defend his camp. The young Duc d'Enghien, son of the Prince de Condé, approached from Picardy with an army of 23,000 horse and foot. De Melo decided not to wait for reinforcements that were close by and deployed his army to face the French. No earthworks were raised that might have strengthened his position against cavalry. When the battle commenced on 19 May 1643, the Spanish infantry and artillery devastated the French left wing and forced it back. The French horse on the right wing brushed aside the weaker cavalry opposing it and wheeled around to attack the German and Walloon infantry regiments in the rear, scattering them. The main French line then battered the tercios with musketry and cannonballs for hours, trying to force them to flee. Unable to leave the field, the Spanish tercios finally surrendered, with the Habsburg army losing 3,500 men dead and 4,000 prisoners, compared to 4,000 casualties among the French. Rocroi was the most significant defeat of a Spanish field army in a hundred years or more.[41]

Milan and Lombardy were left to fend for themselves, as remittances of money from Madrid and Naples were diverted to the Catalan frontier. In northern Italy, France expected the Lombard nobles to rise up and welcome Bourbon armies as liberators, but instead they reached deep into their private purses and raised professional soldiers and militias to hold the invaders back.[42] The pressure on Naples, stripped of its garrisons, to provide men, ships, horses and cash for the war effort increased. Sicily produced few soldiers, but it was a notable source of money and grain for the army and navy. Desperate to raise short-term cash, the king of Spain alienated tax revenues to private collectors, just as he sold royal jurisdictions to nobles and financiers; royal tribunals sold pardons for every crime but treason. In 1647, a tax riot in Palermo led to the momentary loss of Spanish control over most of Sicily. On 7 July it was the turn of the vast population of Naples to rise up behind the fishmonger Masaniello against the tax collectors. Within weeks the furore turned against Spain itself, and the city revolt spread across the kingdom. The nobility declared its loyalty to the king of Spain, and a French pretender to the throne, the Duke de Guise, was quickly sidelined by his pretensions to rule over the Neapolitans. For the better part of a year, the southern kingdom was shaken by bitter local fighting, while in the capital the Neapolitan crowds proved unable to capture the Spanish citadels. On 6 April 1648, a small Spanish sortie of a few hundred men was enough to take back control of the metropolis. Afterwards, the king reduced taxes considerably in order to win back the populace to the Habsburg regime.[43]

By 1643, Olivares' Union of Arms was completely discredited and King Philip IV finally repudiated the minister. Cardinal Richelieu had died the previous year, but the new ministry of the French crown of Louis XIV (five years old), guided by the Italian Cardinal Mazarin, continued a warlike policy now that France was winning. The king of Spain would not countenance a disastrous peace and opted to keep fighting. In the Iberian kingdoms, Philip IV was reduced to raising troops by conscription, in which towns collected men and dispatched them to the theatre of war. Olivares turned to the nobility to raise large contingents from their own revenues. Castile produced about 12,000 recruits annually, whose makeshift levies took their place alongside depleted tercios of Walloons and Neapolitans. Silver remittances from the Indies fell off during the 1640s and 1650s, straining finances even more. The coinage of the kingdom was continually debased, as whatever precious metal arrived from the Indies was already earmarked to pay the interest on new foreign loans. After a new Spanish bankruptcy in 1647, Madrid finally made peace with the Netherlands at the Treaty of Westphalia in 1648, recognizing the independence of the Dutch Republic, and awarding it modest territorial gains.

Fortune finally smiled on Spain when French political elites, supported by the population, rejected a series of new taxes aimed at winning the war. Over the course of the war, the principal direct tax in France, the taille, passed from 11 million *livres tournois* to 53 million in 1643, almost fivefold, and all the other taxes rose simultaneously.[44] Waves of peasant and urban tax rebellion agitated various parts of the kingdom since the war with Spain began. For France as a whole, there was not a single year without a tax revolt between 1623 and 1648. Research on the participants finds them concentrated in the upper spheres of the lower classes, with sympathisers above and below them. Their violence was aimed at the houses and the offices of tax collectors, who were sometimes killed by angry – but not blind – crowds. Some uprisings seized important cities, like Bordeaux, but for never more than a few days. In the countryside, where whole communities were responsible for paying the designated amount, rebellions spread over large districts and could last for weeks and months. In the southwest quarter of the kingdom, where these revolts were endemic, parishes took up arms and converged on walled towns hoping to convert them into protected bases. They often coerced a military aristocrat into leading them and to serve as a spokesman for their demands. In the aftermath of the religious wars, peasants had no difficulty acquiring modern weapons and many of them were former soldiers. The first reaction of royal officials, governors of provinces and the intendants, was to diminish the taxes. In a second phase, troops drawn from the frontiers marched on the troubled zones. A battle between professional troops and peasant rebels was rare: most returned home and hid their weapons. The authorities then arrested scores or hundreds of participants and leaders, but the executions rarely surpassed a dozen, so as not to worsen the climate. Tax revolts worked: just as in Spanish Naples, officials lowered their demands on restless provinces, and in some districts fiscal anarchy reigned for years afterward.[45]

Sensing that Spain was too weak to continue the war in the aftermath of the Peace of Westphalia, ministers of the young Louis XIV opted to keep fighting and to make one final surge to achieve complete victory. Mazarin's sudden tax increase of 1648 was a step too far, for, in addition to antagonizing the general public, it mobilized the Parlement of Paris against him. This triggered a five-year period of instability and localized civil war in France called the *Fronde*, which aimed to unseat Mazarin. The French army broke up into warring factions and only a skeleton force kept the field in Catalonia, Italy and Flanders. This enabled Spanish armies to recover Catalonia completely by 1652, including Barcelona. In Lombardy, the Spanish governor of Milan, Caracena, attracted enough resources to be able to besiege and capture the chief French stronghold of Casale Monferrato, also in 1652.[46] The Spanish fleet retained the initiative in the Mediterranean and kept the French far away from Naples and Sicily. Dunkirk and Arras, lost to the French in the Low Countries, were both recaptured. Only the war against Portugal failed to bring success. There, the campaigns took the form of raids in which large detachments sought to take forts and castles from the enemy. Most bodies of troops on both sides were militia-based units, stiffened with very depleted tercios of foreign professional soldiers. Pay for these soldiers was so low and irregularly paid that many quit to become agricultural workers, as population decline due to famine and plague drove the demand for peasants upward. The levies of vagabonds and peasants in these border armies had no strategic value.[47]

In France, Cardinal Mazarin outlasted his many detractors and bought off most of his enemies. At the same time he emerged as the mentor of the young King Louis XIV and the confidant of his mother, Anne of Austria. Spain's exhaustion was manifest, but France's ability to raise taxes had eroded in the meantime and the size of its armies was scaled back. French armies were defeated in Italy at Pavia in 1655 and at Valenciennes in the Low Countries in 1656, but the tide was beginning to turn again in Paris's favour. What finally tipped the balance was an alliance between the Italian cardinal and the English Protector Oliver Cromwell, who sent a modest expeditionary force of English troops to serve under the direction of the French Marshal Turenne, a Protestant. After Spanish troops lost a set-piece battle on the North Sea coast near Dunkirk on 21 June 1658, Philip IV was finally ready to make peace. Despite 38 years of unrelenting war, and after three bankruptcies, four major revolts and many defeats, Spanish territorial losses to the French and English were very small, limited to the towns of Dunkirk (to England) and Arras in the Low Countries and the district of Roussillon in northern Catalonia (to France). An important part of the peace process, however, resided in the marriage of Louis XIV to Philip IV's daughter, Maria Theresa. Mazarin was far-sighted enough to anticipate that there might one day be an interruption of the Spanish Habsburg line, and it was fragile in Germany, too, such that France might be well positioned to inherit Spain's rich legacy. The war between Spain and Portugal continued, with England and France supplying the Portuguese with just enough support to prevent a Spanish victory.[48] That low-intensity war ended only in 1668.

British civil war 1639–1653

Britain remained neutral during this long period, although Britons served in all the continental armies in large numbers. Scots are thought to have numbered

30,000 in Swedish service and 8,000 in Danish armies, and still 5,000 more in the Dutch provinces. Others fought for France and for the Holy Roman Empire. Some of these might have been the same individuals moving from one army to another, but, given that Scotland's population numbered only a million people, this proportion of soldiers was enormous.[49] Tens of thousands of Englishmen fought on the continent, although not as consistently for the Protestant cause.[50] If one were to include the Irish serving in Spanish and French armies, then the number of Britons in continental armies over the period surpassed 100,000 men.[51]

King Charles I of the Scottish house of Stuart was a particularly inept sovereign whose congenital lack of political acumen was the chief contributor to his demise. In a system of hereditary monarchy, rulers occasionally appeared who lacked sufficient self-control and cunning to govern and inspire obedience. (Today, of course, it is completely different.) He entered into two maritime wars with Spain and France between 1625 and 1630, and lost both of them. To raise taxes to support a fleet and an army, he bypassed the fractious Parliament that was increasingly anti-Catholic and raised so-called 'Ship Money' without the assembly's consent. It was not enough. When he tried to impose Anglican rituals on the Scots' Church in 1639, the affair ended in war that was lost through lack of preparation and sheer military incompetence. The king recruited a largely Catholic Irish army to impose his policy but, in the context of Protestant disasters on the continent in the 1620s and 1630s, Parliament refused to fund it. Then, in October 1641, in reaction to the expulsion of native Irish from the east of Ireland and their replacement by Scottish Protestants, the former rose up in Ulster and massacred several thousand of the intruders. Many others died of disease and exposure. Parliament demanded action against Popery, but denied its resources to the discredited king. Charles tried arresting Puritan leaders (the radical, Calvinist-leaning wing of the Church of England) but this only spurred Parliament to raise troops instead, to defend its prerogatives.

In 1642, King Charles raised a large army in both Ireland and England in order to reassert his authority. Since he would not fight one enemy at a time, he failed to seize London after his first victory at Edgehill in October, when he had the opportunity, and without the capital city he could not control the navy or benefit from rich customs revenue. Charles also spurned peace initiatives from the Parliamentary camp in the aftermath of the battle. Fighting spread all over England in 1643 and the year ended with Parliament dominating the rich southeast and a corridor to Liverpool, while King Charles held Wales and the southwest, and Yorkshire in the north. The financial and industrial resources of London, which might have accrued to the king early in the war, were at the root of final Parliamentarian victory. The early royalist and parliamentarian armies were *ad hoc* affairs of green troops and semi-trained militia bands hesitant to fight. The return of tens of thousands of veterans from the continent quickly gave a more professional form to these men. Both sides imported their weapons from the continent, either from the Netherlands or from Saint-Malo in Brittany.[52] There was no network of fortresses in the interior that might anchor armies to a single theatre. Fighting ranged across much of the kingdom, while medieval town walls and castles underwent transformation with earthworks, 'à la huguenotte'.[53] Garrisons planted there were usually content enough to dominate the countryside and collect provisions, while leaving enemy garrisons in peace. Royalist armies tended to aristocratic direction, but this often resulted in chaos and uncoordinated operations by officers unwilling to follow orders, while the king proved powerless to impose order himself in his capital, Oxford.

Parliamentarian generals Sir Thomas Fairfax and Oliver Cromwell fashioned a much more disciplined force in 1644–1645, which they named the New Model Army. It began by raising pressed men, half of whom deserted, and, like continental armies, it was a revolving door of new recruits and deserters. However, over time, the more strident Puritans tended to dominate its ranks and, by 1647, it had become a political force in the hands of its commander, Oliver Cromwell. It soon acquired an effective engineer establishment (principally Dutch) and an array of cannons and mortars. They proved much more expert than the royalists at formal sieges and, by 1645, they were capturing towns in a systematic fashion. The New Model Army numbered about 15,000 men in the field in 1645, while the king's army shrank. Parliament's victory at Naseby on 14 June permitted Fairfax to overrun the West of England later that year. By early 1646, the Royalists lost almost all their remaining cities in England and the king capitulated in June, although he was not ready to relinquish authority to Parliament. A new royalist rising with Scottish support in 1648 was quickly repressed by Cromwell and the king was tried and executed by a slimmed-down radical rump of republican Parliamentarians. Cromwell then unleashed the New Model Army on Scotland in 1650, where it took control of the kingdom via a number of bastioned forts and garrison towns. This English army effectively suppressed Scottish autonomy for a decade.

Irish rebels formed a confederate army intermittently led by a staunch Protestant, James Butler, Earl of Ormond, who would not make concessions to majority Catholics. Their forces numbered around 20,000 men, but they were dispersed into four separate provincial armies and would not unite. They acquired about two-thirds of Ireland, by launching raids resembling medieval *chevauchées* against enemy towns and castles.[54] Of the seven principal field battles fought against royalists, Scots and Parliamentarians, the Irish won only one of them. Their troops were not well drilled in musketry and their pikes were inferior weapons at close quarters. Their Protestant adversaries routinely massacred their Irish prisoners of war, or exiled them to penal servitude in the West Indies. The Confederates made several offers of an army to King Charles in exchange for religious toleration, but he would never consent to it.[55] Years of campaigning by unprofessional bands achieved no strategic result, and lawlessness became endemic. Riven as it was by multiple factions, by the late 1640s the Irish league began to fall apart.

In 1649, Cromwell led his New Model army across the Irish Sea to conduct a re-conquest of the island, where only a few towns in the northeast and the Protestant capital Dublin were in English hands. His war aims were three:

revenge for the massacres of 1641, the expropriation of the Irish gentry and their replacement by Protestant settlers (with the systematic expulsion of as many Irish natives as possible to the west of the island) and the permanent abolition of Roman Catholicism. From his base in Scotland, King Charles II would not consent to public Catholic worship and he, too, advocated re-conquest of the island, fearful of alienating the militant Protestant majority in England and Scotland. Cromwell's New Model Army landed in Ireland in 1649 and proceeded to occupy the eastern and south-eastern coasts by besieging the port towns. At Drogheda, he saw the Irish garrison and much of the civilian population slaughtered in order to set an example, which resulted in about 3,500 victims. At Wexford, his soldiers butchered 2,000 defenders without receiving explicit orders to do so. Protestant troops destroyed crops and seized animals, burned houses and provoked widespread famine. Towns in the west of Ireland fell to Cromwellian troops in the course of 1652 and, by 1653, the Irish resisted mainly through guerrilla raiding. Civilians were often rounded up and moved to 'protected' zones, a classic counter-insurgency technique. Strategic terror encouraged desperate resistance by the disunited Irish, however. The cost to the Anglo-Protestant army was also high, as typhus and dysentery carried off the soldiers, sometimes thousands at a time, especially during sieges. A severe plague outbreak in Dublin in 1649 spread outward and lasted until 1654. Starting in 1651, most of the Irish troops departed to the continent to enlist in armies there, first for Spain (with a tradition dating back to 1600). After 1650, an increasing number migrated to France, where there were perhaps 34,000 of them by 1653, representing over ten per cent of adult Irishmen. Following the war, more than half of the Irish landmass was granted to the Protestant volunteers and the financial backers of the enterprise.[56]

Estimates of the death toll in Ireland over the course of the 1650s stand at about a quarter of a million people, of a pre-war population of 1.4 million. Another 30,000–40,000 troops and their camp followers fled to the continent, and 12,000 prisoners were transported to Caribbean colonies. Working from the research of Padraig Lenihan, who concludes that the island lost over 20% of its population, Carlton pegs the number of victims at 325,000 people.[57] Some areas of Ireland, as in Germany or Lorraine, lost over half their population during a decade of fighting.[58] Scotland lost proportionately fewer, about 28,000 military casualties and 15,000 non-combatant victims of the fighting, which represented about four per cent of its million inhabitants; Charles Carlton suggests that another 60,000 people died from disease or deportation.[59] Parish registers have not been systematically studied in Great Britain.[60] In England and Wales, the death toll in battle plus army mortality during the war might have been as high as 230,000 individuals, not counting civilian excess mortality wherever armies passed by or garrisons ate up supplies and spread their illnesses, out of a total population of 5.2 million.[61] For the British Isles combined, the death toll from hostilities over a decade would have amounted to about 600,000 people, out of a population of 7.5 million.[62]

In conclusion, four decades of unrelenting conflict in Western Europe resembled a continental civil war as much as a struggle for hegemony. Bohemian political elites, French *parlement* dignitaries, Catalan and Portuguese aristocrats, Neapolitan urban leaders, English members of Parliament and Scottish nobles took up arms against their rightful rulers over questions of local autonomy and liberty in the face of arbitrary taxation. The results were decidedly mixed, since, in most countries (including Great Britain), the monarchs finally prevailed.

Notes

1   Laurence Spring, 2017: xiii–xvii.
2   Peter Brightwell, 1982.
3   Olivier Chaline,1999: 114–38.
4   Joachim Whaley, 2012: 575.
5   Geoff Mortimer, 2010: 42, 96.
6   Lars Ericson, 1998.
7   Mortimer, 2010: 154.
8   Golo Mann, 1976: 342.
9   Richard Brzezinski, 2001.
10 Brzezinski, 2001: 219.
11 Peter Engerisser & Pavel Hrnčirik, 2009: 186–95.
12 William P Guthrie, 2003: 22–4.
13 Jean Bérenger, 2004.
14 Thomas Barker, 1975: 73–173.
15 David Parrott, 1985.
16 Steve Murdoch, Katherin Zuckermann & Adam Marks, 2012.
17 Derek McKay, 2001: 18–41.
18 John Thiebault, 1997.
19 Quentin Outram, 2002.
20 Ronald G Asch, 2000.
21 Geoff Mortimer, 2002.
22 Bernhard Kroener, 1998.
23 Spring, 2017 : 49.
24 Philippe Martin, 2002; Stéphane Gaber, 1991; Gérard Louis, 1998.
25 Otto Ulbricht, 2004.
26 Peter Brightwell, 1974
27 Robert Stradling, 1981: 57.
28 Robert Stradling, 1992: 66.
29 J.H. Elliott, 1984: 87.
30 Jean-Pierre Antoine Bazy, 1864: 53.
31 Jonathan I Israel, 1995.
32 Alain Hugon, 2000.
33 John Lynn, 1994: 881–906
34 Gregory Hanlon, 2014; Gregory Hanlon, 2016.
35 Giuliano Ferretti, 2014.
36 David Parrott, 1987.
37 Alan James, 2004.
38 J.H. Elliott, 1991.
39 Jean-Frédéric Schaub, 1994.
40 Fernando Sanchez-Marcos, 1998.
41 Laurent Henninger, 1993; Fernando Gonzalez de Leon, 2009; Antonio Jimenez Estrella, 2015.
42 Davide Maffi, 2007: 28–46.
43 Alain Hugon, 2011.

44 Joël Cornette, 2000: 57.
45 Gautier Aubert, 2015: 39–48.
46 Gianvittorio Signorotto, 1993.
47 Antonio Dominguez Ortiz, 1969.
48 Henry Kamen, 1980: 350; Michel Devèze, 1971.
49 Peter H. Wilson, 2010: 322.
50 Charles Carlton, 1992: 19.
51 Barbara Donagan, 2008: 51.
52 Christopher Duffy, 1979:, 147.
53 Ronald Hutton and Wylie Reeves, 1998, 195–233.
54 John Jeremiah Cronin and Padraig Lenihan, 2017: 246.
55 Jane Ohlmeyer, 1998.
56 Ian Gentles, 2007: 452.
57 Charles Carlton, 2011: 149.
58 Padraig Lenihan, 1997; John Jeremiah Cronin & Padraig Lenihan, 2017: 246.
59 Carlton, 2011: 148.
60 Martyn Bennett, 2000: 96.
61 Carlton, 1992: 206–10.
62 Gentles, 2007:, 436.

6   The age of military entrepreneurs

Where soldiers came from

Reciprocity is the iron law of anthropology: people in society who derive a benefit from living with others must give enough back in return so that they will not be shunned. This is useful to keep in mind when we consider why men risked their lives in war, and why so many of them volunteered to participate in such a perilous business. Seventeenth-century armies were arguably composed of mercenaries, who were paid by a diversity of warlords to fight a variety of enemies. But modern armies are little different, except for the fact that most of the soldiers originate in the state that employs them. Even now, some armies employ foreigners in elite units, and numerous states are privatizing some military activities. Mercenaries fight for money; apart from that, why would they join armies? There was a time when historians explained such behaviour in terms of alienation and class exploitation (the soldier had nothing to lose but his life). But such interpretations were rarely based on a close examination of army recruitment. It also assumed that humans are recipients shaped principally by their experiences and by prevailing ideologies. Progress in the behavioural sciences sheds much light on the diverse inclinations and personalities of people that is true for all times and places. People are born with distinct personalities that manifest themselves soon after birth: these innate dispositions influence life choices at every age.[1]

Early modern professional armies were based overwhelmingly on the recruitment of volunteers: there was increasing emphasis on conscription, as in Sweden under Gustavus Adolphus, but leaders found that unwilling soldiers would soon desert and nullify the considerable cost of raising them.[2] Young men signed up in the army and received the initial cash bonus, or bounty. A quarter or a third of the men then disappeared, often to enlist in another army and so receive another bonus.[3] Nevertheless, there were attractions enticing them into the army way of life; these included the taste for adventure, the desire to travel, some chance of rising to the rank of sergeant or higher, the hope of windfall booty. Many were also desirous to change their current predicaments, such as bad relations with one's parents or siblings, the drudgery of daily life in the fields or shops, dissatisfaction with a master, female trouble of various kinds, or the need to escape from debt or criminal proceedings. We should also not rule out the attraction armies held for men who enjoyed risk-taking, that is, fellows who deliberately sought out strong emotions and novel and intense experiences.[4]

Governments have not left many records enabling us to see exactly who became a soldier before the eighteenth century, but surviving muster rolls help historians a great deal. Iain Thompson assembled rosters of 29 Spanish companies from the late sixteenth and early seventeenth centuries, when perhaps 8–10,000 men enlisted annually. First-time soldiers would probably encounter a recruiting team, which in Spain consisted of the captain with his licence, or *asiento*, to engage men, an ensign assistant, a sergeant who carried the halberd and kept the books, and a drummer. This little group set up a table in a public space in a city or small town and planted the flag there. Former soldiers, many of whom bore *noms de guerre*, or nicknames, wishing to enlist again would haunt inns and taverns, certain to hear about the arrival of recruiters.[5] Veteran soldiers knew themselves to be highly marketable commodities, sure to be snapped up by other rulers if their prince made peace or laid them off.[6] Of the Spanish volunteers who came forward to take the signing bonus, almost 90% hailed from the kingdom of Castile, and only ten per cent from the Aragonese territories. The great majority identified themselves as town-dwellers, and few seemed to be of peasant origin. Perhaps one in eight or ten was a *hidalgo*, enjoying minor noble status. They were almost never children, with a median age for enlisting at 22, a quarter below age 20 and a smaller fraction over the age of 30.[7] We have close to 70 company rosters for the Duke of Parma's army in 1635–1636, whose details overlap a great deal with those from Spain. This sample of about 13,000 Italian and French soldiers confirms that recruits were disproportionately urban, if one includes in that definition a multitude of small towns where the social range was diverse and the better placed could live with decorum. The evidence suggests that these men were not drawn from the bottom of the social hierarchy, but emerged from every social group.[8] The armies were not looking for skilled men, or even particularly strong ones, for firearms did not require great strength or years of practice to master.[9] They wanted willing subjects without excessive antisocial traits.

The wages advertised were good for the times, given that the great majority of these were single men at the time of enlistment, without the burden of wives or children, whose food, clothing and lodging were provided for them at subsidized rates. The diet was usually varied and entailed copious amounts of meat, fish and cheese, along with liberal portions of wine and beer. Judging from the bills they ran up, French soldiers wintering in Northern Italy in 1636 consumed more than a kilogram of meat every day, in addition to bread and other foodstuffs of every description.[10] Garrison soldiers lived a fairly comfortable life in civilian houses, being subject to sentry duty and periodic drill, but they enjoyed free time in which they might earn money on the side. Marching and campaigning was more arduous, but this is where soldiers learned to compensate themselves for the risks. Digging entrenchments or other unpleasant work often entailed bonus pay, while some units could demand rewards for capturing fortified towns or winning battles.[11] Unit cohesion depended upon many things, such as tribal loyalties of men belonging to a similar ethnic group raised together. New regiments and those raised from men assembled from many different places fell apart quickly.[12] In most armies, the soldiers congregated in small ten-man sections living around a cooking pot, and shared their individual skills with their messmates. Cavalrymen enjoyed the highest standard of living, and often employed grooms and lackeys in their quarters.[13] In addition to the loot, soldiers expected that their promised wages would eventually be paid (Image 6.1). Even well-paid soldiers were not often good with money: they tended to live for the moment and gambled incessantly. If they were dissatisfied with their lot, usually because provisioning broke down, soldiers deserted. The enemy sometimes rewarded them for doing so, by giving them passports and some pocket-money to send them on their way. In Richelieu's French armies in Italy after 1635, something close to 75% of the army deserted their original unit over the campaign, although many enlisted in another regiment. Regulations prescribed hanging deserters, but neither soldiers nor officers would comply with such severe rules.[14] To stanch the flow of desertion, only relentless additional recruitment throughout the year kept the army in the field. Desertion dropped off considerably in the cold season, when men stayed on in exchange for modest cash payments, food and comfortable lodgings.[15] At the end of a war, soldiers still on the books expected to receive the money that was due to them. Governments recognized that it was best to keep veterans happy, for they would be needed again soon enough.

In enemy territory, the men were entitled to take what food they wanted, and other property, too. Some observers gave the impression that rape was very widespread, but closer examination in Germany and Italy has not confirmed this.[16]

Image 6.1 Jacques Callot: Pay Muster ca. 1630. Soldiers were assembled and counted periodically, then issued pay, while an assistant paymaster called each man by name. A summary description of each soldier on the roster was a check against fraud. MET Museum

The worst excesses must be explained by the psychology of individual soldiers, writes Ronald Asch. Looting was an integral part of reward for soldiers. In medieval times (in the absence of proper tribunals dispensing objective justice), an injured nobleman went to war to obtain vengeance or redress, and he would damage his enemy until his rights were recognized. The direct subjects, servants and employees of the adversary – and the adversary's allies, kin and underlings – were all legitimate targets. The aim of war was to inflict maximum damage on them, and to derive the maximum benefit for oneself. This included seizing the enemy's subjects and then ransoming them back to their families.[17] Soldiers had a bad reputation for their attitudes towards civilians, particularly in Germany and France.[18] They were permitted to ransack peasant houses and carry away food and textiles and metal of all sorts. They might torture the inhabitants to force them to reveal where they hid their treasure. They seized chests and bedding and linens if they were portable, and they particularly prized solid footwear. They made houses uninhabitable by ripping off doors and window shutters, and smashing roof tiles, while breaking ovens and cutting vines and fruit trees.[19] Tombs of notables in churches would be pried open and searched for treasure. Even 'friendly' soldiers had to take precautions in order to avoid ambush by disgruntled civilians wielding weapons. Soldiers who lodged within reach of enemy parties would need to cut down vines and trees in order to have proper fields of fire and a view of the approaches. Rather than wander in vulnerable little groups collecting firewood, they would instead burn their hosts' furniture to keep warm and cook their food.[20] Civilians could be stopped and robbed on the roads at myriad army checkpoints, very much like today. 'Merchants who travelled in a theatre of war would have to be convoyed like merchantmen on the high seas.'[21]

Cavalry soldiers were detached every day to collect forage for their horses, and they pilfered houses and barns while they were at it. Cavalry seized oxen, cattle and horses that they prodded into camp for the army butchers or sold for cash. Women and boys following the army (horses required grooms in large numbers) assisted the men in their hunt for loot. Iron hoops around barrels were particularly valuable, which entailed smashing the containers even before they were empty. Anything not nailed down or carefully hidden was taken, but even nails were pried out individually and recycled. In battle, the soldiers might break formation at any time to strip enemy casualties of their armour and weapons, clothing and other valuables. Typically, this was not permitted until the battle was won and the general gave the signal, but this rule required better discipline than most armies enjoyed. Then these trophies were brought to camp and sold to army sutlers who provided choice food and other items the soldiers wanted. In some armies, there was some attempt to share out the booty, providing the officers with a large portion of it. In Switzerland and Germany this was never admitted, as it was held to dampen the men's enterprise and daring. Preferring cash to non-perishable goods, whatever the soldiers stole was usually sold to a sutler or an officer, who then sold it elsewhere for a profit. Army lifestyle pushed soldiers to spend quickly whatever money they managed to collect. Women were central to the care and feeding of soldiers in camp, especially

German soldiers, whose 'tail' of civilians was very numerous. Women in camp were thought to make the men more rapacious: soldiers competed for women's services and plunder was the currency they employed.[22]

Starting in the sixteenth century, warlords began to limit and regulate looting, in the interest of good order. The Imperial Articles of 1570 constitute a long list of rules governing army life and permissible behaviour towards civilians. It was natural that arms and weapons captured in battle should belong to the captor, including the precious horse. Symbols of valour such as standards and drums, and artillery with its munitions and stores, should be given up to the Emperor as his share. The rules also specified that soldiers were not to steal ploughs or damage mills and ovens, and there was a ban on cutting trees and vines, but these strictures were widely ignored in practice. The Imperial Articles of Leopold I in 1668 prohibited the deliberate destruction of houses and fences, and required that all prisoners should be given up to the general instead of being ransomed at lower levels, but there, too, it took time for soldiers to comply. In the absence of regular pay, looting was a necessary part of the military system. Unpaid soldiers were likely to behave in friendly and neutral territory in the same way as they did in enemy lands until late in the seventeenth century. Once they became accustomed to looting, soldiers would not restrain themselves, plundering the baggage trains even of friendly and allied troops. Looting soldiers devastated the theatre of war until it could no longer sustain an army.[23]

Contracting out war

Starting in the late Middle Ages, high-level warriors were both functionaries of a state paying for their services and businessmen who bought and sold goods and services. They earned a salary from their employer and received a profit from their management. The Italian condottieri were the first genuine military contractors, emerging in the fifteenth century as purveyors of smallish professional armies to territorial states in Italy. Sixteenth-century monarchs such as King Henry VIII of England and German princes called upon entrepreneurs to provide them with troops already armed and fit to fight in a matter of weeks. Under a military contract, a government negotiated with a military leader (colonel or captain) for the delivery of a specific number of men typically raised outside its boundaries.[24] Before long, states provided such commanders with a retainer fee called the *dienstgeld*, so that they would quickly spring into action. The Duke of Savoy relied on a cadre of such men, the offspring of feudal dynasties of Northern and Central Italy. He also maintained contacts with Swiss colonels in the neighbouring Valais canton, who could provide him with contingents of 1,000 men or more. He then filled out expensive foreign cavalry companies with contingents of peasant cavalry militia. It was not in the duke's interest, or within his financial capacity, to maintain stable formations of men over a longer term. Hiring large numbers of French, Swiss and Italian regiments (18 in 1632) and then laying them off after a year or two permitted the duke to grasp opportunities of conquest as they appeared.[25] Venice similarly bulked up its skeleton army with Balkan mercenary companies of light horse, and companies of Swiss, Neapolitan and Corsican infantry raised by condottieri based in those territories, to meet the crisis of Cyprus in 1570–1571.[26] Some countries, like the Dutch Republic or England, preferred just to dabble in war by raising expeditionary forces to help allies. They would be able to keep an arm's length from direct involvement in war by allowing private contractors to recruit in their territories for another power without hindrance.[27] Spain, in the Dutch Revolt and the Lepanto crisis, relied in part on permanent tercios enlisting the king's own subjects, alongside more ephemeral contract regiments of German and Walloon soldiers, supplemented after 1600 by Irishmen. Similarly, in the Thirteen Years' War in Hungary, the emperor adopted the contract system, whereby the captains raising troops could usually finance the operation themselves and then recouped their outlay over several campaigns. The men being hired often had enough corporate identity, like the landsknechts, to insert clauses into the contract specifying their perquisites and their rights.[28] These units were private or semi-private revenue-bearing properties, loosely under state control, that enabled the captain or colonel to raise money. The warlord or ruler delegated his authority to military commanders to supply food, clothes and equipment to mercenaries, and to oversee the manufacture and distribution of weapons and munitions to the same.

Military entrepreneurship went hand in hand with the expansion of private credit, which increased much more quickly than tax revenues. Bankers consented to turn short-term debt into long-term debt, with lower rates of interest: the additional capital available had the result of lengthening war.[29] The precursor again was Ambrogio Spinola, a banker from the ambitious second family of Genoa (after the Doria) who virtually purchased the command of the Army of Flanders from a prostrate Spain in 1603. Spinola's gesture had the effect of connecting the army more directly to the Genoese international financial system, the world's most important between 1550 and 1630. Spain placed financial and administrative control in the hands of a few contractors, chiefly Genoese, before the bankruptcies of 1628 and 1647.[30] For over a century thereafter, the port city derived a large part of its fortune from the Spanish empire and its Italian viceroyalties such as Naples, Sicily and Sardinia.

Sometimes, an ally would provide money and raise regiments that they would turn over to a warlord's direction under officers they themselves recommended. The Pope provided money and men to the Emperor during the Thirty Years' War before 1635, when it was still a crusade of Catholic versus Protestant states.[31] The Grand Dukes of Tuscany similarly provided regiments for Medici princes in Imperial service so that they might acquire military expertise that might one day serve the dynasty, while the Duke of Modena similarly subsidized his uncle, Borso d'Este, one of Wallenstein's colonels.[32] Some nobles would also recruit men at their own expense and deliver them to the warlord as a way to purchase forgiveness for some crime, or to come out of disfavour at court. Olivares in Madrid leaned so heavily on Spanish aristocrats to provide regiments for the king that their backlash chased him from power.[33]

These 'military enterprisers' were sufficiently numerous in Germany during the Thirty Years' War (1,500 individuals) to permit a business historian, Fritz Redlich, to undertake a proper *prosopography* of proprietary colonels, that is, a collective biography emphasizing their common traits. Colonels undertook myriad business transactions that formed part of their normal working regimen, requiring organizational skills and access to partners who could liquidate booty and transform it into cash. This had always been part of command, but, in the early seventeenth century, their autonomy increased, like their numbers. The enterpriser contracted to serve a warlord and committed himself to finance out of his own resources enlistment bounties, subsistence and travel costs of the men. If he enjoyed the right to nominate captains to each company, these also added their resources to his. Advancing his own funds gave the colonel a kind of proprietary right over the regiment. It was up to the colonel to recruit the men to his regiment, to equip them, to feed and supply them every day, and to provide their wages, too (Image 6.2). In exchange, colonels reimbursed themselves in many different ways. Warlords rewarded colonels by inviting them to purchase the confiscated estates of traitors at knockdown prices. Officers could recover their outlay and make a profit by trading in armour and weapons and by pocketing part of the money the warlord assigned for soldiers' wages. The colonels could raise additional money by selling commissions to captains and lesser officers, charging fees for promotion (often disguised as 'gifts'), taking a percentage of soldiers' pay, charging the men for clothing and food, defrauding the government through false musters and padded accounts, levying

Image 6.2 Stefano Della Bella: Commander, MET Museum. The general observes his army on the move. In all armies, to varying degrees, the commanders and their officers invested their private fortunes to keep the force operational, and fretted over the means of forestalling personal ruin

a percentage on plunder, all in addition to acquiring legitimate booty. Colonels pocketed the wages owed to deserters, as they did the money owed to dead soldiers. Enterpriser colonels exercised jurisdiction and penal authority over the soldiers under his command, but also over the women and the sutlers, who might have to pay fees to follow the men. They could also be persuaded through fat bribes from cities or monasteries in the path of their troops to lodge them elsewhere. Colonels made additional money by selling safe-conducts and safeguards to individuals and communities, which did not entirely shield them from looting by disorderly soldiers.

Some of these condottieri provided an entire army to several prospective warlords, such as Ernst von Mansfeld, Christian of Brunswick and Bernhard of Saxe-Weimar. The leading Protestant enterpriser of the 1620s, Mansfeld, raised multiple armies using credit and subsidies from England, France, Venice, Savoy and the Palatine Elector, but the forces he assembled until his death in 1626 belonged to him, and not enough to the states backing him. This limited their size and the quality of their supply, and they fell apart quickly.[34] One could not be an independent contractor ready to flog an army to the highest bidder, for without state backing, the army did not have room to grow.[35] This was also the experience of Bernhard von Saxe-Weimar, who tried to lease his personal army to France. He drew financing from Lyonnais bankers, but the force he led was never large enough to weigh decisively on the conflict. Most enterprisers supplied a regiment, in which they had a 'majority interest', to use David Parrott's felicitous phrase, to a particular ruler and expected rewards for loyalty. They were also shareholders in larger armies assembled by Wallenstein and his peers. It was common practice in Germany to enlist captive soldiers into the victor's army in the aftermath of battle. However, very few military entrepreneurs ever changed sides during the Thirty Years' War, although it was common for them to serve allies of their natural sovereign or their original employer.

The entry of Sweden into the war in 1630 and the extension of looting to all of Germany ultimately rendered the system unworkable. Sweden's expansion derived from the internationalization of its iron and copper mines, its armaments factories and shipbuilding yards, financed after 1621 with Dutch capital and technical expertise. The Dutch managed the Swedish forges producing iron and collected abundant saltpetre in the Indies.[36] This new power enabled Gustavus Adolphus to seize the toll stations collecting dues on grain exports in northern Poland, revenues he devoted to raising troops for his German ambitions. Sweden also relied heavily on French subsidies and the threat of occupying the territories of Protestant princes if they failed to support his armies. After the king's death in 1632, the ethnic Swedes numbered only 3,000 of 85,000 men serving the Protestant cause in Germany, the rest being North Germans and Scots. Swedish armies had the reputation of being the most rapacious, for their troops had been promised plunder on their enlistment.[37] Swedish contractors were often paid with conquered lands and feudal rights over the local population, which they exploited to the utmost. Upon Gustavus Adolphus' death, the Swedish Crown transferred its debts to the proprietor colonels who became responsible for paying and feeding the junior officers and soldiers. Each of them suddenly acquired debts between 200,000 and 300,000 thalers, on which they were obliged to pay the interest. They had a strong incentive to carry the war into enemy territory to extend their resource base, in order to keep their unit operational.

Nevertheless, the enterprisers were not mere businessmen, for they had to serve their lord faithfully and were expected to brave the dangers of campaigning in person. Redlich estimates that about 300 such contractors were serving in Germany in the early 1630s (that is, excluding contractors serving in other theatres), and there were never fewer than 100 in each subsequent year. Most German military enterprisers were born Protestants, although, like Wallenstein, many converted to Catholicism over their lifetime. An important minority of them were not Germans at all, but Walloons, Spaniards and, above all, Italians, who were conspicuously Catholic and were cherished by the Emperor for their hawkish views towards heretics. Whatever their ethnic background, they shared type A personality traits of alpha males.

> The vast majority of these men were insensitive, but shrewd, and great organizers. They were big men, generally, and also mercenary, rapacious, brutal, inclined to violence, unrestrained, cantankerous, addicted to playing for large sums, to drinking hard and to other vices.[38]

Most of these men had no other education but military training. The best prepared were often attached to princely courts as pages in their youth, where they acquired social graces and rubbed shoulders with influential people of varied backgrounds.

A 'good' general, notes Parrott, was someone who had enough charisma to persuade his troops to march and campaign longer, who could control the junior officers and ensure everyone's obedience to orders.[39] Generals with access to rich contributions and who proved successful in battle looked like good credit risks for bankers seeking to employ their capital. Albrecht von Wallenstein, backed by the Imperial War Council and the tax resources of the Habsburg lands emerged as an *über* enterpriser during the Thirty Years' War. An ambitious convert to Catholicism, Wallenstein made a modest initial investment in 1618 of 40,000 florins (half was borrowed) in order to raise and equip 1,000 Flemish cuirassiers to help the emperor in time of crisis.[40] By 1624, he proposed an entire army to Ferdinand II, who at first refused, but the offer was accepted a year later and, by 1626, he started issuing recruiting patents in his own name. Wallenstein's personal credit sustained the Imperial military edifice in the late 1620s: with a personal fortune of 'only' 1.5 million florins in 1628, he lent the emperor 8.1 million, channelling the credit and the capital of a host of people, both military and civilian. All the colonels, and all the captains in Wallenstein's army were compelled to invest their own money to support their units. Wherever he imposed contributions, he tried to extract the maximum amount in cash, so that he could pay his soldiers with regularity. In order to raise capital quickly, the condottiere turned to Hans de Witte, a Protestant international banker, who borrowed money in the financial centres of Linz, Frankfurt, Augsburg, Leipzig and Antwerp in order to recruit and equip soldiers. Wallenstein also ruthlessly exploited his own estates in Bohemia and Mecklemberg to provide food, clothes, weapons and ammunition to outfit them. His duchy of Friedland, northeast of Prague, measured a 100 km across and englobed 1,200 km^2, making it a convenient place to locate productive assets. Vast quantities of grain were stored there for shipment to the army. Around Reichenberg (modern Liberec) he set all the cobblers, tailors and cloth-makers to work in order to outfit his soldiers. He imported Italian armaments specialists to supervise local gunsmiths and iron-workers producing weapons between 1627 and 1634.[41] This army was well supplied along the River Elbe axis, which made transport easier and cheaper.

De Witte further supported him by visiting the German money fairs four times a year, building his own network of lenders. Financiers and their merchant correspondents coordinated bulk purchases and ensured their transport to where they were needed. Sutlers on their own were not enough to satisfy a military market. There had to be agents with deep pockets working farther away. The task of the emperor then was to pay the interest on this great debt from the Imperial treasury and from army contributions. Wallenstein held a mountain of credits on the emperor, but also on cities that promised contributions paid out over several years.[42] However, when Ferdinand II cashiered Wallenstein in August 1630 for strenuously opposing the Mantua war, the edifice collapsed and de Witte, who was faced with personal ruin, committed suicide. But the indispensable Wallenstein was back in command the next year, promising to raise an army of 100,000 men. This time, it was Wallenstein's army, for he chose all the colonels under his command. He prized competent officers as well as wealthy ones: hence his partiality for German Protestant and Italian colonels. The step too far that sealed his fate in January 1634 was to demand that the colonels swear an oath of personal loyalty to him. Acquiring a princely territory in Mecklemburg, erecting several palaces and maintaining a conspicuous personal court in Prague all worked in his disfavour, in the end.

Typically, the enterprisers were already noble, although not all of them inherited conspicuous fortunes. Ottavio Piccolomini, from a Sienese family at the court in Florence, was the son of a Knight of Santo Stefano and Tuscan military adventurer in the Mediterranean. He left home at age 17 to serve as a gentleman volunteer fighting for Spain in Piedmont. In 1618, he and a brother left for Austria, then for Flanders as captains of cavalry. He spent his allowance outfitting his troopers, who were present at the battle of White Mountain. His first regiment served under Spinola in the famous siege of Breda in 1625, then marched with Imperial reinforcements to aid Spain in Milan. By 1627, he commanded Wallenstein's elite bodyguard company until he was demoted for squeezing excessive contributions from his Pomeranian base at Stargard. By 1630, back in favour and with Wallenstein sidelined, he owned two cavalry regiments, employed his own information network and promoted his own clients. He is credited with saving the day at Lützen with his seven cavalry charges against Gustavus Adolphus and the Swedish horse. One of the leading conspirators in the death of Wallenstein in early 1634, Piccolomini next led an Imperial contingent to help Spain in the Low Countries, where he distinguished himself against France. After his victory over the French at Thionville in 1639, he committed himself to Spanish service completely, and was awarded the collar of the Golden Fleece in 1645, together with a rich Abruzzo fief in the kingdom of Naples. Returning to Vienna in 1648, in the last months of the war, Emperor Ferdinand III appointed him supreme commander of all German Habsburg forces, which he led to modest victories against the Swedes in Bavaria. He retired to his palaces in Vienna, Prague and rural Bohemia, filled with art and luxuries of every kind. His Bohemian line continued through his nephews after his death in 1657.[43]

Raimondo Montecuccoli, of a feudal warrior dynasty from the mountains near Modena, had a more chequered career. The Imperial emissary Rambaldo Collalto noticed him at the court of Modena in 1625 and engaged him as a gentleman volunteer serving in the infantry at age 17. Paying his first ransom from his own resources in 1631, he rose through the ranks with the aid of family connections. Acting colonel in 1635, when his cavalry troopers plundered the personal possessions of an ally, the Elector of Brandenburg, he was arrested for it. Captured again in 1639, he spent several years at Stettin penning the most successful military manual of the era. He then served the Duke of Modena in a brief war against the Pope in 1642–1644, where, using the last revenues of his house, he raised a cavalry regiment at his own expense. Ferdinand III appointed him to the Imperial War Council in 1645, a roving ambassador after 1648 and, finally, head of the Imperial army on the death of Marshal Hatzfeld in 1658. He salvaged his fortune by marrying a Dietrichstein countess in Vienna, and, due to his piety and his austere lifestyle, he got on well at court under the pious Emperor Leopold I. Old and gouty, he was still able to lead the Imperial army against France in 1675. After his death in 1680, his only son, Leopoldo, was awarded a cavalry regiment and the order of the Golden Fleece as a gift, thanks to his father's merit.[44]

Exceptional individuals could rise in social status if they were lucky, but these were very few. Johann Aldringen from Luxembourg came from a modest background of petty nobility. In 1630, along with Matteo Galasso, he roped off the ducal palace in Mantua as his share of the sack of the city. It contained a colossal fortune in paintings and statues, tapestries, furniture, carpets, jewellery, silver tableware and a golden dinner service. Aldringen deposited 800,000 crowns with Venetian bankers soon after. Peter Melander, a Bavarian enterpriser of peasant stock who served the Protestant duchess of Hesse-Cassel, left a fortune of 770,000 florins at his death.[45] Gil de Haes, a baker's apprentice from Ghent, son of a brush-maker, spent his youth carrying baskets of bread and flour, then enlisted in the Spanish Army of Flanders at age 27 after a romantic disappointment. Serving as Aldringen's lieutenant-colonel at Mantua, he collected enough booty to recruit and equip a thousand soldiers for Wallenstein's new army the next year. He profited again from the plunder of Saxony in 1632. In 1636, he raised a cavalry regiment to serve Spain in Lombardy, and was badly wounded at Tornavento, where his regiment was mauled in the stubborn engagement. While still recovering from his wounds, his regiment unfurled over the rich duchy of Piacenza, collecting 1,000 oxen and 50,000 Spanish doubloons. In 1643, de Haes passed into Venetian service with the title of Excellency, but soon left it to raise 3,000 men for Spain in Flanders. Briefly passing into Bavarian service in 1644, he returned to Venice in 1645 to fight in Crete. He died childless in Dalmatia in 1657, aged 60, with the title Patrician of Ghent.[46]

The social and commercial contacts of these enterprisers were hugely important to their careers. They could not always wait for the right moment to start out, since an army commander gave them deadlines to meet. Otto Henrich von Fugger, scion of the great mercantile dynasty of Augsburg, borrowed money from his relatives at the standard rate of five or six per cent, and was still paying interest on it twenty years later. Before Pappenheim's Westphalian campaign, each of his colonels had to provide 10–12,000 thalers to outfit the army. Colonels often had cash-flow problems that they tried to offload on their financial backers. Officers collecting booty in kind could not easily dispose of it at a good price in wartime, and exchanged plunder for cash, often at a fraction of its real value. The Flemish banker Hans de Witte and the Geiger brothers of Nuremburg made their fortunes by bankrolling generals, by liquidating the assets of the contributions in kind collected from civilians, and then made purchases of munitions, weaponry, artillery and clothing. Many colonels and generals hired their own business agents who took care of the details of regimental business with supply contractors, provisioners and *munitionnaires*. In a long war, colonels and their accountants were able to develop streamlined armies with procedures for procuring supplies quickly. Each developed a system of subcontracting at the regimental level, with captains managing companies. Careful enterprisers made sure that they hired fewer men than the number they promised in the original contract. On inspection day, they might pad each mustered company with a few false soldiers, or men borrowed from other units. They often inflated their accounts to provide a cushion against inadequate payment or non-payment by the government, which was itself constantly looking for ways to save money. Delaying payment to the real soldiers in their employ was a kind of forced loan from the men, who would have to cope in other ways until they were paid off. In this system, everybody cheated. If they were defeated in the field, if their warlord dismissed them, as Wallenstein was in 1630, they and their bankers faced ruin.[47]

Notwithstanding all of these expedients, often considered abuses, contracting for war was a risky venture, for kings and ministers were always close to insolvency. The system could not have functioned without permitting the contractors to levy 'contributions' on civilians wherever the army operated. These are first noted in the Low Countries, collected by Requesens in the 1570s and then imitated by the Dutch rebels.[48] They were not originally intended to be for the private gain of the officers, and at first there was talk of later compensation and repayment to the victims, or a reduction of their taxes, although this concern quickly lapsed.[49] In the sixteenth century, the commander and his soldiers had a clear right to the property of the enemy as their main remuneration. But disorderly looting severely limited the territory an army controlled and it was harmful to military discipline, since soldiers foraging for booty were almost impossible to recall in the event of a crisis. The best defence for civilians was to run and hide, or hold some protected spaces and to fight for them. Dutch and Spanish troops behaved better in comparison with those of other nations. Under Ambrogio Spinola, contributions became a form of extortion whereby army authorities negotiated with local government to turn over money and other resources on the threat of burning the villages for non-compliance. Army commanders refused to recognize legal privileges and exempt status accruing to nobles or the clergy.[50] Negotiation with civilians was the norm for contributions, not the exception; typically, the authorities promised to pay large sums over many months. Local government also knew which people might have cash to lend or reserves of grain. Wallenstein's strategy was to plant garrisons in walled towns and castles over a wide area, and then use the resources collected there to finance the field army. The more territory one controlled, the more men could be hired, and those same resources would be denied to the enemy. In areas caught between opposing armies, village authorities purchased safe-conducts and safeguards from both friendly and enemy garrison commanders, who relied on these revenues to pay their men. It was easier, safer and cheaper to pay contributions than to try to defend one's village.[51] War levies purportedly raked in three or four times as much money as taxation, at least during the 1620s.[52] Orderly contributions did not completely prevent plundering by soldiers, however, particularly during the disorderly 1630s.[53]

Even contributions were often not enough to keep a regiment in being, particularly when the war was going badly. When the troops were not paid on time or mutinied for the wages owing, the enterpriser had to pay them from his own purse or from money he borrowed on the spot. This is why colonels liked to have large quantities of silver plate, tapestries and other precious goods that they could pawn in order to raise cash. If the war endured, the colonel or captain had to make new investments to keep his unit combat-worthy. Clothing and weapons quickly wore out on campaign. During periods of demobilization, it was in his interest to retain a cadre of veterans and non-commissioned officers as part of his overhead. A cavalry regiment required expensive remounts, as equine casualties were always heavier than human ones. Armour had to be purchased in appropriate quantities: a cavalry trooper's armour of 25–40 kg, proofed against musketballs, represented a considerable financial outlay, particularly for Imperial armies that wore more of it.[54]

As active commanders of their regiments, enterprisers underwent other risks, too. Redlich notes that 214 of his sample of 1,500 enterprisers in Germany were killed in battle or died of wounds, without including those who died of exposure or disease while on campaign. If they were captured, they often had to pay their own ransom, too. This happened to Raimondo Montecuccoli twice, held captive for six months after he was taken prisoner near Magdeburg in 1630, and for over two years after being taken in a rearguard action in 1639. Worse, an enterpriser in disfavour for some misstep might suddenly see the warlord refuse to pay the money owed to them. The warlord retained the right to transfer proprietorship of a unit from one colonel to another, or to disband the unit when its strength declined, leaving the contractor with a pile of unpaid debts. This was a potent threat that served to keep the enterprisers in line.

'War was a business built upon complex calculations of potential profit, systems of credit, networks of subcontractors.'[55] Danish, Dutch, Bavarian and Venetian armies hiring them employed state accountants and ministers to review the books. The bureaucracy functioned to supply the men with pay, and the more efficient the bureaucracy, the less the contractor was forced to improvise. The Emperor lacked a numerous bureaucracy in his territories, and regional Estates controlled the tax machinery, so he gave the enterprisers a great deal of discretionary power. The contractor might suffer periodic financial loss, but the law of reciprocity did not fall into abeyance: he became eligible for social bonuses worth more than money, such as a viceroyalty, a cardinal's hat for a son, nomination to a vacant fief, a high-profile marriage with a rich dowry, award of a title with high rank and precedence at the court – in short, all the perks that sovereign princes could confer on deserving vassals. Princes also had oversight of the judicial system, enabling them to halt lawsuits or grant pardons to delinquents. Reciprocity applied to generals and colonels, just as it governed relations between the soldiers and their officers.

Decline of entrepreneurial scope

Fritz Redlich, in the 1960s, thought that the system of military enterprise contained the seeds of its own decline, by compelling the participants to consume for short term gain the resource base they required. As Germany's resources contracted along with its population, war could no longer be fought on the same scale. A field army of 10–15,000 men became the operational norm, about half the previous size.[56] The Swedish armies, like the Imperial and Bavarian ones, were forced to downsize, too, and were better able to live off the land. By the 1640s, armies, composed largely of veterans who chose this lifestyle, waged a more 'sustainable' war of occupying land and moving around. Cavalry units were also compelled to downsize, as dragoons with less armour and smaller and cheaper horses became the new norm.[57] But small-scale warfare led to strategic stalemate. After the 1630s, the number of contractors tended to diminish, while some military men established dynasties. Regiments were not hereditary, strictly speaking, but they might still pass from uncle to nephew, or through in-laws and kinship groups. Professional and aristocratic endogamy resulted in smaller numbers of contractors after two generations. There was a concentration of military entrepreneurship into fewer hands, with a number of rich bankers behind them.[58]

Recent research by British scholars led by David Parrott stresses the military superiority of privately-funded armies over those held more tightly in hand by political rulers. In support of this argument, they compare them with those of Spain and France. In a state commission army, the central government appointed a captain to raise a certain number of men from within state boundaries. Local officials were instructed to assist the captain to find men, and to subsidize their transit to a place of embarkation. In theory, alongside the captain, the state nominated subordinate officers such as the lieutenant and the ensign. This royal control required an extensive and reasonably efficient bureaucracy and the funds to pay and equip the new recruits. Until after 1600, the Iberian kingdoms could raise about 12,000 men annually for Italy and the Low Countries.[59] As indebtedness grew, the size of the companies began to shrink, from 2–300 men to 100 or fewer by the 1630s, and perhaps only 4,000 men were raised each year by the late 1630s. Rich and high-born patrons with no military experience might also raise money to enlist troops; Olivares encouraged this and, indeed, later insisted on it.[60] After 1635, when France entered the war, the decadence of the commission system and the inadequacy of its results were plain.[61] Spain was compelled to contract out for mercenaries in Germany, and increasingly in Ireland. An enterpriser would finance the enlistment bounties, the subsistence and travel costs with the help of the captains. This gave the colonel a property right, making his removal difficult, and he would then siphon off pay for non-existent soldiers. Spanish military justice was more advanced than in other states, however, and its troops did not inflict the same damage on the Low Countries.

David Parrott emphasizes that invasive control by Cardinal Richelieu turned out to be a major handicap to French armies, too. The rationale was clear enough: during the wars of religion, the turbulent Grands were able to extort resources and favours of all sorts from a Crown in difficulty. Cardinal Richelieu was at the height of his power and prestige during the siege of La Rochelle, which was a popular war in a kingdom that was 95% Catholic. His policy of making war on Catholic powers of the House of Austria after 1630 was widely unpopular, on the other hand. He applied his policies through a clientèle consisting of relatives, Protestants and courtiers who shared his outlook, and he sidelined talented commanders who did not, had them executed or sent to the Bastille. (The French court seethed with discontent over Richelieu's war aims, and the cardinal was indeed lucky to have avoided assassination: it was not for want of trying, with the active collaboration of members of the royal family.) France, after 1635, required five or six different armies, each one larger than it could afford. The result was military fiasco and a string of defeats that continued until the death of the cardinal in 1642. French taxes increased prodigiously, triggering widespread outbreaks of revolt, but there was never enough money to pay the soldiers. Richelieu followed an explicit policy not to pay the men in full, but just to give them enough to keep the units from disbanding.[62] Whatever cash came in from taxes was used to make interest payments on the growing debt in order to maintain the confidence of financiers.[63] The expedients were to raise heavy contributions in the field on civilians, and to encourage the officers and the army administrators to spend their own money to keep the units operational. This, in turn, made it difficult for officers to serve for many years without ruining the family fortune. After 1635, and especially under Cardinal Mazarin after 1643, the Crown owed colossal sums to its officers in back pay and reimbursement.[64] The Italian minister of state likewise avoided giving military commanders a free hand.[65]

In order to keep better track of the sums sent to the army, Louis XIII and Richelieu appointed civilian administrators, the *army intendants*, whose purview covered recruitment, discipline, pay, accounting, provisioning, lodging, winter quarters and even fortification. These officials then dispatched their itemized accounts to Paris on a regular basis. They had no means of enforcing their will on the generals, whose councils of war they attended.[66] The intendants developed a system of *étapes* by which soldiers on the march need not pay for their lodgings or their food. Flour was collected via local requisitioning and then hauled to pre-arranged depots by teamsters earmarked for it. But, as often as not, these preparations were inadequate, for many munitionnaires who promised to provide set amounts on specific days in specific locations could not meet their commitments. France's wary allies, the Dukes of Savoy, of Mantua and the Catalan rebels insisted the French armies pay dearly for the fodder they consumed. Success was fleeting for French troops in the field, and, apart from hapless Lorraine, their enemies were successful in keeping them at a distance until the 1650s. During the chaotic period of the Fronde, French armies were compelled to raise resources directly from territories at home under their control, something John Lynn has called a 'tax of violence'.[67] Therefore, even France could not escape the necessity of recourse to private investment to maintain its armies. In the 1620s, it was considered good policy to leave the mobilization and demobilization of troops to rich and influential men. District aristocrats and military governors were ready to raise men in their provinces at a moment's notice. Each captain had to recruit, outfit and equip his soldiers in weapons and horses, with a personal outlay. From about 1620, French officers had to purchase their colonel's and captain's commissions on a shadowy market. It was understood that their successor would reimburse them when they ceased active service.[68]

Military enterprise did not disappear after 1650 or 1660, but the state became everywhere more invasive. First of all, the custom of soldiers taking civilians for ransom was discontinued after 1650. Neither were soldiers or officers authorized to ransom enemy combatants for private benefit. Spain and the Dutch Republic established the first regular prisoner exchanges in 1602, and established a tariff for each captive by rank. Officers made greater efforts to control foraging, not for humanitarian reasons, but for greater operational efficiency. Districts were cordoned off and systematically 'eaten' to supply one's own horses and to deny the same resources to the enemy. In place of individual enterprisers leasing single regiments or cavalry squadrons to a warlord, minor states and princes established permanent military forces that they rented to a larger power under the guise of an alliance. It was a business transaction between two states, usually sharing the same confession. One notable figure was

Christoph von Galen, Catholic bishop of Munster, who leased large contingents to France, Spain, Denmark and the Empire between 1665 and 1678. Other German princes maintained peacetime armies and then rented them out, such as the Dukes of Wurttemburg and Hesse-Cassel, who handed sizeable contingents to Sweden and the Dutch Republic, but prince-bishops in Cologne and Trier participated, too. The three sons of the Duke of Brunswick rented troops to the Netherlands, to France, to the Emperor, and especially to Venice, which, in the 1680s, was fighting the Ottomans in the Aegean theatre. The money earned and prestige derived from leading troops in the field in a just war enabled the duke to purchase the title of Elector in 1692, and then to figure as a credible candidate to the throne of England in 1714. Princes kept as many soldiers as they could afford between rental opportunities, negotiating for their upkeep from nobles and burghers in their Estates, or commanding that their civil servants should lend them money for this purpose. But the standing army was a new phenomenon for most states, and deserves a separate chapter.[69]

Privateer navies in the Atlantic and the Mediterranean

Naval warfare also operated on the tight interlocking of private money and state strategic objectives. Venice had a long tradition of contracting out to condottieri for military service, but, for reasons of excessive risk and prohibitive insurance costs, it ceased to build roundships that could be converted into warships. The Republic of Saint Mark enjoyed warm relations with the Dutch Republic, since both were hostile to the House of Habsburg. To compel the Empire to curtail the activity of Uskok pirates in the Adriatic in 1617, Venice raised whole regiments of German troops under Georg Ludwig von Lowenstein in the Netherlands and contracted their transport to Northern Italy.[70] Venice required a fleet of armed merchantmen to confront the vessels of the Viceroy of Naples. Dutch vessels could be rented more cheaply than anywhere else, armed with iron cannon costing only a quarter of bronze pieces. The Amsterdam Admiralty rented 16 of these to Venice in 1617, then 11 more the following year, all ferrying troops hired in the Netherlands. A third flotilla of a dozen ships fought and won an engagement with the Spanish off Gibraltar, allowing Venice to conclude its conflict with the House of Austria on favourable terms. In 1649, Venice again raised a fleet largely consisting of Dutch and English ships to fight the Turks in the Aegean Sea, and these fought a successful large-scale battle at Focchies, near Smyrna. This time, Amsterdam ship-owners formed a cartel in order to drive up the prices per ship, and negotiated through a single spokesman. Venice obtained the ships it wanted by turning to owners in Rotterdam and Enkhuizen instead, which had their own Admiralties. The ship-owners themselves served on the Admiralty Boards (which today would be considered a conflict of interest). These were eager to outfit the ships with state-owned cannon, munitions and crews made redundant by the peace with Spain. The Turks came calling not long after to rent Dutch and English flotillas in order to fight the Venetians.[71] Another expedient manner by which to acquire ships was to seize foreign vessels in port and to arrest the crews, only to negotiate with the owners soon after to come to an agreement profitable to them. In 1643, Louis de Geer rented another whole fleet of Dutch vessels to Sweden, when it was challenged by Denmark, and threatened to raise the tolls through the Sound.

Privateers were archetypal military entrepreneurs, encouraged by the state to undermine an opponent's trade and to seize additional resources from the enemy. It differed from piracy by the obligation of the enterpriser to purchase a licence, or *letters of marque*, authorizing them to capture vessels flying specific flags, and promising to turn over a portion of the prize money (typically a fifth) to the government. Incentives were often paid for privateers to capture enemy warships, which compelled captains to work in flotillas. A privateer ship required more guns, a heavier frame and a bigger crew – up to a hundred men – than a normal merchant vessel. Flemish captains operating out of Dunkirk, a major base, developed a specialized warship, the frigate, armed with 10–30 cannon to engage in this business with advantage. Flemish privateers took 1,500 Dutch ships between 1627 and 1634, and another 500 between 1642 and 1646.[72] Merchant ship-owners formed partnerships (in order to spread the risk) to fit out a vessel for seven or eight months, paying the crews and supplying them with food.[73] Dutch privateers primarily based in Zeeland raided English shipping during the three Anglo-Dutch Wars in the twenty years between 1655 and 1674. They tended to hunt in packs, and took advantage of government incentives to attack enemy corsairs or warships. From 1665 to 1667, they captured one English merchant ship every three days, on average, including small colliers supplying London, fishing boats from Newfoundland, sugar and tobacco ships from the Caribbean and a treasure ship from the East Indies. Auctions in Zeeland brought in at least 1,000,000 gulden annually to private investors, of which 50% went to the outfitter, the capitalist, who had to pay wages to the crew. The crews received a share of the booty as well as their pay. In addition to auctioning ships and cargos, they held captive seamen to ransom. Until the early 1660s, the Portuguese-hired ships bringing sugar from Brazil were the chief target, 220 were captured in 1647–1648 alone, which had the effect of driving prices down in a glutted market. Privateers did not declare all their prizes, and often sold their captures in foreign ports, in Spain or France, in order to obtain better prices.

During the great wars against France at the end of the seventeenth century, between 200 and 300 Dutch privateers operated at any one time. Of course, English privateers flourished, too, in waters teeming with Dutch vessels. In their three wars against the Dutch, the English captured 1,500, 522 and 500 Dutch ships, respectively. French privateers captured about 700 British ships annually between 1702 and 1712, in addition to Dutch, Portuguese, or Danish vessels. In that period, the British intercepted between 15 and 20% of all French merchant ships, but these were fewer in number. Privateers exemplified military entrepreneurship, but they incurred numerous indirect costs to the owning power, by driving down legitimate customs revenues. By the eighteenth century, legitimate trade finally became a more attractive investment.

Notes

1 Jerome Kagan, 1994.
2 Frank Tallett, 1992: 69.
3 Tallett, 1992: 96.
4 Marvin Zuckerman, 2007.
5 Fritz Redlich, 1964: 117.
6 David Parrott, 2012: 162.
7 I.A.A. Thompson, 2003.
8 Gregory Hanlon, 2014: 42–78.
9 Geoff Mortimer, 2004.
10 Hanlon, 2014: 136.
11 Bernhard Kroener, 1987; Tallett, 1992: 71.
12 Hanlon, 2012: 109–10.
13 Bernhard Kroener, 1998; Jean Chagniot, 2001: 141.
14 Bernard Masson, 1986.
15 Hanlon, 2014: 75.
16 Ronald G. Asch, 2000; Gregory Hanlon, 2016: 164–5; Geoff Mortimer, 2002.
17 Fritz Redlich, 1956: 4.
18 Asch, 2000.
19 Ruth Mohrmann, 1998.
20 Gregory Hanlon, 2016.
21 Redlich, 1956: 22.
22 Asch, 2000.
23 Redlich, 1956: 60.
24 Redlich, 1964: 72.
25 Claudio De Consoli, 1999: 196.
26 J.R. Hale, 1974.
27 Tallett, 1992: 75.
28 Zoltan Bagi, 2018: 4.
29 Parrott, 2012: 75.
30 Parrott, 2012: 222.
31 Giampiero Brunelli, 2003: 206.
32 Carla Sodini, 2001.
33 Jose Contreras Gay, 1981.
34 Redlich, 1964: 295.
35 Parrott, 2012: 105.
36 Parrott, 2012: 125.
37 Stéphane Gaber, 1991 : 35.
38 Redlich, 1964: 64.
39 David Parrott, 2001: 77.
40 David Parrott, 2014.
41 Parrott, 2012: 234.
42 Redlich, 1964: 256.
43 Thomas M Barker, 1982.
44 Tommaso Sandonnini, 1913.
45 Redlich, 1956: 50.
46 Charles Rahlenbeck, 1854.
47 Parrott, 2014.
48 Geoffrey Parker, 1984: 204.
49 Geoff Mortimer, 2004.
50 Parrott, 2001 : 281.
51 Martial Gantelet, 2009.
52 Mortimer, 2004.

53 Tryntje Helfferich & Paul Sonnino, 2007.
54 Vladimir Brnardic, 2010: 15–18.
55 David Parrott, 2005.
56 Parrott, 2012: 179.
57 Brnardic, 2010: 35–42.
58 Redlich, 1964: 221.
59 Thompson, 2003.
60 Fernando Gonzalez de Leon, 2009: 160.
61 José Contreras Gay, 1996.
62 Parrott, 2001: 346.
63 David Parrott, 1987.
64 Chagniot, 2001: 104.
65 Parrott, 2012: 101.
66 Douglas Clark Baxter, 1976: 25.
67 John Lynn, 1993.
68 Chagniot, 2001: 105.
69 Andrea Thiele, 2014.
70 Redlich, 1964: 128.
71 Louis Sicking, 2013.
72 Jaap R Bruijn, 1978; Roberto Barazzutti, 2004.
73 Henning Hillmann & Christina Gathmann, 2011.

7 The advent of standing armies and navies

Birth of a giant: the French army

Standing armies were not a new invention in the aftermath of the Peace of Westphalia in 1648 but most were small affairs of a handful of regiments and palace guards. The young Dutch Republic, whose independence Spain finally recognized, was an exception. The matter of how far to scale down the army and navy led to a resurgence of the basic tensions underlying the state. The Republic was organized as a decentralized federation of almost sovereign provinces, but the Republic's defence was coordinated by the stadtholders of the House of Orange, a high-ranking warrior dynasty that held for generations a monopoly over the appointment of army officers. Frederick Henry of Orange-Nassau was the *de facto* head of state during the last phase of the Eighty Years War, and increasingly lived like a prince with a palace and court at The Hague. On his death in 1647, William II of Orange, brother-in-law of the King of England stepped into his place. William was appalled by the States of Holland's plan to cut back the army to only 39,000 men. William seized Amsterdam and planned to overthrow the States and remove from office the families who opposed him. Weeks after this triumph, he died of smallpox in November 1650, and the five richest provinces decided not to appoint a successor to the stadtholder's office. In lieu of a single army under an incipient monarch, the remaining troops were divided up into seven provincial forces with no central control.[1] They spent most of the next two decades performing sentry duty, and large units no longer trained together. The difficulty of repelling an invasion of the eastern provinces by the Bishop of Munster in 1665, an ally of England, underscored how inefficient the Dutch army had become. After France attacked Spain in the Low Countries and annexed some important towns in 1667, the States General voted to increase the army to 30,000 men, but never carried out their levies. France was considered a friend and an ally since the birth of the Republic, but it was best to keep it at a distance. The Dutch fought maritime wars against England (1652–1654, and 1665–1667), and they also intervened in the Baltic area (1655–1660) in order to ensure that their ships enjoyed preferentially low tolls through the Danish straits. Most of all, they redoubled their efforts to seize as much of the Portuguese Empire in America and Asia as they could. Jan de

Witte, Pensionary of Holland and the leading Dutch politician of the era, was the founding force behind the Netherlands' navy, but he allowed the army and the fortifications to decay.[2]

French troops had been fighting almost continually since the advent of Cardinal Richelieu as chief minister of France in 1624, but, in the early years, this entailed single campaigns against limited objectives with the king leading his men in person. French entry into the Thirty Years' War in 1635, against both the Spanish and the German Habsburgs, forced the kingdom to mobilize all its resources, in a conflict lasting without interruption for twenty-four years. France might have been able to prevail quickly against the Habsburgs as Richelieu hoped, but the army was characterized by a number of traditional inefficiencies that he and Mazarin were never able to overcome during wartime. The French army was administered and led by dynasties of great aristocratic families, the *Grands*, who invested their own money and nominated officers both high and low in order to gratify their personal clientèles. To better constrain the autonomy of these dignitaries, Richelieu flanked them with his own clients, or *créatures*, but the result was to sow discord. He also established a cadre of *army intendants* who managed the daily administration of each campaign, and introduced a Secretary of State for War, who served as a centre for the transmission of orders.[3]

Richelieu's successor as minister of state, the Italian Cardinal Jules Mazarin, in 1643 appointed as Secretary of State for war a young army Intendant, Michel Le Tellier. During the long regency of Louis XIV (1643–1661) this single civilian administrator, diligent and routine-bound, acquired the expertise by which to improve the functioning of the army. What bothered him most was an absence of order (perhaps the dominant preoccupation in late seventeenth-century politics) and a weak hierarchy. To curry favour with the Grands, Mazarin increased the number of field marshals to a total of 16 in 1651, who proved incompatible with each other on campaign. By 1656, Le Tellier and Mazarin established seniority rules for senior officers to observe. To curtail absenteeism, the minister introduced the requirement of residence for officers and men, both in garrison and in the field.[4] The minister devised a whole body of regulations in the course of the 1650s, which were not commonly applied until the Peace of the Pyrenees in 1659. After 1661, he also established a clear hierarchy of regiments, in order to eliminate bickering over precedence and widespread insubordination among titled aristocrats.

Young King Louis XIV only partially demobilized the army after the Peace of the Pyrenees in 1659, letting the numbers slide to about 50,000 men by 1665.[5] Under the Finance minister, Jean-Baptiste Colbert, the kingdom succeeded in establishing budgetary surpluses every year between 1660 and 1672, while the provincial Intendants 'verified' the debts communities owed to their creditors and pruned them back. Manufactures and exports soared under the minister's direction and the king was able to maintain the number of men he wanted without strain. In 1667, about 60,000 men invaded the Spanish Netherlands, exclusive of garrisons, far more than Madrid could field in the theatre. By 1672, army expansion effortlessly reached 125,000 men, more than the kingdom's full mobilization during the Thirty Years' War. Another novelty, 87% were, henceforth, French subjects. This instrument of the king's glory was what John Lynn calls a state commission army, in which the Crown appointed the vast majority of officers and governed the training and the tactics by means of royal ordinances. Even the Swiss and German regiments were raised and maintained like the French ones. Most of these units also remained in being for long periods.[6]

Louis XIV displayed an intense personal interest in drill and devoted much of his time inspecting model military units like the Régiment du Roi, created in 1663. After 1660, the number of parades for recruits greatly increased, as did the amount of drill, at least twice weekly, under professional drillmasters such as Jean Martinet, whose name became a byword for rules and precision. Marching together in large groups inculcated in the men a sense of pervasive well-being, a swelling out and more assertive bearing that William McNeill calls 'muscular bonding'. The euphoric emotional resonance drill imparted resulted in an 'esprit de corps' that bound the recruits to each other, and gave them the sense that they belonged to an elite. Sergeants drilled soldiers to obey short, stylized verbal commands, and constant practice ingrained habits of obedience (Image 7.1).[7] The army's prestigious leader, the Protestant Vicomte de Turenne, established the first modern training camp at Compiegne, north of Paris, where he invited the young king to watch the soldiers train. Military march-pasts and manoeuvres were part of the court calendar at Paris and Versailles, and officers competed to make a good impression on the monarch.

Michel Le Tellier, his son François-Michel Comte de Louvois (1661–1691) and his grandson, Louis François de Barbézieux (1691–1701) oversaw the

Image 7.1 Jacques Callot: La Revue, Harvard Fogg Museum M12584. Colonels and generals laid increasing emphasis on marching and fighting in tight formations, enabling both the horse and the foot to use their firearms to maximum effect

French army administration for almost sixty years. Their activity can be expressed in the annual number of letters crossing the minister's desk. Under Abel Servien in the 1630s, these averaged just over two per day. By 1640, the volume increased to three dispatches, but, in 1690, correspondence arrived at a rate of 27 letters daily, or about 10,000 annually.[8] Le Tellier and Louvois also created general inspectors of infantry who supplied them with a constant stream of reports.[9] The high level of readiness was maintained not only by inspecting the men, but also their accommodations and their dress. After 1680, troops started residing in barracks rather than private houses; more than 160 barracks complexes were built during the reign, mostly in fortresses, but they were not nearly enough to house the entire army during wartime.[10] Deserving old soldiers, 3,000 of them, were pensioned off with dignity with the establishment of the Invalides in Paris, completed in 1676 (Image 7.2).[11] Uniforms were introduced at the regimental level in 1666, although variety ruled until the 1690s. French clothing manufactures produced uniforms in the hundreds of thousands, first in Sedan, then in Languedoc. Uniforms helped keep the men healthy, but they also improved their bearing by fitting them out like gentlemen, and they definitely enhanced the esprit de corps. Even if the French uniforms, like most

Image 7.2 Gabriel Perelle: Les Invalides 1674, Musée de l'Armée. On the edge of Paris, located on the River Seine facing the Louvre Palace, the institution proclaimed King Louis XIV's solidarity with deserving career soldiers. Admission was based on a curriculum vitae as well as on letters of recommendation

armies, adopted drab tones of grey or beige for reasons of cost, the flared garments sported distinctive brass buttons, braid and lapels of brighter hues. Designed to impress the wearers and spectators alike, uniforms were an asset to recruitment.[12]

Until he handed over full control to his son in 1677, Michel Le Tellier increased the king's control over the disbursement of money, by reviewing the accounts closely and demanding detailed explanations.[13] The king's inspectors for infantry and cavalry were hard at work trying to uncover fraud.[14] The entire system of supply and munitions remained in the hands of private contractors or *munitionnaires*, into the eighteenth century.[15] Half a dozen venal officials, *commissaires-généraux* for munitions, determined march routes and étapes for troops and horses on the move, and contacted the munitionnaires to make preparations. The commissaires had the right to requisition ovens, mills, granaries, carts, lodgings and workers, and they advanced funds to meet their goals. The non-venal army Intendants and the 30-odd provincial Intendants dispatched letters daily to about 40 functionaries working under the minister at Versailles.[16] Outside France, the army still levied contributions on enemy villages, but the whole system became more bureaucratized and less lethal for the inhabitants.[17] French troops sometimes got out of hand, but they and their officers were punished if it appeared necessary to avoid exasperating civilians. Because the discipline and the supply had truly improved, army mutinies disappeared under Louis XIV, and the rate of desertion in the eighteenth century was lower than in the Prussian army, which was held to be the model.[18]

Following the models of Venice and the Dutch East Indies Company, the team of Louis XIV, Colbert and Louvois created a national armaments industry between 1664 and 1676, erecting several musket factories at the Bastille in Paris, at Charleville near the Spanish Netherlands and at St-Etienne near Lyon. The Charleville establishment alone assembled a hundred muskets daily. During the 1690s, French foundries produced 2,000 iron cannon every year, principally for the navy. Land armies still predominantly used more expensive bronze pieces. Royal foundries existed in Paris, in military ports, but also in fortresses. Le Tellier centralized the artillery and made a specialized corps out of it in 1671, and founded powder-works and forges to equip it.[19] By the 1690s, more than four million pounds of gunpowder was produced in the kingdom's powder works. From then on, the Crown furnished equipment and weapons directly.[20]

A standing army could constantly experiment with weapons and kit, and programme their introduction. Plug bayonets (inserted into the musket barrel) were first introduced in 1669, followed by the ring bayonet in 1684, which permitted the soldier to fire, and the socket bayonet after 1700, on a design by the engineer Vauban. The bayonet made it possible to phase out the pikes, which finally disappeared in 1703. The lighter flintlock rifle began to be introduced during the 1670s but, as in other armies, the conversion took time, only complete in 1699, due to their greater expense and fragility.[21] The cartridge was introduced for muskets after 1692, those already containing the ball in 1705. Cavalry was traditionally the French strong suit. Acquiring sufficient horses for tens of thousands of troopers was a major problem; royal stud farms adopted a programme to increase the animals' size, as well as their numbers. War horses had to carry a load of 175 kg, including the rider, the saddle and tack and the various implements each cavalier required. Cavalry armour and weapons were standardized: troopers were equipped with carbines, with rifled barrels for greater accuracy, by 1678. Uniforms were adopted in 1690.

The first real test of the army's efficiency was the Dutch War (1672–1678), which aligned much of Europe against France. Le Tellier ceded much of the daily control to his son Louvois, also a civilian. It was Louvois who helped the king formulate the orders and oversee daily operations. Jules-Louis de Bolé, Marquis de Chamlay, who conducted personal inspections and reported back with recommendations for improvement, seconded the minister.[22] After the death of Marshal Turenne in 1675, there was greater emphasis on centralizing authority in the king and his minister, and to designate theatre commanders with rank over everyone else, including field marshals. The jealous king had total authority to confer responsibility wherever he wished. He did not expect outstanding abilities of those who received his gift, but he refused to promote individuals who proved quarrelsome or disobedient.[23]

The French officer corps grew to a prodigious size in the generation after 1660, such that Louvois managed at least 20,000 of them in 1690, that is, 16,000 in French line regiments, and 3,700 in the new provincial militia units. Adding the 32 foreign infantry and seven cavalry regiments, this meant that about 23–24,000 officers served in the army, and another 1,000 individuals served in the navy.[24] To oversee promotion at the higher levels, to reduce the patronage exercised by the senior aristocracy, and to lessen the importance of high birth, Louis instituted the *Ordre du Tableau* in 1675.[25] This measure was part of his campaign to accentuate hierarchy and to reduce the rivalries among high-ranking commanders. In addition to the field marshals, there were whole teams of lieutenant-generals and colonels who comprised what we might call the 'general staff'.[26] In 1668, Louis also created the rank of brigadier, the lowest grade of general officer, who commanded a corps of four to six battalions; he appointed 564 of these during his long reign.[27]

Competition for promotion was a serious problem for nobles who chose a military career, and the Crown needed to find a way to compensate colonels and captains so that they would invest their own money in their units. The solution was military venality, wherein a newcomer approved by the Crown paid money to a retiree to acquire a captaincy or a colonelcy when they retired. The practice, which was not strictly legal, flourished under Richelieu and Mazarin, who turned a blind eye to it. As for the judiciary, the monarch always retained a right of veto over the individual acceding to the post. Louis XIV sold very few army offices during his reign: the purchase of a commission was a private matter between the retiring officer and the individual seeking to acquire it. Allowing the private sale of an office was a way of compensating someone for money they had already invested to keep their unit operational.[28] If the holder was killed or otherwise incapacitated, the office became vacant and the king could grant it to someone else without compensating the family of the victim. The king could also 'reform' or disband the unit and its officers, without compensating them.[29] This was a way of punishing incompetent officers and served warning to the others. In many new regiments, the king conceded the colonelcy free of charge, but he expected the beneficiary to advance the money to recruit and to equip the men, with permission until 1705 to sell the captaincies to eager candidates. The newest regiments were the ones most likely to be disbanded at the end of the war. An officer's commission was a good investment if a family desired to establish or reinforce its noble standing, which entailed legal privilege and some degree of tax exemption.[30] Competitive aristocrats dominated the upper echelons of every army. Early in the eighteenth century, the army was relatively open socially, since, at the conclusion of every battle, scores or hundreds of officers needed to be replaced. Even in the elite Gardes Françaises, a quarter of the officers were either *roturiers* or new nobles. Outside the elite regiments, the cost of an infantry regiment was about 10,000 livres tournois, when many provincial noble families made do with annual revenues of 1,000. Money alone was not enough to rise in the military hierarchy, with or without noble credentials. One needed connections and to establish a professional reputation at least of non-incompetence. Officers of fortune without money of their own, whose rise was slow and difficult, might rise to major or lieutenant-colonel, which were not ranks acquired by purchase.[31]

Officers' formal remuneration was not nearly enough to maintain their rank and social position in the army. Vauban considered that the average infantry captain spent half his army income on incidentals to keep his company functioning. Hervé Drévillon, who has studied some 5,000 officers' dossiers from the later reign of Louis XIV, calculates that every infantry captain spent several hundred livres a year of their own money in this way (a peasant family could live on 100 livres tournois annually). This was not a fortune, but it was not a trifle either. To keep afloat, the officers borrowed money from their families and from their fellow officers.[32] On campaign, these officers had to live above their income, in order to attract attention and favour and to command the respect of their peers and their subordinates, whose social status might exceed their own. A field marshal would attach worthy underlings to his personal retinue and have them dine at his table as a subsidy.[33] In order to be seen and to present a solvent façade, it was necessary for them to appear occasionally at court, and to participate in its expensive social engagements. An army career led to material ruin more often than to wealth, and John Lynn considers it a *de facto* tax on nobility.[34] Raising and equipping a cavalry company was more expensive still: it cost 520 livres for each trooper, for which the king allotted only 150 livres. The war ministry usually paid these sums with bills of exchange, meaning that the officers had to pay conversion fees of 15–25%. A cavalry officer typically was a thousand livres out of pocket for his company every year, raising and equipping new troopers. The officer's subsistence costs also amounted to at least several hundred livres annually, not offset by the commission.[35] What's more, in order to get ahead, the officers were compelled to risk their lives, as well as their fortunes, something that contemporaries called a blood tax on the nobility. Officers made up about ten per cent of all the casualties, a higher proportion than among the rank and file.[36]

In appointing officers below the rank of general, the king and his ministers tried to strike a balance between various considerations; birth and noble pedigree, faithful service of the candidate's forebears, letters of recommendation from influential courtiers, the applicant's financial solvency and obvious signs of talent. Any heredity of a captaincy or colonelcy was a royal favour, not a right. Such rules sought to grant more regular promotion to long-serving lieutenants and captains. The lieutenant-colonels had, on average, 33 years of service, and the captains all more than ten years.[37] Colonels were still high-born, as a rule, but non-venal lieutenant-colonels managed the regiment's daily routine, and administration and discipline was placed increasingly in the hands of majors. The ministers and the high-ranking officers felt that promotion needed to be deserved, and whenever superior candidates were passed over, the injustice demoralized many rising candidates.[38] The king assisted this process in 1682 by creating companies of cadets that introduced thousands of budding officers to the basics of military science, including mathematics and drawing. (These companies were eliminated in 1696.) Elite regiments served as a nursery of officers: the King's Household troops (the *Maison du Roi*) consisted of 10,000 men, of whom 2,700 were posted to the court and provided 70–80% of the officer corps (higher in the cavalry than the infantry). Commoners or new nobles were occasionally appointed to the highest posts, and their social superiors were compelled to obey them, out of fear of displeasing Louvois and the king.

French noblemen continued to be liable to compulsory personal military service throughout the seventeenth century, through a feudal relic, the arrière-ban. In 1674, as the Dutch War widened to include theatres in Germany, Louis called up the nobility from a number of provinces, of whom 6,000 cavaliers assembled at Nancy. The operation was repeated twice more, in 1689 and 1690, at the outset of the War of the League of Augsburg. Generals assigned to organize this rabble were appalled by the lack of cohesion and combativeness, and convinced the king to encourage nobles to purchase exemption from mustering instead.[39] By one calculation, something like 35–42% of all French noble families had at least one member serving in the army in 1693, which is an enormous proportion.[40] The king created the Royal Military Order of St Louis in 1693 as a recompense to the most deserving officers, including commoners.[41]

It is more difficult to identify the rank and file, for complete records with the age, place of origin, a summary physical description and sometimes a profession were kept only after 1716. From the admission records to the Invalides after 1670, we can determine that about 40–50% of Louis XIV's soldiers hailed from towns, depending in part on how one defines these. Almost half the men married before or during their service, but this denotes long-term soldiers only. If they possessed a trade, they were usually artisans, that is, not from the most impoverished families.[42] Starting in the eighteenth century, administrators began measuring the height of recruits, who averaged 168 cm. There was no set term of enlistment, but it was understood that three years was a normal term of service.[43] When soldiers were not on duty, they had the right to hold part-time jobs in order to earn extra money. During wartime, the French army lost 25,-000–30,000 men annually, but not all of these were casualties, and about half that number left or died in peacetime. Famines in 1694 and 1709 spurred recruitment, for the administration ensured that there was always bread and meat for soldiers.

Foreign troops, Swiss, Germans and Irish principally, continued to comprise a significant portion of the French army, about 15–25%. After the Thirty Years' War, general contractors no longer raised foreign units. The French raised foreign regiments individually and trained them in the same manner as the native infantry. The Irish were no longer hired by Spain after 1653, the date we find them in French service; nine regiments, or about 6,000 men, were on the rosters in 1654. About the same number served during the Dutch War in the 1670s. In 1692, after the disaster of the Williamite wars, 15,000 Irish soldiers and 4,000 women and children arrived *en masse* in France. They were considered excellent troops when disciplinarian officers held them in hand, but they had a penchant for turbulence and rapine. Until 1697, they were organized separately under James II as a British army in France. After 1702, they served as part of the French army, and about 1,000 recruits arrived annually from the island.[44]

It is true, as Guy Rowlands claims, that private interests flourished at every level of the French army, but this was true of every other army, too. Putting a very large force into the field, and keeping it operational was a sign of good organization. The ability of the French monarchy to do this had its peaks (the 1680s and 1690s) and its troughs. Already numbering 250,000 men (on paper) at the end of the Dutch War in 1678, army effectives soared to nearly 340,000 in the early 1690s, augmented by 60,000 militiamen in 1697, and still exclusive of the navy. In 1701 began the practice of mixing militiamen into combat units. After 1703, it was impossible to support such large numbers. At the end of the War of the Spanish Succession, the standing army was fixed at approximately 150,000 men.

Competing armies

Emperor Ferdinand III did not completely disband his army after the Peace of Westphalia in 1648, but kept a cadre of men and officers, about 25,000 in 1650, who accepted demotion in order to continue serving. There were also 10,000 to 20,000 irregular troops, or *grenzers*, along the Ottoman military frontier.[45] This force soon increased to assist Spain in defending Lombardy against France in 1655, and an Imperial contingent drove the Swedes from Poland in 1658. Army strength expanded with each crisis and contracted following peace, such as that occasioned by the Treaty of Vasvar with the Ottomans in 1664 and the Treaty of Nijmegen with France in 1678. The professional soldiers numbered about 40,000 men around 1660 just before the Hungarian crisis, and 60,000 in 1675 when the

Empire entered the war against France. There was no decisive shift away from employing military entrepreneurs in Central Europe until the 1670s. Colonels had much more power and influence than in France: the regiment bore the proprietor's name and reflected his social status. They could still sell the junior positions in their regiments and raised money by selling all kinds of permissions, like leaves and security certificates. Each colonel also applied his own tactical preferences, in the absence of an army doctrine.[46]

The Catholic Habsburg emperors were such ardent proponents of the Counter-Reformation that the court welcomed the contributions of German Catholics outside the Habsburg hereditary lands, and from outside Germany as well. Vienna employed one of the most cosmopolitan general staffs in Europe, although army commanders such as Raimondo Montecuccoli recommended maintaining a German homogeneity and common insignia among the rank and file.[47] A large proportion of field marshals at the head of Imperial armies were Italians like Montecuccoli, or Francophones from Lorraine, Burgundy or the Low Countries. In 1699, foreign infantry officers constituted 25% of the corps and fully 40% of the cavalry officers. The army officers were also 80% commoners, but these were concentrated at lower levels. All the Imperial colonels and generals were bona fide aristocrats.[48]

Fritz Redlich's study of military entrepreneurship concluded that 'it defeated its purpose, the efficiency of armies'.[49] By the 1680s, colonels had little to do with recruiting, which was assigned to specialists at the behest of the provinces (Image 7.3). Imperial regiments were neither hereditary nor purchased in this period, but it was customary to offer a very expensive gift to one's patron upon promotion. The Hofkriegsrat gradually took over the supply of weapons, clothing and horses, and a General War Commissariat was set up to oversee troop quartering, recruitment and supply, whose 100 officials inspected units and the records of their administration. The Hofkreigsrat itself became a largely civilian body working under the direction of senior commanders.[50] Army supply was completely left to private contractors, but the Crown established weapons manufactures, and after 1700, it generalized the use of uniforms for the rank and file.[51] 'Austrian' logistics were famously inefficient; colonels competed with each other to get their hands on supplies, and often hired special agents whose task it was to bother functionaries in Vienna and prioritize their own needs. Provisions and pay were channelled through the colonel, who could rake off some of the proceeds, but the manipulation of supplies for private profit was an abuse considered worthy of punishment. When Vienna was short of funds (which was almost all the time), colonels advanced their own money and then reimbursed themselves from the civilian population around them. Colonels and generals might be repaid with promotion, but were later granted large landed estates in Southern Hungary re-conquered from the Turks in the course of the 1680s and 1690s. Montecuccoli, considered an 'honest general' by Bérenger, left a fortune of three million florins upon his death in 1680.

Emperor Leopold was a distinctly pious and unwarlike sovereign, who had a tendency to curtail the number of troops even in the face of enemy military preparations, so the army expanded and contracted continually until the final Ottoman

Image 7.3 Friedrich von Flemming, Prussian Recruiting, Preussischen Bild. A Prussian recruiting team at work on a town square. By the eighteenth century, army recruitment was entrusted to specialists who operated throughout the year. Art Resource

advance on Vienna in 1683. In 1695, dispersed across multiple theatres, the Emperor had 94,000 men under arms, 58,000 foot and 36,000 horse. Of these, 20,500 were part of an international army posted to northern Italy, 7,100 were serving as a component of a German army fighting France along the Rhine, 14,300 were imposing Habsburg rule on Transylvania, and 50,600 operated against the Ottomans in Hungary and the Balkans.[52] In 1715, as the Empire prepared for a new offensive war against the Ottomans, there were fully 144,000 men (on paper); 23,500 posted around the Empire outside Habsburg borders, 18,000 distributed across the hereditary lands of Austria, Bohemia and Hungary, 20,000 stationed in Lombardy and another 14,000 in Naples (newly acquired) and 7,000 in the Southern Low Countries, also newly obtained. This still left 60,000 men mobilized in Hungary and Transylvania.[53] These do not include the 10,000–20,000 irregular soldiers posted along the Ottoman frontier.

Elsewhere in Central Europe, standing armies were on the agenda in many of the larger territories of the Empire, and some of the smaller ones, too. The Treaty of Westphalia established that German princes were free to make treaties with other powers, as long as they did not threaten the Imperial institution. Many German princes wished to expand their lands, and to prevent their rivals from doing so.[54] In the early 1660s, Brandenburg, Hanover, Saxony, the Rhine Palatinate and Bavaria, and the prince-bishops of Mainz, Cologne and Munster all maintained modest armies of a few thousand men. Before long, princes were using their troops to collect taxes and to impose their authority on autonomous towns and stubborn Estates. More revenue resulted in larger numbers of soldiers at their command. War between the Emperor and the Ottomans in 1663 spurred the creation of *Reichs contingents*, wherein each state contributed money and troops to assist the 'Austrian' troops in the field. The Empire, since the sixteenth century, had been sub-divided into large 'Circles' that oversaw the collection of money and men for wars. It became clear that if a state did not have a standing army of its own, the largest prince in the Circle would extract resources from the smaller ones against their will or without their control. Brandenburg and Hanover, in particular, looted their neighbours to provide for their men. The message was that even smaller states should create their own armies to prevent such exploitation.[55] By 1700, Bavaria, Saxony, Hanover, Brandenburg and the Palatinate all employed well-drilled standing armies of over 10,000 men that were intended to raise the status of the dynasty in Europe. To those, one could add the standing army of the Duke of Savoy in northern Italy. Princes throughout the Empire passed rental contracts with great powers seeking additional troops. There were three cost items worked into the contract: (1) recruiting and equipping the men with arms and uniforms, (2) the wages for each rank of soldier and officer and (3) replacing lost men and equipment. By the late seventeenth century, the nominal wages of soldiers were lower than before, but payment was fairly regular.[56]

Bavaria was one of the earliest, raising its first units in 1657: however, its growth was not continuous and numbers dropped to below 2,000 men in 1670. The Elector Max Emmanuel (r. 1679–1726) expanded it afresh, to provide 8,000 troops to fight the Turks in Hungary, and then to assist Spain in Flanders, where he was governor-general during the League of Augsburg war. When he joined the French alliance in the Spanish Succession conflict, hoping to expand his states into the Tyrolese Alps, the Bavarian army reached 30,000 men.[57] Despite its considerable size, army careers were not very attractive to native Bavarians, who gravitated towards careers in the Church or at the court in Munich. In 1705, two fifths of the officers were non-German foreigners, French and Italians, many of whom never mastered the German language.[58] In the late 1690s, a Bavarian prince was designated to inherit a large part of the Spanish empire, and, in 1742, Max Emanuel's son, Charles Albert, was elected Holy Roman Emperor.

Saxony's Electors also used the standing army as an instrument of dynastic ambition after its first expansion in 1682. Until then, the Elector raised contingents of infantry that he leased to Venice, as did Bavaria.[59] The army grew to 20,000 men during the Turkish wars of the 1690s, a Reichs contingent second only to Brandenburg-Prussia's in Hungary. In 1694, the new elector, Frederick Augustus, adopted the Prussian model of organization. With the prestige accruing from his participation in Hungarian campaigns, the Elector was elected King of Poland in 1697, and the army expanded yet again. The Polish army was, for the most part, based in Saxony and financed from there. With Russian subsidies it numbered about 36,000 men in 1710, then dropped to about 26,000 in the aftermath.[60]

One of these ambitious princes was Elector Frederick William of Branden-burg, who ruled a far-flung composite state at his accession in 1640. He man-aged to employ only a few thousand undisciplined men in the years after the Treaty of Westphalia, due to his inability to extract more money from the reluctant Estates of his several territories. Swedish intervention in Poland gave him the pretext to impose his demands on them in 1655 and when the emer-gency ended in 1660 he was determined to keep a strong body of men. He did not hesitate to use force to impose additional taxes to finance the levies.[61] He established a General War Commissariat that owed much to Louvois, which drew up recruiting, supply and billeting contracts for troop mainten-ance. The Elector surrounded himself with a small staff of military-orientated bureaucrats who dominated the entire administration. In 1660, Frederick Wil-liam retained about 12,000 men. To help earn their keep, soldiers were com-mitted to infrastructure projects such as canal construction and fortifications work.[62] The Elector also took subsidies from Louis XIV, hoping to replace Sweden in France's foreign policy in northern Europe. The Elector's Calvinist allegiance made him a Dutch and Imperial ally in the 1670s, employing his large, well-trained force against the French on the Rhine and against the Swedes in the Baltic. After the Treaty of Nijmegen in 1678, the Elector main-tained a force of 25,000 men, the second in the Empire after the Emperor's own. Thousands of Huguenots arriving after 1685 cemented the Elector's anti-Catholic policies, while hundreds of French Protestant officers imported the practices of Louis XIV's army.[63] After the Elector's death, his successor, Frederick, leveraged the availability of this great army to obtain a royal title, King in Prussia, from the Emperor Leopold I.

The three brothers who held the inheritance of the duchies of Brunswick, Hanover and Lunenburg in the 1660s produced only one heir, Ernst Augus-tus, who endowed the emperor with generous subsidies and several regiments to fight the Turks in the 1680s, and his designated heir, Prince George, volun-teered in the force to relieve Vienna. Another of his sons, Prince Frederick Augustus, died in combat in 1690 in an Imperial regiment in Hungary. In order to obtain Hanoverian regiments in the War of the League of Augsburg, and to balance the increase of Catholic Electors with an additional Lutheran, Emperor Leopold conferred the electoral title on Ernst Augustus in 1692. George inherited the combined states of his father and uncles in 1698, and then contributed generously to the coalition cause against France after 1702. He commanded an independent corps of troops along the Rhine in 1707, which gave him a veneer of military competence although the French marshal Villars defeated him in the field. He deeply resented not being party to stra-tegic plans drawn up by Prince Eugene and the Duke of Marlborough. His mother, Sophie, had a distant claim to the English succession, the Protestant frontrunner behind 56 more closely related Catholics. The high profile military and diplomatic activities made Elector George of Hanover an attractive candidate to the English Parliament in search of a Protestant successor to the ageing Queen Anne.[64]

The dynastic advantages to German princes with large military establishments were clear even at the time. Other German princes relied heavily on foreign subsidies to maintain large peacetime establishments. The Protestant Duke of Hesse-Kassel created an army of 3,000 men in 1683, but increased it to 10,000 in 1688 at the beginning of the War of the League of Augsburg. To support this force, he rented regiments to Venice and to the Netherlands. In 1727, he rented the entire Hessian army of 12,000 men to King George II of England, and it remained in the British sphere of influence for the rest of the century.[65] A relative latecomer was Wurttemberg, a smallish state in southwestern Germany. Duke Eberhard Ludwig used money from the Circle of Swabia to levy up to three regiments, leased via the Duke of Hanover to Venice for operations against the Ottomans in Greece. In 1691, he furnished 10,000 recruits to serve several employers, such as the Dutch Republic and Venice, but this was still his private force, not raised from ducal revenues. Wurttemberg troops were not sufficiently numerous to prevent the duchy from being devastated by French troops based nearby in Alsace. In 1698, the duke dissolved the regional Estates and raised a new standing army with extraordinary taxes, which served like the new palace and the court as an instrument of the sovereign's glory.[66]

Outside Germany, the emblematic example was the Duchy of Savoy, ruled by one of the continent's most ambitious and warlike dynasties. Duke Charles-Emmanuel II established a standing army of six regiments organized on the French model in 1664, then raised it to eight in 1670, augmented by some Swiss companies. Not all the soldiers were Piedmontese or Savoyard subjects, since many recruits were native Frenchmen. The duke leased regiments to Venice to fight the Ottomans on Crete, as well as to Louis XIV, which enabled the officers to acquire combat experience. Charles-Emmanuel profited from the distraction of the French invasion of Holland in 1672 to invade the Republic of Genoa in 1672, whose conquest was a long-standing ambition. The invasion ended in fiasco and a quick retreat. At the expansion of the Dutch War in 1673, Duke Charles-Emmanuel II leased four regiments to France, where they were virtually incorporated into the French army until they were released in 1679. Four other regiments passed into French service in 1688. This reflected Savoy's satellite status during the period, despite the dynasty's royal aspirations.

By 1690, the Savoyard army still numbered only 8,000 men, but young Duke Victor Amadeus II increased it with foreign subsidies when he joined the Augsburg League against France. When the duke passed into the coalition against France again in 1703, the force swelled with money from the Empire, from England and the Netherlands. Victor Amadeus defended his duchy with various Swiss, German, Dutch and Huguenot regiments of professional soldiers alongside his Piedmontese and Savoyard subjects. The advent of the large peacetime standing army emerged after 1710, with a base level of 22,000 men, which included a number of provincial regiments of chosen militia on the French example. These were first incorporated in 1704 and served adequately in the defence of Turin in 1706. In peacetime, the soldiers garrisoned a network of powerful fortresses that controlled the Alpine passes. In 1733, Charles-Emmanuel III (now king of Sardinia) could oppose 40,000 soldiers and 1,000 officers against the Emperor; against the Bourbons of France and Spain in 1747, the king aligned 55,000 men. In these wars, the dynasty finally acquired a royal title, expanded the borders of the state and substantially increased its population and its taxation base.[67] The eighteenth century standing army was still made up of foreigners for one-third, mostly Germans and Swiss. About two-thirds of the Piedmontese and Savoyard soldiers were volunteers, the remainder pressed men. The provincial regiments, reorganized in 1713, were mustered twice a year. Most of the professional soldiers were now lodged in barracks, where the mortality rate was three times that of civilians. The army was a hotbed of heresy and atheism but, at the same time, a conduit of international technical expertise. The soldiers, who served on average for two to three years, came from diverse backgrounds, more rootless than impoverished. Their sentry obligations left them a lot of free time and many exercised commerce or a trade. The officers were usually, but not always, nobles, and a third of noble families had at least one member serving in the army. Ambitious commoners found that service in the 'Sardinian' army was the fastest way to obtain legal nobility and social influence.[68]

Spain's once prestigious army shrivelled over the course of the later seventeenth century, still numbering 100,000 troops on paper in 1676 but perhaps only 50,000 remained around 1690, woefully insufficient to protect the Low Countries, Lombardy and the south Italian kingdoms from France. The best Spanish units were generally posted outside Iberia, while at home the best troops were Italian and Walloon tercios and German mercenary regiments.[69] Part of the problem was the difficulty of convincing nobles to invest their private resources into the imperial project. When they did join, they preferred to serve in the cavalry. Infantry tercios were often skeletal forces containing only a few men per company. The army campaigning in the Low Countries was bedevilled by ongoing competition among different nationalities.[70] One field in which Spain retained an advance on its competitors was in the realm of military hospitals; the first had been established near Antwerp at Mechelen in 1585, but others appeared in large cities close to military theatres, like Barcelona, or in major ports such as Cadiz and Palermo, and every large garrison possessed its own. But in this period they were all plagued by inadequate funding and relative neglect.[71] The nadir must have been the Dutch War of the 1670s, when only small forces could be raised to protect the Pyrenees border or recover rebellious Messina in Sicily. There was a marked improvement of Spain's finances in the 1680s, when Naples and Sicily began to contribute to Imperial defence once again.[72] In Milan, field troops and garrisons averaged about 10,000 men in peacetime, and double that in periods of tension, which was larger than any other Italian state. The soldiers consisted of oscillating proportions of Spaniards, Germans, Swiss, Lombards and Neapolitans.[73] Fortresses contained substantial amounts of siege artillery and powder, and the works themselves were still considerable. But this was essentially a holding force against Louis XIV, reliant on allies in sufficient numbers to prevent French expansion. Fortunately for Spain, Louis XIV and Louvois accorded much less attention to the Italian theatre than in the time of Cardinal Mazarin.[74] In unthreatened lands such as the kingdom of Naples, the number of professional soldiers fit for active duty was very small, underscoring the fact that these lands were not held in Habsburg captivity by armed force. Circa 1700, only 4,000 men were on the rosters, and half of those were assigned to Tuscan coastal fortresses. The garrison tercios were notionally Spanish, but a third of those soldiers were drawn from Italy, and only one officer in three was effectively Iberian. The kingdom's militia existed only on paper, and it proved impossible to raise soldiers from it.[75] With the onset of the War of the Spanish Succession against the maritime powers of Britain and the Netherlands, new regiments were raised and shipped off to fight in Spain or Lombardy. When a German Imperial army marched down the peninsula to re-establish Habsburg rule in 1707, there was no means of resisting it.

The Spanish army was recast on French lines by the Bourbon King Philip V, starting in 1702; the tercios were transformed into regiments of two or three battalions. The king and his ministers issued uniforms and standardized equipment and training across the board. The French practice of selling commissions to officers also became widespread policy under Philip V. Unlike the Habsburg army, which was dispersed and multi-ethnic, the Bourbon army was fundamentally Hispanic and limited to the peninsula.[76] In 1704, a reserve was established based on obligatory militia service, as in France, then organized into 34 regiments in 1734. This reformed army served alongside French troops to consolidate Bourbon rule in Iberia and to repel the international coalition of Portuguese, Imperial, Dutch and British troops in the decade after 1704. Nobles constituted only half the officer corps in 1700, but, as the prestige of the corps increased, nobles more readily embraced military careers.[77]

We can complete our survey with the creation of a British standing army, founded in 1661 after disbanding Cromwell's hated New Model Army, a republican institution dominated by the unpopular Puritans. Initially, there were only two regiments of foot and 400 horse guards, soon raised to six regiments (four foot and two horse). It was designed to be a ceremonial army of royal guards based on the model of the French guards. The men continued to wear red coats from Cromwellian days, and the term eventually became synonymous with the British soldier. There were also separate armies in Scotland and Ireland, but these were merely castle garrisons scattered in small establishments paid out of the taxes of those nations. Officers purchased their commissions, after being selected by royal favour, but military experience was not a prerequisite. This was the king's army, not Parliament's, since it was financed from the excise taxes or from French subsidies.[78] In addition to these units, England sent a series of expeditionary forces abroad: a small contingent left to help defend Portugal from Spanish re-conquest in the early 1660s, and another to garrison Tangier in Morocco until it finally abandoned the town in 1680.

New regiments were hurriedly commissioned after the Dutch fleet raided the mouth of the Thames in 1667, but the war ended before the units were raised. By the secret Treaty of Dover in 1670, King Charles undertook to send a corps of 6,000 men to fight under the French flag against the Dutch. The force was divided among the various theatres of war and never fought together as a corps. England dropped out of the war in 1674 but most of the men remained in France on French pay.[79] The peacetime armies of the three Stuart kingdoms totalled about 10,000 men in 1680, of which the largest force was based in Ireland (5,000 foot and 2,500 horse), but hired in England to ensure the troops would be Protestants. Despite their numbers they were not considered an efficient military force. The Scottish army numbered fewer than 2,000 professional soldiers but they were easily the most warlike, and even the Scottish militia could be relied upon to fight.[80]

King James II, a devout Catholic, raised the number of troops in England to 20,000 men by the end of 1685. He was soon challenged by William III of Orange (married to his daughter, Mary), who desired to employ the resources of the British Isles in his league of Protestant states challenging France. For the Dutch stadtholder this project was part of a divinely inspired Holy War against Catholicism. The English navy did not leave port to challenge William's fleet of 463 ships (53 warships) carrying 40,000 men in November 1688 until it was too late. The invasion army disembarking in the west of England numbered 14,000 foot and 3,600 cavalry, the great majority of which were foreign soldiers, plus 5,000 volunteers, largely financed by the States of Holland. King James mobilized his army, with Scottish and Irish reinforcements, to confront William on Salisbury plain, but in mere days, three-quarters of the English officers changed sides (but few of the rank and file). Once he was in command of the kingdom, William convinced the English Parliament to expand the army to five times its previous size, largely raised by impressment like the navy.[81] The Dutch monarch was not about to distribute officers' commissions to inexperienced Englishmen; the highest posts were mostly given to experienced Dutch generals, and 10–15% went to Huguenots. The artillery and engineering components of the army were overwhelmingly Dutch, and Dutch Sephardic Jews ensured the army's provisioning and transport.[82]

British troops sent to Flanders to fight the French constituted a quarter of William's field army by 1691, but the king (who had a prickly personality) had only contempt for their poor discipline and lack of training. They were soon drilled and organized in the Dutch manner. In 1692, the British expeditionary force grew to 21,000 men, while England leased 19,000 more soldiers from Germany and Denmark. The French repeatedly bested William's Anglo–Dutch and German armies in the field, however. The king was lucky to fight the French to a draw in 1697 when hostilities ended, but this raised his prestige in Britain. An array of new taxes made the large army viable, and the Bank of England was created on the Dutch model in 1694 to help borrow money for it. The standing army employed 5,000 commissioned officers at its height, with the most prestigious positions going to those with court connections. Scotland contributed disproportionately to the army, but needed to find men using conscription and impressment. In 1698, Parliament tried to cut the army back to 10,000 men, the level of 1680, but there was now a consensus that Britain should retain a standing force financed by that body.[83]

Before we leave the standing armies, we should understand that being in readiness to fight foreign wars permitted them to fulfil other tasks in peacetime. Parcelled out in numerous small garrisons, professional soldiers assisted their rulers in squeezing taxes from restive subjects. Taxes were levied not on individuals, but on communities, whose authorities were compelled to collect or borrow the entire sum demanded of them. Companies of light horse were billeted on villages unable or unwilling to raise the amount, and their lodging costs were added to the sum. Up to a point, soldiers could misbehave to the point of making themselves intolerable. Rape and murder were definitely not permitted, but destruction of furniture and appropriation of food and drink certainly were. In the aftermath of sweeping new taxes to fight the Dutch war in 1675, French anti-fiscal rebellions broke out in rural Brittany and in Bordeaux. Royal regiments quickly put these down, and similar rebellions became quite rare and isolated in the aftermath.[84] In the early 1680s, the Intendant of Poitou learned that Protestants would soon convert to Catholicism if dragoons lodged in their houses, and Louis XIV generalized the technique across the kingdom in 1685. The French king was certainly not alone in using troops to restore religious unity: only the scale and the duration of the repression, until his death in 1715, were different.[85]

Standing armies were also an essential ingredient in one other process of enormous importance: the internal pacification of states. Medieval and sixteenth-century violent crime was many times more frequent than in our own time, because the means to combat it were makeshift and local. A great wave of rural banditry engulfed much of Europe in the second half of the sixteenth century, forcing rulers to mobilize militiamen against it and to apply draconian penalties. In Western Europe, the homicide rate (the easiest crime to measure) began to fall after 1600, although it is difficult to pinpoint where this first began because the archives are so spotty. In Italy, the various duchies began to implement extradition treaties by the 1630s, permitting task forces to eliminate outlaw refuges. The viceroys of Naples, Pedro Fajardo, Marques de los Velez (1675–1683) and Gaspar Mendez de Haro, Marquis of Carpio (1683–1687), used the army to eliminate rural banditry and to browbeat the feudatories who tolerated it.[86] By the seventeenth century, professional soldiers, together with special tribunals, were employed to crack down on lawless districts where social elites tormented their underlings. After 1670, lethal violence was in full retreat across most of Western Europe, such that by the middle decades of the eighteenth century modern homicide rates were attained. (Mobile phones, ambulances and surgical teams in well-equipped hospitals to save the badly wounded were still far in the future.)[87]

Also, on a positive note, rulers with standing armies did not wish to keep them idle. Brandenburg's soldiers spun wool and helped weave their new blue uniforms. Military work crews raised the new walls of Berlin, and excavated a ten-kilometre canal connecting the River Oder to the Elbe. Louis XIV employed army labour to erect Versailles and its great gardens in the 1660s. Finally, soldiers constituted an essential element in the fight against contagious epidemics such as the bubonic plague, for they erected a *cordon sanitaire* around infected areas and prevented people from leaving. Plague could not be cured until the twentieth century, but it could be contained to prevent its spread, and soldiers were employed to effect this. The disease was endemic in the Ottoman Empire, and continued to kill millions of people in Central and Eastern Europe until the early eighteenth century. In 1690, an outbreak of the disease on the coast of Puglia prompted Spain to mobilize troops and the galley flotilla to prevent its spread, which proved successful (Image 7.4). Emperor Joseph I established a 'Pestfront' of quarantine posts along the Ottoman border in 1710, after the plague struck Vienna and much of Central Europe.[88] Similarly, in France in 1720, when a plague killed half the population of Marseille, troops cordoned off most of Provence on land, while the galleys blockaded the coast, thus saving the lives of millions of Europeans.

Era of standing navies

The decade after the end of the Thirty Years' War witnessed another truly important innovation, the creation of whole navies of purpose-built warships

Image 7.4 Filippo Arrieta: Plague containment in Puglia 1690–1692, BNF 30031657, p. 183. A Spanish cordon sanitaire isolates districts of the province of Bari in the Kingdom of Naples. Army checkpoints were stretched out in two rows behind infected towns, while the navy blockaded the coast. In this way, armies prevented the spread of a deadly plague pandemic originating in the Ottoman Empire

taking over from armed merchantmen. The large warship was not itself an innovation, for most navies periodically built one for purposes of prestige. They were top-heavy and sailed poorly: the Swedish *Vasa* sank almost as soon as it left Stockholm on its maiden voyage in 1628. But, by the 1650s, England launched the first modern fleet of *ships of the line*, aggressively seeking to deprive the Dutch Republic of its maritime supremacy. Parliament inherited most of the warships built for King Charles I in the 1630s. It augmented this with 54 new vessels built between 1649 and 1654, and Cromwell's regime built dry docks, magazines and even a hospital as part of the new infrastructure, with several dockyards in the vicinity of London.[89] All modern navies relied on well-stocked state arsenals. In the first Anglo–Dutch War, the English fleet demonstrated its superiority by inflicting severe defeat on the Dutch in the North Sea, although Dutch ships bested the English ones in the Baltic and in distant colonies, where such warships were not deployed.[90] The English fleet raised crews by subjecting merchant ships to embargoes (not permitted to sail until the navy had finished recruiting sailors), and by resorting to press gangs, more common than on the continent.[91] One considerable advantage of the Royal Navy was that it was governed by a single committee, the Navy Board, and so was spared the political wrangling and the duplication of effort that characterized the Dutch, who were cursed with five separate admiralties and the two large trading companies with their own heavily-armed flotillas. With the restoration of the British monarchy in 1660, the Royal Navy was taken over by King Charles II and his brother, James, Duke of York. Both were passionate about ships and intended to deprive the Dutch of their commercial primacy by dispatching ships to attack Dutch possessions in peacetime. They kept the navy efficient and budget-conscious so that they would be able to prevent Parliamentary oversight.[92]

Dutch fleets overwhelmingly comprised converted merchant vessels that were quickly demobilized. They responded immediately to the English threat by laying down the keels of similar warships, so that by 1660 the Republic could deploy scores of ships of the line. These were still not as large as their English adversaries because they needed to navigate shallow waters.[93] The new Dutch vessels were confided to the care of the States-General, not destined to be privatized with the return of peace. Jan de Witt, Pensionary of the States of Holland, who expanded the battle fleet and embarked frequently on the ships himself, provided the political direction. The old navy was officered by admirals and captains who were close to the city governments and merchants of their home base, and there was much indiscipline and disobedience among their number. New officers were no longer merchants and were trained to fight with line tactics. Dutch seamen were not compelled to join the navy, and their pay and food was perhaps the best anywhere. Many of the crews comprised Germans and Scandinavians, and many of the officers were foreigners.[94] This navy inflicted sharp defeat on the English in the war of 1665–1667. Anglo-Dutch rivalry to 1678 served as a stimulus to naval expansion. After William of Orange took direction of the Dutch Navy, he sponsored the launching of more and bigger ships, with adequate port facilities at Flushing and the Texel passage.[95]

Jean-Baptiste Colbert urged the king to create a French navy equal to Louis XIV's ambitions. In charge of French colonies and fisheries from 1661, the navy fell naturally under Colbert's purview. Cardinal Richelieu established the first modern French navy in 1626, mainly by purchasing large Dutch merchant ships, converted to carry cannon and troops. The fleets collected to fight England and Spain in the 1620s and 1630s were very large, but they were not enough to deprive Spain of the initiative in the Mediterranean and, following the cardinal's death in 1642, there was little continuity.[96] Unlike the army, the navy was the king's creation and he was less obliged to contend with competing interest groups. Louis XIV launched his shipbuilding programme in 1665–1667, with four categories of warships, but only three were heavy enough to take their place in the line. The fleet comprised only 20 converted merchantmen under Mazarin in 1661, but 80 ships of the line a decade later, when it challenged the Dutch in the Mediterranean. Frigates were built in sizeable numbers in order to scout and to relay messages. The French invented a specialized warship, the bomb ketch, to fire explosive bombs at stationary targets, tested on Algiers in 1682–1683, and on Genoa in 1684. In addition to the sailing vessels, France maintained a flotilla of up to 40 galleys based in Marseille, propelled by convicts and captives. The galleys were instrumental in gaining strategic superiority in Sicily in the 1670s and Catalonia in the 1690s. This navy was mostly a Mediterranean instrument designed to combat Barbary corsairs. Toulon, France's naval base in the Mediterranean, a well-protected and capacious harbour, employed 10,000 people in the shipyards. Harbours on the Atlantic façade were not as capacious as Toulon, or were not protected enough from attack by sea. Brest, the principal base in Brittany, was considerably expanded in the 1670s, and employed 3,000 people. A model arsenal and shipyard was created from nothing at Rochefort on the Charente River in 1665. By century's end, it was a city of 12,000 inhabitants, a third of whom were employed in the arsenal. These arsenals were not only places to build ships, but to outfit them also, so they contained artillery parks, munitions depots, huge surfaces for sails and cables, a giant barrel works, where convicts worked alongside artisans. A slaughterhouse fed a saltworks for curing meat, while a great bakery supplied biscuit. When necessary, production could be accelerated by hiring sub-contractors.[97]

From the 1670s on, all the French vessels were built in the kingdom in a handful of important arsenals, and they were outfitted with guns, sails and cables produced domestically. Only the masts had to be imported from species of trees growing in the Baltic. (Other countries were forced to do the same.)[98] Colbert relied at first on naval arsenals owned by the Crown, but turned soon enough to private forges. The state was a major customer of hardware, and demanded high-quality products, but it was not a good payer.[99] In 1690, a French second-line vessel carried 500 men, equal to a battalion of infantry. A first-rank ship carrying 74 iron cannons contained 600 men. The largest vessels bristled with 100 cannon, equivalent to two major fortresses, and carried a complement of 1,000 men, with six or seven crewmen for each piece of artillery.[100] Each vessel was also a floating naval yard carrying specialized tradesmen, while the soldiers aboard often had useful skills, too. Forests had to be managed and harvested rationally across the entire kingdom. Intendants in the ports supervised construction and provisioning, and determined how many ships should be armed every year.[101] The masts, cannon and provisions were removed from vessels and stored at the end of every campaign, in order to better preserve the ships, which had a lifespan of thirty or forty years. There was always a disparity between the number of existing vessels and those that could be armed for a new campaign.

In the navy, the king paid for everything, which meant that he enjoyed complete control over the appointment of about a thousand officers. These were periodically moved from one ship to another, and given various kinds of missions. Naval commissions could not be purchased, and were granted to people of diverse social status.[102] Seafaring skills earned their holder a premium, such that about a third of the officers were commoners, hailing especially from Brittany and Normandy. Filling the vessels with skilled seamen was the principal difficulty, however. Following the Spanish example, Colbert developed in 1668 a census of eligible seamen that included employees of river boats, but these were never enough to man a large fleet. The merchant marine was still too small relative to the navy to enable large-scale impressment.

France's principal strategic difficulty was that it required two autonomous navies, one for each coast. Combining the two flotillas into one for large-scale operations was a considerable problem. Nevertheless, the navy's success was measurable in several ways. Barbary Coast corsairs were less likely to attack French ships than those of other nations, which led to a busy international carrying trade from Marseille. In the Mediterranean, only Venice launched a similar fleet of warships of the line in the 1660s, such that there was no competition to French naval hegemony in southern Europe before 1700. In the Channel, the French navy defeated the combined English and Dutch fleet off Beachy Head in 1690. It suffered a reverse at the Hogue in 1692 but its losses were quickly made up. The only great sea battle in the war of the Spanish Succession, against an Anglo-Dutch fleet off Malaga in 1704, was effectively a draw. When the navy was not strong enough to challenge the combined fleets of the maritime powers, after 1692, the warships were leased out to privateers, who inflicted huge losses on British and Dutch shipping. After 1709, however, the lack of funds meant that the fleet was largely mothballed. In the space of a few decades, Western Europe created at least a score of substantial standing armies, well drilled and committed to battle on a fairly regular basis, and a half-dozen modern navies. Shortcomings were addressed and corrected and the weaponry improved over the same period. However, in a tournament model wherein the principal protagonists with standing armies and navies periodically recomposed their alliances, no continental hegemon emerged that could impose peace by its great size.[103]

Notes

1 Olaf van Nimwegen, 2010: 306.
2 Marjolein 't Hart, 2014: 31; van Nimwegen, 2010: 409.
3 Olivier Chaline, 2016: 18; David Parrott, 1992.

4   Louis André, 1906: 159.
5   John A Lynn, 1997: 33.
6   Lynn, 1997: 7.
7   William H. McNeill, 1995: 130–31.
8   Lynn, 1999: 53.
9   Lionel Marquis, 2015: 31.
10 Cornette, 2000: 63.
11 Cornette, 2000: 92.
12 Chaline, 2016: 85; Roche, 2007: 211–23; Ilya Berkovich, 2017: 134–5.
13 Guy Rowlands, 2002: 137.
14 Hervé Drévillon, 2005: 159.
15 David Parrott, 2012: 275.
16 Marquis, 2015: 58–61.
17 Myron P Gutmann, 1980: 44–52.
18 Chaline, 2016: 180.
19 André, 1906: 497; Chaline, 2016: 88–93.
20 Drévillon, 2005: 101.
21 Drévillon, 2005: 370.
22 Drévillon, 2005: 31.
23 Rowlands, 2002: 300.
24 André Corvisier, 1983: 341.
25 Marquis, 2015: 25.
26 Guy Rowlands, 2015.
27 Marquis, 2015: 32.
28 Drévillon, 2005: 191.
29 Jean Chagniot, 1979.
30 Lynn, 1997: 230; Rowlands, 2002.
31 Jean Chagniot, 1991.
32 Rowlands, 2002: 243.
33 Lynn, 1997: 239; Rowlands, 2016.
34 Lynn, 1997: 222.
35 Drévillon, 2005: 129–41.
36 Drévillon, 2005: 385.
37 Drévillon, 2005: 225.
38 Drévillon, 2005: 209.
39 Marquis, 2015: 27.
40 Hervé Drévillon, 2015; Michel Nassiet, 1998.
41 Chaline, 2016: 42.
42 Robert Chaboche, 1973.
43 Drévillon, 2005: 107.
44 Nathalie Genet-Rouffiac, 2015.
45 Jean Nouzille, 2012: 41.
46 Fritz Redlich, 1964: 50; Michael Hochedlinger, 2003 109–114, 140.
47 Thomas M Barker, 1975: 52, 68.
48 Jean Bérenger, 2004: 305.
49 Redlich, 1964: 87.
50 Hochedlinger, 2003: 120.
51 Jean Bérenger, 2005–2006.
52 Nouzille, 2012: 135.
53 Nouzille, 2012: 631.
54 Peter H Wilson, 1998: 14.
55 Wilson, 1998: 41–53.
56 Redlich, 1964: 114.

57 F. L. Carsten, 1959: 421.
58 Redlich, 1964: 156.
59 Redlich, 1964: 229.
60 Carsten, 1959: 239–47.
61 Derek McKay, 2001: 124.
62 McKay, 2001: 173.
63 McKay, 2001: 227.
64 Ragnhild Hatton, 1978: 43–6, 72, 84.
65 Carsten, 1959: 183.
66 Carsten, 1959: 96; James A Vann, 1984: 178.
67 Geoffrey Symcox, 1983: 169.
68 Sabina Loriga, 1991: 85.
69 Davide Maffi, 2006.
70 Fernando Gonzalez de Leon, 2009: 167.
71 Christopher Storrs, 2006.
72 Giuseppe Tricoli, 1980: 47.
73 Davide Maffi, 2010: 48.
74 Jean Meuvret, 1960.
75 Tommaso Astarita, 1982–83.
76 Antonio José Rodriguez Hernandez, 2009.
77 Francisco Andujar Castillo, 1991: 159.
78 John Childs, 1976.
79 Childs, 1976: 176–79.
80 Childs, 1976: 198.
81 Roger Manning, 2006: 359.
82 John M Stapleton, 2007.
83 Manning, 2006: 428; John Childs, 1991.
84 Yves-Marie Bercé, 1974.
85 Jean Quéniart, 1985: 118–28; Janine Garrisson, 1985: 215–37.
86 Giuseppe Galasso, 1982: 221.
87 Gregory Hanlon, 2013.
88 Charles W Ingrao, 1979: 216; Michael Flinn, 1981: 58–61.
89 N.A.M. Rodger, 2004: 43.
90 Jonathan I Israel, 1995: 721; James R Jones, 1996.
91 Rodger, 2004: 57.
92 Rodger, 2004: 68, 106.
93 Jaap Bruijn, 1989.
94 Jaap Bruijn, 2011: 33, 59.
95 Bruijn, 2011: 85.
96 Alan James, 2004.
97 Chaline, 2016: 230.
98 Chaline, 2016: 28.
99 Chaline, 2016: 210.
100 Chaline, 2016: 63.
101 Lynn, 1999: 85.
102 Chaline, 2016: 42.
103 Philip Hoffman, 2015: 20, 66.

8   Ottoman wars in the seventeenth and early eighteenth centuries

End of the classical era after 1610

The Sunni Ottoman state was designed for religious war with the Christian West and with Shi'a Persia, for long-term peace with unbelievers and miscreants was un-Islamic. The sultan declared war by solemnly planting horse-tail standards in Istanbul or in Edirne, but few sultans rode with their armies farther than the hinterland of the capital city. Murad IV, who led his men to the extremely distant Mesopotamian border and captured Baghdad in 1638, constituted the exception. Notwithstanding his success, it became clear that the great hosts of sipahi cavalry and janissary infantry that enabled the Ottoman sultans to expand their empire from Hungary to Morocco and from the Ukraine to Yemen in less than a century lost their decisive edge after 1606. There was a marked decline in the frequency of victory in the seventeenth century that contemporaries could not fail to notice. The principal missing ingredient was money to hire infantry, to cast cannon and to build ships, to stock magazines. According to Philip Hoffman, Ottoman taxes – that is, those destined for the central treasury, were far lower than those levied in Western Europe. There were no mechanisms for borrowing money at low rates of interest (for interest was contrary to Islam, too).[1] Taxes raised by the sultan's servants were always inferior to those of Austria, its major opponent in the West, and most of the resources squeezed from the peasantry and the commercial sectors were channelled into private hands or to local power brokers.[2] Western European states were in the process of concentrating power in the monarchs and elites in capital cities. The Ottoman trend after 1600 was in the opposite direction.

Ottoman military technology did not appear to be markedly inferior to their European adversaries in the first half of the seventeenth century or perhaps later. They were self-sufficient in the production of cannon and powder into the eighteenth century, but were open to Western influences in their use. The artillery corps numbered some 6,000 men in the 1680s. An Italian renegade who built a great foundry in Istanbul helped modernize the artillery. A Venetian deserter at Negroponte in 1688 improved the process of casting and firing mortars.[3] If the Venetians routinely melted down Ottoman guns after capturing them, it was in order to reduce the variety of pieces to a few convenient calibres. Neither did the

Ottomans lag behind Western technology in infantry weapons. Their muskets were longer and heavier than the Western ones, and better steel enabled them to use larger powder charges, which made them more accurate at longer range.[4] These muskets also had a small knife planted in the butt for close combat.[5] By the late seventeenth century, janissaries no longer employed bows, and used muskets and sabres almost exclusively, although sipahis, Tatars and infantry auxiliaries were experienced archers. Turkish cavalry rode smaller steeds than their European adversaries, but they sat more firmly in their saddles and were difficult to unhorse. Cavalry attacked in loose order, seeking an opening to break the enemy formation down into small nuclei for individual combat. Turks still wore chain mail armour and carried shields of wood, but German cavalry wore plate armour, hard enough to deflect arrows and sabre strokes.[6] On the march, Ottoman soldiers lived in big cotton tents, which were much sturdier than the canvas versions in western armies. They raised ablution tents for frequent bathing and dug latrines, both practices uncommon in the West. There was also an execution tent for spies, criminals and often for captives, too. Ottoman camps were not laid out in streets and regular squares like Western armies, but tents were raised in confused order, explained as a way to better defend the position.[7]

Ottoman campaigns could still concentrate and feed as many as 80,000 combatants in one place, plus a large number of camp followers. The Ottomans maintained several military corridors in order to mobilize great armies on distant frontiers. Two great magazines existed near the points of departure, at Edirne (for Hungarian or Ukrainian campaigns) and Salonika (for Greece and its islands). Distances along the routes emanating from them were carefully measured out, with materials on hand for road repair and bridge-building. The nearby populations were obliged to furnish means of transport, while peasants not far away supplied food and fodder. There were also capacious staging magazines in Belgrade (for Hungary) and Bender (for the Ukraine).[8] Tens of thousands of camels ensured supply over long distances, while water buffalo pulled heavy cannon and wagons along primitive roads. Tradesmen and city artisans also accompanied the troops to supply goods and services, to cook, to heal, to purchase slaves and move them out on carts and boats plying the Danube, the Tisza and their tributaries.

Battlefield tactics, on the other hand, remained deeply conservative. The host would assemble in a half-moon formation with the cavalry posted to each wing. Ottoman janissaries employed a marching band with great kettledrums and cymbals, bagpipes and oboes playing in order to create a terrifying din. Despite their considerable firepower, Ottoman tactics relied in large part on hand-to-hand encounters by sabre-wielding soldiers with weak command structures.[9] There were no pikes offering shelter to the lead troops, and they did not employ battalion-style formations. Soldiers, wearing talisman shirts, advanced in a great mass shrieking 'Allah, Allah', hoping to unnerve their adversaries enough to see them flee. The cavalry roved about continually, trying to draw the tight Western formations out of their positions. Combatants ingested opium tablets that gave them a rush of elation and confidence for a half-hour or hour, before the negative effects were felt.[10] Some historians claim that, man for man, Ottoman soldiers were qualitatively and quantitatively superior to their Western adversaries, better fed and benefiting from superior sanitation. If the Ottomans greatly outnumbered their adversaries, they were likely to win.[11] However, the Ottomans never developed bastioned fortifications, or a Western officer corps, and they invested little in military technology or training.[12] Luigi Ferdinando Marsigli, who spent almost two decades observing Ottoman ways of war, doubted that they were, man for man, better than Western soldiers. We need some close scholarship on the dozen or so pitched battles in the two generations after 1660 that looks more closely at the mechanics of operations and tactics from eyewitness sources on both sides.

The breakdown of the timar system was the first notable symptom of military decline. Timar holders and the local kadi judges who assisted them were not participants in local life over generations, as in Western Europe where feudal paternalism was widespread. Both were regularly rotated, with a lack of predictability of tenure. Officials had no particular concern for the local population, who existed only to provide resources. The short terms made office holding in the Ottoman empire a precarious business enterprise requiring bribes. Timars were increasingly left vacant in order to serve as tax farms; that is, a well-placed dignitary would advance cash or provisions to the Porte, and then be assigned a timar in order to reimburse himself. Since money sent to Istanbul replaced compulsory military service, the number of timar holders required to join the army declined to about 20–30,000 in 1610.[13] Marsigli estimated that the timars, with their retainers, could field 65,000 soldiers in 1683, but only a portion of it was sipahi cavalry, whose quality gradually declined along with their revenues.[14] The additional income in the hands of the central government permitted the Grand Viziers to increase the number of janissaries, to provide more musketeer mercenaries and to multiply frontier garrisons.

The janissary institution eroded simultaneously, given the pressure to provide more and more of them. The devshirme was gradually discontinued as a means of recruitment during the seventeenth century. Murad IV commanded the last big levy in 1637, and a smaller one followed in 1663. Only 1,000 boys were raised by this method in 1705. The devshirme was never applied to all non-Moslems in the empire, such as the Romanians (not technically subjects of the sultan), the Greeks and Jews. The most eager to serve, apart from some Italian renegades, were the Albanians, followed by Serbs, Bosnians and Croats.[15] Rather than collecting adolescents who were more or less forcibly taken from their parents, there was a drift towards admitting sons of janissaries and other Moslems, apart from Sunni Arabs, who were not admitted.[16] These recruits acquired a corporate identity and a special tax status, and, across Rumelia, they collected and managed local taxes. There was an ongoing process of voluntary conversion to Islam throughout the Balkans, especially after 1650, by families who hoped thereby to accede to janissary status. After they enlisted, they continued their daily occupations as before and remained part of the rural population.[17] In the army, they prized their special tax-exempt status, and their communal meals with the sultan and the Grand Vizier on the eve of battle.[18] Janissaries enjoyed no restriction to barracks, no compulsory roll-call, and experienced no regular drill or training beyond archery practice. In fact, there did not appear to be a time of military training at all. It was mainly in the field, under the eyes of the veterans, that janissaries learned how to fight.[19] By the seventeenth century, the janissary corps lost its fighting edge and became more like ordinary line infantry possessing basic skills.[20] A corps of household cavalry, which expanded more quickly than the janissaries, numbered some 15,000 troopers in the 1690s.[21] Another serious defect of the janissaries was their tendency to mutiny if the campaign lasted too long, or if their pay was delayed.[22] The mustered fighting force of the sultan's professional infantry may never have exceeded 40,000 men after 1606. The infantry were supposed to number 70,000 in the late seventeenth century, but fewer than half of those would have been fit to fight. Marsigli estimated that there were still 30,000 Janissary soldiers in the field army in 1683, but one Ottoman source claims that only half of these were combatants.[23]

Alongside the sultan's soldiers, the provinces provided ever larger numbers of men who were not quite professionals. Frontier defence relied increasingly on 'azebs', 'levends' or 'sekbans', who were volunteer musketeers paid from provincial funds, often Bosnians and Albanians, reputed to be robust and fierce.[24] While most of these volunteers were mounted troops, they carried long muskets as their principal weapon and fought very much as dragoons did in the West.[25] The Grand Vizier compelled the pashas to join the army with all the forces they could muster: in case of absence or bungling, they would be purged.[26] These tended to enlist private armies assigned to their households in the administrative towns when not on campaign. Pashas resembled military contractors who provided bands of musketeers and light cavalry, reimbursed by the treasury after the campaign. Mercenary volunteers and auxiliaries comprised half the provincial troops in 1609, but two-thirds in 1700, outnumbering the Janissaries.[27] The cavalry equivalent was the akinji light horse recruited from the Balkans or from Vlach frontier tribes, who foraged for booty and captives in lieu of pay. These might number as many as 20,000 men. Auxiliary soldiers were often eager to make their mark in order to be admitted to the janissary corps or granted a timar. However, once demobilized, they often became bandits or henchmen of local officials. To curb rural brigands, called *klephts* in the Balkans, the Ottomans raised armed Christian bands, the 'armatoles', only loosely controlled by the pashas. Klephts and armatoles were largely interchangeable, with the result that lawlessness flourished in the Balkan lands.[28] Under Moslem commanders they also raided the Christian borderlands in Hungary and Venetian Dalmatia. The sultan could still rely on allies to swell his host throughout the seventeenth century. The Tatars, who routinely raided in Russia and the Ukraine, could be bribed into sending contingents to Hungary, occasionally surpassing 20,000 horsemen, but in the field they operated autonomously from the main army.[29] Princes of Wallachia and Moldavia also provided contingents of a few thousand semi-professional soldiers, who were more often spectators than combatants.

The majority of armed men (perhaps only a small majority) were still cavalry, with the prodigious requirements for fodder that that entailed. Given the coming and going of volunteers and auxiliaries, there was no way for an Ottoman commander to know how many men in the army could fight.[30]

Venetian epic in the Mediterranean 1638–1718

Ever since the end of the Lepanto war in the 1570s, relations between the Ottoman Porte and the Venetian Republic were cordial. Italian traders held their own in the Levant commerce alongside their English, Dutch and French competitors until the 1640s.[31] Plagued by recurrent Barbary corsair penetration of the Adriatic Sea in 1638, a Venetian squadron forced its way into Valona harbour in Albania and destroyed a whole fleet in port. This might have served as a convenient *casus belli*, but the Ottoman focus then was on the Iranian enemy. In 1644, however, a Maltese flotilla seized part of the crucial Istanbul–Alexandria convoy carrying members of the sultan's entourage, and put into Venetian Crete for repairs. Malta's flotilla of five or six galleys was supplemented by 20–25 corsair ships under the command of French or Italian owners, often ex-knights.[32] The favourite hunting grounds of both were off the estuary of the Nile in Egypt, which provided rice and other foodstuffs for Istanbul. Greek merchants and seamen could not be enslaved and so were marooned on small islands or abandoned at sea in skiffs. The knights took about 200 captives every year, mostly male Moslems destined to row the galleys, and there might have been as many as 10,000 slaves in its bagno, the highest concentration anywhere in Europe.[33] Alongside the Maltese were the knights of Santo Stefano and corsairs operating out of Tuscan Livorno. The Ottomans maintained a fleet of about 70 or 80 galleys in the 1630s. Most of the oarsmen were captive Ukrainians and Poles, with a sizeable minority of Italians seized at sea or on the coast.[34] But normally, the galleys remained moored in the Arsenal in Istanbul. The galley fleet made an occasional tour of the Aegean islands in order to levy tribute there. Western corsairs in those waters withdrew briefly until the Turks went home. The sultan rented Barbary corsair flotillas to chase interlopers from these strategic channels, but these created havoc by attacking islands inhabited by Ottoman subjects. By the 1620s, the waters of the Greek archipelago were a no-man's-land where corsairs created a permanent climate of insecurity.[35]

Sultan Ibrahim directed his ire towards Malta, the ostensible target of ships collected in the course of 1645. Even in the Ottoman fleet, no-one knew that Crete was the objective until after the armada left port at the end of April. The Republic of Saint Mark suspected that it was the likely target and hastily improved the island's defences. The Ottoman amphibious force reputedly carried 7,000 janissaries, 14,000 sipahis, 50,000 irregulars together with 20,000 miners and pioneers who specialized in siege warfare.[36] The garrison at La Canea was massacred after it surrendered in August, to induce terror in the other strongholds. The Cretan rural militia of 12,000 men melted away and had no more than nuisance value against the Turks. The Venetians collected their own galleys, rented a dozen

Dutch vessels and united with the flotillas of its Mediterranean allies, Malta, the Papacy and Tuscany, but the combined fleet was not large enough to engage the Ottoman navy with any likelihood of success. Part of the problem was that such a coalition entailed negotiating with multiple semi-independent entities, each with its own agenda.[37] In 1646, the Ottomans laid siege to the town and port of Rettimo, which surrendered in November. Husseyn Pasha, in command of the Ottoman fleet and army, blockaded the island's capital and principal port, Candia (modern Heraklion) in the summer of 1647, but began a formal siege of the city only in April 1648. The Venetians had time to improve the city's considerable fortifications, where Italian, French and Dutch engineers built a series of hornworks, using corvée labour, to keep the besiegers far back from the walls. The garrison consisted of several thousand Italians and Greeks, supplied and reinforced by sea. The Ottomans were unable to concentrate many troops there. Venetian countermines slowed down their progress, and, by the end of the season, the attackers numbered only 6,000 men. They undertook another fruitless effort the following year.[38]

Venice prepared for a long war by opening access to coveted patrician status to commoners for 100,000 ducats. By this and other means, the Republic of Saint Mark was still capable of aligning between 30,000 and 35,000 professional soldiers, plus the irregular Croat and Greek forces living in its Adriatic empire.[39] All fit men aged 18–50 were enrolled in the militia under their own leaders. Ottoman armies invaded Dalmatia in 1646, capturing the small port of Novigrad in order to open a second front and divert Venetian resources from Crete. They attacked the larger port of Sebenico the following year, without success. Instead of funnelling their resources into a single besieged city (Candia), the Venetians hit back all along the Balkan frontier. Small contingents of professional Venetian soldiers and Dalmatian militiamen marched for several days deep into Bosnia and Hercegovina, launching surprise attacks on local castles and laying ambushes against the janissaries and militias of the zone.[40] By 1647, these forces immobilized 20,000 Ottoman troops in the Balkans.[41] After 1648, when it became easier to hire mercenaries freshly disbanded in Germany, Venice shipped a steady stream of reinforcements to its beleaguered colonies. Up to 2,000 workers staffed the great arsenal in the capital, while smaller dockyards operated in Corfu and elsewhere.[42]

The Republic's best strategy was to try to choke off supplies and reinforcements for the Ottoman army on Crete, by year-round blockade of the Dardanelles and the west coast of Anatolia. A fleet of sailing ships first attempted this in 1646, but they could not prevent the passage of Ottoman galleys in calm weather. Blockades were a hazardous operation for oared vessels, which were vulnerable to rough seas. Venice lost 18 galleys and nine sailing vessels in a single March storm off the island of Paros in 1648, along with thousands of men. The republic responded by renting Dutch and English armed merchantmen, complete with their crews, and packing them with soldiers. Venice possessed great stocks of weaponry and the means to outfit 65 galleys and several galeasses, which manoeuvred alongside the sailing ships. After several years of false starts, Admiral Giacomo Riva took 19 ships (mostly Dutch, French and English rentals) into Focchies port near Smyrna (modern Izmir) on 12 May 1649 and inflicted heavy losses on the Ottoman convoy. The Ottoman war fleet emerged from the Dardanelles in July 1651, only to be defeated off Santorini, another decisive Venetian victory at sea. They repeated the success off the island of Samos the following year. These were actions of sailing vessels (principally armed merchantmen) with the support of galleys, which kept their role as troop transports and anti-corsair vessels in the Greek archipelago. Venice levied abundant contributions and seamen in Greek waters almost unopposed. The Venetian navy effectively closed the straits between 1654 and 1657, but the strategy worked only partially. It was still possible for the Ottomans to supply and reinforce the besiegers on Crete by hopping the short distance from Chios and western Anatolia, via Rhodes and the few islands they garrisoned.[43] Nevertheless, the Turks could only maintain on average about 15,000 men at Candia, not including their other garrisons on Crete, which were always at risk of a surprise attack.

Unanticipated Venetian resistance greatly disturbed the populace of Istanbul, which suffered, as did countries everywhere, from adverse atmospheric conditions during those years. The giant city was on the verge of continual revolt because, in addition to interrupting the Egyptian convoy, the Venetian navy threatened to penetrate the Sea of Marmara to attack the capital directly. Lacking regular pay, the janissaries in the capital rose and overthrew Sultan Ibrahim, and killed several Grand Viziers in succession, causing general chaos from 1648 to 1656. Under the boy-Sultan Mehmed IV, the finances of the empire were utterly exhausted: estates of rich people and viziers were confiscated, their owners executed.[44] On account of the Venetian blockade of the Dardanelles, prices in the capital soared, although there was never fear of famine, for most foodstuffs arrived by the River Danube and the Black Sea. On 26 June 1656, a great fleet of 98 Ottoman ships was destroyed in the Dardanelles by the Venetian and Maltese squadron under Lorenzo Marcello, and 5,000 Christian slaves were freed. This was the largest Ottoman defeat since Lepanto, which was followed by the occupation of Lemnos and Tenedos, islands controlling the exit of the straits. Defeat triggered unrest in Egypt and Syria and a revolt in Transylvania, all of which diminished the flow of taxes to Istanbul. The bishop of Cetinje in rugged Montenegro connived with foreign powers, and local bands began to ambush Turks.[45] It was not until September 1656 that the Sultana Regent Turhan conferred absolute power on the Albanian vizier Koprulu Mehmed Pasha, who killed hundreds, if not thousands, of janissaries to restore order, as well as officers of the fleet and officials throughout the empire. In the meantime, Venetian success attracted ongoing support from its allies: in 1659, the Papacy provided a flotilla of ten ships and Malta 12 others, still, for the most part, Dutch armed merchantmen carrying Italian and French soldiers.[46] Success revived European crusader instincts and covered the participants in glory. Successive Koprulu Grand Viziers, the elderly and stern Mehmed to 1661, and then his talented son Fazil Ahmed, who eased up on the politics of terror, obtained the first Ottoman successes. In 1657, the Venetians were ejected from Lemnos and Tenedos, thus easing the supply of the Cretan army. New artillery forts were erected in the Dardanelles narrows below Gallipoli, reducing the chances of future enemy penetration. Venetian forces were never strong enough at Candia to chase the Turks from their trenches, so a long stalemate ensued. The Ottomans were then distracted from the theatre between 1658 and 1664 by events in Transylvania and Hungary that required their attention.

In 1667, the Grand Vizier Fazil Ahmed Pasha landed in person and made the complete conquest of Crete a priority once more. The combat before Candia was more than a mere siege if only because of its vast scale. Between May and November, the Ottomans exploded 618 mines (three daily) and launched 32 attacks. The Venetians sallied forth 17 times, but lost 3,500 dead contesting the place. Anyone who fell captive to the besiegers was quickly beheaded. The defenders created a new kind of unit for close assault, elite grenade-throwing infantry, who became common across Europe.[47] Whenever the defenders received a relief convoy, they raised their banners, fired noisy salutes, beat the drums and sounded the trumpets in triumph, whose effect was to demoralize the Turks still more, whose trenches were still out of range of the walls.[48] Continual replenishment of the garrison and abundant provisions meant that the defenders could explode powerful mines under the Turkish trenches, allegedly killing thousands at a time. Pitch and naptha illumination revealed Ottoman troops burrowing towards the outworks at night.

In 1668, a Cretan–Venetian engineer, Andrea Barozzi, passed over to the Ottomans with plans of the fortress, and convinced the Vizier to shift the attacks to the seaward bastions where the exposed rock was free of Venetian mine tunnels (Image 8.1). He taught the Ottomans to dig long trenches that could be more easily defended, and widened them so that cannon could be brought closer to the ramparts.[49] That year saw the Venetians and their allies lose 7,000 soldiers, 2,400 oarsmen and 400 civilians. Only a continuous supply of troops from Italy and Germany could keep the defence going, under the direction of Francesco Morosini. Over the winter of 1668–1669, the Ottomans multiplied their batteries of heavy cannon and mortars, whose constant bombardment gradually destroyed the city (and made it unhealthy for the garrison). They mined and demolished two of the city's bastions, and multiplied murderous assaults of infantry wielding sabres. A French contingent of 7,000 men under the Papal flag arriving in 1669 looked as if it might save the city, but, against the advice of experienced Venetians, they launched a sortie headlong against the Ottoman trenches. The besiegers learned to give way to the initial assault in order to draw the attackers farther out, before turning on them with overwhelming numbers. After losing the commander and almost a thousand men, the contingent withdrew not long after. On 27 September 1669, Morosini surrendered what remained of the fortress, fearful of wholesale slaughter of his garrison if the Ottomans carried off a successful storm. The last three years of the siege resulted in over 100,000 Ottoman dead and 29,000 Christian fatalities, of whom 280 were Venetian patricians, equal to a quarter of the ruling

Image 8.1 Antoine de Fer: Siege of Candia 1669, BNF Registre C 19375 (16). For two decades, the Ottoman approaches from the right gradually demolished the city's massive walls. A Venetian renegade engineer convinced the Grand Vizier to make his approaches in the rocky ground close to the port, on the left. The dots at the end of lines emerging from the walls represent pre-positioned mine chambers

group.[50] Fighting continued in Bosnia until the following year. By the final treaty, the Venetians managed to retain some coastal fortifications on Crete.

The peace did not change the balance of power in the region, because Venice retained naval superiority. Corsairs in Aegean waters flourished in the absence of an Ottoman administration. A score of large Western corsair ships operated with impunity, often manned by French and Venetian subjects sailing under Maltese or Papal banners.[51] After a pause of little more than a decade, in which the Republic paid off most of its debt, the Venetians, in 1684, joined the Empire and Poland against the Turks to recover the island. Starting in the 1660s, Venice built a modest flotilla of purpose-built warships, like England, the Netherlands and France. The first fleet, under Francesco Morosini, consisted of 24 ships (14 of which were ships of the line), six galeasses and 28 galleys. They could count on the Maltese galley flotilla of 7–8 units and several warships operated by the Knights of Saint John as well as the Tuscan Knights of Santo Stefano. The fleet and its transports ferried a sizeable polyglot army of Venetian troops (Italians, Croatians and Greeks), along with Brunswickers and Saxons hired from German princes and Lombards released by the king of Spain. Malta, the Papacy and Tuscany provided 2,000 additional men. Venice's total amphibious forces numbered between 25,000 and 30,000 men, of whom 16,000 were infantry, half Italian and Slav, and the other half mercenaries rented from Brunswick, Hanover and other German Protestant states. In addition to the professional troops and naval vessels, Christian corsairs (mostly French) circulated among the Greek islands, levying contributions and bringing maritime commerce to a halt.[52] The Ottoman administration virtually vanished from these territories for the duration of the war. The period 1660–1690 constituted the high-water mark for several thousand Christian pirates and corsairs in the Aegean, who greatly resembled their Caribbean counterparts. In the islands, they could repair their ships and purchase stores, hide their captives and organize ransoms, divide or sell their booty.[53] Louis Sicking compares them to land-based military entrepreneurs who extended the military capacity of the Republic of Saint Mark.

The Italian professional soldiers were drawn not just from the Venetian Terraferma, but also from Corsica and the entire Adriatic watershed of Italy. Periodically, the Republic paid for pressed men from the Dukes of Parma and Modena. It also purchased outlaw gangs from the Kingdom of Naples for service in Dalmatia.[54] The Ultramarine troops (Oltremarini, that is, from across the sea) were Venetian subjects principally, but not exclusively, Croats and Morlacchi Vlachs, as well as Montenegrins and Albanians, used as light infantry and shock troops. The Venetian light cavalry (about 600 men, often Albanians called *stradiotti*) joined with insurgent Greeks and Macedonians, sacking Ottoman towns and villages and waging guerrilla war in Bosnia. Unable to recapture Crete, which was too strongly garrisoned, the fleet began to occupy the ports of the Morea (Peloponnesis peninsula). At Koron in 1685, the soldiers lost their discipline and slaughtered up to 3,000 surrendering Ottomans. This success triggered a Greek revolt against their Moslem overlords that spread outward.[55] Navarino was captured with the help of new bomb-ketches, galeots firing mortars. With its fall, the Ottomans retired to Thebes on the mainland. Athens, which was a secondary city in the seventeenth century, fell to the Venetians in 1687: a lucky mortar shot on the Parthenon, where the Turks stored their ammunition, produced the ruin we see today.[56] By the late 1680s, Christian populations rose in rebellion across Epirus (north-western Greece), the Morea, and then Albania. Thousands of Greek irregulars marched with and beyond the Venetian troops, pinning down Ottoman garrisons and intercepting supplies. Morosini's first failure was Negroponte (modern Euboea) in 1688, following an outbreak of contagious disease that killed and incapacitated both the landing force and the seamen and galley crews.

After 1690, when Austrian armies were redirected away from the Danube, the Turks were able to allocate more resources to the Mediterranean theatre, and so Venetian successes ceased entirely. Morosini died early in 1694 and was succeeded by lesser lights. The Ottomans built modern warships in the yards of Istanbul, under the direction of Admiral Huseyin Pasha, known as Mezzomorto. In 1694, Venice sent a large fleet of 34 galleys, six galeasses and 21 warships to the large island of Chios, just off the western coast of Anatolia. There they were forced to fight indecisive fleet battles against the Ottomans, in 1694, 1695 and 1697. In the first of these, they required at least 3,000 soldiers to serve on the 28 ships and the galleys, against 40 Ottoman vessels. Several major vessels were blown up or captured in the bloody engagements. Chios had to be abandoned in 1695, and there were no new conquests until the final peace of 1699 that awarded Venice all of the Morea (Map 6).[57]

The Morean population was loyal enough to their new Venetian masters at first, despite their irritating habit of raising the minority of Greek Catholics to command over the majority Orthodox population. Worse, the Venetians were much more efficient than the Turks at collecting taxes, which the Greeks deeply resented. Venice transformed the Ottoman castles and medieval town walls into state-of-the-art bastioned fortresses at Arcocorinth, Nauplia, Modon and Koron. The Venetian peacetime army was refashioned into 18 Italian and 11 Ultramarine regiments totalling almost 25,000 men, equal to about one per cent of the

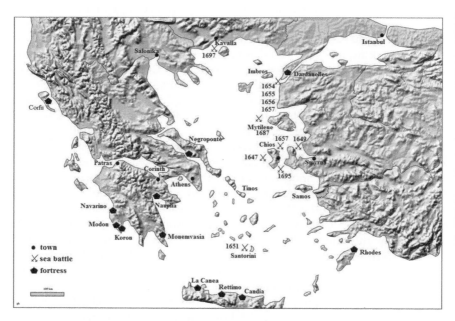

Map 6 The Aegean Theatre 1645–1699

empire's population. The infantry adopted fusil muskets and bayonets and wore uniforms. There was only one regiment of real cavalry, not much used, but several regiments of light cavalry served in the Greek and Albanian manner. The artillery was abundant and well served.[58] Since the Republic's standing army had to be scattered in garrisons across north-eastern Italy, and along the Croatian coast, only a few thousand were based in the Morea.

The Ottomans were never reconciled to losing the Morea in the heart of their Greek territories, which made the Dardanelles vulnerable to blockade. After 1699, ever more Montenegrins refused to pay tribute to the Turks, which was prelude to a religious uprising in 1711. Thousands of Orthodox refugees swarmed into Venetian territory, where they organized further resistance. The Venetians refused to arm and supply them, fearing a new war with the Ottoman Empire. The Turks fought a brief, successful war against Peter the Great and Russia in 1711, recapturing land in the Ukraine they had lost in 1699. In the aftermath, they collected a fleet of warships and assembled an army of 60,000 infantry and 15,000 cavalry at Salonika in 1715. An Ottoman fleet of 58 ships and 30 galleys repelled 19 Venetian ships and 15 galleys off the Morea coast, cutting the demoralized garrisons off from reinforcements. At Arcocorinth and Nauplia, the Grand Vizier could not restrain his janissaries from a rush to pillage the towns, where civilians and soldiers were massacred. At Nauplia, the Grand Vizier decided to behead the prisoners in order to spread terror in the remaining outposts. Despite desertion and heavy losses in uncoordinated attacks, the Ottomans recaptured all the Morea fortresses in just a hundred days. The Turks relied increasingly on Albanian irregular troops, ferocious and undisciplined to the point of creating havoc. Control broke down over enslaving the local population and enforcing the conditions of capitulation.[59] Ottoman authorities also beheaded apostates, formerly Moslem peasants who, instead of emigrating, remained under Venetian rule and converted to Christianity.[60]

In 1716, the confident Ottomans dispatched an army of 55,000 men to capture Corfu, the last and most important of the Greek possessions of the Republic. The outer works of the powerful fortress fell to the besiegers, but the Ottoman navy of 72 sailing ships (50 ships of the line) fought Venice's 27 vessels to a draw. Galleys, after 1700, receded in importance and played only a marginal role in naval battles. Later, more Venetian, Papal and allied warships arrived to reinforce the fortress. Despite its massive fortifications and its abundant artillery, Corfu might have fallen had the entry of Austria into the war not forced the Turks to lift the siege in August. In the aftermath, Venetian and allied warships and galleys numbering 60 units fought two multi-day naval battles with the Ottoman navy of comparable size off the Dardanelles and Cape Matapan, with heavy casualties on both sides.[61] At the peace of 1718, Venice retained Corfu and some coastal villages in Epirus, but the rest of its Greek empire vanished.

New Hungary wars

After the Peace of 1606, the Habsburgs relied on their militia auxiliaries to defend the 1,000 kilometres of frontier with the Turks that Jean Nouzille calls the 'Iron Curtain of Christendom'. This band of territory, detached from royal Hungary 30–90 kilometres deep, stretching from the Adriatic Sea to the Carpathian Mountains, was inhabited mainly by Serbian Orthodox refugees from the Balkans.[62] Peasant freedom there attracted serfs from Hungarian and Croatian estates, infuriating the kingdom's magnates. These irregulars formed a light infantry the Germans called *grenzers*, who protected their districts from Ottoman raids and then carried the war into Bosnia and Ottoman Hungary. On the Christian side of the border, villages were often abandoned due to insecurity and few communities had permanent houses. People tried to protect themselves from raiders on horseback by barricading themselves in churches or castles.[63] On the Ottoman side, janissaries received pay from the treasury, but irregular soldiers and auxiliaries relied on raiding for a living.[64] These forays were clear violations of the treaty, but the ghazi tradition of holy war against miscreants was irrepressible. Ransom slavery reached its peak in Hungary in the decades prior to 1663. Many men were ready to participate, in the hope of bringing home rich captives. Prisoners able to pay a steep ransom were confined to forts and towns not too far from the border. Poor captives were simply shipped off to Sarajevo or Istanbul to be sold as slaves. Considerable numbers of captives were taken by Tatars or by local irregular bands of armed men. Auxiliary Tatars scoured Transylvania and Slovakia and ventured as far west as Moravia in 1658, 1660, 1663 and 1683. The last raid by Tatars, in 1717, carried off 1,500 people. Following each of these sweeps, captives were sold at Buda or in the river ports along the Danube or the Tisza, from where they were shipped to Anatolia. Common soldiers taking prisoners could not afford to pay gaolers to keep them during the period of negotiation, so officers and district leaders bought them up in the meantime. Some prisoners found freedom by converting to the religion of their captors. Catholic charity encouraged people to contribute money to redeem captives in Moslem lands: there were boxes for this purpose in thousands of churches. There were also mutual prisoner exchanges for people of equal value, similar to mechanisms already common in Western Europe. A captive would be released often after their relatives paid only a deposit (about half), letting them pay the rest upon their return home. A customary law also developed based on reciprocity that forbade either side from torturing prisoners excessively to extract money from them.[65] Similar slaving practices continued on a large scale east of the Carpathians. Duties on Russian, Polish and Circassian slaves collected in the Crimea by the Tatars were very high, and well recorded. After 1650, the Russians and Poles reduced the onslaught of Tatar raiders by turning to Cossaks and Kalmuks to defend the frontiers. When Ottoman and Tatar raiders moved into Russian lands, authorities herded tens of thousands of people away from the frontier. The Belgorod line of wooded and earthen fortifications erected across the steppe in 1679–1680 ran for 530 kilometres.[66] Smaller numbers of Moslems fell into Christian hands and were ransomed similarly; their treatment could vary considerably depending upon the personality of their captor.[67]

Poland descended into chaos in 1648 in the aftermath of a Cossack revolt. In the subsequent decade, the kingdom's weakness attracted Swedish and Brandenburg armies seeking permanent conquest. Revolt in Turkey itself, and the collapse of Ottoman finances in the early 1650s led Istanbul to 'rotate' the Romanian princes on the edge of the empire, sometimes confiscating their estates and executing them, like the viziers. The Prince of Transylvania, Ferenc Rakoczi, joined the fray in 1655, hoping to be elected King of Poland, but the Ottomans ordered him to desist. Impressed by the inability of the Turks to capture Venetian Candia, the prince ceased paying the annual tribute to Istanbul in the wake of momentous unrest in the Ottoman Empire, thinking the Porte was too weak to force him to comply. Then he invaded the Romanian principalities of Wallachia and Moldavia. There was a feeling in Balkan Christendom that the Moslem empire would soon collapse.[68] Grand Vizier Mehmed Koprulu decided to make an example of Transylvania in order to prevent further centrifugal forces from breaking the empire apart. The prince of Transylvania typically employed a small mercenary army of several thousand German soldiers, and Rakoczi raised a feudal army drawn from the Magyar and German population. They were no match for the Ottoman invasion of 1658 and 1659. Large numbers of ethnic Hungarians were captured in order to teach the rebellious principality a lesson; 4,000 were seized in just one place, Tremblova. So many captives were taken that it might have finally shifted the ethnic balance of the region in favour of Orthodox Romanians. The Transylvanians elected a new prince, Janos Kemeny, in 1661 and carried on the war, but he was killed the following year and the Porte's new champion, Mihail Apafy, restored Ottoman suzerainty.

Into this maelstrom, Emperor Leopold I sent his leading general, Raimondo Montecuccoli, in 1662, with an army too small to turn the tide. Transylvania was too far from Vienna to control effectively, and, lacking adequate provisions, Imperial troops retreated. The emperor and his leading minister, Count Portia, detested war and would rather have negotiated with the Ottomans, but they were conspicuous for their lack of diplomatic acumen and provoked the Turks to retaliate for their interference.[69] Emperor Leopold I pursued what many considered to be a wrongheaded programme of Counter-Reformation Catholicism and absolutism in central Europe, and wished to reduce Hungary to the level of Bohemia, whose autonomy had been crushed in 1620. The powerful feudal families were often Protestants and jealous of their prerogatives. Leopold aimed to transform the constitution of the kingdom of Hungary, whose monarchs were elected and whose nobles met continually to limit royal power, as in Poland. The result was that the Hungarian nobles were always on the edge of open revolt. Leopold was also wilfully blind with regard to the Turkish threat. He disbanded several regiments from his service in 1661, even while the fighting raged in Transylvania.

For a century and a half following the Habsburg takeover of eastern and northern Hungary, the magnates provided few men and negligible tax resources to the emperor.[70] When war finally erupted between the Ottomans and the

Habsburgs in 1663, many Hungarian magnates refused to cooperate with Leopold or his field marshals. They proposed a levée en masse, or *insurrection*, by the nobility with their retainers, mounted *hussars* and infantry *haiduks*. In 1663, only 28,000 professional soldiers were available in Hungary to serve in field armies, against perhaps 80,000 Ottomans. Fortunately, it took the Ottoman army 119 days to march from Istanbul to Esztergom, their advance base. Montecuccoli, leading barely 5,000 men, developed an intense dislike of Hungarians who hampered his operations and refused to help his troops.[71] The magnates raised a force of 8,500 cavalry and haiduks under Miklos Zrinyi at Zrinivar, a makeshift stronghold hundreds of kilometres south-west of the main threat in Upper Hungary. This division of forces and command enabled the Turks to capture the bastioned fortress of Neuhausel (Nove Zamky in Slovakia) after a two-month siege, and then to lay waste to the Moravian frontier, collecting booty and slaves less than 100 kilometres from Vienna. In January–February 1664, Zrinyi threw 25,000 Hungarians, Croats and Germans against the strategic Ottoman bridge at Osijek, a round trip of 500 kilometres, without accomplishing anything significant.

In the spring of 1664, with the assistance of Reichs Contingents from western Germany, Emperor Leopold mustered 90,000 men for the entire theatre, of whom 36,000 infantry and 15,000 horse were divided into three distinct field armies widely separated from each other. Miklos Zrinyi commanded a force covering his native Croatia; the marshal Souches operated in Upper Hungary (modern Slovakia) and the third army blocked the Danube avenue towards Vienna. Its commander, Raimondo Montecuccoli, waited for the main Ottoman army behind the narrow River Raab with only 25,000 men, widely dispersed, including a contingent of 6,000 French soldiers sent by Louis XIV. An Ottoman army, allegedly 100,000 strong, captured Zrinivar and dispersed the Croatian force in a siege of 20 days, demolishing the fortifications there and the palanka forts in the vicinity. The diminished host then proceeded north along the Raba river valley, taking captives and plundering villages. Montecuccoli's force marched parallel to them, as far as the monastery of Saint Gotthard. We have two concordant accounts of the event, from the French contingent commander, Coligny, and from an Ottoman participant, Evliya Chelebi. On 1 August 1664, the Turks advanced units across the river and threw up semi-circular earthworks to protect their position. Troops built a bridge to enable the rest of the army to join them, but battle was not anticipated that day and many men were dispersed in raiding and foraging parties. An advance force of sipahis on the wings with janissaries in the centre surged beyond the bridgehead to the sound of drums and trumpets and stormed the Hanoverian troops nearby, who froze on the spot and let themselves be slaughtered. Men withdrew from the firing line to bring severed heads to the Grand Vizier across the river for reward while others dispersed to loot the nearby village of Mogersdorf. A gap of almost two kilometres opened in the Christian line. Coligny's French troops and German cavalry appeared at that juncture, hemming in the Ottoman advance, while Montecuccoli deployed infantry to the left and the right of the gap.

Concentrating their forces, Christians formed two lines of infantry about two kilometres across with just 12–13,000 men. These advanced unhurriedly, in good order, firing in salvos. The sipahis and sekban infantry collapsed first, followed by the janissaries, who retired across their earthworks to the bridge, which then collapsed under the weight of the crowd. Luckily for Montecuccoli, recent rain had swollen the River Raba, making it impossible for the Ottomans to advance reinforcements across the river, or to enable those facing the Christians to retreat. Many of the invaders drowned in the swollen stream, while the Christians shot at them from the bank, then turned about, dropped their breeches and slapped their bare buttocks to taunt their victims – 'hey, Turks!' Coligny counted 6,000 Ottomans killed in the battle, approximately ten per cent of their force, but including their best troops. Christian losses were 5,000, a much larger proportion of their force, and many more soldiers died of disease in their camp in the aftermath.[72] Saint Gotthard was the first significant victory of Western troops against the Ottomans in a field battle in centuries, but it was a defensive success only, acquired by luck as well as superior tactics and organization. Emperor Leopold was happy to make peace with the Ottomans at Vasvar only days later, relinquishing to them the fortresses of Neuhausel and Varad (modern Oradea).[73]

Leopold's hurried peace enraged the Hungarian magnates. They and the Transylvanian nobles dreamed of a great coalition that would drive out the hated Germans and restore the medieval kingdom, even as an Ottoman protectorate. Several leading dignitaries around Petar Zriny and Fran Krsto Frankopan, with the support of hundreds of nobles, planned a rebellion to expel the Habsburgs. Emperor Leopold had Zriny, Frankopan and two other magnate leaders executed for treason in 1671. Habsburg rule was anchored by some 47 fortifications in 1674, with garrisons numbering 13,000 men.[74] Leopold used the planned rebellion to repudiate the medieval Hungarian constitution of elected monarchy and the right of armed resistance, intent on imposing instead hereditary Habsburg rule and Counter-Reformation Catholicism. Hundreds of Protestant ministers were arrested and sentenced to row on the galleys of Naples. 'Malcontent' or *kuruç* rebels massed on the north-eastern fringes of Hungary and began to loot churches and castles. Montecuccoli's army was deployed against this anti-German and anti-Habsburg movement. When Leopold entered the Dutch war against France in 1675, Louis XIV sent money and other assistance to the rebels from Poland, while Mihail Apafi, Prince of Transylvania, sent thousands of soldiers to assist the Malcontents, but they could not prevail against professional soldiers.

The Ottomans went from success to success under the Koprulu Grand Viziers in the 1660s and 1670s, first against Crete, then Hungary and finally Poland. The siege of Candia had sharpened the Ottoman abilities at besieging strong fortresses. In 1672, a large army supported by Tatars and 15,000 Cossacks invaded south-east Poland, captured the modern fortress of Kamenec and advanced almost as far as Lemberg (modern Lvov), one of the kingdom's principal cities. The Polish general, Jan Sobieski, slowed down their advance by a local victory at Chotin, but it was a brief success. The Polish royal army was pitifully small by design of the kingdom's magnates, who relied on an 'insurrectio' of feudal troops to counter invasions. Sobieski's victory led to his election as king in 1674. The Ottomans conquered the district of Podolia (today in northwest Ukraine), which they retained in the peace of 1676. Fazil Ahmed Koprulu, the Grand Vizier, died soon after, having achieved the greatest extension of the Ottoman empire. Kara Mustafa Pasha, who had married a Koprulu daughter, succeeded him to the position. He successfully repelled a Cossack attack in the Ukraine in 1678.

A fresh rebellion of Hungarian nobles against Emperor Leopold, under Imre Thokoly, drew support from the Grand Vizier, Kara Mustafa, whose aim was to reconstitute a Hungarian kingdom under Ottoman suzerainty. Mihail Apafi sent over 5,000 Transylvanians to reinforce Thokoly's insurgent army and Habsburg rule collapsed outside the fortress towns.[75] Mobile rebel armies dominated all of eastern Hungary in 1681, and the next year they raided Moravia and Silesia, almost to the gates of Vienna. In 1682 the sultan declared war on the emperor and Kara Mustafa prepared a new army for the following year. The private armies of rebel Hungarian aristocrats provided about 10,000–12,000 men, but consisting principally of haiduk infantry and hussar cavalry without siege equipment.[76] Leopold had retained in service many veterans of the recent Dutch War that ended in 1678, who were able to staff some 20 new regiments. The Imperial Diet voted to raise Reichs Contingents who would fight under Imperial command alongside the Emperor's regiments. Pope Innocent XI then worked to create a league of crusading states to overwhelm the Ottomans everywhere. The Papacy sent considerable sums of cash to assist the levy of soldiers in Vienna and Warsaw, a Habsburg ally, equal to about ten per cent of total military expenses. Spain and Italian principalities also sent money and supplies to assist the cause, while hundreds of nobles and aristocratic volunteers from much of Europe (including a young Franco-Italian aristocrat, Eugene of Savoy) converged on Austria to offer their services. This Imperial army, while consisting mainly of German troops, was led by officers who were Catholic, first and foremost: the titular head of the army was the Virgin Mary.[77]

Kara Mustafa made an exceptional effort to assemble the largest Ottoman force ever in Hungary, estimated at over 100,000 combatants, although not all were deployed in the principal field army. As many as 40,000 janissaries, and about the same number of provincial troops, converged on the theatre from Istanbul and the Balkan forts. Egypt and Syria sent 6,000 elite troops, and an equal number of soldiers in the Grand Vizier's retinue marched from Istanbul along with 2,000 elite janissaries under their commander, the Aga. This vast army and its camp followers reached the forward base of Osijek, near the Danube between Belgrade and Buda, on 2 June. Tens of thousands of Tatars and the Hungarian cavalry under Thokoly joined the force, before dispersing to attack the Habsburgs over a wide arc. Romanian contingents from Moldavia and Wallachia, probably limited to a few thousand horsemen, joined the host out of obligation. They were looking for ways to join the Christians, and

confined their activities to blockading German fortresses on the flanks or building palanka forts and bridges.[78] Vienna was not revealed to be the principal
Ottoman target until the army reached Buda. With so many men, it was possible
to bypass and screen the fortress of Raab, held by a mere 750 men and march
directly into Germany. Kara Mustafa moved slowly towards the target and gave
time for the capital city to prepare its defences.[79]

The Christian forces in Hungary in 1683 numbered, on paper, 45,000 foot
and 17,500 horse, plus the grenzers on the Hungarian frontier. At Pressburg
early in the campaign, it was possible to parade a field army of only 21,600
infantry and 11,000 cavalry, whose leaders quarrelled. Once the Turks passed
the River Raba, panic seized Vienna and the emperor thought it judicious to
flee up the Danube to Linz.[80] The city garrison numbered 10,000 professional
soldiers and a few thousand militiamen, who placed over 300 cannon on the
ramparts, with abundant provisions and ammunition. The extensive suburbs
were quickly demolished.[81] Kara Mustafa had decided to leave the heavy artillery
behind and to tackle the Viennese fortifications using professional miners. Despite having learned much from the Candia siege, their saps, or trenches, were
not well designed, being enfiladed in many places. The trenches, while deep,
were too narrow to drag cannon closer to the walls to erect batteries at close
range as Western armies did, so the artillery remained in batteries to the rear.[82]
Cavalry scoured the district to feed the animals, and helped prepare gabions, fascines and sandbags to protect the saps. Armed with sabres and bows they also
participated in storming parties.

By themselves, the Habsburg lands in Germany and Bohemia numbered
fewer than six million inhabitants, and the rebellious Hungarians under
two million more.[83] German Reichs Contingents were absolutely critical to the
defence of the empire, but they required time to assemble. The saviour was Jan
Sobieski, King of Poland, who had long experience of fighting the Turks: they
had decapitated his brother and grandfather on the battlefield. Sobieski's ambition was to create a strike force of heavy Polish hussar cavalry (who sported
winged armour).[84] He was able to bring 20,000 men from Krakow to join the
Germans assembled under Prince Louis of Baden at Tulln, 30 kilometres
upstream from Vienna, constituting a combined force of more than 65,000
men. They arrived just in time. Vienna's garrison fought stubbornly for 59 days,
inflicting heavy casualties on the besiegers, but the losses mounted week after
week. By 11 September, the Ottomans had demolished a ravelin and created
breaches in two bastions. Kara Mustafa came within a day or two of forcing the
city's last defences, accelerating the pressure with repeat assaults up the crum-
bling bastions. The Grand Vizier proved excessively overconfident in that he
neglected to erect lines of circumvallation to protect his camp. His screening
force of 6,000 men was inadequate to hold back the Imperial and Polish troops
as they converged upriver on the Danube above Vienna, where they were soon
joined by Reichs Contingents from Saxony and Bavaria. When, on 12 September, the Christian horse and foot occupied the heights of Kahlenberg overlooking the city from the north, the Grand Vizier deployed only 28,000

uncoordinated men to stop them. Two months' siege had reduced the Ottoman army considerably, as poor hygiene and the burial of corpses in shallow graves made conditions in the camp intolerable.[85] The Tatars, the Hungarian rebels and the contingents of Wallachians and Moldavians who assisted the Ottomans left the camp just before the decisive fight. Soldiers began to behead the male captives on the edge of the Ottoman camp, and moved the captive women and children away from the city. Once the Poles and Germans broke through the Ottoman line and descended on the camp, the Turkish rout was complete (Image 8.2). Nevertheless, in those two months, some 40,000 to 70,000 people had been carried off from Lower Austria alone, leaving another 30,000 dead among the civilians.[86] The Christians purportedly slaughtered 3,000 Ottoman sick and injured left behind.

Christian success in 1683 was total, as the Ottoman army scurried downstream to reform. Kara Mustafa blamed his subordinates for the defeat and executed about 50 of them, but he was himself strangled before the year was out. Thokoly's Hungarian rebels retreated, too, for they relied entirely on Turkish support. The Danube fortress of Esztergom fell to the Habsburgs in October, opening the way to Buda. In 1684, General Caprara took a field army to recover Upper Hungary from the rebels, who escaped into Ottoman territory. Jan Sobieski, with Polish troops, pressed hard to recover Podolia, hoping to occupy Moldavia, too. The Venetians launched amphibious attacks in the Aegean Sea and along the Montenegrin coast. The Habsburg army, the strongest contingent in the alliance, began to unfurl over the great Danubian plain. Neuhausel fell to the Imperials in 1685, who slaughtered most of the Ottoman garrison. In 1686, Buda fell to the Germans for the first time, after a long and bloody siege unfolding in the presence of an Ottoman relief army unable to pierce the lines. The Ottoman garrison relied on strong sorties armed with grenades and sabres, but they could not withstand the German battery fire. At Buda, too, most of the garrison was slaughtered or reduced to slavery. German troops won a field battle near Mohacs the following year, butchering some 20,000 Ottomans (Image 8.3). Western military specialists such as Marsigli, noted that Turkish troops were unable to withstand Western troops in good order.[87] On the defensive, the German infantry fought behind movable barriers, 'Spanish riders' or 'chevaux de frise', which were a spear-and-beam assembly that allowed the men behind them to fire uninterruptedly.[88] German musketeers used bayonets, but pikemen served, too, at close quarters, until 1703. The Imperials interspersed drilled infantry formations with squadrons of armoured cavalry that rushed the Ottoman foot. Western troops were trained to verbal commands and to drum beats, and could quickly shift from column into a firing line. They obeyed elaborate signals given by flags and drums. They fired disciplined volleys at increasingly shorter intervals, and they used the bayonet to good advantage. Against the sipahis, European cavalry retained enough heavy armour to protect themselves from arrows and sabres and manoeuvred in tight squadrons to avoid being surrounded.[89] Horsemen constituted about a third of the field army in the 1690s, a superior proportion relative to the West. Most of all, German troops were more numerous than ever before; in 1690, on paper, the Imperial soldiers numbered

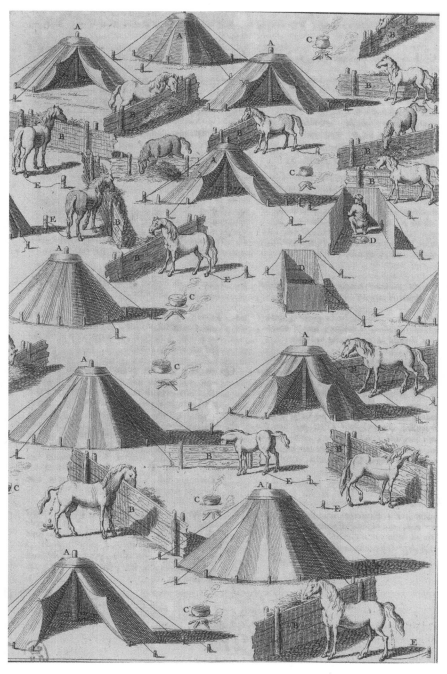

Image 8.2 Luigi Ferdinando Marsigli: Camp turc, Etat militaire de l'Empire Ottoman, Amsterdam 1732, BNF 41612558, p. 80. The presence of non-combatants in Ottoman field armies swelled the size of the encampment, which was not laid out in neat rows like those of Western armies

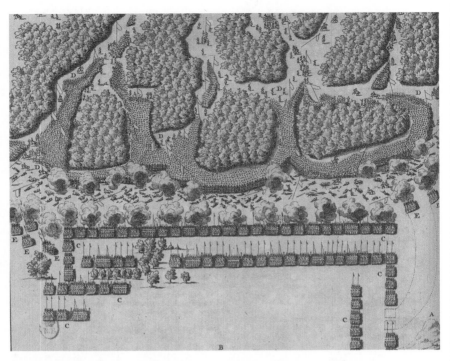

Image 8.3 Marsigli: Second battle of Mohacs 12 August 1687, Etat militaire de l'Empire Ottoman, Amsterdam 1732, BNF 41612558, Planche XXVIII, description vol. 2, 89-90. Note the contrast between the great crowd of Ottoman combatants at the edge of the woods and the tight German formations pressing them back. The disparity of fatal casualties was ten to one in favour of the Imperial army and its Reichs Contingent allies

63,000 men, plus another 40,000 from the Reichs Contingents.[90] By 1687, Habsburg armies had recovered most of the rebel strongholds and Ottoman Hungary, too. Emperor Leopold, who had suspended his policy of forced religious conversion, felt the time was ripe to impose his views on the kingdom at a Diet in Pressburg. The Hungarian Crown was declared hereditary in the Habsburg male and female line. In 1697, Transylvania also ceased to be an autonomous principality; its towns were occupied by German troops and the Counter-Reformation priests and friars soon joined the soldiers.

The German soldiers were poorly supplied and were forced to live from plunder and contributions, since the Austrian lands lacked an efficient bureaucracy compared to other states. Imperial soldiers were the worst paid in all of Germany, and the wages suffered long delays.[91] General Antonio Carafa, in particular, was notorious for his brutality against recalcitrant town councils consisting of Magyar Protestants who wintered his troops. At Eperjes (modern Presov), he hanged a score of town dignitaries for disloyalty. Leopold also angered the nobility by rewarding his generals with great estates in conquered lands, which were almost completely deserted at the time. The Serbs tended to be hostile to the Magyar feudal lords and never joined the rebellions.[92] The wars occasioned massive population shifts; some 130,000 Slavonian and Croatian Muslims were uprooted from their homes and were driven into the Balkans.[93] Those taken captive by the Germans were condemned to build fortifications. Simultaneously, tens of thousands of Serbian, Bulgarian and Albanian Christians moved north, leaving the depopulated Serbian heartland of Kosovo to be resettled by Moslem Albanians. Large zones of the Balkan peninsula lost half their population.

Hungary was a difficult theatre for armies, because rain swelled the rivers and water covered much of the vast, sparsely populated plain, making malaria a problem. The Ottomans, now reliant on their fortifications to slow down Habsburg progress, had fallen far behind their adversaries in this regard. The Ottomans were content to repair the Byzantine and Hungarian medieval fortresses, rectangular castles. At best, the Ottomans added circular artillery platforms to medieval walls. The palanka fortifications of wood and earth were not designed to resist for very long.[94] In the early 1690s, French engineers arrived to help modernize the Ottoman fortifications, but it was too late. In 1689, it was the turn of Belgrade to fall, enabling the Habsburg columns to penetrate Kosovo and march as far south as Macedonia. A small army under General Piccolomini reached Prizren and was rapturously received by Christian populations. He marched as far as Skopje in Macedonia, which he set ablaze. However, an alliance with Serbs and Albanian Christians fell apart when the Ottomans regrouped. The Turks were still adept at cutting off and destroying smaller detachments, if they fell victim to faulty intelligence or poor reconnoitring. After more Habsburg troops were withdrawn to the west, the theatre stabilized.[95]

In 1690, Emperor Leopold shifted troops to Italy and to the Rhine to confront a new offensive by Louis XIV, which placed the Habsburg armies in Hungary on the defensive. The new Grand Vizier, Fazil Mustafa Koprulu, displayed conspicuous military talent. The Ottomans advanced, retaking Nis and then Belgrade without difficulty in 1690. After they recovered the key Danube fortress of Vidin, they pushed the Germans back into Transylvania. Even outnumbered, the Imperials could inflict severe defeats on Ottoman armies, as at Slankamen in August 1691, where the Grand Vizier was killed. East of the Carpathian mountains, Jan Sobieski continued to press against Moldavia, but the Polish Diet refused to grant funding to pay his troops, who never surpassed 30,000 men. For years the Ottomans held the Germans and the Poles at bay, while they committed resources to create a modern navy to repel the Venetians from Greece.

In 1697, peace with France enabled Emperor Leopold to reinforce his Hungarian theatre with veterans, placed under the young Prince Eugene of Savoy. Sultan Mustafa II led his army in person to confront the reinforced enemy. Prince Eugene sensed that a great field battle would decide the war, and he stormed the Ottoman camp when that army was halfway across the wide River Tisza at Zenta. This battle, where Ottoman dead surpassed the Germans by ten to one, marked the clear superiority of Western tactics on an open battlefield. In the aftermath, Eugene invaded Bosnia, where he set fire to Sarajevo on 22 October, as well as burning all the Moslem settlements he could find. In these final years of the Ottoman wars, Peter the Great sought access to the Black Sea. Large Russian armies (which resembled Ottoman ones) were occasionally formed but they could not be supplied on the steppe and just melted away. Peter captured the port of Azov in 1696, supplying his army by river with the support of a fleet of galleys, but there was no breakout to the Black Sea.[96]

The Turkish wars were the scene of large-scale atrocities on both sides, as it was not yet systematic to take prisoners on the battlefield.[97] The greater likelihood of massacre or slavery stiffened the will of soldiers on both sides to fight. Ottoman sources, as well as Westerners in Turkish camps, stressed the custom of beheading of prisoners and of civilians unsuitable for slavery or ransom, as well as paying soldiers for delivering the heads of enemy dead and wounded. After the victory against the Cossacks at Özü (modern Ochakiv) in 1656, some 6,000 heads were collected, then singed and salted for transport back to Istanbul, where they were piled in front of the Imperial gate at the end of a victory parade where city Christians were compelled to carry them impaled on pikes.[98] Elsewhere, Ottoman armies piled mounds of severed heads in cities in order to cow the population. Many captives were decapitated after battle, despite their value, sometimes even after they were promised their lives to induce them to surrender.[99] Ottoman soldiers taking prisoners sometimes hid them from the viziers, fearful that they would lose the ransom value. It would be useful to find burial pits at the site of important battles and sieges in order to ascertain the extent of the practice from archaeological remains.

Sultan Mustafa signed the Treaty of Karlowitz in 1699, whereby he relinquished the entire kingdom of Hungary (minus the district of Timisoara in the southeast, called the Banat) to the victorious emperor (Map 7). The Ottomans were forced, for the first time, to use the language of equality when referring to other states. Jurists were now reinterpreting the concept of Holy War to permit a legal state of peace with unbelievers. The ghazi tradition would have to be curtailed to avoid provoking war with a stronger power. Poland was another victor, reclaiming the lost province of Podolia and threatening the crucial Danube estuary. The Ottomans, therefore, ended the autonomy of Romanian princes and supplanted them with Greek appointees from Istanbul, called Phanariotes. One consequence of the general distemper in Istanbul was that the janissaries deposed Sultan Mustafa in 1703 and placed his brother Ahmed (1703–1730) on the throne, in the hope of reversing the tide.

Leopold now subjected Hungary to significant taxation, without the consent of the Diet. The problem of the Spanish Succession was now looming and the emperor was determined to impose the Habsburg claimant by force of arms. As soon as the troops disappeared to Italy and the Rhine to fight the French, the Hungarian magnates rallied again to Ferenc Rakoczi's malcontents. At the outset, he led the serfs to understand that they would be freed from their feudal obligations, and all religions would be tolerated. He quickly disposed of a large army of Hungarians, Ukrainians and Slovaks who, with French money and technical support,

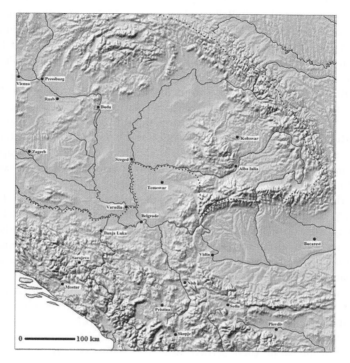

Map 7 Retreat of the Ottoman Empire in Hungary 1699

waged small war against the Habsburg garrisons. Leopold refused to make concessions and when he died in 1705, almost half of Hungary was in rebel hands. His son, Joseph, had a more secular outlook and phased out forced conversions to Catholicism. England and Holland pressured him to grant concessions to the rebels, which annoyed him intensely, for the British would make no concessions to Catholics in Ireland. After the Imperial victory at Turin, in 1706 Joseph shifted regiments to the Hungarian theatre, about 50,000 men, or half the army. General Heister and the Slav grenzers committed many atrocities and alienated most of the population. The rebel armies of irregulars were never able to defeat the Germans in the open field, and neither were they able to capture fortified towns with adequate garrisons.[100] By 1710, the Kuruc army had dwindled from 70,000 men to only 15,000, confined to the north-east part of the kingdom. Joseph was willing to recognize Hungarian autonomy from Austria (unlike Bohemia after White Mountain) but nothing more. Between the widespread devastation and the plague of 1710, about half a million Hungarians died during the rebellion, 80% of them civilians, out of a total population of about 2.5 million.[101]

An expansionist Russia under the Czar Peter the Great made another appearance. By 1705, Peter had created a standing army of 130,000 foot and 38,000 horse, a much bigger army than he could supply. Peter conspired with the Romanian princes and with Balkan Christians with the intention of expanding his empire south-east as far as the Mediterranean. He was momentarily distracted by the threat from Sweden, whose King Charles XII invaded Russia in 1709, but after destroying the latter's army deep in the Ukraine at Poltava, he prepared a campaign against the Ottomans. Early in 1711, the sultan declared war on Russia and moved troops from the Danube and Anatolia to the lower Danube estuary, reaching Izmail by 28 June, more quickly than Peter thought possible. A great host of 200,000 Ottoman troops soon made contact with 40,000 Russians on the Pruth river frontier and hemmed them in. Reinforced, but soon surrounded, Peter's army fought for three days and then capitulated. The Russians were happy to restore to Turkish control the Black Sea areas they acquired in 1699.

When the Ottomans marked new successes against the Venetians in 1715 and 1716, they laid themselves open to a new attack by the Habsburgs in Hungary. Prince Eugene won a field battle against the Ottomans at Peterwardein, then captured in quick succession Temesvar and Belgrade in 1716. Imperial troops marched deep into Serbia, and into western Wallachia. As they marched south of the Danube they were welcomed by the Serbs. The Austrians commented on the poor discipline of the Ottoman troops, no longer capable of facing drilled European regulars. The Ottomans changed Grand Viziers four times in a short period, and quickly consented to peace with the Habsburgs with the loss of more territory in 1718.[102] German colonists and others from various parts of Western Europe were then settled near the Serbs on Hungary's southern border, reducing the rebellious Magyars to barely 50% of the kingdom's population. This would hold the restive kingdom in check until 1848.

Notes

1 Philip T Hoffman, 2015: 12.
2 Hoffman, 2015: 49, 87–92.
3 Marsigli, 1732, II: 23
4 Thomas M Barker, 1967: 192.
5 Agoston, 2014: 106.
6 Brent Nosworthy, 1990: 37.
7 Marsigli, 1732, II: 80.
8 Mesut Uyar & Edward J Erickson, 2009: 82–86.
9 A.N. Kurat & J.S. Bromley, 1976.
10 Barker, 1967: 192–97; Marsigli, 1732, I: 37, II: 132.
11 Uyar & Erickson, 2009: 86; Agoston, 2014; Rhoads Murphey, 1999.
12 Virginia Aksan, 2007: 116.
13 Karen Barkey, 1997: 33, 65–80.
14 Aksan, 2007: 53.
15 Geoffrey Goodwin, 1997: 40.
16 Marsigli, 1732, I: 103.
17 Evgeni Radushev, 2008.
18 Aksan, 2007: 50.
19 Gilles Veinstein, 2013.

20 Uyar & Erickson, 2009: 91
21 Agoston, 2014: 113
22 Goodwin, 1997: 101.
23 Aksan, 2007: 49.
24 Mark L Stein, 2007: 78; Marsigli, 1732, II: 6.
25 Özgűr Kolçak, 2017.
26 Aksan, 2007: 74.
27 Uyar & Erickson, 2009: 95.
28 Apostolos Vacalopoulos, 1976: 219.
29 Aksan, 2007: 30.
30 Marsigli, 1732, I : 103.
31 Robert Mantran, 1970.
32 Pal Fodor, 2007.
33 Molly Greene, 2010: 100, 117.
34 Michel Fontenay, 1981, vol. 2.
35 B.J. Slot, 1982, vol. 1: 120, 158.
36 Charles Terlinden, 1904: 3.
37 R.C. Anderson, 1952: 125.
38 Paolo Moracchiello, 1986.
39 Luciano Pezzolo, 1986.
40 C.W. Bracewell, 1982.
41 Thierry Giappiconi, 2018: 87; F Sassi, 1936–1937, 1937–1938.
42 Ennio Concina, 1986.
43 Slot, 1982: 172.
44 A.N. Kurat, 1976: 163.
45 Wayne S. Vucinich, 1982.
46 Anderson, 1952: 167.
47 Hochedlinger, 2003: 127.
48 Evliya Tchélébi, 2000 : 171–87.
49 Tchélébi, 2000: 200.
50 Giuseppe Gullino, 1986; Gregory Hanlon, 1998a.
51 Slot, 1982: 194–200.
52 Vacalopoulos, 1976: 85.
53 Louis Sicking, 2014.
54 Ennio Concina, 1971: 21–31.
55 Giappiconi, 2018: 101.
56 William Miller, 1921: 223; James M Paton, 1940.
57 Philip Argenti, 1935.
58 Concina, 1971: 101.
59 Dionysios Hatzopoulos, 1999: 56–90.
60 Hatzopoulos, 1999: 92–3.
61 Anderson, 1952, 249–69.
62 Jean Nouzille, 2012: 61.
63 Maria Ivanics, 2007.
64 Stein, 2007: 114.
65 Geza Palffy, 2007.
66 Brian Davies, 2007: 171.
67 Osmân Aga de Temechvar, 1998.
68 Radu Paun, 2013.
69 Jean Bérenger, 1975: 43, 80
70 Ferenc Toth, 2007: 44–8.
71 John A Mears, 1986.
72 Tchélébi, 2000: 31–42, 131–53.

73   Toth, 2007, 82–107.
74   Bérenger, 1975: 337.
75   Janos Szabo, 2013.
76   Gabor Agoston, 2015.
77   Jean Bérenger, 2004: 353–56.
78   Ovidiu Cristea, 2013.
79   Uyar & Erickson, 2009: 99–102.
80   John Stoye, 1964: 94–138.
81   Andrew Wheatcroft, 2008: 131.
82   Marsigli, 1732, II: 37 & 140.
83   Bérenger, 2004, 172–97.
84   Norman Davies, 1982: 477–81.
85   Wheatcroft, 2008: 152.
86   Thomas M Barker, 1967: 284.
87   Marsigli, 1732, II: 151.
88   Hochedlinger, 2003: 127–40.
89   Wheatcroft, 2008: 63.
90   Bérenger, 1975: 371.
91   Bérenger, 1975: 360.
92   Nouzille, 2012: 45–61.
93   Noel Malcolm, 1994: 83.
94   David Nicolle, 2010: 4–23.
95   Kurat & Bromley, 1976: 192.
96   Davies, 2007: 180–85.
97   Peter H Wilson, 1998: 85; Hochedlinger, 2003: 142.
98   Tchelebi, 2000: 111.
99   Benjamin Lellouch, 2005.
100 Charles W Ingrao, 1979: 124–57.
101 Ingrao, 1979: 149–57.
102 Nouzille, 2012: 178

9   The wars against French ascendancy 1667–1714

French potential unleashed

The first effect of the interminable international and civil strife of the central decades of the seventeenth century was to enhance France's natural preponderance in Europe (Chart 2). Due to wars and from the effects of epidemic and a cooling climate, the populations of Germany, Spain, Italy and the British Isles contracted by almost 10–40% between 1630 and 1660. France, too, was hard hit by plague and famine, but not to the same degree and it recovered more quickly. Frontier regions like Champagne and Burgundy had been scorched by

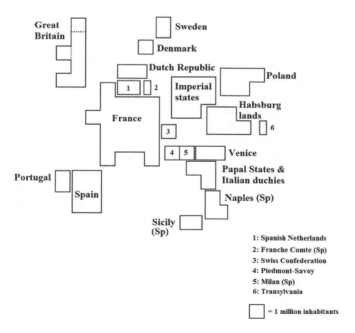

Chart 2 French demographic preponderance in Europe in the 1660s

the fighting, but not nearly to the same extent as neighbouring Lorraine and Germany. The kingdom's population in the early 1660s would have approached 20 million inhabitants, subjects of a monarch whose direct power had been enhanced by the war. Louis XIV was happy to let Cardinal Mazarin direct policy until his death in 1661, but, from that day forward, he came into his own and imposed his own personality and directives on the court.

Louis was motivated by 'gloire', in the sense of the pursuit of renown, reputation and prestige that would withstand the test of time. Future generations would look back on his accomplishments in many different fields and marvel. The functioning of early modern monarchies was heavily influenced by the personality of the sovereign, and their natural ability to inspire obedience and govern effectively varied greatly from one to another. The French king stood head and shoulders above his peers, the pious Emperor Leopold, the two unscrupulous Stuart kings, William of Orange and the invalid Charles II of Spain. Louis's influence extended far beyond absolutist government and a desire for military efficiency, because he gave form and content to the concept of grandeur. All his contemporaries and most future kings imitated his manner of ruling. Early in his reign, his aim was to extend French boundaries in almost every direction. By the Peace of the Pyrenees in 1659, Spain ceded very modest territories to France, despite the duration and scale of the conflict: Artois, Roussillon, in addition to parts of Alsace acquired in the Peace of Westphalia. In his declining years, Philip IV of Spain lurched from bankruptcy to bankruptcy, suspending payments on the debt in August 1662, and again in May 1666, shortly after his death.[1] The kingdom could no longer afford to reconquer Portugal. By the Treaty of the Pyrenees in 1659, Louis XIV promised to discontinue military assistance to the breakaway kingdom, but he never intended to observe this clause. French 'volunteer' soldiers and technical assistants continued to fight in Portugal by passing through England.[2] Spain also found it increasingly difficult to defend its loyal provinces in Flanders. The Spanish Low Countries remained the coveted prize, with its populous cities, flourishing manufactures and advanced agriculture. It was no longer feasible for Madrid to dispatch tercios from Lombardy to the Low Countries via the Alps. The Crown relied increasingly on the nobility to raise men, paying the Grandees and the cities to recruit and supply them in the field, but there was no longer a serious army administration to keep them in order, and the infrequency of victories entailed that military service held a very weak attraction. Spanish fiscal institutions had largely been privatized from the 1630s onwards, and the Crown retained little direct power over them. On Philip's death in 1665, the kingdom passed to a sickly infant, Charles II, who was not expected to live for long. The regency governed the kingdom through an aristocracy that had largely demilitarized in Spain and in Italy.[3]

Louis and his ministers laid plans for the conquest of Flanders and justified it legally with the claim that, since the dowry of his Spanish queen, Maria Theresa, was never paid, that the queen herself should be able to inherit the Spanish Netherlands from her father, which would then devolve to France: the resulting conflict is, therefore, called the War of Devolution. Starting in 1665, Michel Le Tellier and Marshal Turenne added new regiments to the standing army, raising the total to about 80,000 men. Turenne, who acted as a mentor to young Louis XIV on military affairs, invaded the Spanish Netherlands in May 1667 and quickly occupied a dozen fortified cities. Only Lille resisted for longer than a few weeks. The Spanish army in the theatre numbered only about 40,000 men, mostly confined to garrison duty. Walloon and German units were paid only fitfully and proved unreliable in the field. Another 30,000 soldiers, seen as undisciplined rabble, fruitlessly continued the border war against Portugal. In early 1668, a French army occupied the Spanish Franche-Comté, which was completely defenceless. Another 100,000 men prepared to complete the conquest of Flanders, when Louis decided to end the war, returning the Franche-Comté to Spanish rule but keeping a dozen fortified towns, including Lille.

French success in 1667 had convinced two adversaries, Restoration England and the Dutch Republic, to patch up their bitter commercial quarrels and to join with Sweden in a Triple Alliance to halt French expansion. All three countries were informally French allies. Mazarin arbitrated the Peace of Oliva in January 1660, by which Sweden occupied parts of Denmark, and the Elector of Brandenburg, Frederick William, acquired full sovereignty from Poland over Prussia.[4] Brandenburg and some Catholic prince-bishops in Westphalia and the Lower Rhineland became part of the French alliance. England had always opposed French control over the North Sea coast and acquired the privateer base of Dunkirk in the peace of 1659. However, the newly restored King Charles II, frustrated by Parliament's penny-pinching, sold the fortress to Louis in 1662 and received French money in order to govern. The Netherlands had been a French ally since the birth of the Republic, but the States-General considered that France should be a friend, and not a neighbour. Dutch 'betrayal' deeply annoyed Louis XIV, who, for the first time, contemplated punishing the Republic for its action. What really convinced the king to halt the war with Spain so suddenly was a secret treaty signed in January 1668 with the Habsburg emperor, Leopold I, which prepared the partition of the Spanish empire in the likely event that King Charles should soon die without an heir. Louis would acquire the Spanish Low Countries, the Franche-Comté, the kingdom of Navarre in the Pyrenees, the kingdom of Naples and the far-off Philippines, all without fighting. The German Habsburgs would receive the rest. Not long after making peace, in 1670, Louis, without legal title, occupied the entire duchy of Lorraine, though without annexing it formally to the kingdom. It would only be returned to its legitimate rulers in 1697.

In addition to war over dynastic competition and in defence of religious principles, the seventeenth century saw the unmistakable rise of war for economic hegemony. The Dutch mastery of seaborne trade relied as much on soldiers and cannon as on prices and markets. The first voyages of the Dutch East Indies Company borrowed weapons and munitions from the States of Holland in order to impose themselves on Indian principalities and their Portuguese rivals. After Portugal seceded from the Spanish empire in 1640, it hoped that the

Dutch predation of its ships and colonies would cease. For almost two decades, the Dutch attacks continued relentlessly, failing to conquer Brazil, but eventually capturing all of Ceylon. The Republic was also prepared to employ its naval muscle in order to preserve its trading advantages in Europe. After King Christian IV of Denmark raised the tolls through the Baltic Sound and on the River Elbe near Hamburg in 1638, Dutch merchants demanded retaliation. In the summer of 1645, a Dutch fleet forced the Danes to reverse their policies. On the other hand, when Sweden seemed set to overwhelm the Danish kingdom and control the Sound in 1658, the Republic dispatched another fleet to prevent the kingdom's collapse.[5] When the Netherlands returned to peace with Spain in 1648, its ships and manufactures overwhelmed most of its foreign competitors, such as England, in southern Europe. In the later seventeenth century, the Dutch Republic had, no doubt, the highest proportion of the population devoted to manufacturing, well ahead of England. The Spanish Netherlands also retained much of its previous craft infrastructure, in the era before machine manufacturing.[6]

England developed a modern textile industry during the later Elizabethan era, imitating the 'New Draperies' emerging in Flanders and in Holland; these were shoddier and less durable than the prized woollens produced in Italy, but they were much cheaper. After the 1620s, English drapers produced a series of 'anti-Venetian' cloths that bore all the markings of their Italian competitors, but were designed to drive the latter out of business in the Levant and South European markets.[7] Cromwell and the Stuart kings saw the Dutch as the next obstacle to their maritime trade supremacy and intended to reduce the Republic to a simple dependency, or protectorate. They argued (not without reason) that the Dutch had imposed a dominant trade position in the world by force, and that England should take it away from them, also by force. The younger brother of King Charles II, James, Duke of York, appointed admiral of the fleet, built up the British navy in view of a great maritime war. Given that Charles had no legitimate offspring, James was the heir to the throne, and he had his own ambitious court in London comprising military men and people connected with foreign trade. This naval lobby pressed for war with the Dutch, which they assumed would be victorious. The Second Dutch War of 1665–1667, provoked by England, was concluded with a Dutch descent on the Thames estuary, where the English fleet was moored. Charles was forced to conclude a humiliating peace, and then join his adversary in an alliance against France.

The English were, nevertheless, keen to join France in a third war against the Netherlands republic when Louis proposed it to them in 1668. The French finance, trade and navy minister, Jean-Baptiste Colbert, raised the profile of French manufactures after 1662, and, like the English, he determined to curtail the number of Dutch ships and products in French ports. He first imposed high tariffs on Dutch products in 1664, and then raised them to punitive levels in 1667.[8] It is little recognized that France was Europe's leading manufacturer *by volume* at least until the 1780s, with a wide array of products produced across many different regions, and Colbert's mercantilist policies spurred its growth.

The minister recommended to Louis XIV the complete conquest of the Republic, which would result in the French takeover of its international trade.[9] England and France signed a secret Treaty of Dover in June 1670, and began preparations to invade the Republic by land and sea. For the Stuarts, commerce was only a pretext for war: the sovereign and his brother hoped that the acquisition of Dutch trade and colonies around the world would enable them to break free of the financial chains imposed on them by Parliament, and to free them also of the pro-Protestant policies of the Church of England. Charles II was a secret Catholic; his brother James was an incautious public one. Victory against the Dutch would enable the dynasty to overturn the results of the English Civil War and enhance the royal prerogative at the expense of Parliament.[10] The Elector of Brandenburg, ignorant of these plans, also joined the French alliance in 1670 in the hope of obtaining slivers of the Spanish Netherlands in the lower Rhineland.

French preparations for the invasion stand as a Machiavellian masterpiece. The Dutch government, under the brothers de Witt, was amply informed of the French intentions but refused to comprehend the seriousness of the threat. The Marquis de Louvois, as secretary for war, took most of these preparations in hand, first raising the standing army from its floor of 70,000 men in 1670 to three field armies totalling 120,000 men in the winter of 1672. To enable the French army to strike its enemy across 100 kilometres of neutral territory, he stocked several great magazines in the Lower Rhine area, at Neuss, Kaiserswerth, Bonn and Dorsten, employing foreign agents (often of Dutch origin) to discreetly purchase military stores. That meant that the French army on the way north would be marching *toward* its supplies. Louvois stocked enough grain for 200,000 daily rations for six months, plus all the heavy weapons the army would require for major sieges. In addition to England, France recruited two German allies on the Republic's exposed eastern border, the Archbishop of Cologne (who raised 17,000 men) and the Bishop of Munster, with an additional corps. The Dutch, in 1671, finally began to raise men, who numbered about 80,000 when the invasion began, but most of them were confined to fortresses. The Dutch Republic remained very decentralized: there was no stadtholder designated after 1650, so there was no centre of military decision, or of finance. The States-General anxiously appointed Prince William of Orange to the position on 25 February 1672, but Johan de Witt tried to block the young man's ascent.

The king and Louvois rode off to join the army on 24 April 1672, which mustered at Cologne on the Rhine. Two armies descended the Meuse river bishopric of Liège and bypassed the southernmost Dutch fortress of Maastricht, and combined with the third force. They attacked the republic from the east, not the better fortified south, and the undermanned Dutch garrisons surrendered their fortresses in mere days. French troops crossed the smaller branch of the Rhine in the direction of Holland almost unopposed, under the eyes of Louis XIV. While one army pushed forward, the others laid siege to important cities like Nijmegen and Utrecht in the Dutch heartland. Until 22 June, the invasion was a complete success, coming to within a day's march of Amsterdam and total victory. William III of Orange, now firmly in charge of the government as stadtholder, opened the sluices at Muiden, flooding a good portion of the land east of the capital at tremendous cost to the population. The Dutch were fortunate that the English fleet had made no plans for landing troops on the Holland or Zeeland coast. The de Witt brothers were blamed for the fiasco and were brutally murdered by an Orangeist mob on 20 August.

The Dutch regents clamoured for peace at this juncture. They were ready to relinquish to France the Generality Lands south of the River Waal, perhaps a quarter of the Republic, adjacent to the Spanish Netherlands. Louis XIV and Louvois demanded much more, such as three eastern provinces, complete freedom for the Catholic religion, an enormous war indemnity of 24 million livres tournois, and the removal of all restrictions on French traders and products.[11] A Dutch naval victory against the English fleet in the channel lifted the Republic's spirits. The Elector of Brandenburg then attacked the French and allied German troops from the east with an army of 23,000 men; Spain offered some regiments in support of the republic, and, in September, a force of 16,000 Imperial troops joined them all in Westphalia. The French offensive came to a halt on the edge of the flooded area. The army, under the Duc de Luxembourg, ravaged the territory under French occupation, extracting as many contributions as he could squeeze.[12] Louis hoped to conclude the war by returning some 20,000 prisoners of war to the Dutch, who quickly re-enlisted. This turned out to be a major error.

In 1673, Marshal Turenne vigorously attacked the Brandenburg troops assisting the Dutch and soon drove the Elector out of the war. The French project now focused on acquiring the key enemy stronghold blocking the Meuse river highway at Maastricht, with Louis XIV present in person to animate the besiegers. It was here that the young Vicomte de Vauban was given a free hand to introduce his improved method of taking fortresses by digging several parallel trenches that gave better protection to the sappers. Maastricht capitulated after just three weeks. William III hovered not far away with a Dutch field army: he was keen to be in complete control, but he had no experience of planning military operations.[13] Recapturing the town of Naarden, not far from Amsterdam, was the lone Dutch success. The capture of Bonn on the Rhine by an Imperial contingent was another turning point: it rendered vulnerable the French forces planted deep inside the Dutch Republic, and convinced the king that he would need to withdraw his armies to less exposed positions. They withdrew from the Netherlands in the first weeks of 1674, but not before having inflicted immense damage.

The war widened considerably in 1674: Spain joined the growing coalition of states assisting the Dutch, forcing France to divert men to other theatres. England feared the loss of access to the Mediterranean and Spain's Caribbean markets, so dropped out of the war soon after, which had not pleased Protestant public opinion. A modest expeditionary corps of English troops remained behind, fighting under French direction. Emperor Leopold joined the war formally and ordered an army to the Rhine to pressure France in Alsace, while the Elector of Brandenburg re-joined the struggle with a corps fighting alongside the Imperials. Almost all the German princes aligned with Leopold and consented to raise troops for the defence of the Empire. Habsburg intervention shifted the balance of power away from the French king, especially on the eastern frontier. Very early in the year, the French army occupied the Franche-Comté again, with little effort, netting Louis almost a half-million new subjects. Despite being outnumbered by a German army of 55,000 men on the Rhine, Turenne fended off the German attacks in Alsace, and then chased the Imperials and Brandenburgers out of the region completely in a brilliant winter campaign ending early in January. Sweden then invaded northern Germany, profiting from the chaos, forcing Elector Frederick William to rush his men to the Baltic to confront them. Louis XIV had maintained contact with Hungarian magnate rebels throughout the period, and was now able to send them arms and troops. Hungarian magnate forces drew off important German contingents from the Rhine frontier. Montecuccoli conscripted thousands of peasants to erect fortified lines, hoping it would be sufficient to fight a defensive campaign at the foot of the Black Forest.[14] Turenne was killed while taking the offensive in 1675, but the German army was unable to push the French back.

The main French blows fell now on Spain, which required Dutch support to defend its own Low Countries territories. Between July 1673 and the end of 1675, Spain established twelve defensive treaties with European allies.[15] The Spanish army in the theatre was increased to 50,000 men, but it was scattered across dozens of fortresses.[16] The Germans and Walloons no longer enjoyed a high reputation.[17] The Dutch, under William, kept an army of at least 30,000 men in the field, but, unlike Louis XIV, he was unwilling to leave control of it to better generals. William insisted on fighting field battles against the French, who bested him every time. Neither was he more successful in forcing the French to lift their sieges. The French armies grew steadily under the greater pressure, reaching the unprecedented size of 250,000 men and 100 warships in the later period of the war. Thanks to Louvois's well-stocked magazines, French armies began their campaigns very early, even in March, before the Dutch were ready to oppose them.

In 1674, the war spread to the Mediterranean as well, where a Dutch squadron under Admiral de Ruyter assisted the Spanish fleet. On 7–8 July 1674, the great mercantile city of Messina rose up against the Spanish regime and its ever-increasing taxes. Messina was the economic capital of Sicily, blessed with extensive economic privileges. The revolt, like urban rebellions elsewhere, was rooted in the violation of its privileges and the defence of its autonomy with respect to its rival, Palermo. The city contained a garrison of only a few hundred soldiers, and throughout Sicily and in the neighbouring kingdom of Naples, professional troops were very scarce. Spain reacted to the rebellion by blockading the city with a couple of thousand Spanish, Lombard, Neapolitan and German soldiers, and levied large bodies of local militia that were almost uncontrollable. This new theatre of war meant that the considerable resources of Naples and Sicily would not be available for Spain's war effort elsewhere. Louis XIV ordered his Mediterranean fleet to land a small expeditionary force to assist the rebels, hoping to spread the rebellion across the island. The revolt did not, in fact, spread beyond Messina's hinterland. The fleet commander, Duc de Vivonne, could have occupied Naples itself, had he wished, given the skeleton Spanish garrison in its several citadels. French ships landed shore parties around Sicily and on the mainland, too, in order to pin down Spanish forces everywhere. In 1675 and 1676, the combined Spanish and Dutch flotilla tried to drive off the French fleet. Three bloody sea-battles between the French and the Hispano–Dutch flotillas were fought in Sicilian waters and after the final one at Palermo, the French seized the initiative. A stalemate developed around Messina itself, where Spain still had only 4,500 professional soldiers two years after the onset of the revolt. By 1677, both sides maintained about 11,000 troops in the theatre, as French professionals gradually disarmed and replaced the local militia. Naples became an active base for the recovery of Messina, with nobles volunteering their services to try to transform local militiamen into real soldiers.[18]

Notwithstanding the multiplication of theatres of war, the French were still able to capture towns in the Low Countries and to keep relief armies at bay. William of Orange could not recapture Maastricht in 1676 and failed to win any field battles either. The Imperial army continued expanding on the Rhine frontier after 1675, eventually numbering 77,000 men on paper. German states raised their own troops from the Circles, the Reichs Contingents, to reinforce the Imperial army. The French still consolidated their hold on the upper Rhineland.[19] Louis was ready to end the war in 1677, when the English public pushed Charles II to re-enter the war on the Dutch side. The Duke of Savoy, Charles Emmanuel, signed a treaty with Louis XIV to enter the war as a French ally, with the design to seize Milan. Both of these situations constituted diplomatic manoeuvring rather than active campaigning. Louis then brought his troops home from Messina in April 1678, along with the most compromised citizens. The principal opponent to peace was William of Orange, who attacked the French (and was repulsed) four days after the peace was signed at Nijmegen, 17 September 1678. France returned Maastricht to the Dutch, their last remaining piece of the Republic's territory. The Dutch also recovered their commercial dominance as soon as the war ended, although it was careful to devote more money to defence. French support compelled the Elector of Brandenburg to evacuate all the territory in Pomerania seized from Sweden. France retained the Franche-Comté and a few towns in the Spanish Netherlands, so the king's reputation as a conqueror remained intact.

French defence by aggression 1680–1697

France displayed bad faith with its former adversaries as soon as the Treaty of Nijmegen was signed, by seizing outlying territories by increments. Louis aimed to expand his territory in Italy and Germany by acquiring gateways and bridgeheads, a strategy France had long practised. Here, he was advised and supported by Louvois, who was more than merely an intermediary or an adviser, like Chamlay or Vauban. The two shared views on strategy, which was mostly defensive and focused on logistical details.[20] The king established *Chambers of Reunion* in Metz, Besançon and Breisach on the Rhine, in which magistrates were instructed to find the legal basis under which important towns and districts outside French boundaries were designated as dependencies of small places inside the kingdom. Once the legal claim was established, the French army seized and 'reunited' them with the kingdom. One of the first to fall was Orange, in 1680, ancestral seat of William III, deep in southern France. A putative fief of the Bishop of Metz, the sizeable duchy of Zweibrucken, north of Lorraine, was annexed the same year. In September 1681, the tribunal pronounced in favour of recovering Strasbourg in Alsace, and French troops carefully hidden in the vicinity occupied the city, its bridge and the Rhine bridgehead of Kehl the next day. A citadel was soon erected to better hold it under French control. Louis also purchased the fortress of Casale Monferrato in northern Italy from the spendthrift Duke of Mantua, and entered that stronghold the same day as Strasbourg. Spanish Luxembourg and its large district was the next target, object of a foray by a French army in 1683. After several months of fending off similar attacks on his territory, the king of Spain declared war on France at the end of 1683. But the larger context was very bad: the Turks were at the gates of Vienna and the Emperor and German princes could send no assistance. Louis then claimed the important city of Ghent and other towns in Flanders. A French army took Luxembourg by siege in 1684 and compelled Spain to sue for peace in August. The policy of Reunions and the discreet French entente with the Ottomans turned the great majority of German princes against Louis in the 1680s.

Less controversially, the French king made demonstrations of force along the Barbary Coast, ostensibly to deter corsair attacks on French shipping. Specially designed barges designed to fire explosive shells on stationary targets were towed close to Algiers and bombarded the city in 1682 and 1683, inducing it to seek peace. The treaty placed French merchant ships off limits to Barbary corsairs and gave the kingdom an added advantage in its growing Levant trade.

As tensions mounted, Louis sought to place his kingdom off limits to enemy armies by erecting a great barrier. Vauban proposed to build strong fortresses in two rows across France's northern frontier, placed 25 or 30 kilometres apart in order to sustain each other (Map 8). In the course of the 1680s, the budget for fortress construction quadrupled, not including the money spent by town governments on the walls and defensive landscaping. Breisach, Landau and Philippsburg on the Rhine, and Casale Monferrato in northern Italy, beyond the kingdom's borders, enabled France to carry its military operations more easily deep into enemy territory.[21]

Louis XIV ignored the Italian states for most of his early reign, although the major ducal dynasties in Turin, Parma, Modena, Mantua and Florence eagerly sought his friendship.[22] There was a fresh project to reduce Piedmont-Savoy to satellite status, as under Cardinal Richelieu, a prelude to eventual annexation.[23]

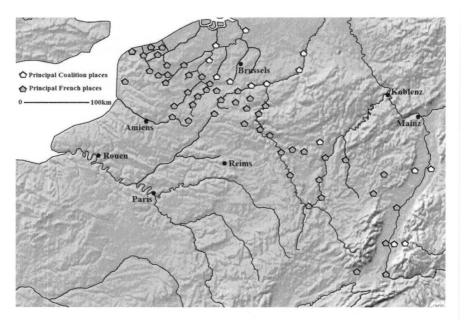

Map 8 Vauban's Barrier of French Fortresses circa 1700

Holding Casale Monferrato to the east, and Pinerolo to the west of Turin were two large garrisons hemming in the duchy's royal ambitions. Genoese patricians still served as senior dignitaries in the Spanish Empire, and the city deliberated joining Spain in a formal alliance in 1678 and in 1683. In 1684, to punish Genoa for its logistical assistance to Spain during the war of the Reunions, the French navy cruised off the coast and placed its bomb ketches in position. The fleet bombarded the city with 2,000 explosive shells and 13,000 stone cannon-balls, damaging or destroying most of the houses. The garrison and local militia repulsed a French landing party of 3,500 troops, but it was never the king's intention to hold the great port. Spain sent reinforcements from Milan in order to impede looting, and in the first moment the city rallied around Madrid. But in the aftermath the Republic kept its distance from European power politics, which was the original French intention.[24]

In the 1680s, the middle-aged king also desired to end the anomaly whereby the Calvinist minority retained extensive legal toleration, which no other European state observed. The vexatious laws pushing Calvinists to convert were harshened in the late 1670s, then again in the early 1680s, but Colbert was hostile to them. Louis waited until after the minister's death in September 1683 before accelerating the persecution process. Languedoc was a powder-keg of religious tension, as the persecution whipped up the anti-Protestant zeal of nearby Catholics. A brief Calvinist revolt in the Languedoc

Cevennes region irritated the king even more. However, it was discovered that billeting soldiers in the homes of Protestants was an efficient way of inciting them to convert. Such methods had long been used in villages owing back taxes, and not only in France.[25] Louis thought the procedure abhorrent when first used in Poitou in 1681, but, in 1685, he resolved to revoke the Edict of Nantes, expel all the Protestant ministers, and lodge dragoons in Protestant households until the inhabitants embraced Catholicism. The method worked, after a fashion. While emigration was illegal, something like 150,000 French Protestants (maybe one in five) fled the kingdom in the following years, seeking safe haven in the Netherlands, Germany, Switzerland and England. The measure was only mildly applauded by the Pope and fellow Catholic monarchs, but it irritated Protestant states far more, who embraced the refugees as they arrived. About a third of the 1,000 officers in the fledgling Brandenburg army were Huguenots in the 1690s.[26] The Brandenburg Elector, Frederick William, passively supported the French Reunions in the 1680s, in exchange for French subsidies for his army. But the Revocation of the Edict of Nantes forced the pious Calvinist prince to reassess his policy. One should keep in mind that Europe's Protestant crowned heads often found resurgent Baroque Catholicism, its grandeur and its pageantry, very seductive. Queen Christine of Sweden was the first to convert in 1654, but she was forced to abdicate. Charles II of England was a secret convert in the 1660s and his brother James was a public one. The Elector of Saxony, Frederick Augustus, converted in order to be a candidate to the throne of Poland in 1697, and Duke Antony Ulrich of Brunswick, an admirer of Louis XIV, in 1707. Catholicism's emphasis on authority, its calendar of special occasions and its geography of sacred spaces fit absolutist ceremoniousness like a glove.

New crises emerged in the later 1680s, especially in Germany, where Louis hoped to maintain some client states. With the death of the Protestant Elector Palatine in 1685, the emperor awarded the strategic Rhine Protestant principality to the Catholic Duke Philip William of Neuburg, a Wittelsbach closely linked by marriage with the Habsburgs. Louis opposed the choice. The Archbishop of Cologne, another French client, died in 1688, and the Pope would not replace him with the Bavarian candidate favoured by France. The Habsburg Emperor, Leopold I, began to unite states into an alliance concluded at Augsburg in 1686, to which Spain adhered. Fearing an international Catholic conspiracy in Europe, Brandenburg joined the league in 1688.Confessional tensions rose suddenly in England in June 1688, when the Italian queen of King James II gave birth to a son and successor. James considered himself a French ally, and in his brief three years' reign, he fashioned a substantial professional army to add to the great navy. Both were his own creation and owed allegiance to him. Parliament shared the public's rabid anti-Catholic sentiment that reached a fever pitch with the arrival of Huguenot refugees. A handful of English political worthies went to Holland to beg William of Orange and his Stuart wife Mary (James' eldest daughter) to overthrow the legitimate king and thereby ensure a Protestant succession. James was not fearful, believing that his army would easily repel the foreigners.[27] Louis XIV was informed of these developments and offered the English ally French ships to repel the Dutch fleet, but the offer was refused. In the event, the English fleet simply stayed in port and was not ordered to try to intercept the Dutch navy when it arrived in November 1688. The Dutch were allowed to disembark their troops on the south coast. James advanced to confront it with his army, assembled on Salisbury plain. There, three-quarters of the English officers deserted and joined the Prince of Orange in a single night, although the rank and file did not follow them. James lost his nerve and fled to the continent seeking French protection and support. Louvois and Louis XIV presumed that this war of the British Succession would play out over a much longer time, and were, therefore, caught off guard.

In order to impose his will, Louis XIV, Louvois and Chamlay decided to make an example of the Palatinate, with the aim of intimidating German princes to remain neutral, and fully conscious that they were acting in support of the Ottoman armies in Hungary.[28] In October 1688, a French army crossed the Rhine and captured the Imperial fortress of Philippsburg. French troops occupied the Palatinate on both sides of the Rhine, and imposed enormous contributions on the population. At the end of 1688, Louvois gave the order to dismantle the fortifications in the towns of the district, between Koblenz and Freiburg. This measure was not uncommon at the time. Chamlay and Louvois then recommended demolishing some of the towns and transplanting the population in France to create a devastated zone that would prevent a German counter-attack. This, too, had a precedent. In 1674, Marshal Turenne emptied Palatinate villages of their inhabitants and burned the buildings, in order to prevent Imperial troops from operating in the region and in order to strike terror among the German princes. The novelty was that this scorched earth policy was decided by the French high command and carried out systematically.[29] As winter took hold of the Rhineland in 1688, troops set to work burning the cities and demolishing the ruins. This 'rape of the Palatinate' was deliberate policy, imposed on generals in the field by Louvois, usually against their better judgement. It took place across four waves of destruction from December 1688 to October 1689, and when it was finished, a score of significant towns, such as Speyer, Worms and Oppenheim were largely razed to the ground. The crops and villages of the rural districts were also plundered, then burned by French troops. One of the aims was successful, to deny a German army the resources to operate against France, for Imperial armies lacked proper logistics systems and still relied on local fodder and food. However, instead of intimidating the German states, the devastation energized them to defeat Louis XIV.[30]

As soon as he was in control of England, William III committed the kingdom and the Dutch Republic to the League of Augsburg, and commenced full-scale operations in the Spanish Low Countries. Louis recalled the Duc de Luxembourg from disgrace to command the forces in the theatre, who trounced William in a set-piece battle at Fleurus in 1690. French armies, on Louvois' instructions, began to bombard fortified cities in order to intimidate them into submission. This practice, which Luxembourg and Vauban both

deplored, rarely worked. A frantic recruitment drive in France raised unprecedented numbers of troops, dispatched to Flanders, to the Rhine, to the Pyrenees and to Savoy. With the assistance of new royal militia regiments
(25,000 men at the outset, then 60,000 by 1697), French professional troops
probably numbered over 350,000 men, not counting the fleet and the coastguard. Year after year, there were perhaps 190,000 men in several field
armies, and as many as 80,000 troops under Luxembourg fought stubborn
battles against the Anglo–Dutch in a single engagement. In the campaign of
1692, Louis XIV placed himself at the head of a giant army that besieged
and captured the strong fortress of Namur.

French strength was unprecedented at sea also; Colbert's creation had
become Europe's largest navy by 1690, with 130 warships in 1688, most of
them of recent construction. From 1690 to 1693, it held the upper hand in the
English Channel against the English and Dutch fleet combined, winning a sea
battle off Beachy Head in 1690. But neither Louis XIV nor his naval minister,
Colbert de Seignelay, gave much thought to grand maritime strategy.[31] They
neglected to prevent William III from sending an army to Ireland to chase
James II from the turbulent island, nor did they try to impede the arrival of
allied supplies and reinforcements. The Protestant army of English, Dutch and
Huguenot regiments bested the undisciplined levies of the Stuart monarch and
conquered the kingdom by the end of 1691. The combined French Atlantic
and Mediterranean fleet, under Tourville, hunted and found off the coast of
Portugal the great Smyrna convoy of Anglo–Dutch ships destined for the Mediterranean, inflicting a colossal 30 million livres tournois damage on allied commerce. William III, on the other hand, commanded two navies, an English one
with 100 ships of the line, and a Dutch one with 69 purpose-built warships. He
combined both in great fleets and worked out ways to make their individual
naval styles compatible, under the command of English admirals.[32] Over time,
the allied superiority in existing vessels, and the greater rate of replacement,
limited French opportunities.

A new theatre of war opened up in northern Italy after the young Duke of
Savoy, Victor Amadeus, joined the League of Augsburg in 1690 and used allied
subsidies to expand his standing army. The Savoy dynasty lusted after royal
status throughout the seventeenth century, and was prepared to take military
risks to acquire it. Louis XIV considered this move to be a betrayal, and
unleashed his army, under Marshal Catinat, on Piedmont, with instructions to
ravage it, while Savoy itself was completely occupied. Louis had sent French
troops to the region to suppress Calvinist Vaudois villagers already in 1685 and
1686, with Piedmontese assistance. It was in the wake of this intervention that
the young duke began to challenge the duchy's dependency on France. Victor
Amadeus II was a hard, rigid man, with a passion for soldiers, like his contemporaries William of Orange and Frederick William of Prussia.[33] Generations of
warfare had endowed the duchy with a patrimony of fortresses blocking Alpine
passes and holding key areas of the plain. Turin, with its 45,000 inhabitants,
was especially well fortified and crowned with a stout citadel. Marshal Catinat

used a scorched-earth policy as a means of drawing Victor Amadeus into battle with his Spanish and German allies, and succeeded by this method in thrashing them at Staffarda in August 1690. The technique worked again on a larger scale at La Marsaglia in October 1693. Catinat lacked the troops necessary to penetrate farther beyond the edge of the Alps, however. Piedmont remained a secondary theatre.[34]

The Italian theatre took on new significance to the degree that it attracted the attention of Emperor Leopold. Austria's claims to northern Italy became increasingly theoretical at the end of the Middle Ages, but they were not forgotten. Leopold periodically demanded money from Italian princes to fight the Turks, but they always politely refused, or had to be compensated with titles and honours. Spain represented Habsburg interests in Italy for most of the century, but Spanish power was quickly waning, even in Milan. In 1690, the emperor sent Marshal Antonio Carafa to northern Italy with a substantial army destined to join Spain and Savoy. However, the marshal had instructions to draw heavy contributions from Italian states in his path, and to assert Austria's precedence everywhere. Imperial fief-holders were summoned to pay considerable sums on pain of seizure of their estates. The Italian states, except for Savoy, which had the military strength to refuse, paid for the German army in the theatre.[35] Carafa was soon replaced in the field by Eugene of Savoy, nephew of Victor Amadeus, who showered estates and revenues on him. The combined Savoyard, German and Spanish force was insufficient to drive the French from their Alpine base at Pinerolo, so a stalemate developed.

In the principal theatre of 'Flanders', the war continued year after year. Until 1693, the French king spent part of each campaign at the head of his army, but he did not presume to instruct the generals how to manage the details. From Versailles, Louis and Louvois dispatched letters and instructions to the generals in the field, confident that they would be followed. This defensive *stratégie de cabinet* worked well enough in a war marked more by sieges than by battles.[36] Louvois managed very well the logistical details until his sudden death in 1691. For the remainder of the decade he was replaced by his son, Barbézieux, who did not wield the political influence of his father. The machine functioned well nevertheless, since French field armies alone totalled almost 200,000 men in the early 1690s, with local concentrations of 70,000 or more under Marshal Luxembourg.[37] Allied armies expanded in the same proportion: there were perhaps 140,000 German troops fighting in the West, exclusive of those facing the Ottomans in Hungary.[38] In 1695, the Allied army recovered Namur from the French in an epic siege (although the French made countervailing gains elsewhere) and Louis began to consider winding down the war. It was easy enough to induce Duke Victor Amadeus not merely to make peace, but to change sides by secret treaty in 1696, after demolishing the fortress of Casale and turning Pinerolo over to Savoy. France also recognized the dynasty's royal titles in its court protocol, an important concession for the ambitious duke.[39]

The last holdout was Spain, still very weak in the last years of the reign of Charles II. There were moments when the kingdom seemed to rally, as in 1677 when the bastard prince Don Juan imposed himself as prime minister (but he died soon after), or again in 1686, when thousands of men volunteered to join the Imperial army to capture Buda. Spanish troops in Flanders were ever less numerous as time went on, and had to admit Dutch troops to defend the fortresses there. In the 1690s, Naples began to contribute new weapons and ships, and troops in greater numbers to hold the Catalan theatre against French encroachment. The last phase of the war saw both French and Spanish armies build up to unprecedented size in Catalonia, culminating in a new siege of Barcelona. The fall of the city to the French General Vendôme, with the help of the navy, on 10 August 1697 marked the conclusion of the momentous war.

The threat of Bourbon world hegemony

By 1697, all the belligerents were financially exhausted and needed a pause. Looming on the horizon was the poor health of Spain's invalid King Charles II. He proved unable to sire children from either of his queens and the problem of the Spanish succession took on new urgency. France had prepared for this moment since the time of Cardinal Mazarin, who arranged the marriage between Louis XIV and the Spanish princess, Maria Theresa. Louis XIV's mother, Anne of Austria, was also a Spanish Habsburg. Since 1668, France was well placed to dispute the Spanish inheritance with the Habsburgs in Vienna, who exchanged princesses with Madrid in every generation. King Charles of Spain outlived everyone's predictions, but he was clearly waning in his early thirties. Louis XIV reached out to Vienna in 1698 to negotiate a new accord by which a child candidate, Joseph Ferdinand from Bavaria (also closely related to Madrid), would inherit most of the Empire while France and Austria would each be compensated. But the inopportune death of the Bavarian prince in 1699 ruined all these plans. Leopold of Austria claimed the entire Spanish inheritance for his second son, Archduke Charles, and made it clear that he would fight to acquire it. This was neglecting the interests of the Spanish political class, which had no desire to see the empire partitioned among competing powers. Shortly before he expired on 1 November 1700, Charles II specified in his testament that he wished that all his territories should pass undivided to the Bourbon candidate, Louis's adolescent grandson, Philip of Anjou (the name of Spanish kings assigned to him at birth was not accidental). The Bourbons, with their powerful navy, were seen as better able to keep mastery of such a vast empire, instead of Austria, which was virtually landlocked. Louis debated with his council to reach a decision, and decided to accept the Spanish testament. Prince Philip was presented with a retinue of French military, judicial and financial experts and packed off to Madrid to assume the crown. This development served as a *casus belli* for Emperor Leopold. Fighting began in northern Italy in 1701, when a German army under Prince Eugene of Savoy tried to capture Milan. Political elites in Milan, Naples, Sicily and Sardinia now had to predict the likely winner of the contest. At the outset, the great majority chose the Bourbon King Philip V, who soon journeyed to Italy to solicit support. With

Bourbon possessions to the east and to the west, Duke Victor Amadeus of Savoy was compelled to join them in an alliance, but he contrived to make his troops scarce whenever they were needed. France sent a field army to Italy under Marshal Catinat, who was repulsed by Eugene in a couple of battles but kept the field. His successor, Marshal Villeroy, did not enjoy the confidence of his troops.

A Bourbon king of Spain was a nightmare scenario for the Protestant maritime powers, who had inserted themselves into the Spanish Caribbean economy. If it were possible to unite the incredible potential of weak Spain's planetary empire with the administrative efficiency and economic breadth of France, then the Bourbons would acquire a global primacy that none could challenge. English and Dutch merchants in Cadiz (now Spain's principal commercial window on the wider world) feared they would quickly be replaced by French traders and products. There was much at stake in the succession crisis. William of Orange, King of England and Stadtholder of the Dutch Republic, contemplated supporting Austria in its struggle. Maladroit French initiatives soon made up his mind. By the treaty of 1697, the Dutch established garrisons in a dozen fortresses of the Spanish Netherlands in order to constitute a barrier to French expansion. Louis sent French troops to join the Spanish garrisons in the Low Countries and they expelled the Dutch soldiery immediately. This rendered the Netherlands Republic very vulnerable. Second, Louis recognized James II, the Stuart exile, as the legitimate king of the British Isles, and lodged him and his Jacobite court in the Saint Germain palace near Paris. A large portion of the British political elite harboured Jacobite sentiments, and the sour Dutch sovereign was not a popular man. In Scotland and Ireland, the overwhelming majority of the population desired the return of the Stuart dynasty. This determined William to join the alliance against the Bourbons and to send a British expeditionary corps to fight alongside the Dutch. A number of German princes lined up in support of Emperor Leopold. Elector Frederick of Brandenburg promised to provide troops in exchange for the concession of royal status, and the title of King in Prussia (for Prussia lay outside the Empire). William was preparing to join the war when he died after being unhorsed. This turned out to be a stroke of good fortune for the coalition, for as a military commander, he proved markedly inferior in talent to his French adversaries. King James' youngest daughter, Anne, Protestant wife of Prince George of Denmark, mounted the throne in Britain, while the Dutch Republic decided not to fill the position of stadtholder. The British corps was confided to an aristocrat who had not yet exercised significant command, John Churchill, Duke of Marlborough, and, from June 1702, he obtained supreme command over the Confederate army in the Low Countries theatre. This achievement was not without its drawbacks: the English general displayed tactical competence, but he had no experience of organizing marches, had never planned a campaign or coordinated operations among several corps. He had never commanded forage operations, or led contribution raids, or commanded a wing of an army in battle, unlike a number of Dutch generals whom he was reluctant to consult.[40] Dutch and English money purchased a large number of German regiments, who brought experienced officers and men to the alliance. Military operations began on the lower Rhine and the frontier near Antwerp in 1702.

Strategically, the Bourbons held the upper hand: it sufficed to fight their adversaries to exhaustion in a war of sieges for a few years until the bankrupt coalition recognized the Bourbon regime in Spain. Huge field armies in the Low Countries and the Rhine manoeuvred for advantage and the Bourbons ceded the furthest outposts, but they lost little territory of their own. The alignment of Elector Max Emanuel of Bavaria with France at the outset of the war made it possible for a French army under Marshal Villars to penetrate deep into southern Germany in 1703. In northern Italy, the French Marshal Vendôme proved equal to Prince Eugene and pushed the Germans back into the Alps as far as Tirol. French contributions there triggered a major peasant revolt, to which Vendôme responded by killing peasants and burning villages.[41] Both sides solicited the aid of Italian states. Only the Duke of Mantua joined the Bourbons, while the others, including the Venetian Republic, watched nervously from the sidelines. Both the Franco–Spaniards (called *Gallispans*) and the German–Imperial troops raised contributions wherever they passed, although without inflicting too much damage. Duke Victor Amadeus actively negotiated to change sides at the first convenient opportunity, but it was an ill-guarded secret and, in 1703, Bourbon troops disarmed his best regiments.

Bourbon fortunes suddenly worsened everywhere in 1704. Two important allies, Savoy and Portugal, passed over to the Allied camp, bringing sizeable armies into the balance. The Duke of Marlborough then conceived a plan to march 400 kilometres from Brabant to the Danube and to join with Prince Eugene to knock Bavaria out of the war. The British–Imperial army of about 52,000 men attacked the Franco–Bavarian slightly smaller force along the Danube at Blenheim on 13 August 1704, broke through its centre and pinned a third of it along the river, forcing it to surrender. Blenheim was the worst French defeat in the field in several generations, and in the aftermath Bavaria was overrun and sacked. Elector Max Emanuel retreated to Flanders with the debris of his army and, now in exile, depended on French support. Austria imposed such heavy contributions on the conquered duchy (equal to ten per cent of Imperial military spending) that the population rose in revolt the following year that required an entire army to repress it.[42]

Each alliance did its best to foment revolt in the other camp. Fresh pressure on Protestants in Languedoc triggered a widespread revolt in the rugged Cevennes region in 1702. This inaugurated a classic counter-insurgency campaign against the Camisards (men who fought wearing shirts) entailing the deployment of 10,000 professional troops. The French commander Montrevel planned to displace whole populations in order to starve a few thousand guerrillas who made hit-and-run strikes against isolated posts. Catholic militias launched retaliatory raids with ever larger bands, bringing the region close to civil war. By 1704, the rebels were being supplied by English arms shipments unloaded on nearby Mediterranean beaches. Marshal Villars was then sent with ample reinforcements to pacify the region, assisted by the intendant, Basville, who gathered an extraordinary amount of intelligence. Villars allowed a discreet level of open Calvinist devotion, in exchange for disarmament, and most of the rebel leaders enlisted in the army with a pardon.[43]

France helped the Stuarts reignite the embers of rebellion in Scotland, and attempted to land a military force there in 1708, but to no avail. They were much more successful in assisting a general eight-year revolt in Habsburg Hungary. Emperor Leopold's policy of absolutism, Counter-Reformation intolerance and German military occupation alienated most of the Hungarian kingdom and Transylvania, which erupted in a Kuruç (Malcontents) revolt led by Ferenc II Rakoczy in 1703. The French king sent money, artillery specialists and military engineers to assist them in 1704, but the rebels could not win field battles against professional armies. Nevertheless, an average of 25–30,000 Habsburg troops were tied down in counter-insurgency war in Hungary, and as many as 52,000 in 1711, half the total army.

Still, in 1704, a British fleet under Admiral George Rooke cruised in the Mediterranean while an Anglo–Dutch–Portuguese army invaded Castile from the west. Unable to capture Cadiz, too well garrisoned, the fleet seized the virtually undefended nearby port of Gibraltar on 4 August. Rooke was soon forced to confront the French Mediterranean fleet under the Comte de Toulouse (Louis XIV's bastard son) off Malaga, in a long and indecisive battle, after which both sides retired to base. Philip V in Spain urgently raised men to confront the invasion, assisted by French troops sent by his grandfather. Forces fighting for King Philip in Spain numbered barely 25,000 in the vast Iberian Peninsula, and the regiments in Italy and Flanders were also few in number. Louis XIV dispatched some 20 French military engineers to press attacks against the Portuguese fortresses, while 120 artillery officers from France were attached to the fortresses and field armies, not without incurring the jealousy of their Spanish colleagues.[44] Scores of French engineers made their careers in Spain over the next decade, serving to train native cadres.

Bourbon troops held their own or better in the Low Countries, the Rhine and Italy in 1705, but a fresh Allied fleet landed an expeditionary force in Catalonia, where Archduke Charles established his court after capturing Barcelona. While the majority of the Castilians rallied around King Philip in Madrid, the Catalans fervently aligned themselves with the Habsburg claimant. From this moment, Spanish aristocrats were forced to back the Bourbon or the Habsburg rival. Some of the Spanish garrisons declared for Charles and the allies, especially in Valencia and along the Mediterranean coast.[45] A second Allied army began to operate in Catalonia and Aragon, pressing towards Madrid from the east. By now, the allies enjoyed uncontested superiority at sea. Along with British troops, arrived Germans, while thousands of Catalans enlisted in fresh regiments to support the popular German pretender, Charles III.

The Bourbon situation worsened sharply again in 1706, as the financial strain made it impossible for them to match the growing armies of their adversaries. From 1701, French militia were allotted to combat units, although their numbers were modest. After starting out with very large armies, Louis found it ever more difficult to recruit men as the war dragged on. In May, the combined Dutch and British army (the majority of which was constituted by German auxiliaries) caught the Bourbon army under the inept Marshal Villeroy and Elector Max Emanuel at Ramillies, at the eastern edge of the Spanish Low Countries, close to Liège. The Bourbon army was routed after several hours, and, for two weeks, Marlborough pressed forward and occupied a dozen towns. Some of them, like Brussels, were indefensible; at Antwerp, the Spanish citadel commander proclaimed for King Charles. Once he reached the North Sea coast, Marlborough captured Ostend and gained thereby a much shorter route for his supplies. Half of the Spanish Low Countries was now in coalition hands.[46] The weight of numbers was now clearly to the allied advantage. Britain mobilized some 50,000 native troops in 1706, in addition to a large number of German auxiliary regiments. Austria contributed 129,000 men to the coalition, without counting the Circle contingents of smaller German states. The Dutch employed 110,000 men already in 1702 (many of these German auxiliaries) and supervised the provisioning of armies in the Low Countries. Brandenburgers, Hanoverians, Danish and Palatine regiments, among many others, furnished substantial contingents year over year to the alliance. Portugal and Savoy added standing armies close to 30,000 men each, partly funded by Britain and the Netherlands. Against these, France supported eight different armies in 1706, in the Low Countries, on the Moselle, along the Rhine, one in Lombardy and another in Piedmont, and three Iberian forces, in Roussillon, in Catalonia and in Extremadura. Spanish troops in Italy and the Low Countries proved to be underfunded and unreliable allies.[47]

In Italy, Marshal Vendôme gradually occupied the Piedmontese fortresses, pushing Duke Victor Amadeus into the district around Turin. The French general then trounced the Imperial army in Lombardy at Calcinato on 19 April and pushed it back behind the River Adige, where it was reinforced and reorganized under Prince Eugene. But, in the aftermath of Ramillies, the French marshal was called north and command of the Italian theatre passed into the less capable hands of Marshals La Feuillade and Prince Philippe d'Orléans, nephew of Louis XIV. These initiated the critical siege of Turin in the summer of 1706. Vauban sent them instructions from Paris to capture the city first so as to shorten their siege lines. They ignored the recommendation, perhaps at Vendôme's behest, and concentrated on the citadel, the strongest point. Victor Amadeus still commanded an army of over 20,000 professional soldiers, but only by virtue of receiving considerable subsidies from the Allies. The French showed no urgency in pushing their approaches forward, and the Piedmontese made a very active defence, while Victor Amadeus harassed the besiegers from the countryside nearby. At the end of August, Prince Eugene re-emerged from the Lake Garda district with a large German contingent that out-manoeuvred Bourbon troops in Lombardy, joined Victor Amadeus and then arrived outside the Bourbon camp on 7 September, after a prodigious march of 400 kilometres. The Allied attack on the over-extended Bourbon siegeworks from the west succeeded and the Gallispan army retreated in haste towards Milan, since their retreat towards the Alps was cut off. The siege and battle of Turin was one of the significant political events in Italian history, for it meant that Austria now had the upper hand militarily. The Imperial army then deployed over northern Italy and extracted heavy contributions from the various duchies and the nearby Papal States. The Gonzaga Dukes of Mantua, who had openly sided with the Bourbons, forfeited their duchy to the Empire. In 1707, a German Imperial army marched the length of the peninsula and occupied the Kingdom of Naples, while Bourbon regiments departed for Spain.

Philip V tried to recover Barcelona during the course of 1706, but the coalition navy provided everything necessary to the defenders and the Bourbon army just melted away. The Habsburg pretender, Charles, established his rule over all of Catalonia, and as the Bourbon army withdrew, Aragon and Valencia also rose in his support. Bereft of troops and money, Philip had to evacuate Madrid as coalition troops advancing from Portugal entered it and proclaimed the rule of Charles III. However, the population soon rallied in favour of Philip, who collected reinforcements returning from Italy. In order not to be cut off in deepest Castile, the Anglo–Portuguese army evacuated Madrid and marched eastward towards Valencia. At Almansa on 25 April 1707, a Bourbon army under Marshal Berwick (illegitimate son of King James II of England, whose mother was Marlborough's sister!) smashed the coalition army utterly and pushed the remnants back into Catalonia. Aragon and Valencia were soon reoccupied, and Habsburg control receded into the northeast corner of Spain.

In the Low Countries, French armies were able to contain the Allied advance, but without being able to draw resources from outside France. This made the French financial situation increasingly dire. Along the Rhine frontier, the Imperials were undermanned because of their ongoing campaigns in Hungary. Marshal Villars stormed the German lines at Stollhofen and pushed the outnumbered enemy northward. French forces then fanned out over a vast area of Franconia and Swabia, almost as far as Bavaria, collecting millions of livres tournois in contributions. But this success could not offset the heavy cost of constant war in multiple theatres.

The year 1708 brought fresh disasters for the Bourbon cause. Louis XIV imposed his grandson, the Duc de Bourgogne, on the Duc de Vendôme as co-commander, each in charge of half the field army on the Low Countries frontier. The two men did not get along. Marlborough and Prince Eugene, who were famously compatible, marched west and attacked them just north of the fortress of Oudenaarde on 11 July. An aggressive general, Vendôme advanced to strike back, but half the army, under the Duc de Bourgogne, just stood fast on his left flank and watched. This debacle forced the Bourbons to retreat toward France, while the Allies next laid siege to Lille, the strongest of all the French fortresses. The city and its citadel, Vauban's masterpiece, held out for sixteen long weeks, inflicting grievous losses on the Allies, but governor Marshal Boufflers eventually surrendered. All the French efforts to cut the Allied supply line north of the city came to naught. The Walloons and

Flemings had initially cheered the arrival of Dutch and English garrisons as the Bourbons retreated, but their sentiments soon swung back in the other direction under the weight of heavy contributions, by the Protestantism of the occupiers, and of the Dutch intentions to impose its products on local markets.[48]

In Italy, indiscriminate heavy contributions levied on all the territories where Imperial troops were quartered finally provoked the irate Pope to declare war on the Emperor. His general, Luigi Ferdinando Marsigli, hastily collected a ragtag force to oppose the German professional army, and he was forced to retreat southwards along the Adriatic coast to avoid giving battle. The Pope conceded defeat by the next year. Emperor Joseph I resolved, after the Coalition defeat at Almansa, to send German troops (paid out of the British treasury) to Catalonia to defend his brother's claim to the throne of Madrid.[49] By this time, Louis XIV was desperate for peace and consented to abandon his support for Philip V. Reeling from the effects of a disastrous harvest and plummeting revenues, Louis was ready to admit defeat. He moved to withdraw some 15,000 French troops from the Iberian Peninsula that made offensive operations impossible for Madrid. For the allied negotiators at Gertruidenburg (and the Dutch in particular), this was still not enough. They demanded that Louis employ the French army to drive his grandson from his throne. For Louis this was a demand too far, which he explained in an appeal to France as he made preparations for a new campaign.

Early in 1709, a polar air mass settled on most of Europe for six weeks, killing trees and vines, the seeds in the ground, the birds and small animals. It did not inflict the same mortality as the previous famine of 1693–1694, but it created tremendous hardship. Desperate men signed up in the French army in unprecedented numbers, where they were sure of finding food. Marlborough and Eugene captured the powerful fortress of Tournai, and then moved on to Mons, working their way methodically through Vauban's forward line of fortresses. Marshal Villars deployed his army nearby at Malplaquet in order to harass the besiegers, and had permission from Versailles to fight a defensive battle if attacked. About 75,000 French troops raised earthworks about four kilometres long between two large woods on each flank, which were blocked with felled trees, or *abattis*. On 11 September, Marlborough and Eugene launched almost 100,000 men against troops in prepared positions, who mowed down the assailants over the course of several hours. Allied cavalry eventually broke through the line and Villars amassed French horse to repel them, when he was hit. His subordinate, Marshal Boufflers, then organized a proper withdrawal and the French army marched away in good order. A technical victory for the Allies, who incurred as many as 24,000 casualties compared to only 12,000 for the French, Malplaquet was a sobering warning that Louis XIV's armies were not yet in disarray and that they had recovered from their previous demoralization. The Allies were, therefore, forced to lay siege to Vauban's great fortresses one by one, at enormous cost of blood and treasure (Map 9).

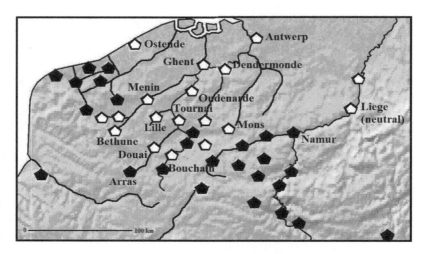

Map 9 Coalition sieges in the Low Countries

Deprived of most of his French regiments, in 1710 Philip V felt strong enough to invade Catalonia with his Castilian army, but he was quickly checked and withdrew to Zaragoza, where his army was defeated a second time by the advancing British and German troops. He withdrew deep into northwest Castile while the Allies occupied Madrid a second time. Most of the Spanish nobility left the capital so as not to pay homage to the Archduke Charles. The population of the capital murdered dozens of sentries every night, until, on 9 November, the Allies decided they must evacuate the city and return to Barcelona. Louis XIV instructed General Vendôme, with fresh French regiments, to combine with the forces of the Spanish king. Advancing the whole army at breakneck speed in a forced march three days long, Vendôme and Philip surprised the British contingent at Brihuega on 8 December. The entire army was killed or captured after a brief struggle. Vendôme pounced on the German and Catalan force the next day at Vilaviciosa and battered it, too. The Allied cause outside Catalonia collapsed completely.

The recovery of Spanish military power under King Philip was, in itself, a remarkable success. At the beginning of the war, the troops were demoralized and poorly financed. There was no unified treasury for all of Spain, and no financial figures available for any place but Castile. This reflected the lack of centralization of the Habsburg monarchy, where each component was a separate entity with its own constitution and administration. After remodelling the army on French lines in 1703, Philip raised new regiments. We should speak of a Bourbon army rather than a Spanish one, for regiments of both kingdoms served side by side in the field and in garrison. French generals such as Berwick and Vendôme held the ascendancy until the very end of the fighting in 1715.

Spanish contingents arrived from the Low Countries and from Italy as those territories were occupied by the coalition, which had the result of stiffening resistance in Iberia. When France withdrew its troops in 1709 in order to make peace with the Allies, Philip retained a field army of 19,000 men, almost all Spaniards. Allied field armies rarely numbered more than 25,000 men due to the difficulty of finding forage in such a dry country, and, apart from Catalan auxiliaries, the great majority were foreigners and frequently Protestants, too. French troops returning in 1710 under Vendôme tipped the balance back towards the Bourbons.

During this crisis, the French advisers, the ambassador Michel Amelot, the chief finance minister Jean Orry and the Fleming Jean de Brouchoven, Count of Bergeyck, supervised the financial recovery of Spain. The financiers themselves were more often Spaniards, who accepted reimbursement in the debased coin of the realm. The silver fleet arrived intermittently throughout the war, despite the best efforts of the Allies to intercept it, and, notwithstanding the Spanish civil war, the king's revenues increased year on year. In 1702, Spanish revenues were about 12 million crowns, but amounted to 26 million in 1713, even without Barcelona, of which the great majority was assigned to the war effort. In 1707, Philip abolished the *fueros*, or the tax privileges of Valencia and Aragon as punishment for their rebellion, placed new gabelles on salt and tobacco and recovered taxes that had been privatized by his predecessors. Early in the war, Philip regularly received instructions from his grandfather at Versailles, but, over time, French interference rankled the Castilian political elites. From 1711, Italians began to move into key positions, which increased after 1713 when Philip married Elisabeth Farnese, from the ducal family of Parma. She and her countryman adviser, Cardinal Alberoni (a close companion of Marshal Vendôme), gradually took greater control over the court and its policies. Very few Castilians adhered to the cause of the Habsburg pretender, Charles.[50]

The political context of the war changed suddenly in April 1711 when Joseph I died at the age of 33, which made Archduke Charles the Holy Roman Emperor. Joseph hated France and spent his entire reign trying to rally German states against Louis XIV. He proved more conciliatory towards the Hungarians than his father, Leopold, and was finally able to end the rebellion there by the time he died. The Habsburg states raised over 100,000 professional soldiers from their very decentralized territories, but they were scattered over multiple theatres of war, including about 12,000 men in Catalonia.[51] The new emperor, Charles VI, quit Barcelona for Vienna, without abandoning his claim to the throne of Spain and the Americas. England suddenly acquired cold feet, not wishing to replace a Bourbon hegemony with a Habsburg one. The British Parliamentary election in 1710 returned a landslide number of MPs wishing to end the war so that the country might resume commerce in Spain. Marlborough lost influence after the butchery of Malplaquet and the disaster befalling the Allies in Spain, and his wife's close relationship with Queen Anne soured. At the end of 1711, still blocked by fortresses in northern France, Marlborough had to relinquish command of the British contingent. Britain withdrew from active hostilities without informing its allies: its regiments kept the field, but they attended the field operations as spectators, while Prince Eugene assumed overall Allied command.

With the fall of Lille in 1708, Allied armies opened a path through Vauban's first line of fortresses and they began to besiege the second line in 1711 and 1712, in the face of stiff resistance. Prince Eugene besieged Landrécies with German and Dutch regiments in 1712, when Marshal Villars, after a frantic night march, stormed the Allied fortified camp at Denain on his flank, which contained most of the supplies for the campaign. Having separated Eugene from his line of supply, French armies recaptured a dozen lost fortresses in a period of weeks, setting the Coalition progress back by years. A fleet of French naval warships acting as privateers attacked Rio de Janeiro in 1711 and scooped up millions of crowns in booty. During the war, French privateers, from Dunkirk, St Malo and La Rochelle particularly, had captured more than 4,500 ships belonging to Allied nations, crippling their overseas commerce.[52] By now, the diplomats were close to peace. The British and Dutch concluded the war at Utrecht in 1713, by which France lost very little territory (keeping Strasbourg and recovering Lille). France was to repudiate definitively the Stuart claim to the British thrones. Philip V retained the throne of Spain, but on condition that it might never be joined with France. English and Dutch financiers obtained the *asiento* to supply Spanish colonies with slaves and were conceded a modest level of legitimate commerce with the Spanish Indies. The Holy Roman Empire fought alone for another year, but Marshal Villars carried the war across the Rhine into Germany and captured the strongholds of Landau and Freiburg. By the Treaty of Rastatt in March 1714, the Empire made final peace with the Bourbons. Austria acquired the former Spanish Netherlands and allowed the Dutch to garrison the major fortresses there, as before. Milan, Sardinia and Naples also passed to the Habsburg emperor, Charles VI, while the Duke of Savoy, Victor Amadeus, acquired some adjoining territories in Italy and the kingdom of Sicily, finally realizing the dynastic dream of royal status. In the war's last act, Philip V, with Spanish and French troops, besieged Barcelona, after having suppressed Catalonia's liberties, or *fueros*. With the surrender of the Catalan capital on 11 September 1714, the continent was again at peace.

Notes

1   Henry Kamen, 1993: 265.
2   Jean Bérenger, 1987: 350.
3   Antonio Dominguez Ortiz, 1980.
4   Derek McKay, 2001: 104.
5   Jonathan Israel, 1995: 543–44, 736–38.
6   Myron P Gutmann, 1988: 117–120.
7   Richard Rapp, 1975.
8   Jean-Philippe Cénat, 2015: 131.
9   Michel Vergé-Franceschi, 2003: 219–20, 386–90.
10 James R Jones, 1996: 96.

11 Cénat, 2015: 138.
12 Bertrand Fonck, 2014: 240.
13 Olaf van Nimwegen, 2010: 324.
14 Peter H Wilson, 1988: 45.
15 J Alcalà Zamora and Queipo de Llano, 1976.
16 Antonio José Rodriguez Hernandez, 2009.
17 Dominguez Ortiz, 1980.
18 Giuseppe Galasso, 1982: 189–204; Emile Laloy,1929 vol. 2: 1.
19 Michael Hochedlinger, 2003: 55, 91.
20 Cénat, 2015: 198.
21 John A Lynn, 1999: 161–4.
22 Jean Meuvret, 1960.
23 Geoffrey Symcox, 1983: 69.
24 Carlo Bitossi, 1988: 39–69; Gianni Galliani, 1984.
25 Roy L McCullough, 2007: 33.
26 McKay, 2001: 114.
27 Stephen Ede-Barrett, 2017: 15.
28 Jean Bérenger, 2004: 376.
29 Jean Bérenger, 1987: 403.
30 Jean-Philippe Cénat, 2005; Hermann Weber, 1994.
31 Olivier Chaline, 2011.
32 Jaap R Bruijn, 1989.
33 Symcox, 1983: 69.
34 Emmanuel de Broglie, 1902: 52–155.
35 Christopher Storrs, 2006.
36 Jean-Philippe Cénat, 2015.
37 John A Lynn, 1997: 258.
38 Peter H Wilson, 1998: 91.
39 Robert Oresko, 1997.
40 John M Stapleton, 2012.
41 Fadi el-Hage, 2017.
42 Charles W Ingrao, 1979: 47.
43 McCullough, 2007, 193–228.
44 Catherine Desos, 2016.
45 David Francis, 1975: 205.
46 Jamel Ostwald, 2000.
47 Clément Oury, 2011: 371.
48 Oury, 2011: 371.
49 Ingrao, 1979: 162.
50 Henry Kamen, 1969; Francis, 1975.
51 Hochedlinger, 2003: 185.
52 Lynn, 1997: 347.

10 The classical campaign

Winter preparations

Whoever reads accounts of multiple campaigns in the late seventeenth and early eighteenth century will be struck by a certain repetition of situations and events. Warfare, writes John Lynn, was a *process* that unfolded year after year according to well-established operational procedures.[1] Battles were not very frequent and even fewer proved decisive, such that campaigns evolved with regularity over the summer. With the onset of autumn and winter, it became impossible to transport heavy charges on unpaved roads or find sufficient fodder for animals in the fields. The cold, wet weather also exposed the soldiers to the elements, which multiplied the number of sick and invalid men. There was no solution but to discontinue active campaigning and to assign as many men as possible into comfortable winter quarters. Soldiers and animals made their way back from the theatre of operations into the interior and functionaries dispersed them in towns and villages over a wide area so as not to overburden the resources of small communities. Not the entire army, however: fortresses near the frontier with the enemy needed to be strongly held, and generals assigned part of the army to large winter camps not far away in order to monitor enemy activities over the winter, which were always possible. Near the edge of the theatre of operations, units in winter quarters lodged in walled towns almost exclusively, for greater security. Some towns assigned the men to stables, store-rooms and barns to lodge over winter, instead of barracks or inhabitants' houses, which, owing to the heat radiating from the animals, must have been cosy enough. These men had many diverse tasks to carry out over the winter, done by rotation so as not to tax particular regiments. If troop pay was not forthcoming, the officers would have to pay the men from their own pockets, or borrow money locally in their own name, to keep the men warm and fed. But winter imposed a general hiatus in military activity.[2]

A portion of the officers left the army to hunt for men, usually in their home territories, in order to fill the gaps in their company complement. Ambitious officers would make their presence known in the capital, to 'work the court' in search of patrons who would vouch for their promotion. A drawn-out siege or a large-scale battle opened hundreds of vacancies that the war ministers needed to fill. Senior commanders also returned to court in order to discuss plans for the next campaign with princes and their ministers. Belligerents also used the winter months to exchange prisoners, having agreed to a monetary value, typically a month's pay, for each rank. The side with the smallest number of prisoners was then 'owed' a sum for the remainder by their adversaries. These negotiations were not based on concerns of morality or religious sentiment, but on reciprocity; one could recover experienced men lost in the previous campaign by making a bargain with the other side.[3] None of the belligerents had the facilities, the financial means or the desire to hold and guard prisoners over the war's duration. Many of them might be induced to join the army that captured them, by making captivity uncomfortable for those who remained stubbornly loyal.[4]

Winter was a time when peace negotiations accelerated, taking into account the results of the previous campaign. If these discussions were not conclusive, princes, ministers and generals set about planning the next one. If fighting was anticipated in several theatres simultaneously, they designated how many troops to mobilize in each area and where to fix the assembly points. In the allied coalitions against France, the various powers debated the financial burden of each of the belligerents, and, for a fee, minor princes offered their regiments to each of the great powers. Not expecting to break through enemy fortress barriers completely, planners discussed the best sieges to undertake and studied plans of strongholds. If they expected to fight a defensive campaign, they needed to hurry improvements to their own places before the next summer. Maps played an increasing role in elaborating these projects. The increased diffusion of printed maps in the late seventeenth century, and marked improvements in their accuracy around 1700, tended to accentuate the drift to positional warfare. All the belligerents possessed the same black and white printed maps, and a good stock of coloured pen-and-ink sketches of varying elaborateness. Ambitious projects such as long marches or organizing the efficient delivery of supplies were impossible without good maps.[5] Some officers had, as their sole responsibility, the preparation of new maps and plans of campaign, in order to assist senior commanders and ministers. The Netherlands Republic and the Spanish Low Countries were particularly well mapped, along with Northern Italy and the Rhineland. Writing planning documents and appending maps and sketches to them absorbed a considerable amount of time for these officers, who, like the Marquis de Chamlay at Versailles, or Luigi Ferdinando Marsigli in Vienna, could rise quickly by virtue of these skills.[6] French war ministers employed a number of engineers specialized in geography and cartography. Maps were also indispensable to diplomats, whose task was to fix the frontiers after the peace. Military staffs also collected intelligence from spies planted abroad. Prisoners and deserters tended to possess little useful information, so it was better to aim higher. Louvois possessed a formidable network of such agents, who included the Prince William of Orange's personal valet, Lannoy. Proper spies needed to present well in society and have a good education, in order to mingle among important people. They must also be multilingual, to overhear conversation in polyglot armies. Among them one also encounters civilian commissaires, or army contractors and forage specialists, whose business contacts gave them knowledge of military camps. Most information came from rumours, or news indiscreetly published in gazettes.[7]

Once the number of troops in each theatre had been determined, it was urgent to stock the magazines with the proper amount of stores. An army of 60,000 men required 90,000 food rations a day for the soldiers, and more for the horses. Stabled working horses required considerable quantities of oats and other cereal as well as roughage such as bran and straw. If enough dry fodder was available, the army could enter the field in March, long before the enemy was ready. Generals could draw on these stocks until the grass was high enough to feed their animals in the field, usually in late May. Fortresses served as supply depots and the point of departure for field armies. To fill the store-rooms, ministers turned to private contractors, the *munitionnaires*, who were familiar with market conditions, and enjoyed access to cash and credit through their connections. Using false names, they purchased provisions in enemy territory, too, particularly in the great emporium of Amsterdam. While they sometimes defrauded the state, they were no more guilty of this than state officials and commanders.[8] By 1700, France's competitors also adopted the use of advanced magazines, like the ones in Tirol and Friuli, to feed and supply Prince Eugene's men in northern Italy.[9] The foremost great Dutch magazine at Maastricht could feed armies 60 kilometres away if they operated close to the navigable River Meuse. Fortresses also stored the heavy artillery of the siege trains, which were too cumbersome to accompany an army's daily movement.[10] As the convoys of provisions trundled towards the magazines, parties of cavalry emerged from towns along the way to meet the previous escort half-way.

The men camped in winter quarters close to the enemy were not usually inactive: if they could disrupt enemy preparations, it might give them a decisive advantage. In December 1711, a French force of 40,000 men collected from the camps and nearby garrisons converged on the Scarpe and the Deule rivers connecting the enemy magazine at Douai, wrecking the embankments undisturbed for three days and flooding the zone. This delayed the Allied timetable by weeks, and required 20,000 men to restore the navigability of the waterways and to resume stocking the fortress. Numerous smaller parties were sent out to attack enemy convoys and posts, sometimes located 100 kilometres away. Soldiers in the frontier zone were also employed building fortified lines over considerable distances, in part as barriers to enemy armies, but mostly in order to curtail raiding parties and to protect the communities behind them from contributions. Earthworks, raised with earth tightly tamped around a timber frame, were increasingly central to campaigns. Raimondo Montecuccoli conscripted thousands of peasants to construct field fortifications to block Black Forest passes and river crossings in 1675: these consisted of interconnected earth walls and ditches, redoubts and batteries, palisades and blockhouses stretching 90 kilometres in all.[11] In 1690, the French erected 20 kilometres of lines between the Lys and Scheldt rivers, supported by 34 independent redoubts. By 1694, they had greatly extended these, in order to place the villages behind it out of reach of enemy patrols, and traced

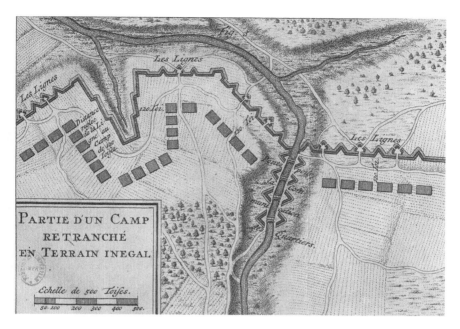

Image 10.1 Vauban, Field Lines. Field lines consisting of raised earthworks and detached redoubts, sometimes extending 50 kilometres or more, gave some protection to villages behind them. They could also block an enemy advance, if they were manned sufficiently. Traité des sièges et de l'attaque des places, BNF V-9323

a network of roads behind them to shift troops quickly to threatened places (Image 10.1). Units spending the winter close to the frontier occupied many small posts in order to keep an eye on the enemy and to control the border. Detachments typically spent five days in exposed positions, and were then replaced by other troops based in nearby fortresses. A good commander of winter quarters could intuit where the enemy might wish to advance in force, and when they might be ready to move, so he would make plans to strengthen those posts just before the campaign began. With luck the enemy might have to change their plans and incur further delays.[12]

In March, the French provincial intendants established the *étapes* along which troops in distant winter quarters would march to the point of assembly (Image 10.2). This system was not adequate for the movement of large contingents but it worked well for single companies and their officers. Infantry moved 16 kilometres and cavalry 24 kilometres daily (Image 10.3). Since they often strayed off route and inflicted damage on fields and houses, these roads were the scourge of peasants who lived near them, but most of the violence customary during the Thirty Years' War disappeared after 1675.[13] Munitions

Image 10.2 Nicolas Guerard (le jeune?): Sortie du quartier d'hiver. Troops leave their winter quarters, filling their sacks with food and drink purloined or purchased from their village hosts. The latter were usually happy to see them depart. Art Resource

Image 10.3 Nicolas Guerard (le jeune?): La Marche. Infantry soldiers march to or from the theatre of operations. Individuals in a section (chambrée) of five or six men who messed together, took turns carrying heavy gear. Their approach triggered an alarm rung from church steeples. Art Resource

converged at the frontier in April, along with recruits and reinforcements, and whatever militia units had been assigned to the theatre arrived, too (Image 10.4). Troop and magazine inspections then began in earnest. The presumed beginning of the campaign was late in May, but the exact date

Image 10.4 Nicolas Guerard (le jeune?): Le Bouteselle. The trumpet and drum (on the left) broadcast the order for the cavalry troopers to saddle up and assemble at the head of the camp. Art Resource

depended largely on the whims of Mother Nature. A wet spring would render roads impassable and swell each creek. A crucial factor was the growth of vegetation; before a campaign, horses were released into meadows to be 'grassed' with vitamin-rich fodder to give them strength to work. Once the horses had been restored to vigour after surviving for months on dry fodder and hay, the campaign was ready to begin.[14] In Spain and Portugal, the timetable was completely different, due to the inability to campaign in July and August because of the extreme heat and lack of water. Mild Octobers and Novembers and an early spring compensated for the inconvenience.

Small war and foraging

The army could not move very far without sending cavalry to collect fodder in the field, the equivalent of petrol in modern times (Image 10.5). A small army with only 4,000 horses would still require 100 cartloads of grass or hay every day. An army 10–15 times that number had enormous daily requirements that could not be improvised. The general rule, which was built into the army routine, was to gather supplies for four or five days. Cavalry would be sent as far away from camp as possible to start, and then moved in closer (Image 10.6). Forage officers required knowledge of the most nutritious plants, based on their study of botany and agriculture. Soldiers scythed the grass in the field amid stands of muskets, watched by friends mounted on horses, to prevent surprise attack by enemy cavalry patrols. Foragers scythed the standing grain in the field, and then collected local grain stocks from attics (Image 10.7). These they

Image 10.5 Ravenet: Farm and fodder in the Parmigiano. Farms such as these were the equivalent of modern petrol stations for advancing armies. Oxen were also driven off to feed the soldiers, who liked meat. Archivio di Stato Parma

Image 10.6 Stefano Della Bella: Cavalry Reconnaissance. Cavalry served as the eyes of every army, and patrols avidly questioned people they encountered, and snatched prisoners to interrogate. MET Museum

loaded on the rumps of horses or into carts and trundled back to camp.[15] Great foraging parties, in addition to ammunition convoys, required considerable cavalry and dragoon escorts to remain safe (Image 10.8). Enemy cavalry patrols did their utmost to interrupt these tasks. They were convenient opportunities for

Image 10.7 Nicolas Guerard (le jeune?): Fourageurs. Foragers enabled armies to keep the field, by reaping grass and grain in quantities sufficient to feed all the horses in the army, and to deny the same to enemy parties. Troopers would have wielded scythes more often than sabres. Art Resource

Image 10.8 Nicolas Guerard (le jeune?): Cavaliers et Dragons. Both played an important scouting role, but dragoons were multi-purpose mounted infantry who excelled at skirmishing. Art Resource

soldiers to slip away and hide, and so army provosts and their executioners joined such parties to hang offenders.[16]

Low-intensity fighting called 'small war' – *guerrilla* in Spanish – took place on a daily basis. Henri IV, who was an expert in the matter himself, published the first army ordinances governing this in France in 1595. This manner of fighting is as old as war itself, but official histories and most modern historians neglect its existence (Image 10.9).[17] Seventeenth-century military writers dealt with it increasingly, such as Montecuccoli, who encountered it in Hungary on a large scale. His writings reached an enormous international public. The Marquis de Feuquières (died 1711) was another expert, whose writings on the subject were published only in 1730. Skirmishing constituted the majority of soldiers' experience of combat. Officers leading these *parties* (the technical term) proved their bravery and their spirit of initiative, and derived reputation and honour from it. The best of these '*partisans*' were highly sought after. Small war served multiple purposes: to collect contributions from enemy territory, to harass enemy strongpoints, to blockade enemy fortresses and to collect intelligence.[18]

Forward fortresses levied contributions on the enemy or neutral communities within reach, and commanders organized armed visits to collect money and provisions from them. Fortress governors also issued licences for partisan raids, to seize booty from the enemy and to burn whatever valuable supplies could not be transported. They might consist of ad hoc members of regular infantry and cavalry regiments, or form free companies specialized in such activities. A typical party numbered 20 or 30 men, but hundreds or even thousands of troops set out on more ambitious projects, pulling carts filled with tools and explosive devices to open town gates. Map-reading was a special skill required in partisan warfare, to judge the

Image 10.9 Nicolas Guerard (le jeune?): Embuscade, or Ambush. 'Partisans' surprise an enemy detachment. This kind of war was practised by both sides on a large scale, but historians until recently gave it little consideration. Art Resource

distance to sheltered places. If peasants refused to pay contributions, a fire raid could be organized. Such parties were very active in winter, when the enemy field army was not present. Typically, they burned a house or two and seized a few notables for ransom. If the inhabitants ran away, their houses were looted and burned to make an example. Parties tended to visit several villages almost simultaneously, setting fires or damaging houses in one in order to induce the others to pay quickly. Usually, they were structured into two groups: the 'hunter' section, and the covering force lurking nearby to prevent surprise and to facilitate the escape. Their preferred prizes were horses, easily carried off and possessing decent resale value. Prizes taken by partisans had to be sold at well-publicized auctions, where the officers often took the best pieces for themselves and redistributed the rest.[19] The booty obtained this way could double or triple a soldier's pay if the target, such as a convoy, contained valuable assets. The army was a place of circulation of second-hand goods of all kinds, from building materials, to household goods, to leather. As Sandberg explains, the army itself was a great magazine that assembled new and used goods. It recycled metal on a large scale, melting down bells and agricultural implements in order for army blacksmiths and armourers to repair firearms. Soldiers smashed casks of wine or beer in order to make off with the iron hoops. Musket-balls were retrieved and reused. The army also scavenged clothing and the personal effects of prisoners and of casualties. Camp followers and officers with coins in their purses snapped up plundered goods for a fraction of their normal value and then resold them farther away.[20]

By the 1670s, these practices had become so routine that contribution notices were presented on printed leaflets, with blanks to place the name of the community and the amount of cash or provisions demanded. Typically, the officer of a contribution party dealt with the local lord or town council, who then raised the money and disbursed it. They might have to lodge the soldiers overnight and billet them on houses. The owner was supposed to keep records so as to have the expenses deducted from his taxes. Communities usually borrowed money from city dwellers, and then paid interest on it, which fed urban prosperity and gave business to lawyers, who could sue villages for non-payment. A community that delivered contributions to one army was liable to pay an equal amount to the other side, however. Because these contributions effectively doubled or tripled the rural tax burden, in 1677 French and Spanish delegates met at Deynze, outside Ghent, and agreed to fix some general principles governing the practice. The amount demanded should not exceed the community's normal tax bill, and it should be deducted from the money they owed their own government. Execution by fire should only be applied to people who had fled their homes. These measures were only really applied after 1700, with the primary intention to maintain discipline among the soldiers rather than some humanitarian concern.[21] During the Dutch War between 1674 and 1678, French contributions and related war taxes on the Spanish Netherlands and the United Provinces amounted to 13 million livres tournois annually, or 16% of annual military expenditures.[22] For the 1690s, Guy Rowlands has calculated that contributions raised about 12% of the money the French army required on campaign, and it deprived the enemy of the same resources.[23] In

1689, the Marquis de Feuquières issued forth from Heilbronn near the central Rhine with 1,000 cavaliers, raided to the gates of Nuremburg, crossed the Danube and returned to camp via Augsburg, having raised between three and four million livres tournois, equal to two per cent of the King of France's total tax revenues in a single adventure!

Larger parties aimed to seize towns and castles, or attacked the enemy in their quarters even in the dead of winter. Parties could lie in ambush in the woods, or lurk between two enemy contingents, or between the enemy camp and its magazines to the rear. Armies enhanced the roles given to troops who fought in this way; the grenzers, Cossacks and hussars, whose methods were familiar to raiders everywhere. Partisans were better armed than most troops, carrying flintlocks rather than matchlocks (with no glowing match at night), pistols and swords for fighting on horseback and grenades carried in pouches, as well as axes for battering down doors. Imperial armies were dangerous adversaries, as their Croats scoured the theatre of operations. Imperial Hungarian hussars numbered 5,700 men in eight regiments in 1702, operating in Italy, Germany and the Low Countries. Following the great *Kuruç* revolt against the emperor, the French raised hussar regiments (three in 1706) from Magyar deserters. Walled towns and isolated castles occupied by regular troops were frequently the target of daring raids in which soldiers swam moats and escaladed walls. In attacks on convoys, most of the party assailed the escort troops, while a detachment briskly seized wagons and horses and made their escape. The French Marshal Luxembourg strongly encouraged these forays to harass Spanish and, especially, Dutch generals, like the plodding Waldeck or the Prince of Orange. They kept the enemy off balance and helped gather precious intelligence.

Parties could constitute small armies in some operations. In 1691, after a long night march, the Marquis de Feuquières seized Savigliano in Piedmont with 800 cavalry and 500 infantry riding on the rumps behind the troopers. In 1693, Marshal Luxembourg assembled 10,000 men, mostly cavalry, to advance 80 kilometres across the Spanish Low Countries to surprise the contingent of General Tilly, who just barely escaped. In 1675, one French raid from Maastricht penetrated deep into Holland in order to set fire to the houses of members of the Dutch government. The operations were by no means always successful. One near-success was Prince Eugene's project of infiltrating 500 German grenadiers crawling through a sewer into the Gallispan fortress of Cremona in Lombardy in February 1702. There were not enough sentries on the walls, and not enough scouts patrolling outside to prevent the approach of the grenadiers or detect the supporting force behind them. They had captured the French commander, Marshal Villeroy, but were interrupted by Irish troops who gave the alert before enough Austrian reinforcements could enter the gates. Villeroy's capture was perhaps the most important consequence of the failure, for his replacement, General Vendôme, was a much tougher opponent.[24] In September 1708, General Lamothe marched 20,000 men to attack an Allied munitions convoy bringing supplies to the critical siege of Lille. Though heavily outnumbering his prey, Lamothe bungled the manoeuvre and the siege went on to its successful conclusion.

War of manoeuvre

A war of positions and limited objectives did not imply that armies stood still: they might march hundreds of kilometres during the season, although remaining boxed into a relatively small area. French armies in the Low Countries received letters from Versailles, in which the king, Louvois and his successors instructed the generals where to move next. This was the *guerre de cabinet*, which applied particularly to the northern theatre that the king knew well. Marches and campsites were entrusted to specialist officers, the marshals-general, who discussed these in conjunction with the minister, Chamlay, who had a pleasing talent for sketching out these plans and explaining them to the king. Given the very large dimensions of field armies by this time, routinely superior to 60,000 men, marches had to be organized in eight or nine columns, plus a covering force. An efficient highway network, such as the one that enabled Napoleon Bonaparte to subdivide the great force into autonomous corps moving by separate roads, did not yet exist. Every day, cavalry received the order where it must patrol and dispatch scouts. In case of trouble, a cannon shot alerted the outlying detachments. Scouts were eager to capture enemy prisoners who might inform them of nearby contingents, but they also stopped and interrogated passers-by.

The men could not march farther than 20 kilometres for more than a few days in succession, and it was customary to stop every four or five days to rest, and to bake bread. Troops had to arrive at the new campsite early enough in the day to set up tents, search for forage and scout enemy activity. They might erect entrenchments two metres high around the perimeter, like the Romans, or simply use empty carts as barricades deployed around the circumference of the

Image 10.10 Nicolas Guerard (le jeune?): Discipline de la baguette. A wayward soldier runs the gauntlet, reduced to his shirt and breeches, then struck by rods wielded by his comrades. Officers considered that soldiers feared only corporal punishment. Art Resource

camp. The *maréchal de camp* would lay out the army in such a manner that the units could emerge from it in the order they would fight in battle, in lines.[25] Soldiers erected canvas tents or huts made of branches and straw, sited about three metres apart in long rows, with a cooking pot for every three or four shelters. Soldiers lived in sociable groups of about a dozen men who would aid each other and they made army service bearable.[26] Keeping soldiers within the bounds of the camp and not abroad causing trouble was a prime concern, the remedy for which was taking frequent roll-call. Soldiers were still prone to looting on the march, and even the churches were not respected, despite strict orders. Officers occasionally searched the huts and tents for plunder. Outside camp security was maintained by detachments occupying villages and fords.

The army commander on the move searched for ways to fool his adversary. He might mark out several dummy camps simultaneously on the afternoon before his army moved, seeking to instil doubt in the mind of his opposite number. Roads and bridges needed to be repaired for the march, and making these preparations in several directions could also create uncertainty. The army then moved in two wings, each subdivided into columns in order to use all the available roads.[27] Guides and peasant pioneers were hired, and often paid handsomely, to facilitate the march forward. In the centre of the columns moved the baggage, the heavy guns and the sutlers with their civilian helpers. The wagon-master imposed a march order for the wagons and any vehicle in the wrong place, or that created an obstacle, could be immediately looted. Aristocratic officers required a considerable amount of baggage for themselves and their servants. Generals were allotted three wagons and a coach, drawn by a good stable of horses.[28] The staff officers had to solve the practical problem of ensuring that men and vehicles on the roads in multiple columns would never cross each other's path. By the later seventeenth century, this specialized knowledge was the domain of army furriers. Battalions that had become intermingled would be completely disorganized and slow down the entire process.[29] In a large army, each unit needed its own route and timetable, so that not all the army marched at once. The vanguard left just before dawn in the direction of the next camp, while the main body trundled out behind them later in the morning. The rear guard packed up the remainder, and by the time it reached the next camp, everything was in place to receive them.

Armies moved by a command cycle, wherein headquarters reacted to intelligence, brought by letters and reports and plotted on maps.[30] The senior officers then decided on a response and delivered instructions to myriad subordinate officers for action. The faster the cycle, the more efficient the army. Victory belonged to the force with the superior organization, especially since the technological level of Western European armies was virtually the same. Each general was encouraged to maintain his personal spy service. Marshal Luxembourg employed one precious spy, Jacquet, secretary of the Elector of Bavaria, military commander of the Spanish Low Countries and close collaborator of William of Orange. He was paid a fortune for each letter he sent. Generals spent a good portion of their day at their camp table, reading and dictating letters and interviewing people. They would have to sign passports, safeguards for villages and monasteries, requisition orders of vehicles for the army, and issue a variety of correspondence with their political masters. Prisoners might be brought before the commander-in-chief for interrogation. Marshal Luxembourg was punctilious in this regard, coaxing information by his natural authority and high social and military rank. The records give no hint of torture on these occasions, but he was generous with alcohol to loosen tongues.[31] Communication was undertaken by written letter, delivered by hand by a postal service or carried by aristocratic attachés or young aides-de-camp. Correspondents in the field made use of ciphers, substituting numbers for whole words, for names of persons or places.

Senior commanders were surrounded by numerous officers with the rank of lieutenant-general, along with hand-picked advisers who served as a kind of general staff. There were so many lieutenants-general that they rotated as 'officer of the day', supervising the different tasks of the army. The generals also kept open tables for their underlings (who appreciated the savings and the opportunity to maintain visibility and connections) and other guests.[32] The Coalition army in the Low Countries worked smoothly on the whole, perhaps because the senior commanders were fluent in French. William of Orange, Stadtholder of the Netherlands, was, at the same time, King of England, while his successor, Marlborough, made an effort to accommodate the Grand Pensionary of Holland, Anthonie Heinsius, who ensured the army's supply. The German auxiliary troops in English or Dutch pay fulfilled their tasks under officers of various ethnic groups. The English and Dutch got along well together in the field, while the Spanish commander in both wars confined most of his troops to garrisons. The degree of collaboration by the Imperial commander depended upon his personality. During the war of the Spanish Succession, Marlborough and Eugene shared a similar outlook and co-operated seamlessly.

A clever commander would detach sizeable forces from the main army to constitute a *flying camp*, which occupied a position ten or twelve hours' march away in order to supervise a nearby sector. These contained a larger proportion of cavalry and dragoons, who could react quickly to an opening in the enemy deployment. Cavalry moved at the rate of 4–5 kilometres an hour, where infantry marched more slowly, at 3.5. When called to join the main army to fight a battle, they would leave their tents standing and their campfires burning to induce the enemy into error, as at Fleurus.[33] Fast-moving forces could also break an enemy blockade and reinforce a fortress threatened with investment. About half the troops in the theatre were assigned to garrison duty, but strong parties of men marched out of nearby fortresses to augment the main force if a major action was looming. Thus, the opposing general was never completely sure of the number of men in the enemy array. Marshal Vendôme recommended remaining close to the enemy army to keep a better eye on them, and, typically, the opposing camps stood only a day or two apart.

Generals frequently detached troops to erect earthworks in lines and redoubts, of no single shape or size. Redoubts were commonly square, two metres thick and two metres high, or almost three metres if gabions were placed atop of them. Eight hours were enough to erect a redoubt big enough for a company of 68 men. Each one stripped the natural tree cover for 500 or 700 metres around, or about 300 trees, inflicting durable damage of 1000 m^2 to the forest cover.[34] When battle loomed, earthworks were made more solid, with planted stakes or palisades and deeper ditches. Bridges were fortified at both ends (the bridgeheads) and were shielded from floating incendiary devices. Soldiers could also defend themselves by throwing up *abatis*, that is, felling trees to constitute makeshift parapets or to block roads over long distances. Army carpenters and pioneers were crucial here, led by officers who could recognize different kinds of trees and their properties. Much of the soldiers' time was taken up by building things with axe, spade, rope and lumber, under the skilled direction of officers. Recruiters enlisted young rural folk accustomed to manual labour, rewarded with shiny coins and copious food.[35] Dragoons were indispensable in this kind of war, for they carried axes and spades as well as cavalry arms and muskets. They could quickly remove obstacles and render the roads passable for vehicles, or else repel the enemy patrols. There was a vogue for such units in all the armies. The French army contained only two regiments of dragoons in 1672, but 14 in 1678, and 43 in 1690, when they constituted more than a third of all the cavalry. Another advantage of dragoons was that their horses were smaller than the typical voracious cavalry charger (standing only 1 m 40 on average). Armies sought horses that were resistant to fatigue, for long marches and scouting rather than battle. The heavy cavalry was lightened, which was easier on the animal and made the mounted arm more affordable. Only the cuirassiers were still wearing heavy breastplates after 1700.[36]

Given the frequent pauses in the schedule, an army might only march for 30 days in each campaign. If all was prepared in advance, a force could march a distance of 20 kilometres several days in a row. However, long marches were quite exceptional. Marlborough's great 400-kilometre march from the Low Countries to Bavaria in 1704, lasting five weeks, averaged 14 kilometres a day, counting the pauses.[37] Prince Eugene also marched 400 kilometres from the River Adige to rescue Turin in 1706, at a comparable speed. Occasionally, commanders gave their men food for a week, but many soldiers would sell their extra ration on the march without saving it. Armies could march much longer distances in order to effect a surprise. Marshal Boufflers marched his men 45 kilometres in a single day in June 1703 to surround a Dutch force at Ekeren, north of Antwerp, which barely escaped. General Vendôme performed similar feats on several occasions, most decisively at Brihuega, where his men marched over 100 kilometres over three days in time to destroy the Coalition rear-guard. This lax disciplinarian was followed enthusiastically by his men, and was lucky. A general needed to imagine the ability of his columns to manoeuvre across local terrain and to take up position in time. Night marches, like that of Marshal Villars at Denain, were especially risky, for soldiers had to be placed close together so as not to wander in the wrong direction.[38] Even after a victory, it was difficult to pursue the beaten enemy very far, for fear of running out of forage.

Whatever the skill of a commander in manoeuvring his army in the field in the face of the enemy, he must take care not to outrun his supplies, or leave the precious convoys vulnerable to enemy enterprises. The roads also had to be passable to sutlers and other merchants who conveyed livestock, fresh vegetables and creature comforts to the troops. A shuttle service normally connected the army to its magazines to the rear. Considering the largest armies in the 1690s, the daily rations for 90,000 men and 40,000 horses required 8,000 carts and 10,000 civilian drivers and helpers, along with 30,000 draught animals not belonging to the army *per se*. William of Orange's army of 100,000 men required 800,000 kg of green fodder *every day*, 270 mills for grinding grain and 120 field ovens fuelled by 2,800 wagon-loads of wood, served by 480 bakers. The number of cannon on the battlefield increased as well: the Coalition arrayed 120 cannon at the battle of Ramillies in 1706, against only 70 for the French. Each artillery piece required multiple wagons carrying tools, ammunition and baggage for the crew.[39]

Only the most economically developed regions in Europe could support such enormous concentrations of men and animals. The Spanish Low Countries and northern France contained about 50 people/km², surpassed only by Lombardy in northern Italy, with 55/km². The army stopped to build ovens and bake bread it would consume over four or five days. Thereafter, it could not march more than two or three days from its ovens before they would have to move forward to renew the process. Armies needed to grind the grain into flour, which made mills strategic objectives to hold or destroy. As Perjes writes, the army was a fighting machine, but also a milling, baking, foraging and transport device. In addition to the bread, biscuits and beverage (beer or wine), the commanders improvised. Animals taken by foragers and patrols were brought back to camp for sale and slaughter. It has been claimed for British armies that from the late seventeenth century until the end of the Napoleonic period, soldiers were fed only 1,700 calories daily, that is, the bare biological minimum.[40] However, malnourished men were physically and psychologically fragile. The evidence in the Imperial army points to a substantial meat ration on campaign, and a dietary intake above 3,000 calories. French troops in winter quarters in Italy during the Thirty Years' War consumed daily over a kilo of meat per person over and above their bread ration, in addition to other food and drink.[41]

These calculations consider only the number of combatants in each army, and do not include the presence of army sutlers, cavalry grooms and regimental women. Armies in the Thirty Years' War, and German contingents in particular, travelled with great numbers of women, a few children and a crowd of other non-combatants who occasionally might be as numerous as the soldiers. These were an important part of what John Lynn calls the campaign community who accompanied the men on their marches. Army reforms after the great conflict aimed to reduce their number in order to increase efficiency, to speed up the marches and to reduce the number of wagons in the train. These wives and concubines continued to carry out tasks of cooking, cleaning and mending clothes and nursing men back to health. They frequently sold creature comforts to the men alongside their other duties. Administrative records from Dijon around 1700 suggest they were equal to about five per cent of the number of soldiers, and a smaller portion of people on the move. Female soldiers captured the popular imagination then, as now, but they could not have been very numerous, probably no more than one in 10,000. Some recent authors might claim that women had far greater *symbolic* importance, if one concedes the validity of symbolic logic.[42] The inescapable fact is that soldiers in Europe, as elsewhere, were male, and overwhelmingly so.

After the Thirty Years' War, armies learned not to terrorize the peasants in their path, despite levying contributions on them. Marshal Villars warned his soldiers at the outset of his Bavarian campaign of 1703 that if they drove away the peasants, they would starve. Generals needed to squeeze resources from rural folk, but they needed them to stay in their homes, too. Peasants in the path of armies would often move their livestock to protected towns, and even dismantle mills, by removing the heavy grinding stones, dismantling the precious gears and the water wheels, in order to keep them away from soldiers.[43] Soldiers tended to be spiteful against vacant houses where there was no one to lodge them properly.[44] Peasants learned that it was best to keep soldiers happy in order not to arouse their anger. The decline in violence towards civilians was particularly notable in the Spanish Low Countries, where the pillage and arson of towns became very rare. Town authorities did not hesitate to complain to the high command if soldiers overstepped the bounds of decorum.[45] Armies issued passports and safeguards in order to protect private property from the clutches of patrols. The French and Spanish respected the safeguards sold to villages, but Imperial troops ignored the ones issued by their Spanish allies and continued to plunder and kidnap notables in friendly territory.[46] Troops were frequently lodged in the houses as well as in the barns, whose inhabitants owed them wood, vinegar, bedding, a bowl and a cooking pot. For longer stays, civilians had to provide shoes as well, which wore out quickly from the rigour of campaigning. Finding enough food for the soldiers distracted them from their other duties, even if they were paid for it. Peasants also had to provide carts and animals for army haulage, which was a considerable inconvenience. If they had not been frightened away by unruly troops, peasants could also provide manpower in sieges, for raising earthworks and digging ditches, a task for which they were paid. Fully 20,000 of them were hired by Vauban to expedite the French siege of Maastricht in 1673.

The officers lived in more comfortable conditions on campaign, with more spacious and better-constructed tents equipped with their own furniture. Valets and coachmen formed part of their normal campaign retinue. Near towns, officers were often invited to attend balls and ceremonies and rubbed elbows with the leading families. Wounded officers were evacuated to large cities and would be lodged in aristocratic houses as a courtesy. Over the seventeenth century, one cannot

overlook a notable increase in aristocratic gentility in the army, and the fraternization among men of good pedigree and education across national lines, embracing
all the belligerents except for the Ottomans. This codification of *bonne guerre* had
deep roots, due, in Catholic countries, to the widespread influence of Jesuit institutions, but the Dutch writer, Hugo Grotius, sketched out its legal basis in 1625.[47]
Jesuit-managed colleges for aristocrats in Italy attracted pupils from much of Central Europe to learn not only Latin, the art of public speaking and elegant writing,
but to undergo a regimen of corporal deportment, dance, fencing, equitation,
mathematics and military theory.[48] French academies multiplied in the seventeenth
century, with an even broader European appeal. It was considered unseemly to subject captured enemy officers to harsh confinement, if they would give their word
(parole) not to escape. French became the language of military science and coalition armies required that officers should be able to converse in the courtly dialect of
that language.[49] The observation of aristocratic decorum was one check on the
uninhibited expression of dominance by the assertive males who made up the campaign community.

Commanders, nevertheless, might have explicit orders to punish the civilian
population in the theatre of operations and to inflict wholesale destruction of
livestock and buildings. The Duc de Luxembourg carried out instructions
from the court to devastate the zone of the Netherlands under his control
from 1672 to 1674. Louis XIV and Louvois's destruction of the Palatinate in
1688–1692 was mirrored in similar scorched earth strategy inflicted by Marshal Catinat on Piedmont, which had just joined the League of Augsburg. The
Williamite Anglo–Dutch army in Ireland in 1690 thought the best way to
repress the Jacobite uprising was to burn the towns and to destroy the forage,
while the Imperial army ravaged Upper Hungary (modern Slovakia) and Bavaria after 1704. Warfare might revert to wholesale destruction, when policy
dictated it.[50]

Winding down the campaign

Operations tended to slow down towards the end of summer, especially if it
was judged that the army was unlikely to successfully complete a new project,
such as a siege, before the weather turned. Soldiers tended to be vulnerable to
infection at the end of summer and early in the autumn, like the civilian population. Lesser mobility meant that armies spent longer periods in their camps,
which gave rise to a new set of problems. The seventeenth century was famously insensitive to hygiene and it is doubtful that camp latrines became
common before 1700 (Image 10.11), except among the Turks, who, moreover, erected ablutions tents for frequent washing. An earlier generation of
commanders, such as Montecuccoli, recommended that when the air became
'corrupted' it was necessary to move the camp, but he made specific mention
only of butchers' waste. Dead horses and refuse were supposed to be quickly
buried and removed from the camp. Hygiene was the weak link of camps,
rarely mentioned in the sources. The tents and other materials employed there

Image 10.11 Moncornet: Le chieur. Western armies immobilized in camps did not customarily dig latrines until the end of the seventeenth century, with deadly
consequences if it remained there very long. BNF FOL-QB-201 (28)

wore out in bad weather or from constant use. The armies could dissolve
under the hot sun as well as from heavy rains, due to the basic lack of sanitation. About three-quarters of campaign mortality stemmed from disease, not
combat. The season of sickness began in the latter part of August, especially if
an army was encamped in too small an area, or campaigned in waterlogged
country where malaria was endemic.

This whole topic, hugely important, has rarely been explored in detail until
the recent publication of Padraig Lenihan's study.[51] The Neapolitan doctor
Luca Porzio's 1685 book on how to maintain cleanliness in camps appears to
be the first text devoted to the subject. He accompanied the Imperial army in
Hungary and was appalled by the universal laxity of German troops compared
to the Turks.[52] Lenihan's study of the self-destruction of Marshal Schomberg's
Orangeist army in Ireland in the fall of 1689 is an excellent illustration of this
problem. The ten-week stay at Dundalk provoked the death of half the army
from disease, given that the camp was normally a source of pathogens, and hospital conditions were too neglected or too derisory to cope with the situation.

Perhaps 8,000 men of the 16,000 in the camp perished from bacillary dysentery, or e-coli infection from tainted water, or else fell sick with typhus, which was typical of camps and overcrowded conditions in colder weather. There was no sense among the English officers that faecal run-off in the local water supply could be dangerous. Filthy clothes and bedding concentrated contagious pathogens, too, spread by lice. There was a fatal casual attitude to human waste and to unburied bodies in the camp. Dutch soldiers posted away from the main camp, who were wiser in field lore and knew enough to drink running water, were largely spared.[53] The Spanish army of the Low Countries was the first to establish proper military hospitals, but these were generally confided to Flemish nuns, who would treat only Catholics. The Dutch organized proper field hospitals from 1674, but no permanent structure until the 1690s, while the British wounded were evacuated across the Channel and confined to the Tower of London to prevent their escape![54]

The French army posted to the Pyrenees theatre in the Dutch War similarly made no attempt to avoid disease through proper sanitation. Those who perished from disease were seven or eight times more numerous than those who died from combat. The hospitals were more lethal than a battlefield, for multiple men were placed in a bed, with little clean linen, and, due to the lack of personnel, the dead were sometimes removed days after their decease, their clothes quickly redistributed. Concentrating sick men in city hospitals often had the perverse result of spreading epidemic more widely among the civilian population. In the garrison of Collioure, the straw in the soldiers' quarters had purportedly not been changed for years. It was full of pathogens, to the point that the officers could no longer bear the stench. The surmortality among the troops and even members of the French and Spanish high command, then spread to the entire population. In this Mediterranean theatre, horses and men could also die of heat stroke, which closed down operations at the height of summer. It was an innovation when Marshal Navailles proceeded to remove rubbish from the streets of Perpignan, a famously filthy city. Men were detached to keep barracks and beds clean, while latrines were multiplied to prevent infection. The commander then isolated the men stricken with dysentery from the other patients and from the convalescents. A proper health service was only organized in 1708.[55] By 1700, latrines had become common in the camps, too, and fresh ones were dug about 100 metres from the edge of the camp every six days when the army was immobile.[56] Sentinels were posted to prevent the men from excreting in more convenient places.[57] Dysentery, which could kill up to 20% of men stricken with it, was only a 'gateway' disease that might be fatally aggravated by typhus, spread by lice living in clothing. Troops crowding together seeking warmth, not changing their shirts or breeches for weeks at a time, were a perfect breeding ground for a typhus epidemic.[58]

Towards the end of the campaign, camps became semi-permanent places, entrenched and palisaded. By the 1690s, peasants could make considerable money from these camps, selling foodstuffs and scrap metal. By this period, the soldiers were an occasional threat to their property but only rarely to their lives. If some people sought refuge in cities when armies contested the region, more and more people stayed on their farms to keep them going until better times.[59] In the Lower Meuse district between Liege and Maastricht, the wars no longer prevented long-term population growth. The worst years of 1675–1676 and 1693–1694 coincided not just with troop lodgings, but with harvest failures on a vast scale that afflicted peaceful regions, too. The total population dropped quickly when the population failed to replace itself, but this was not a long-term phenomenon. Too few military historians have examined the parish registers, as Myron Gutmann has, in order to calculate the effect of war on civilians.

By September and October, the cooling climate and the onset of bad weather made it mandatory to put the men into winter quarters. The operations gradually diminished in frequency and scale, but both sides reduced their men by stages, so as not to give the adversary a temporary advantage. New 'étapes' were fixed to organize the march of men rearward into winter quarters, dispersed over a wide area far away. French cavalry from the Low Countries would be scattered across a vast area north of the Loire, and perhaps even beyond. The army commanders returned to court, and left somebody more junior in command to watch over the frontier until the next assembly in spring.

Notes

1   John A Lynn, 1999: 2.
2   François Royal, 2015.
3   Geoffrey Parker, 2002.
4   Paul Vo-Ha, 2017: 192–99.
5   Simon Pepper, 2000; Bertrand Fonck, 2015.
6   Erik A Lund, 1999: 144–47.
7   Stephane Genêt, 2015.
8   Geza Perjés, 1970.
9   Clément Oury, 2011: 283.
10 Olaf van Nimwegen, 2010: 363.
11 Peter H Wilson, 1998: 54
12 John Childs, 1991: 44–6; François Royal, 2017.
13 Myron Gutmann, 1980: 98; Lionel Marquis, 2015: 61.
14 Perjés, 1970.
15 Lund, 1999: 77.
16 Perjes, 1970.
17 Sandrine Picaud, 2007.
18 Bertrand Fonck & George Satterfield, 2014.
19 George Satterfield, 2003: 145.
20 Brian Sandberg, 2008.
21 Gutmann, 1980: 62.
22 Fonck & Satterfield, 2014.
23 Lynn, 1999: 56; Guy Rowlands, 2002: 127.
24 Sandrine Picaud-Monnerat, 2010: 125.
25 Raimondo Montecuccoli, 1752: 106–12.
26 Hugo O'Donnell & Duque de Estrada, 2006.

27 Childs, 1991: 46.
28 Stewart Stansfield, 2016: 79.
29 Lund, 1999: 144.
30 Lund, 1999: 16.
31 Bertrand Fonck, 2014: 375.
32 Guy Rowlands, 2015.
33 Childs, 1991: 138.
34 Vaclav Matoušek, 2005.
35 Lund, 1999: 10.
36 Frédéric Chauviré, 2017.
37 Oury, 2011: 292.
38 Gérard Lesage, 1992.
39 Pepper, 2000: 193.
40 Childs, 1991: 54; Edward J Coss, 2010; Paul Delsalle, François Pernot & Marie-France Romand, 2007.
41 Gregory Hanlon, 2014: 136
42 John A Lynn, 2008: 212.
43 Satterfield, 2003: 53.
44 Myron Gutmann, 1977.
45 Catherine Denys, 2009.
46 Satterfield, 2003: 73.
47 Vo-Ha, 2017: 34.
48 Gian Paolo Brizzi, 1976: 30.
49 Peter Drake, 1960: 187.
50 John Childs, 2007.
51 Padraig Lenihan, 2019.
52 Luca Antonio Porzio, 1747: 25.
53 Padraig Lenihan, 2007.
54 Childs, 1991: 60; van Nimwegen, 2010: 350
55 Alain Ayats, 2006.
56 Stansfield, 2016: 208.
57 O'Donnell & de Estrada, 2006.
58 Lenihan, 2019: 91.
59 Gutmann, 1977.

11 The classical siege in the age of Vauban

Scaling up the bastioned fortress

Sebastien Le Prestre, Vicomte de Vauban (1633–1707), has come to represent the entire age of siege warfare in the later seventeenth century, both for the design of fortifications and in the refinement of methods to conquer them. Born to the middling aristocracy in rural Burgundy in 1633, this brilliant polymath deployed his curiosity over a wide range of activities. He was one of a number of European writers, called *political arithmeticians*, who prepared studies designed to influence government councils in the late seventeenth century. Vauban was interested in economic development, in agronomy, in fiscal reform, in town planning and a host of other fields. He came to the attention of the Marquis de Louvois in 1667, when he proposed a project to raise a powerful citadel in newly conquered Lille, and then brought it to completion in just three years. All of Europe applauded him in 1673 when he captured the powerful Dutch fortress of Maastricht after just 14 days of open trenches. Louis XIV did not spare his praise for the engineer and appointed him to oversee the fortifications of the entire kingdom. Brigadier-General in 1674 (no engineer had ever risen beyond the rank of captain, in any army), he was appointed Lieutenant-General by King Louis in 1688, then Marshal of France in 1703. In recognition of his encyclopedic interests, he served as president of the *Académie des Sciences* in 1701 and 1705.[1] Vauban directed siege operations 53 times (20 times in the presence of the king), but defended a fortress only once. At the request of Louvois, the master engineer elaborated a manuscript treatise on siege techniques in 1672 which had only limited diffusion, followed by a second book, published in 1706, that acquired a huge international following.[2] Vauban taught armies of the period how to capture fortresses more quickly than ever before. The average duration in days of a Vauban siege, counting from the moment of opening the trenches, or sap, was merely 14: the longest, at Charleroi, took 27 days. He saved lives as well as time: in two important sieges, at Cambrai and Ath, the besiegers lost only a hundred men killed, a mere handful. Namur fell in 1692 at the cost of 3,000 men, but the huge fortress had a strong garrison.[3]

Louis XIV named Vauban *Commissaire général des fortifications* in January 1678, which entailed inspecting and supervising construction projects all over France. As the head of fortifications, Vauban created a structured corps of well-paid engineer officers, numbering about 280 in 1697, without equal in Europe. The great majority of them were 'roturier' (commoner) or only recently ennobled. Only the Dutch, who had their own tradition of military engineering starting with Simon Stevin (1548–1620) and culminating with Vauban's contemporary, Menno van Coehoorn (1641–1704), employed a substantial number of combat specialists. The Dutch United Provinces employed 111 of them in 1696 (although a great many of them were ethnic Germans), and engaged 275 engineers over the duration of Spanish Succession War. In other states, the emergence of professional military engineers was still in its infancy. The Imperial army only employed 27 engineers in 1686 and 66 in 1704, but those who were native to the Empire were quite rare. An engineering academy opened in Vienna only in 1718, with an annual intake of barely a dozen students. Spain had a long tradition of military engineering, but their number was quite inadequate to their needs in 1700. Louis XIV dispatched some 69 French engineers to Spain during the War of Succession, and, even in the aftermath, those serving the Bourbon king in Madrid were often French, Italians or 'Belgians'. English engineers numbered only 37 for all theatres over the same war.[4]

Until Vauban founded the French engineering corps in 1669, these were formed on the apprenticeship model, outside formal institutions. They learned not so much mathematics as simple arithmetic, often displayed in tabular form. But, as time progressed, they required geometry, trigonometry and mechanics, as well as geography, architecture and construction techniques, just as they needed expert knowledge of artillery, ballistics and military science in general. Draughtsmanship was an essential skill: they studied and drew maps using conventional symbols, copied the sketches and designs of colleagues and constructed scale models. Italians dominated modern fortification, as well as cartography, in Europe until the early decades of the seventeenth century. Theoretical education in France was acquired mostly from works translated from Italian, although there were several generations of French military architects preceding Vauban, starting with Jean Errard in the late sixteenth century, and two veterans of the Thirty Years' War, Antoine de Ville and Blaise de Pagan. By the 1640s, French engineers were working for the Papacy and other states in Italy, without displacing Italian competitors entirely.[5]

The diffusion of Dutch fortifications manuals entailed that, in emergencies, governments raised cheap earthen fortifications around threatened towns both large and small. Across Europe, fortresses became more elaborate over the seventeenth century. In place of defending every small town with makeshift earthworks, planners selected fewer sites and fortified those more completely with larger bastions and multiple outworks. Fortresses in good stone or brick were expensive to build, but they were a long-term investment. Elaborate new projects used materials intended to last for decades, or even centuries. Trees were often planted atop the walls, whose roots bound and secured the masonry. Trees gave shade and comfort to the garrison and civilians in time of peace, who could escape the heat and filth of narrow streets by strolling atop the walls. Trees were also a convenient source of timber for gun-carriages and platforms, bridges, barricades and palisades.[6] From a distance, one would only see the top of the wall and what looked like a forest. If there was no particular hurry, fortification projects could unfold over decades, such as the 40-year improvement of Novara, which defended the approach to Milan from the west. There, bastions, ravelins and covered ways were added one-by-one; the project was finally concluded in the 1650s with the demolition of houses, churches and convents outside the city walls.[7] Work accelerated across Piedmont in the 1660s, and in Turin during the 1670s, in order to envelop new city neighbourhoods with strong walls. Straight, wide streets were designed with the intention to move troops and guns more easily.[8] Hard stone was considered to be a poor cladding material, for projectiles shattered it and produced lethal shards. Brickwork was a cheaper material, easier to repair and to modify. A cannonball made a small, neat hole in a brick revetment, or cladding, enabling projectiles to be located and recovered after the siege.

Vauban did not so much invent new styles of fortification as adapt specific modules in ingenious ways, always taking the terrain into account. He continually experimented with fortress design, in search of innovative solutions to practical problems: it is his originality that is most striking. In a number of urban projects, he innovated by erecting a continuous line of outworks, an *enceinte de combat*, in front of the bastions, which constituted an *enceinte de sûreté*, reinforced by multi-level artillery towers. Later, he added casemated towers on top of bastions (called cavaliers) that gave a better view of approaching sappers.[9] These also provided further protection from cannonballs and grenades to defenders posted on the bastion or along the walls. Vauban multiplied the ravelins in the ditch, and dug more elaborate outworks, such as horn and crownworks projecting hundreds of metres from the wall. These were open to the rear in order to prevent the besieger from finding cover there. Vauban preferred the simple triangular ravelin in the ditch protecting the bastion faces. From there, musketeers could pour deadly fire at close range along the ditches and covered ways in front of adjacent bastions. These outworks had the defect of requiring larger garrisons to defend an enlarged perimeter and larger quantities of munitions. If Vauban was guilty of one shortcoming, it was that he paid little attention to expenditure.

Under the influence of the Chevalier Antoine de Ville and Blaise de Pagan, the engineers of Vauban's generation placed greater emphasis on a musketry defence, which was more accurate and less expensive in gunpowder.[10] Fortress designers strengthened the outer perimeter beyond the walls and bastions, in order to delay the enemy along the covered way and in various outworks. The covered way was protected by palisades: traverses, or barriers were raised at intervals along the length of the ledge to prevent enfilading fire. A more expensive, but effective means of defence beyond the wall was to dig counter-mine chambers underneath the glacis and the covered way, to explode once the enemy burrowed to the edge of the ditch. Pre-built mine chambers around Bergen-op-Zoom, and the citadel of Turin greatly added to the strength of the fortress. A few places had wet moats, which normally served as open sewers, and were as much a health hazard for the garrison as a significant obstacle to the besiegers. Most ditches were dry, and subterranean passages might connect the outworks and counter-mine tunnels under the glacis. A cunette, or a simple ditch dug along the bottom of the moat, forced enemy miners to burrow more deeply. Designers might raise a ledge along the bottom of the rampart, called a fausse-braye, to lodge musketeers contesting the besieger's penetration of the moat.

Citadels were erected at the edge of the fortress as a place to which the garrison might retire after it could no longer hold the city. Their fortifications were typically much stronger, and were well stocked with provisions. Citadels were usually built in a pentagon shape, allowing guns to fire at assailants from three bastions, while not requiring many more troops than a square or rectangular shape. Francesco Paciotto, who erected one in Turin, discovered the formula in the 1560s, which was imitated for centuries. It might also contain barracks for the garrison, usually a simple stone structure three storeys high. Nearby was a powder magazine, built for protection against bombs. Not one of Vauban's magazines ever exploded, although they were often targeted.

The brick and masonry fortress was only an envelope, a complete waste of money unless it was adequately manned and supplied. Vauban thought that 500–600 men per bastion was a reasonable garrison for a fortress threatened with siege. A first-rate fortress might require a garrison of 5,000–15,000 men, depending on its circumference, a number equal to the armies of many secondary powers. The walls required enough cannon to delay an enemy advance, but it was best if these were economical with gunpowder. Fortress cannon were often 16–18-pound culverins, which fired almost as far as a 24-pound siege gun, but required much smaller powder charges.[11] Fortress guns, with their wooden carriages, were typically stored away in shelters, to prevent the tubes from rusting and the wood from rotting. Along with the cannon were wall-mounted heavy muskets, which rested on a pivot, which had a faster rate of fire and used little powder.

Vauban's first engineering coup was to update and reinforce the fortifications of Lille after its capture in 1667. He completed it and the powerful adjoining citadel in 1671. Meanwhile, he transformed the nearby towns of Ath, Oudenaard, Charleroi and Dunkirk. Vauban counselled Louis XIV and Louvois to take care to straighten out the border and give up advanced places that were difficult to supply, a policy known as the *pré carré* or 'straight-edge field'. Well-stocked fortresses with great magazines enabled field armies to invade enemy territory nearby, and had their greatest defensive potential when they constituted an interlocking barrier. This view coincided well with the increasingly defensive outlook of the king after 1678. Vauban's *pré carré* consisted of an outer row of 13 large fortresses and two isolated forts, with a second line of 13 fortresses a day or two's march to the rear.[12] As inspector of fortifications, he was called upon to improve works everywhere an enemy army might penetrate the kingdom (Metz and Verdun in Lorraine, Belfort near Alsace, Grenoble and Briançon in the Alps, Antibes along the Mediterranean coast near Italy, Montlouis in Roussillon and Bayonne near the Atlantic Pyrenees). Other projects protected the chief commercial and military ports (Dunkirk, Brest and Lorient in Brittany, Blaye, on the Gironde river downstream from Bordeaux, Marseille and Toulon in Provence). At Dunkirk, an important privateer base, he built a fortified jetty over a kilometre long protecting access to the inner harbour, which was capacious enough for 20 warships. In all, he worked on about 150 fortresses or smaller strongpoints of various description.

A mountain fortress was very difficult to build, replenish and reinforce, like Pinerolo or Montdauphin in the Alps. Briançon was overlooked from several directions, such that mountain outcrops within artillery range had to be fortified and garrisoned. At Villefranche de Conflent in Roussillon, at the very foot of the Pyrenees, Vauban erected a solid wooden roof over the wall, protecting the garrison from mountain sharpshooters peering over the town. Traditionally, the French liked to hold strongpoints beyond the frontier, known as *portes*, or gateways, as at Philippsburg, Freiburg and Landau on the Rhine, Montroyal on the Moselle or Casale Monferrato along the Po in northern Italy. Vauban strengthened all of them over his long career. Reflecting this obsession with defensive positions, the Crown quadrupled its fortifications budget during the 1680s. Louvois kept a special atlas in his cabinet containing up-to-date plans of both friendly and enemy fortresses. In 1668, the minister began to commission realistic scale models, at 1/600, of fortresses set in their adjoining landscape in order to study both the defence and the attack. These also had didactic aims: to explain projects to the king, and younger officers were invited to study them closely. These numbered 144 at the end of the seventeenth century, and are well worth the trip to Paris and Lille to view them today.[13] Vauban and his peers understood, however, that there was no such thing as an impregnable fortress, because garrisons had only finite stamina and would eventually surrender if they were not relieved from the outside. Vauban thought that a fortress should be stocked to hold out for about two months. A longer defence was probably not realistic, and the extra powder and shot in the magazines would only end up in the hands of the enemy.[14] Fortresses were designed to buy time for the owning country to reorganize their army, or to strike back in another location.

The labour of besiegers

Louis XIV and Louvois preferred sieges to other kinds of operations because they were more predictable and rarely put an army at risk. Sieges relied above all on logistics, which was the minister's strong suit. Beyond the importance of capturing fortresses, effecting a breakthrough into enemy territory, sieges were rewarding because they were clear markers as to which side was winning the war. The victor could keep the town or use the place as a pawn to obtain some other benefit when peace was made. Moreover, cities concentrated the manufacturing and commercial capital of an entire district, and were the place of residence of social elites, whose assets were removed from enemy control for the duration of the war. A successful siege hinted to the Dutch States-General or the English Parliament that the expensive war against the Sun King was not in vain and that final victory was within reach.[15]

At first, generals hoped to seize a fortress by surprise, often with the help of sympathizers embedded in the garrison or the town. Bruges and Ghent fell into French hands by such a stratagem in 1708, much to the Allies' annoyance, for it placed their convoys within reach of Bourbon contingents. Obtaining a place in this way also meant that there was no damage to repair. A very large force could intimidate a small garrison into surrendering quickly, or a poorly fortified place, weakly garrisoned, might be simply unable to offer resistance. The great towns of the Spanish Low Countries occupied by the Allies in 1706 were either poorly fortified or poorly defended.[16] Large cities, like Milan, with over 100,000 inhabitants were not likely to resist, for the walls required too many men and guns. Paris, London, Madrid and Rome were open cities, simply too big to fortify. Proper fortresses might be placed in difficulty if they could not draw supplies of food and fodder from the surrounding countryside. The besieger usually sent detachments of dragoons and infantry to occupy the villages and castles in the vicinity, requisitioned the available grain and hay and led away all the available carts and harness animals in order to deny them to the place. Dragoons also tried to stampede villagers towards the safety of the town, filling it with 'useless mouths' drawing on precious food stocks. This preparation often accelerated the subsequent siege itself: following these rules, Flanders towns requiring six weeks' siege in the 1660s gave up in less than three weeks in the later 1670s.[17]

The besieger holding the strategic initiative attempted to trick his adversary into reinforcing the wrong target: planning feigned marches or sending conspicuous reconnaissance missions around one fortress, while preparing to march on another, was easy, for these places were distant from one another by only twenty or thirty kilometres, a long day's march. The true target was then invested by smallish contingents marching from several directions simultaneously. They prevented all but the strongest flying camps from entering the place. The main army followed several days later.[18] To pursue the siege with the proper energy, the besieger would need to outnumber the garrison by five or ten to one, so that he could always keep in the trenches a force equal to three-quarters of the garrison's complement. The besieger would then raise lines of circumvallation to prevent attacks on his camp from outside forces. Since the line of circumvallation erected two kilometres from the target could have a total circumference of 20 kilometres or more, besiegers required several camps. Lines of contravallation were dug about a kilometre distant from the fortress to prevent the attack of the camp by *sorties* from there. If enough peasants were available, these lines could be finished in about ten days. Peasants were expected to provide corvée labour, but they were not always willing. One inducement to work was to pay them daily wages; on the other hand, their villages might be burned if they refused.[19] The complete isolation of the fortress was the most important consideration. Marshal Vendôme's sloppy five-month siege of Verrua in Piedmont in 1705 failed to observe this rule and cost 3,000 men; this had serious consequences for the Bourbon cause in Italy.[20] Instead of immobilizing men along a huge circumference, Vauban thought it was better to deploy an army of observation near the siege works in order to repel any relief force; at Namur in 1692, the active besiegers numbered only 18,000, while an army of 80,000 men camped nearby to prevent the town's rescue.[21]

It required considerable staff work just to bring enough equipment to the staging point of an important siege, often dragging heavy equipment to the principal nearby magazine months in advance. The heavy artillery of 16-, 24- and 33-pound guns moved very slowly: larger sieges consumed impressive quantities of powder and 100,000 cannon balls, ten times what was possible in 1600. A forty-day siege required three million rations for men, and 700,000 rations for the horses. An enormous quantity of lumber had to be amassed, along with enough picks and spades and barrows to shift many tonnes of earth. Kilometres of rope would have to be brought in order to move equipment and fasten objects. Peasant corvées and private transporters were called upon to carry out these tasks as well as to repair roadways and erect solid bridges. The larger the fortress, the more equipment was necessary to capture it. Few siege trains numbered over 50 cannon in 1670, which required about 1,500 horses, but the trend was for bigger numbers: the French siege train for Namur in 1692 included 196 cannon and 67 mortars; the Bourbon army employed 200 guns for the failed siege of Turin in 1706.[22] Until the Dutch war, it was customary for the heavy artillery and its wagons to move with the main contingent in the field. With the greater emphasis on firepower, however, it proved wiser to march the great guns separately in a heavily-guarded siege train, in which 80% of the pieces were 24-pounders or heavier, in addition to the mortars, which were carried on wagons (Image 11.1). The train would not be able to move without a well-equipped road crew of pioneers. On flat terrain, the speed record for moving the train was 130 kilometres in a week, but it rarely travelled more than 20 kilometres

Image 11.1 Stefano Della Bella: Artillery train on the move, ca. 1640. Heavy cannon and the wagons filled with equipment and munitions made huge demands on horses. It was best to move these columns separately from the field army, under strong escorts. MET Museum

in a day, even when using boats. In the Black Forest, the speed was never more than ten kilometres a day, and, with good weather, only five kilometres a day in the Catalan Pyrenees. In the Alps, horses had to be replaced with mules, surer-footed on narrow roads; Vendôme required 2,000 of these expensive animals in 1705.[23]

Once the siege began in earnest, the leading roles fell to the engineers. In the spirit of Vauban, their goal was to conduct the attack by the shortest and least bloody route possible. It was his maxim to attack a fortress always at its weakest point, and never its strongest. At considerable risk to their persons, engineers moved as close to the walls as they dared, together with other high-ranking officers, in order to verify their assumptions about the strength of the defences, and then make detailed sketches of them. Vauban was as economical with men as he was lavish in the expenditure of powder and shot. The French virtuoso preferred a hands-off commander who took his advice and ordered the quartermasters to supply him with everything he needed; King Louis XIV did precisely this when he accompanied the army. Once the engineers selected the sector of approach, and determined where to site the guns, labourers began erecting multiple batteries in a wide arc about a kilometre from the walls, so that they could hit the fortifications from different angles and maximize the damage to the defenders (Image 11.2). It required 48 hours to build an emplacement of six guns. Firing

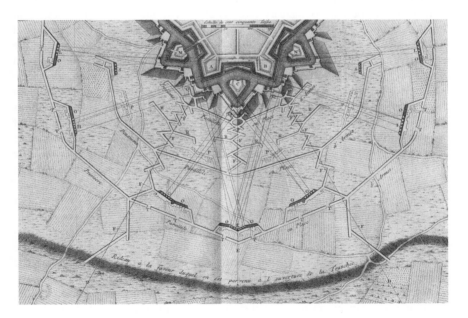

Image 11.2 Vauban, Batteries, approach trenches and parallels. Note the impressive economy and simplicity of the works depicted here. Batteries (shown here) direct their fire from multiple angles to immobilize the defenders. Traité des sièges et de l'attaque des places BNF V-9323

at fortresses from farther than 600 metres did no damage to the masonry, but it reassured the sappers psychologically and, above all, it periodically knocked a fortress gun out of commission. New pieces cast after 1680 had greater range, so that a 24-pounder could fire up to a kilometre. The initial task of the batteries was to knock out the fortress guns, typically by 'dismounting' them, or smashing their carriages. Vauban recommended firing from 600 metres in order not to miss the target or waste precious ammunition. He also deplored damaging houses and other structures inside towns that would soon serve to house the garrison. Meanwhile, thousands of cavalrymen were employed stripping nearby woodlands of branches to make *gabions*, wicker cylinders that, when filled with earth, served to protect the gunners and sappers from small shot (sometimes sandbags were used). Peasants could earn money by lending their hands to this operation. Each gabion took two or three hours to make, for which the men were paid. Many thousands of these gabions went into the construction of batteries and the protection for the trenches. John Lynn writes that cannon barrels were cast long to enable them to fit better in battery or fortress embrasures, so as not to damage them with their blasts.

The artillery was coming into its own at the end of the seventeenth century, promoted in France by Le Tellier and, above all, by Louvois, who was master of the kingdom's ordnance. The first school to teach mathematics to gunners opened at Douai in 1679. The institution was not durable, but mathematics for French officers became obligatory after 1720.[24] The rate of fire of a siege gun was low, from 10–20 shots per hour, depending on the calibre of the piece and the experience of the crew. Specialists were often tempted to decrease the weight of cannon by shortening the barrels, but this only made them inaccurate.[25] Artillery servers placed the piece on a wooden platform, and tethered it to the battery wall with ropes, as on a ship, in order to quickly replace the gun in its embrasure. In addition to the powder charge in a sack, tampons had to be inserted front and rear of the ball in order to increase the power of the explosion. With each shot the gun recoiled, so the officer had the piece replaced in position and aimed anew. After 12 shots it was necessary to cool the piece down by placing wet fleece over the barrel, or, for continuous fire, to reduce the powder charge, which was normally one-third the weight of the ball. According to Pierre Surirey de St-Rémy, master of the French artillery after 1703, one should not fire a gun more than 100 times a day, or every 15 minutes, so as not to ruin it. Continuous firing overheated the cannon and the barrels began to droop, or else fissures developed in the bronze that could be detected with the naked eye. If an overheated gun exploded, it would kill the crew and the officers standing nearby. The Dutch, with their efficient river transport, were able to keep supplying the Coalition army with fresh bronze cannon, and removed spent pieces for recasting. Iron cannon became simple landfill.

Once the batteries were erected, workers opened a ditch in front of the line of contravallation and the sap began to zigzag (so as not to be subject to enfilade fire) towards the part of the fortress to be attacked. Progress was usually rapid at the outset, but slowed considerably near the covered way when the workers came within range of muskets and grenades. The chief engineer made regular inspections and reports on the progress of the sap, to determine the number of men for daily work parties. He was supported by a good number of subaltern engineers whose place was at the head of each trench. Each underling was assisted by a trench-major supervising daily work. Infantry regiments served in the trenches one day a week, rotating regularly so as not to exhaust or over-expose any single unit.[26] Four-man sapper teams laboured at the head of the sap, the lead man protected by a wooden shield and a rolling gabion (Image 11.3). The front man frantically cut away the sod and excavated a narrow ditch, while the men behind him placed empty gabions in a line and filled them up with earth as quickly as they were able. Supervisors relayed the

Image 11.3 Adam Van der Meulen: French Camp before Douai in 1667. Soldiers operated in regular shifts, day and night, to advance the siege works, while cavalry scoured the district to provide fodder and materials to make gabions and fascines. Large-scale sieges denuded the countryside of forest cover. MET Museum

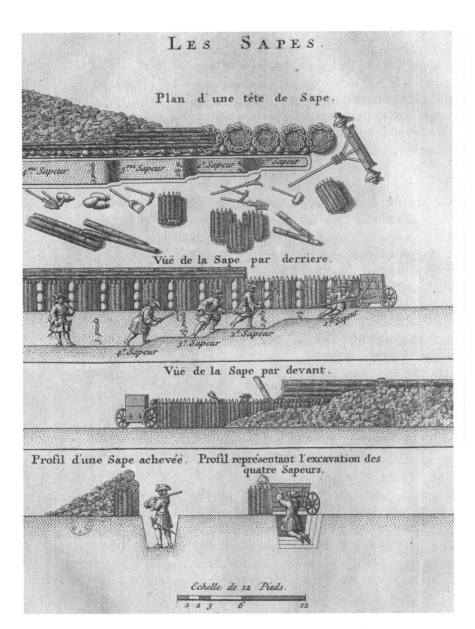

LES SAPES.

Plan d'une tête de Sape.

Vüë de la Sape par derriere.

Vüë de la Sape par devant.

Profil d'une Sape achevée. Profil représentant l'excavation des quatre Sapeurs.

Echelle de 12 Pieds.

Image 11.4 Vauban: Planche VI Les Sapes. Didactic description of the sapping process at the head of the trench. Additional teams widened the ditch to the rear to enable horses to drag heavy cannon and mortars closer to the target, to increase their destructive effect. Traité des sièges et de l'attaque des places BNF V-9323 sapper teams every hour, and each team averaged five or six gabions as it advanced. Other workers behind them then widened the narrow protective ditch to a breadth of four metres, which would permit horses to tow heavy guns into place closer to the wall (Image 11.4). To push forward 150 metres in 24 hours was very good speed, signifying that they could reach the counterscarp in under a week.[27] At night, covering infantry would lie with their bellies on the ground 50 metres ahead of the work crews, with their ears cocked for the sounds of approaching men. These were armed with flintlock muskets in order to avoid the danger of having glowing wicks in the darkness. Fire-pots of burning pitch might be thrown in their direction to illuminate their presence for the defending musketeers. A major siege could employ 50 engineers or more among the besiegers, always close to the action. At Namur, the French lost 22 of their 60 engineers, nine of them killed.

After a short advance, sappers extended a trench parallel to the enemy fortress wall, in which guns and troops would be placed in order to cover the work. This was the first parallel. Vauban did not invent this method, since it first appears in the manual of the Sieur Fabre in 1629; Andrea Barozzi, an Italian renegade engineer, reputedly taught it to the Ottomans in the final phase of the siege of Candia in 1669. About 300 metres from the covered way, sappers dug a second parallel and moved the heavy guns forward again. At this range, several dozen cannon were allocated to ricochet fire, whereby cannonballs would deflect off obstacles in unpredictable ways, which reduced defenders' musketry a great deal.[28] Vauban, who invented the technique at the siege of Philippsburg on the Rhine in 1689, experimented continually to find the right formula for the best bounce, calculating the piece's elevation and the size of the powder charge. Beside the great guns, mortars were now added. An Englishman, one Malthus, produced the first mortar in France in 1634, although the Spanish had used them for half a century already. The 12-inch mortar, the diameter of the heavy piece's bore, was the most common. An 18-inch mortar required 48 pounds of powder just to fire the bomb. France deployed more than 700 of these engines in 1711, designed to smash the rear of the parapet when used by the besieger, and intended to drop bombs inside the trenches when employed by the defenders. Mortars fired bombs of hollow cast-iron, filled with powder and shot, set off with a lit fuse, or else a container filled with incendiary materials that were difficult to extinguish. They were dangerous to operate, for it required lighting the bomb fuse and the mortar fuse almost simultaneously. If the mortar fuse fizzled out while the bomb fuse continued to burn at the edge of the cavity, the crew would have to run for cover. Bursting bombs could destroy smaller defensive works, or else they crashed through roofs of houses and then exploded. Vauban designed a mortar, called a *pierrier*, that fired baskets of stones on a high trajectory (or plunging fire), which dropped on men hiding in the ravelins and along the covered way. Its maximum range was also about 300 metres. Menno van Coehoorn, sometimes called the 'Dutch Vauban', developed a mini-mortar that could be carried by just two men, which could fire grenades up to 150 metres. All of these pieces were placed in short artillery trenches excavated just behind the second parallel. Finally, at about 70 or 100 metres from the covered way, besiegers dug a third parallel across the foot of the glacis. At this point, the fortress projectiles would pass over the heads of the sappers, but they were now moving into range of muskets, wall-mounted heavy muskets and other ingenious devices of trench warfare. The attacker's heavy guns now aimed at the palisades and the edge of the counterscarp where the defending infantry lurked. The unarmed workers in the forward sap ran away at the first sign of danger.[29] The attackers might erect cavaliers, or mounds of earth raised on several layers of gabions behind the parallels to see better into the covered way and the ditch, and from there they could fire on to the wall, but this made them more visible to the defenders, too.[30]

The siege reached the critical point after the third parallel was finished and stocked with men and material. It was now time to attack the covered way and carry it by storm. Grenadiers and shock troops led the way, followed closely by work crews, who frantically dug lodgements, or slit trenches, along the lip of the counterscarp. This was the most hair-raising part of the entire siege, because the troops who stormed and seized the covered way exposed themselves to musketry from the bastions and ravelin embrasures, and from the ledge of the fausse-braye across from them. Storming the covered way often incurred the majority of casualties suffered by the besiegers in the entire operation, often 1,000 men or more. At Lille in 1708, the Allies charged the city's covered way three times, finally establishing four isolated lodgements, but not before incurring some 3,000 casualties. The infantry assault, with engineers among them to direct the works, tried to clear the enemy out of the nooks and crannies of the covered way. Both sides used copious quantities of grenades at this range. The Venetians, at Candia, developed grenades as a weapon suitable for fighting in fixed positions at close quarters, and soon the *grenadiers* formed an elite of assault troops in every Western army.[31] At such close quarters, the besiegers would employ '*forlorn hopes*' of thrill-seekers and rash volunteers to lead the way, like the Crown Prince of Hanover (future King George II).[32] The French employed a take-no-prisoners elite unit, the *Grenadiers à cheval*, which specialized in storming positions with grenades and blade weapons.[33] Generals were always prone to rushing operations by storming the covered way or the ravelins in the ditch without bombarding them first. Coehoorn was known for his love of bombardments and storms, even at the cost of thousands of men, as at Namur in 1695, where large columns of troops assaulted the covered way from 600 metres.[34] The generals wanted quick results, and the public enjoyed stirring gazette accounts of daring attacks. Generals complained of delays, not of casualties; with every pause they blamed the engineers.[35] Once the attackers made lodgements along the outer edge of the counterscarp, they burrowed sloping tunnels down to the ditch or else piled earth and debris there so as to clamber down. Heavy cannon were brought forward and assembled to batter the wall's base from less than 50 metres. Vauban recommended firing forward and obliquely on a single section in the form of the letter H, judging that, after 1,000 shots, the masonry of the bastion or the ravelin would fall into the ditch.

Sharpshooters in the parallels behind them kept the fortress musketry down, while workers laid down fascines or sandbags across the ditch like a causeway, to enable 20 or 30 men to advance abreast.

Eventually, the debris falling into the ditch formed a ramp that men could climb without putting their hands to the ground. An alternative method was for the besiegers to attach a miner to the base of the revetment, who would burrow through the brick or stone cladding, dig out chambers under the bastion, then pack them with gunpowder. Miners could also dig a ditch across the moat, covered over with a roof. These were often professional miners and carpenters who could burrow five or six metres every day. Thirty or forty barrels of powder were enough to blow up a bastion and create a practical breach. If the besiegers faced a wet ditch, parties of daring men threw down thousands of fascines under enemy fire to create a causeway. Once everything was in place, storming parties led by grenadiers and crack troops assembled, along with men carrying gabions. If they could not carry the breach, they might at least dig in at the top of the structure and demoralize the remaining defenders. But it rarely came to that; by that point, the governor was expected to surrender. John Childs notes that there is no recorded instance of besiegers storming a breach and capturing a fortress during the War of the League of Augsburg in the Low Countries. After the surrender, thousands of workers were then drafted to repair the damage. During the War of the Spanish Succession in the same theatre, every major siege was successfully concluded, and only 40% of them surpassed two weeks of open trench.[36] But, depending on the vigour of the defence, things might not progress so smoothly.

Labours of the besieged

The fortress governor was encouraged to have eyes and ears in the distant countryside in order to know when to prepare for a siege, for some of these chores took precious time. Planting palisades along the covered way would require days or weeks. Cannon would have to be moved from storerooms and placed on their carriages, and wooden firing platforms had to be laid down behind the embrasures to facilitate aiming the guns after firing. By damming a river and flooding the low-lying vicinity, the defence could be improved, but this also required days. It was also a good precaution to place the necessary heavy mortars and pierriers in the outworks, together with their ammunition. The commanding general in the theatre might have time to dispatch last-minute reinforcements of men, flour, powder and shot from the field army or nearby fortresses. The governor met with a 'council of defence' every day, made up of representatives of each category of defenders, with some liaison members of the municipality. These conscripted civilians into work parties and made inventories of food stores and building materials. Excess mouths were induced to leave the threatened city, particularly foreigners and the footloose poor.

After being invested, it was not in the defenders' interest to lay down a heavy fire on the besiegers from the outset, although they sometimes attempted to land a few cannonballs in the enemy campsite to sow confusion. The besieger used many guns for the purpose of counterbattery fire. It was, therefore, advisable to move the cannon from place to place, fire several times, and then remove it to another location.[37] The result was that fortress cannon killed few of the enemy from afar. Few fortresses could align more than 50 or 60 guns on the ramparts, and most had only 30. Artillery officers kept many guns in reserve so as not to have them knocked out or dismounted early in the siege. Vauban relied increasingly on mortars to help the defence, but few fortresses had a large number of them and they required copious charges of precious powder. He designed the pierrier similarly, to drop stones on the approaching sappers, but beyond 300 metres these were ineffective.[38] Musketry from the counterscarp had an extreme range of 200 metres, and an effective range only half that. In fact, the garrison inflicted little damage on the approaching sappers at longer ranges. But they could send parties of several hundred infantry at night, in *sorties* designed to chase the sappers from their works and to fill in as much of the trench as they could before they were repulsed by besiegers' infantry deployed in the parallels. Cannon in the parallels fired canister, or grapeshot, which had a longer range, at the exposed defenders.[39] Parallels much reduced the efficiency of sorties, for the garrison could not afford to take many casualties, given their much smaller numbers.

As the sappers approached the covered way, the defenders' muskets became much more effective, as were the larger wall-mounted muskets firing heavier balls. Marksmen armed with fusils, or slow-loading hunting pieces with rifled bores, would pick off exposed besiegers. Within 200 metres, the remaining fortress cannon fell silent as they could no longer hit targets inside that range. The defenders could slow down the work of sappers at night if they catapulted 'fire-pots', or globes filled with tar, which illuminated considerable areas. Barrels of tar were also placed in likely spots after dusk and set alight in order to draw attention to the besiegers' activities.[40] The defending infantry, if they were sufficiently numerous, then put up a stout fight to defend the covered way. Workmen packed the counter-mine chambers with powder if the fortress was built with them. Counter-mines were quite deadly, economical in the lives of the defenders, although expensive in powder. At Douai in 1710, between the counter-mines and disease in a drawn-out siege of 56 days, the Allies lost 8,000 men.[41]

Once the besiegers' batteries on the counterscarp smashed the revetment and began to create a feasible ramp, the defenders could still attempt to dig in behind it, demolishing city houses to furnish the necessary building materials. But few sieges in western Europe reached that point. When the damage was sufficient and the garrison sufficiently depleted and demoralized, the governor typically displayed the white flag, or beat the *chamade* (a specific drumbeat played atop the breach), which indicated willingness to discuss capitulation. In principle, the governor was expected to resist several assaults on the breach, but this was rarely respected. Often, by this time, garrison losses ran from 30–50% killed, wounded and sick, and ammunition was running low. The opening of a breach was usually enough to accelerate the decision to seek terms, and rulers usually approved of the governor's decision not to resist to the bitter end. The commander was faced with a dilemma: too weak a defence and he faced social death and ostracism at court, or exile to his estates by an angry king. Count Arcos, governor of the Imperial fortress of Breisach on the Rhine, was shot by firing squad for having given up his place after only two weeks in 1703, and his second-in-command, Luigi Ferdinando Marsigli, was dismissed from service after a humiliating ceremony. Sieges were highly publicized operations, where ordinary people made casual judgements on the valour of the defenders. The loss of a great fortress without long resistance was a public relations embarrassment for governments, who looked for convenient scapegoats.

The defenders could surrender without disgrace once the besiegers had established lodgements on the counterscarp and readied their batteries to fire on the bastions. The rituals of honourable surrender developed out of the trend towards siege warfare, and appeared in treatise literature in the early seventeenth century. Hostages of officer rank were exchanged as a sign of good faith, and discussions would begin between representatives of the defenders and the attackers, never the commanding officers themselves. The hostages were usually treated with great courtesy. The representatives were often clergymen in Catholic countries, priests or friars who were men of peace and mediators by profession. The negotiators might belong to the same ethnic group, or speak the same mother tongue. There emerged a specialized personnel accustomed to microdiplomacy aimed at avoiding incidents while sensitive issues were discussed politely.[42] Officers might invite each other to dinner, or deliver food and medicine to the garrison to show generosity and esteem. But capitulation talks might also serve to induce the defenders to lower their guard and to leave themselves open to a surprise storm.[43] During capitulation negotiations, both sides put on a brave face; often, neither party had a good understanding of the exact situation of the other. Disease might have broken out among the besiegers, or the commander might fear an impending change in the weather that would render trench life unbearable. The defenders could be short of ammunition; the townspeople might be on the verge of revolt and would have to be guarded, or else the garrison could be on the verge of mutiny. It was a rational act for the besieger to promise good treatment to a vanquished garrison, in order to avoid an assault of the breach. Surrender was a rational act for the garrison, too, which could march away and soon fight again.[44] Over the course of the seventeenth century, capitulation agreements became more detailed and punctilious. If the defenders put up a decent fight, the victors conceded to them the 'honours of war', and permitted them to leave with their personal weapons and marching under their unit banners. Infantry might be permitted to exit via the breach, to prove that it was passable. The victors would form a guard of honour, a salute to the pluck of the defenders, but this ritual served also to better monitor the procession from the place. The departing garrison would receive passports, maybe even an escort to a destination in friendly hands in order to protect them from insult. Garrisons surrendering 'at discretion' would have to lay down their arms and march into captivity without their banners. A surrendered town usually relinquished its bells to the victors, who could either melt them down into artillery, or, more frequently, sell them back to the inhabitants. Only when a fortress was carried by storm were troops permitted by the laws of war to plunder civilians. This rarely happened. When the garrison survivors marched out unarmed, the victor's troops might commit infractions of the agreement, which in this period rarely entailed massacre, though soldiers might be plundered or stripped of their personal possessions. Officers on both sides deplored such outcomes, however, because these outrages, well publicized in the gazettes, were soon followed by reprisals. Reciprocity governed relations between belligerents, and favours granted would be expected in return. With the widespread practice of the honourable surrender, war lost some of its savagery.

In the War of the Spanish Succession, the Allies had good reasons to shorten the sieges and let the garrison depart for friendly territory. Rapid advances across the Spanish Low Countries in 1706 stopped abruptly as they entered French territory and encountered Vauban's great fortress barrier, the *pré carré*. They lost about 12,000 men in the 16-week siege of Lille in 1708. The campaign of 1710 captured four French fortresses, but cost the Allies 20,000 casualties and caused frustration on the home front.[45] When Britain withdrew from active participation in the alliance at the end of 1711, the coalition forces had not yet broken through the barrier, and, a year later, the French had turned the tables on them. During the war, keeping prisoners became the new norm: half the capitulations in Flanders after 1700 stipulated that the garrison would remain captive. This trend accelerated after 1712, when the French went back on the offensive. It was a way of depriving the enemy of trained soldiers and an incitement to speed up peace negotiations. Under Louis XIV, many captives were induced to change sides after a great siege, although these were not very effective soldiers. They might be starved or forced to work on fortress projects in order to vanquish their stubbornness. It was not yet typical, however, to use captives as forced labour. A captor had the power of life and death over the prisoners, but unless they were rebels or deserters, they were not usually harmed. Prisoners were often transferred to towns far away from the frontier, kept in makeshift accommodations like towers, but the guards soon left them in semi-liberty. They might make friends among their captors and perform odd jobs to supplement their rations. Some prison towns were lethal destinations, like Aigues-Mortes in the malarial estuary of the Rhone river, but they were hard on the guards, too.[46]

It became customary to observe these laws of war, handed down over generations of officers and soldiers. Lynn writes that the practice and law governing the exchange of prisoners evolved together over the seventeenth and eighteenth centuries towards a more restrained and rationalized military culture, which was made possible by the greater ability of states to administer, supply and control their own armies.[47] This *guerre en dentelles* was almost becoming genteel.

Notes

1 Martin Barros, Nicole Salat & Thierry Sarmant, 2006: 20–7.
2 Jean-Denis Lepage, 2010: 15.
3 Barros, Salat & Sarmant, 2006: 57.
4 Jamel Ostwald, 2007: 136; Jean Bérenger, 2004: 320; Michael Hochedlinger, 2003: 120; Catherine Desos, 2016.
5 Renzo Chiovelli, 1993.
6 Christopher Duffy, 1975: 51.
7 Paola Piccoli & Simona Pruno, 2010.
8 Martha Pollak, 1991: 170, 217.
9 John Childs, 1991: 90.
10 Lepage, 2010: 69.
11 Duffy, 1975: 81.
12 Barros, Salat & Sarmant, 2006: 78.
13 Jean-Philippe Cénat, 2015: 354.
14 Frédéric Naulet, 2002: 156.
15 Cénat, 2015: 185–99.
16 Jamel Ostwald, 2000.
17 Bertrand Fonck & George Satterfield, 2014.
18 Duffy, 1975: 92.
19 Stewart Stansfield, 2016: 202.
20 Fadi el-Hage, 2017.
21 Barros, Salat & Sarmant, 2006: 51.
22 Childs, 1991: 180–90.
23 Naulet, 2002: 189.
24 Naulet, 2002: 42.
25 Naulet, 2002: 82.
26 Stansfield, 2016: 226.
27 Duffy, 1975: 116.
28 Ostwald, 2000: 32.
29 Ostwald, 2000: 166.
30 Ostwald, 2000: 273.
31 Lepage, 2010: 127.
32 Stansfield, 2016: 235.
33 Paul Vo-Ha, 2017: 318.
34 Padraig Lenihan, 2011.
35 Ostwald, 2000: 186.
36 Ostwald, 2000: 24–32.
37 Naulet, 2002: 151.
38 Naulet, 2002: 161.
39 Duffy, 1975: 116.

40 Childs, 1991: 237.
41 Barros, Salat & Sarmant, 2006: 71.
42 Vo-Ha, 2017: 92.
43 Vo-Ha, 2017: 300.
44 Vo-Ha, 2017: 281; John Childs, 2012; John A Lynn, 2012.
45 Ostwald, 2000: 100.
46 Vo-Ha, 2017: 226.
47 Lynn, 2012: 109.

12 The classical battle

Offering battle

In war as a process, neither successful sieges nor day-long battles were in themselves decisive events likely to end the conflict. Both played out over a backdrop of ongoing negotiation as each side tried to mark points against the other for years on end.[1] If the outcome of a siege was fairly predictable, battles were risky events that could destroy the fruits of a campaign or lead to major losses of one of the belligerents. Despite his attendance at dozens of sieges, Louis XIV never witnessed a field battle in his entire reign, and instructed his generals from Versailles to avoid them when his armies were in enemy territory. He authorized them when the aim was to defend his own realm, but still warned his commanders not to give one without sound reasons.[2] He never absolutely forbade a general to take advantage of an unexpected opportunity to disrupt enemy plans. Individual soldiers might serve for years without once being caught up in a set-piece battle, that is, the deployment of the majority of the field army, with its artillery and baggage, against an adversary arrayed similarly. In this 'classical' period, only a handful of battles could be called decisive: the Boyne (1690) in the War of the League of Augsburg, that resulted in the reconquest of Jacobite Ireland, was one, and in the Spanish Succession conflict, the battle of Blenheim (1704) that deprived Louis XIV of Bavarian support, Turin (1706) that marked the advent of Austrian domination of Italy, and Almansa (1707), where the Habsburg cause in Spain was lost, were three more.

Some aggressive commanders pushed hard to contrive such decisive victories: Marlborough and Prince Eugene in the Coalition camp, Villars and Vendôme for the Bourbons, but even they understood that battles were not always opportune. A victory in the field early in the campaign might permit the winner to occupy considerable territory and capture several towns against an enemy too enfeebled to hold him back. But late in the campaign battles served little purpose, for the adversary would make good his losses over the winter. The opportunity of a decisive battle might present itself at any moment during the campaign, if both sides wished to risk it, but the event was too momentous to undertake lightly. The advantages of victory must be greater than the cost of defeat. On the eve of an impending fight, a general consulted with his senior staff to debate what purpose the battle served and took the pulse of his men. The troops themselves had to be confident that they would win; an army's high confidence was a sign that the enemy was already half-beaten.[3] This optimism rested on past experiences of the soldiers and their officers, and the diffuse sense that they would prevail again.[4] Notwithstanding this positive outlook, which might have reflected overconfidence, the general had to have a good idea of the strength of the enemy, whether their regiments largely comprised veterans or were filled with new recruits, whether his adversary was bold and resourceful, or cautious and passive.[5]

Modern historiography seeks to know more about the experience of the men caught up in the fight. John Keegan's landmark book from 1976, *The Face of Battle* was the first to renew what is the oldest genre of history. Keegan's later work was rich in studies of human and animal behaviour and the anthropology of war, which emphasizes that soldiers in the stress of battle react to their predicament on an emotional level, and that these motivations are universal to the human animal.[6] Keegan's imitators increasingly consult the social and behavioural sciences to understand the subjective experience of soldiers in past times, even though individual soldiers wrote little of their emotional reactions.[7] Battlefield narratives are problematic because single eyewitnesses could not have seen very much and what they thought everybody knew they did not bother to explain. We often lack a coherent chronology of the stages of battles, richer in the beginning and at the end, but confused and uncertain between the two extremities.[8]

Today, we know that the rank and file were neither social misfits nor the scum of the earth, and we must try to understand what motivated them to fight and risk their lives. Keegan and his emulators draw inspiration (whether they realize it or not) from a remarkable nineteenth century observer–participant, Charles Ardant du Picq, who undertook the first scientific studies of men in combat.[9] Men followed their leaders into battle by mutual consent, and the officers had to speak to their self-esteem as professionals. They all shared a culture of honour, a desire to be worthy of the respect of their peers by assuming their fair share of the risks. Primary group cohesion served the interests of the men who underwent the danger, but it served the interest of the military organization, too. Common soldiers who left memoirs from the eighteenth century certainly did not criticize officers who meted out harsh treatment to cowards.[10] Those who failed to take their fair share of risks in battle earned the contempt of their peers, which would one day have to be redeemed through some more noble action, so as not to suffer ostracism. Individuals at all ranks on the battlefield were caught between two contradictory desires, to survive the ordeal unhurt, and to prove themselves in the eyes of their peers.

Commanders organized their march routes half-expecting they would encounter the enemy. The army's march would replicate the position of each regiment in a battlefield array, and they would camp and sleep in combat formation in order to reduce the preparation time necessary for an engagement.[11] Opposing armies might encounter each other in the afternoon, but it was often best to delay a fight until morning, giving time for the soldiers to rest and eat, to give them strength and increase their fortitude. If the men had to march before reaching the battle-field, they would be tired and hungry, and reluctant to make extra exertions. If the men expected to be attacked, they might spend the night raising parapets to defend themselves, though they might be exhausted in the morning.

It required two consenting parties to hold a battle. In a period where larger armies were the rule, battles could not be improvised, since it was easy enough for one of the commanders to slip away during the night or the following morning with arms and baggage intact. He could be pursued by enemy cavalry, but they could only engage with his rear-guard and the main army would be safe. It took hours for an army to ready itself for a major fight, for a battle meant synchronizing the movements of many thousands of men. Generals allocated each unit according to their anticipation of the enemy's intention. They were reluctant to modify the dispositive later, because it was difficult to follow the flow of the battle once it had begun.[12] A general with strong cavalry forces preferred open terrain to capitalize on this advantage. An army lacking good horse, or with inferior numbers of them, preferred a battlefield full of hedgerows, farms and villages, although a battleground too segmented made communication and command control difficult. Approaching the vicinity of an enemy position, troops advanced in column, not employing a cadenced step. Outside the range of enemy artillery (say, about a kilometre) they shifted into line, the slender formation giving the maximum number of soldiers a good view of the enemy, and, thus, the ability to fire at them.[13] Infantry, arrayed eight men deep in 1635, and six deep in 1650, were deployed in five ranks in the War of the League of Augsburg (only the rear row armed with pikes) and then four or three men deep in the War of the Spanish Succession, after pikes were phased out in favour of fusils with bayonets.[14] Additional regiments were drawn up several hundred metres in the rear to serve as a reserve. The battle order of a large army would extend in a line covering three or four kilometres or more, even with two lines and an emergency reserve.[15] Commanding generals would rarely be in a position to see their entire deployment before the shooting started, even with a spy-glass.

Broken terrain and obstacles were exploited to shore up the defence. A general holding the high ground enjoyed several advantages; the enemy could not see his men deployed to the rear, while the officers on the hill had an amphitheatre view of the adversary's array. Cannon firing from a height had a longer range and more effect on the enemy below than cannon firing upwards at their targets. Men attacking downhill also enjoyed a gravitational advantage that accelerated the force of their attack. Water-courses constituted natural defensive advantages, even if they were shallow enough to ford. Troops deployed behind a river or a stream knew that enemy cavalry could not attack them directly across wet ground without becoming disorganized. Villages or walled farms packed with troops were positions not easily broken without a fierce fight, since closed space was more fiercely contested than open ground, and firing holes were poked through outer walls of houses. Furniture was piled up in spaces between the buildings to serve as makeshift barricades. Earthen redoubts similarly gave courage to their defenders: 'a hundred men resist more strenuously in a fort, than a thousand arrayed behind an earthwork', wrote the *maréchal de bataille*, François Dorignac, after decades of campaigning.[16]

Generals preparing for battle divided their armies into several large contingents, a centre and two wings, with a similar deployment behind it forming a reserve. Each segment of the battle line and each reserve had its own commanders to supervise fighting in that sector. Single regiments were combined into brigades several thousand men strong, under a brigadier-general. The general-in-chief could post himself anywhere, but he had to be easily located in order to receive reports and transmit messages.[17] Each regiment or squadron marked its emplacement with flags, carried by young nobles just starting their careers. The banners marked the tangible location of that specific unit, and, in their absence, men would not know where they were to go. Officers and aides, or aristocratic volunteers, were then allocated behind the line in order to observe the performance of the troops, in order to shore up their morale, and to distribute rewards and blame after the fight. If the soldiers understood their general's plan and their own part in it, they enjoyed a moral advantage over men who did not know why they were posted where they were. The men might be confident of victory, but they must still be forced to fight and prevented from running away.

As the men took their positions in the line, individually placed by their sergeants, they often had unimpeded view of the enemy, although this was easier for the horse than for the foot. The men were also trained to recognize several drumbeats in order to reinforce an officer's command, and to set the pace of march.[18] The general and his leading staff and messengers then took their position at the head of the army and gave the order to advance. The attacker tended to have more initiative than the defender, who had to wait anxiously for events to unfold. 'As the battle is close to being joined, the men will display a certain natural levity and eagerness for combat,' wrote Montecuccoli. An army in full battle deployment was an impressive sight, designed to strike dread in the hearts of the adversary and to discourage them before the fighting started. La Colonie was struck by the spectacle at Ramillies, the gorgeous formations' banners, and the fanfares of drums and trumpets. He marvelled at the distinctive colours of uniforms of various regiments on both sides. The participants wore their best uniforms, and the soldiers put on a 'bel air' to impress their adversaries as well as each other of their valour. The uniforms helped clarify the situation; red for English, blue for most Germans, but then beige, white and grey for the Imperials, the Dutch and the French. Elite regiments on both sides wore more vivid colours than the ordinary line units.[19] It was difficult to tell friend from foe by the uniforms alone, since many armies wore predominantly drab colours. Bavarian troops wore both blue and red, which meant they were easy to mistake. For better recognition, soldiers inserted various badges into their hatbands. Senior officers often wore no uniform at all, but instead wrapped coloured sashes across their torsos, red for the Habsburg, orange for the Dutch. We have no statistics concerning officers and men who fell victim to friendly fire, but it was not a rare occurrence.

The fight often began with an artillery duel, before each side had finished aligning their men. French guns were the best in Europe in 1680, and the best served, which reflected Louvois' enthusiasm for them.[20] Prior to 1740, the field artillery averaged one piece for every 1,000 men, ranging from manoeuvrable four-pounders to the large 12-pounders, which had much longer range and greater accuracy. The main problem with cannon was to find the best trade-off between the power and range of the gun and its mobility. Before 1740, the larger ones were simply planted in the most likely spot and remained there for the length of the combat, due to the time and trouble it took to relocate them. The smaller pieces constituted about 70–80% of the guns on the battlefield, which weighed only 600 kg and could be wrestled into place by a small team of soldiers. Light cannon only had a really effective range of 300 metres, or 500 metres for the new pieces cast after 1680 by La Frezelière. These lighter pieces had a fierce recoil, which was hard on the carriages.

Guns were often posted ahead of the infantry, for, if placed behind the foot, the gunners would not be able to fire because they lacked a view of the enemy.[21] Firing commenced perhaps from a kilometre away. This did little damage to the enemy, but served to keep up the spirits of one's own men as the danger drew nearer. Once the two armies began to close, the guns began firing in earnest within 800 metres. It was possible to fire a gun three times per minute, but not for very long; after 12 shots the tube had to be cooled down with water before reloading. It was calculated that only one round-shot or cannonball in ten hit somebody, but the unfortunate victim was splattered all over the vicinity and anybody who saw it was appalled. The operative principal behind artillery fire with round-shot was bowling. The tremendous force behind a cannonball meant that it would kill everyone who happened to be in its path, and it could still cripple someone as it rolled on the ground to a full stop. Skilled gunners aimed the piece in order to knock down the maximum number of 'pins'. Several batteries might converge their fire on a single body of men (a column especially, which was densely packed) and troops who were targeted could not do much to avoid it.[22] Attacking units were unlikely to be broken by artillery fire alone, but the trial unnerved the men, who feared for the worst.

As the attackers closed range with the guns, around 200 metres or less, the gunners working under an officer substituted round-shot with canister (a metal cartridge containing musket balls) or the heavier grapeshot that left the tube as a lethal spray. When the guns were attacked directly, this ammunition mowed down men and horses indiscriminately, and, at 50 metres, the nearby fusiliers detailed to defend the guns added their musket fire. Guns charged by horse or foot were then abandoned by their crews who scurried to the rear for safety. Captured guns could be turned around and fired by the enemy if the munitions and tools were left nearby. Naulet claims that French cannon inflicted about 14% of the Coalition losses at the battle of Malplaquet, which would be equal to about 3,000 Coalition soldiers, or almost 40 casualties per piece. Few men hit by a cannonball would have survived.[23]

Cavalry

Cavalry typically comprised a quarter or a third of the field army, although the proportion gradually diminished. Since horses moved more quickly than men on foot, generals posted them to both flanks where they could cover more ground, or to a single wing if one flank was well anchored in terrain where cavalry could not manoeuvre. For most of the battle, cavalrymen would sit perched atop their animals waiting for orders. That way, a cavalier could better enjoy the view of the fight from where they sat and discern the movement of men back and forth.[24] Squadrons of horse could also be interspersed with infantry along the line for mutual support, as in the time of Wallenstein and Gustavus Adolphus. For cavalry to be at all useful, it had to advance as a tight body in unison, and could not, therefore, charge across streams, through swamp, forests or across hedgerows that separated fields. Cavaliers could sit behind the infantry lines, if the general feared the latter might break under the strain of an enemy attack, and Montecuccoli recommended that they be lined up close enough to discourage infantry soldiers in the rear of their formations running away.

The purpose of a cavalry charge was not to kill their adversaries, but to break the enemy's cohesion and order, and reduce enemy troopers to a formless and ineffectual crowd. 'This tactical axiom is not particular to cavalry but is rather a constant principle of military science', writes Frédéric Chauviré, author of the best study of cavalry tactics to date.[25] Eyewitness accounts about how cavalry charges unfolded are quite rare. There were several types of cavalry at the end of the seventeenth century, but the newest version of light cavalry, the hussars, were not usually employed to fight the enemy on a battlefield. Armies deployed instead a corps of moderately heavy cavalry, the *cuirassiers*, large men who still wore a breastplate and a helmet and who rode larger horses or proper chargers to support the greater weight of their accoutrement. Dragoons were primarily mounted infantry, but they were also trained in basic cavalry tactics and were employed as such in battle. Most of the rest was what used to be called 'light' cavalry, armed with pistols and swords and often carbines, too, for greater accuracy and penetration. A typical regulation cavalry squadron represented 150 men, two to four of which formed a regiment. Horsemanship for most cavalry troopers was fairly basic, and emphasized riding in formation.[26] Nevertheless, cavalry required much more training than infantry, in large part because riders had to master an excitable horse during the chaos of battle.

During the later wars of Louis XIV, cavalry charges might still use the caracole tactic, a mounted version of the counter-march in which troopers would advance in three ranks, fire at the massed enemy horse at short range (perhaps only ten metres) rank by rank, wheel about to the left and ride rearward while the successive ranks advanced similarly. Eventually, the men would draw their swords to charge into the enemy formation. The caracole was challenged by tacticians over the entire century, for musket range was longer than that of pistols and the large horses and their riders were easy targets.[27] At White Mountain in 1620, the horse were eight to ten deep and 40–50 across; the men were armoured from head to knee. The more disciplined force fired their carbines last, from very close range, in order to impose their dominance on the adversary. If one side swerved to avoid close contact, the other pressed home their charge with drawn swords.

Gustavus Adolphus took away the carbine and left the troopers with only pistols and swords, especially recommending the use of the latter. But he also placed musketeers on foot close by, who would close with enemy cavalry, fire and then withdraw to reload. Cavalrymen charging with pistols found it difficult to shoot accurately from a moving horse against a moving target and then reload while riding. Once they fired their pistols at the last moment, the Swedish horse closed the charge with swords, and the Imperial forces did the same (Image 12.1). The thinner order of the Swedish formations made greater speed possible and a larger proportion of the troopers had direct contact with the enemy. Their thinner lines helped envelop the enemy formation from the flank. In 1700, there was no single tactic adopted by any army. Cavaliers were permitted to use the sabre or their firearms, according to their circumstances. Veteran cavalry troopers admitted to the Invalides in Paris had received gunshot and blade weapon wounds in roughly equal proportion. Although it was not described in the drillbooks, the French began to speed up the pace of attack, '*en fourrageurs*'.[28] A cavalry squadron of men arrayed boot against boot formed a living barrier 160 metres across and two to three metres high. It was a moving wall of centaurs, writes one author, whose impact derived from its solidity, not its speed. The largest horses, trained for combat, were supposed to be in the front ranks and were intended to dominate those across from them, in an emotional contagion amongst the animals. A second and third line of

Image 12.1 Jan van Huchtenburg: Combat de Cavalerie. Western troopers would remain in compact formation but in the melee horsemen engaged in individual combat at close range. Pistols were notoriously inaccurate save at very short range. Art Resource

troopers, swords drawn, followed closely.[29] They advanced across the field 'au pas' at 6–7 kilometres/hour, then increased speed to a trot of 8–14 kilometres/ hr, and finally passed to a gallop at only 50 metres from the enemy, 13–19 kilo- metres/hr, still in formation. Marlborough and Villars recommended not gal- loping, but moving at a quickened trot from about 30–40 metres, in order to maintain alignment and so as not to tire the horses.[30] The target formation of cavalry would themselves charge at the last moment, if one side did not swerve away first.

The shock of two mounted formations colliding with each other almost never happened. Both met at a moderate speed in what Chauviré calls an '*abordage*', or boarding. Often, one of the formations, the less resolute one, swerved to avoid a head-on encounter. The success or not of the charge could be felt by both sides in the instants before the contact. As Ardant du Picq wrote about the infantry, 'there are never, ever two equal resolutions face to face'. Both the horse (which is also a sentient animal, bred for docility and the ability to remain in formation) and the trooper obeyed an instinctive restraint. 'Shock does not crush the enemy, it disperses him'.[31] Gaps opened up in the formations into which cavaliers advanced, trying to exploit breaches in the opposite array. The animals pushed away or 'pressed' other horses with their shoulders, which is why larger animals were more effective. The trooper simultaneously tried to push his adversary away or unhorse him. Horses could be seized with fear and refuse to move, or they might panic and run blindly into danger. Cuirassiers, who were big men on big horses and wearing armour, enjoyed practical psycho- logical advantages in a melee. (They sometimes had to be ordered to wear their uncomfortable breastplates, however.) Only the front two rows of troopers would fight, and then only briefly, with the second rank discharging their pistols at those attacking their comrades in front. Troopers would then try to strike their adversaries with the edge of their sword, which would usually wound an enemy rather than kill him, if he really tried to fight in the melee. Wounds received from blade weapons were the least likely to be fatal. With luck and skill, the formation could open up the enemy array and reduce their adversaries to individuals who would have to withdraw. The officers had little or no control over this stage of the action, although buglers would soon call the men to dis- engage and reform if they had not sought to escape already on their own. Cav- alry were trained to rally after a charge, and catch their breath. The beaten formation would hesitate to renew the experience.[32]

Generals only infrequently threw cavalry against bodies of infantry, for the horses could not be trained to impale themselves on bayonets and the animals swerved to avoid colliding with men, and even sidestepped men prone on the ground so as not to tread on them. Austrian regiments, from their Hungarian experience, set up 'Spanish riders', or beams with holes for boar spears two metres long arranged crosswise. These were sufficient to keep enemy horse at bay.[33] The animals presented a very large target to packed musketeers, who might number six or eight for each cavalier. But shaken troops with little experi- ence, or units having suffered many casualties might break up as the horses approached: each fusilier only had time to fire a single shot before the horsemen were upon them. The speed of the charge made infantry fire too soon and inaccurately: weak fire just egged the cavalry on.[34] If the formation began to scatter, cavalry could ride down many times the number of infantrymen and shatter their morale completely. Most of the casualties inflicted by the cavalry on the enemy were when they were already broken and fleeing and gave no thought to resisting. It was cavalry that enabled an army to win a battle outright, if the enemy infantry collapsed. But this was not a sure thing.

Infantry in battle

As in the Napoleonic era, victory was procured by a series of psychological shocks applied in quick succession, which began by impressing the foe with a full view of numbers and magnificence. As the attacker advanced toward the enemy, the men on both sides raised a great shout and emitted frightening noises to induce fear in their adversaries and to bolster their own courage.[35] Generals depended upon the readiness of their men to fight, and the slightest interruption of momentum could stall an attack. Once the foot received the signal to advance, they set off with their officers in front to close with the enemy, muskets not in their hands, but slung over their shoulders. At Neerwinden and Landen on 28 July 1693, Luxembourg did not bother ordering the foot to change formation into line but instead had them advance quickly in column against William of Orange's men, who were not expecting battle. The column had very little firepower and it would suffer heavy casualties in a fight against infantry arrayed in line, but this formation accelerated the speed of attack and allowed the men some measure of dash that a line would not permit. French troops did not often train in column or square formation: the Allies were in closed country behind hedgerows and packed densely into villages and inflicted heavy casualties on the attackers, but it still ended in a rout with the loss of Allied baggage and guns.[36]

Generals more commonly formed their men into long firing lines, increasingly effective as the matchlock was replaced by the flintlock around 1700, or even later in the case of the Imperial army. Between 1650 and 1700, the musketeer's rate of fire passed from one to two shots per minute. A battalion's firepower was ten times smaller in 1600 (when two-thirds of the foot were pikemen) than a century later, when all the foot carried flintlock fusils.[37] Armies experimented with the most effective systems of fire and the best range, but in either case, troops had to be drilled to withhold their fire until the last minute. The Dutch developed the most effective firing system of firing by platoons, which passed to British troops in the 1690s, arrayed in slender formations only three men deep. A Dutch battalion contained 18 platoons, and six of those placed in different parts of the line would unleash a volley from 165 muzzles simultaneously, giving the impression of fire all along the front. Men who had fired then reloaded their weapon in a standing position. The French answered rank by rank, with *aimed* fire from 125 marksmen from a similar battalion of 500 men.

Men who had fired dropped to their knees to reload, although reloading a long-barrelled weapon in this position was awkward, while the men behind them delivered their shot. It became clear to Luxembourg, in his bloody victories against the Coalition armies, that his troops had less firepower than his adversaries. The French adopted the platoon-fire system in 1706–1707, but it required the men to march forward four paces and then back, a more convoluted tactic, and they suffered a mild handicap relative to the coalition armies. Worst of all, the French received insufficient firing practice, in order to curb costs, while the Dutch regiments received the most.[38] French firing was more efficient from broken terrain and from behind entrenchments, and the men were trained to aim their shots individually, rather than deliver volleys.[39] Austrian soldiers employed uninterrupted individual fire when fighting Turks, but switched to volley fire against Western armies.

The above assertions are only generalizations. In fact, various systems of firing coexisted and each colonel employed a specific repertoire of tactics. More important than the system of firing was the officers' ability to get the men to close with the enemy without firing first. Like cavalry engagements, the measuring of infantry regiments against each other was as much psychological as tactical. As the attackers advanced, it was necessary to halt the line every 50 metres and dress it afresh. Officers on horseback did their utmost to keep the ranks moving forward, to avoid men malingering or dropping out. Ideally, they would advance to within 20–50 paces of the enemy before stopping to fire, but this was not often achieved. It was a rule of thumb that 50 metres was an effective range for muskets. If troops fired too soon, they would lose heart, for few of the enemy would be hit. Since a walking advance in line covered 100 metres a minute, this permitted only a single shot from the defenders before closing.[40] Attacking men might halt near their opponents to fire, but the advance risked coming to a stop and develop into an indecisive firefight. Taller men were placed at the front in order to better intimidate the enemy until the shooting started. Certain parts of the uniform, which was large and billowy, were designed to make the soldiers appear bigger than they actually were.[41] The boldest troops should be posted at the front of the formation, so as to give more momentum to the men marching behind them. These battles were largely contests of mental endurance between opposing troops, something Lynn calls 'forbearance'. Soldiers must be drilled to obey and wait for orders, and then advance on waiting guns without flinching. Battle tested the ability of men to endure fire without moving, or advancing without firing themselves as they were being shot at. Once firing commenced, new problems appeared. Each shot contained six grams of black powder that released one cubic metre of thick black smoke from the barrel and more from the firing pan near the marksman's face. Unconsumed powder and cartridge, or tampon paper, stuck to their clothes, their hands, their faces. Downwind, the shooters were soon enveloped in the enemy's smoke as well as their own. Marching forward towards the enemy meant walking into the shadows, where the smoke irritated the eyes and choked the soldiers. Individuals and groups could easily get disorientated in the smoke, especially if they lost touch with senior officers. Crops in the field might inhibit troops marching in formation, or block their visibility: fog also inhibited visibility, but it served more as a protective shroud.

Salvo fire was probably only possible at the beginning of an exchange, after which the men fired individually. Ten muskets firing in unison amount to 100 decibels, which is comparable to a rock concert: 120 decibels for a rank of 100 men, 130 decibels for two battalions firing together. The men endured battle perhaps because they were almost deafened by the noise.[42] They could not have ignored that men beside them were being hit by bullets that they could hear zipping by their own heads, which was no doubt very stressful.[43] Musketry at close ranges might still have been devastating. There is a persistent myth that these early firearms were wildly inaccurate. But trials conducted at the Provincial Armoury of Graz (Austria) in 1988 test-fired matchlock and flintlock weapons, and determined that, at 100 metres, it was possible to hit a man-sized immovable target 61% of the time, which is considerable. That means that two shots from each man would have annihilated an enemy battalion.[44] Musket balls left the muzzle of the weapons at supersonic speed, but then rapidly slowed due to the spherical shape of the projectile. Slow-travelling balls did more damage to the victim by the resulting ricochet effect inside the body than one that passed quickly through at high velocity. The man hit in the torso at 150 metres would still suffer a catastrophic wound, while one hit at 75 metres would probably die from it.[45] An exchange of musketry could last for long minutes that wore down the participants psychologically. Some soldiers in battle mimicked fighting, while others feigned wounds or helped carry wounded comrades to the rear, or left the firing line to seek extra munitions. Apart from the firing, soldiers were enjoined to keep silent in order to better hear their orders, but if they were ordered to charge, they raised a yell to unnerve their adversary. While musketry exchange could be very lethal over a long duration, we know that it required, on average, 200 to 500 shots to hit a single man at fairly close range. This simple arithmetic means that soldiers firing at each other face to face at ranges they found acceptable were deliberately aiming to miss. Killing the adversary was not their principal aim. They were praying that the opposing troops would back away.[46]

Soldiers assaulting enemy entrenchments would have to be organized differently. Fusiliers with their bayonets would lead the charge, followed close behind by work parties instructed to pull down the earthworks at a frantic pace in order to enable cavalry to cross them. The shooters and workers must be organized in order to relay each other. The men not working or firing stood back far enough not to suffer excessive casualties.[47] Earthwork lines were simple enough to penetrate, but the forts and redoubts placed along them were not so easily carried. It was rare for troops to cross bayonets except in buildings and redoubts and, if it occurred, prisoners other than officers were rarely taken. Commanders wrote of the superiority of blade weapons over firepower, and did their utmost to get their men to advance in order not to remain targets. Hand-to-hand combat was exceedingly rare, however, and one specialist has never encountered a single eye-witness example of it. In close actions, manoeuvring and tactics mattered little, certainly less than the confidence of the troops. French infantry, who were not as well drilled as their adversaries, preferred to charge with bayonets, and they often derived good results from it.[48]

Montecuccoli claimed that a unit that withdrew under pressure could not improve its posture. Only a fresh reserve corps would save the position. Troops in the front line, even if they had taken their objectives, were seized with apathy and fatigue, called a *parasympathetic backlash*. 'Once the attacker's fury has been spent and he encounters trouble, he becomes impatient and cowardly and is repulsed easily.'[49] The courage of soldiers oscillated during the battle, and the officers had to monitor the men's fortitude in order to prevent them from breaking under pressure. The art of the general in battle was to manage and contain their men's natural fear of death. Shaky units depleted by casualties or the loss of popular officers would have to be withdrawn, while battalions posted to the reserve line would then advance to renew the fight. Soldiers' perceptions of time were altered under the stress, as interminable waiting was replaced by sudden frantic activity. In hot weather, the men were constantly on the lookout for sources of water. Standing in battalion formation under the hot sun was debilitating. Soldiers could only dimly perceive how the battle was unfolding through the smoke and the chaos. They were alternately encouraged or threatened by their officers posted front and rear, who shared the danger with them. The men up front underwent what is called a 'saturation of perceptions' that focused them entirely.[50] The men to the rear were nervous spectators of the events around them, but, if discipline was maintained there, the army would maintain its viability. Even when suffering heavy losses, good units would show surprising resilience under the strain, but encirclement by the enemy would completely deprive them of their combativeness.[51]

In the heat of battle, some soldiers would engage in daring displays and communicate their bravado to their comrades. They also appreciated the daring of their adversaries, which was information they would spread as anecdotes to their comrades. The longer the battle lasted, however, the more the men were overwhelmed by the chaos and the noise and showed signs of torpor or psychological disengagement. Soldiers' physiological reactions to combat varied, from the stress produced by a state of shock and malaise, to the mobilization of adrenalin, where the heart rate speeds up and sensations suddenly sharpen, improving muscle performance. There is a longer phase of resistance to aggression under enemy fire, in which the soldier responds with lessons learned from drill, but this eventually gives way to apathy and exhaustion, a return to a state of shock and the onset of extreme fatigue.[52] Signs of discouragement at this point could quickly spread through the troops and soldiers looked for ways to stop fighting and withdraw to safety. When soldiers started to withdraw on their own, the task of the officers was to gesticulate and shout in order to bring them out of their daze and to make them regroup. The danger was that disbanded men would spread disorder to other comrades still fighting around the colours.

Soldiers might also throw down their arms, not in order to run faster, but to show that they had ceased fighting and were not a threat.[53]

The general who understood that he would not prevail had to promptly organize an orderly withdrawal, remove the baggage and the cannon to the rear and constitute an effective rear-guard that would keep the victors at a distance. The greatest danger was that the army would disintegrate on the field in the face of excessive pressure. This was the challenge that Marshal Boufflers successfully accomplished at Malplaquet, by marching away in good order with arms and baggage. Normally, the view of the enemy retreating suddenly energized the victors, who forgot their fear and began to chase their enemies with an irrepressible desire to kill as many of them as possible. The soldiers' blood was up, and it was then that most of the killing took place. This phenomenon, called a *forward panic* is a universal form of unthinking fear. To kill enemy fleeing the field was not considered to constitute an atrocity, and generals expected this of their men.[54] It was not uncommon for the victor to have incurred greater casualties than the loser up to that moment. Montecuccoli phrased it thus: 'the sole objective in establishing a battle order is to be able to disrupt, smite, rout, confuse and hound the enemy from the field'. In pursuit, one can massacre him easily because, being disorganized and panic-stricken, he lacks courage to defend himself.[55] Cavalry held back during the fight now came into its own, seeking to strike down as many fleeing men as possible.

Aftermath of carnage

As the firing died down, parties of the defeated enemy that took shelter in a protected space and continued resisting were offered terms by the victors. Men readily surrendered if they felt reasonably secure they would not be harmed. Men who recognized defeat lay down their weapons and gave themselves up as prisoners.[56] Captives were relieved of their valuables and most had the good sense not to complain too loudly. Officers offered their swords to their peers, if they could.[57] If the victorious men gathered booty they could not march away with, they would liquidate it at a great auction before the army continued its travel. Soldiers rarely wrote in their memoirs about the carnage they witnessed on the battlefield. The survivors were assailed by the stench of blood, entrails and decaying bodies, all of which were terribly stress-inducing for men who understood the danger to health they represented (Image 12.2). The collection of the wounded was anything but systematic and if the fighting continued to nightfall, it would have to take place the following day. Soldiers did not carry first-aid pouches that would permit them to assist wounded comrades before taking them to the surgeon. The wounded often succumbed to bleeding, fever and thirst, while looters, both military and civilian, dispatched the lingering victims. Men could be haunted by the cries of the wounded men agonizing after the battle, although few speak of empathetic trauma. If the fight took place in the shadow of a large city, urban hospitals took a portion of the casualties, whose expenses were often paid by the officers. Such hospitals provided the

Image 12.2 Nicolas Guerard (le jeune?): Champ de bataille. Few observers from the era described the carnage which characterized every battle. It is by no means certain that armies buried their dead all the time. Mass graves are beginning to reveal important information to historians. Art Resource

best care available, with clean bedding and adequate clothing and laundries, a general cleanliness and better food. Gunshot wounds were treated by methods elaborated in the sixteenth century by Ambroise Paré, which reduced the incidence of amputation and cauterization.[58] Inflammation of the wound on an arm or a leg required rapid amputation, however, practised without anaesthetic soon after the fight.

Psychological trauma in the aftermath of battle certainly existed, but it was often masked and manifested as other pathologies, such as homesickness or melancholy. Surgeons in Napoleon's army coined the term 'syndrome of the cannonball's wind' to describe the stupor of shocked soldiers. Men overwhelmed by the experience of battle cradled their weapons in their arms and were deaf to the exhortations of their comrades for minutes or hours. Some men went through the motions of fighting like automatons during the entire experience, and then emerged from it afterward as if from a dream.[59] Some might have irrepressible memories of killing specific enemies, but, in fact, the great majority of soldiers never killed anyone (although some killed more than one) and even if they had they would not know it. The risk of being killed in battle was not enormous, ranging from 3–10% of the men involved, because not all the men present were in harm's way.[60]

Afterwards, but not always, began the process of burying the victims, after their belongings were pilfered by soldiers, camp followers and civilians. During hot summer days, especially in Italy, it was not long before bodies began to decay in the hot sun.[61] Horseflies could smell blood from a distance of up to

60 kilometres, and honed in to lay their eggs on cadavers of men and horses. These hatch within four to six hours and commence their feast on subcutaneous fat on the inert corpses. On occasion, nobody bothered to collect and bury the corpses, which decomposed in the open air at speeds dependent on the temperature. In temperate weather of 20 degrees Celsius, a 68 kilogram cadaver reaches an advanced state of decomposition in about three weeks, but the hot summer accelerates the process. Unlike the officers, whose remains might be handed over to ecclesiastical authorities and then to waiting relatives, the men were buried without much ceremony.[62] This was an unrewarding task whereby officers might have to pay extra money to soldiers in order to collect the corpses from the field. Men were laid in pits, without being identified first and local clergy did not record military casualties in their burial records, unless wounded men cared for in the aftermath of combat died at a later date. Army administrations rarely accounted for casualties to the government in a precise way before the nineteenth century, and often gave the losses in round figures.[63] People occasionally uncover the burial pits today, with the assistance of radar that can detect anomalies up to three metres underground. Skeletons are proving to be a precious source of information on the soldiers, including their wounds and their previous illnesses. Those discovered at Wittstock (1636) enable us to calculate the sex (all men), height (average 170 cm) and age (between 17 and 40) of the victims. At Lutzen (1632), battlefield archaeologists have explored one-third of the battlefield, or 1.1 million square metres, and have found dozens or hundreds of men buried in pits. Men were carefully laid to rest, but almost naked. With time, we will be able to identify the specific national origins of soldiers from strontium isotope analysis. To extract the maximum amount of information, however, the scientists are going to require some extra funding.[64]

Notes

1 Lynn, 1999: 2.
2 Jamel Ostwald, 2017.
3 Thomas M Barker, 1975: 73.
4 Rory Muir, 1998: 6.
5 Paul Azan, 1904: 62
6 John Keegan, 1976; John Keegan, 1997.
7 Idan Sherer, 2017: 9–10.
8 Malcolm Wanklyn, 2006: 8–12.
9 Charles Ardant du Picq, 2004 (1904 edn.).
10 Ilya Berkovich, 2017: 101.
11 Barker, 1975: 75.
12 Clément Oury, 2017.
13 John Childs, 1991: 82.
14 Clément Oury, 2015.
15 Giovanni Cerino Badone, 2013.
16 Azan, 1904: 38.
17 Barker, 1975: 113.
18 Keith Roberts, *Matchlock Musketeer 1588–1688* (Oxford & New York, 2002) 21.

19 Dorothée Malfoy-Noël, *L'Epreuve de la bataille (1700–1714)*, Montpellier, 2007, 43; Oury, 'Au cœur de la bataille', 127.
20 Frédéric Naulet, *L'Artillerie française (1665–1765): Naissance d'une arme* (Paris, 2002) 54.
21 Naulet, *L'Artillerie française*, 254.
22 Muir, *Tactics and the experience of battle*, 40.
23 Naulet, *L'Artillerie française*, 258.
24 Malfoy-Noël, *L'Epreuve de la bataille*, 33.
25 Frédéric Chauviré, *Histoire de la Cavalerie* (Paris, 2013) 52.
26 Chauviré, *Histoire de la Cavalerie*, 66; Muir, *Tactics and the experience of battle*, 111.
27 Chauviré, *Histoire de la Cavalerie*, 85.
28 Clément Oury, *Les défaites françaises de la guerre de Succession d'Espagne, 1704–1708*, 2011, 691.
29 Hochedlinger, *Austria's Wars of Emergence*, 140.
30 Frédéric Chauviré, 'Le problème de l'allure dans les charges de cavalerie du XVIe au XVIIIe siècle', *Revue Historique des Armées*, 249, 2007, 16–27.
31 Chauviré, *Histoire de la Cavalerie*, 283; Gavin Robinson, 'Equine battering rams? A reassessment of cavalry charges in the English Civil War', *The Journal of Military History*, 75, 2011, 719–31.
32 Muir, *Tactics and the Experience of Battle*, 122.
33 Hochedlinger, *Austria's Wars of Emergence*, 127.
34 Muir, *Tactics and the experience of battle*, 130.
35 Paddy Griffith, *Forward into Battle: Fighting Tactics from Waterloo to the Near Future* (Novato, CA, 1991) 21–6.
36 Childs, *The Nine Years' War and the British Army*, 37.
37 Philip Hoffman, *Why did Europe Conquer the World ?* (Princeton & Oxford, 2015) 57.
38 Oury, *Les défaites françaises*, 708–30; Boris Bouget, 'D'une guerre à l'autre: le double retard de l'infanterie française, un handicap limité (1688–1715)', *Les Dernières guerres de Louis XIV 1688–1715*, H Drévillon, B Fonck & J-P Cénat eds, Rennes, 2017, 143–56.
39 Oury, *Les défaites françaises*, 756; Hochedlinger, *Austria's Wars of Emergence*, 140.
40 Griffiths, *Forward into battle*, 41.
41 Malfoy-Noël, *L'Epreuve de la bataille*, 29.
42 Oury, 'Au Coeur de la bataille'.
43 Marco Costa, *Psicologia militare: elementi di psicologia per gli appartenenti alle forze armate* (Milan, 2003) 169–73.
44 Peter Krenn, 'Test-firing selected 16th-eighteenth century weapons', *Military Illustrated Past and Present*, 33, February 1991, 34–38.
45 N.A. Roberts, JW Brown, B Hammett & PDF Kingston, 'A detailed study of the effectiveness and capabilities of 18th-century musketry on the battlefield', *Journal of Conflict Archaeology*, 2008, 1–21.
46 Gregory Hanlon, *Italy 1636*, 140–43; Dave Grossman, *On killing: The Psychological Cost of Learning to Kill in War and Society* (Boston, 1995) 50 & 180; Ardant du Picq, *Etudes sur le combat*, 141.
47 *Memoires de Montecuculi, généralissime des troupes de l'Empereur*, Amsterdam 1752, 183.
48 Oury, *Les défaites françaises*, 706–15.
49 Barker, *The Military Intellectual and battle*, 83–4; Dave Grossman, *On Combat: The Psychology and Physiology of Deadly conflict in War and in Peace* (Mascoutah, IL, 2004) 16.
50 Malfoy Noël, *L'Epreuve de la bataille*, 48.
51 Vo-Ha, *Rendre les Armes*, 132.

52 Louis Crocq, *Les Traumatismes psychiques de guerre* (Paris, 1999) 69–76.
53 Oury, 'Au Coeur de la bataille', 135–40.
54 Sherer, *Warriors for a Living*, 154–60; John Childs, 'The laws of war in seventeenth-century Europe and their application to the Jacobite war in Ireland, 1688-91', *Age of Atrocity: Violence and Political Conflict in Early Modern Ireland*, D Edwards, P Lenihan, C Tait eds, Dublin, 2007, 283–300.
55 Barker, *The Military Intellectual and Battle*, 83.
56 Vo-Ha, *Rendre les Armes*, 166.
57 Muir, *Tactics and the Experience of Battle*, 253.
58 Hanlon, *Italy 1636*, 145–48.
59 Crocq, *Les Traumatismes psychiques de guerre*, 79.
60 Muir, *Tactics and the experience of battle*, 7.
61 Malfoy-Noël, *L'Epreuve de la bataille*, 59.
62 Hanlon, *Italy 1636*, 168–76.
63 Alain Guéry, 'Les comptes de la mort vague après la guerre. Pertes de guerre et conjoncture du phénomène guerre', *Histoire et Mesure*, 6, 1991, 289–312.
64 Anja Grothe & Bettina Jungklaus, 'Archaeological and anthropological examinations of a mass grave from the 1636 battle at Wittstock: a preliminary report', *Limping together through the Ages: Joint Afflictions and Bone Infections*, G Grupe, G McGlynn & J Peters eds, Rahden Westfalen, 2008, 127–35; Christoph Seidler, 'Mass grave begins revealing soldiers' secrets', *Der Spiegel Online*, 27 April 2012.

13 War finance in the classical age 1689–1720

Paying taxes in the age of absolutism

Taxation by kings was a crucial innovation at the end of the Middle Ages, when they imposed their demands upon peasants and townspeople already providing resources for noblemen and priests. In France, the most precocious large state, royal taxation emerged during the Hundred Years' War in order to repel the English invaders, and it continued during peacetime from the mid-fifteenth century. Monarchs employed no bureaucracy permitting them to assess the ability of each family to pay its allotted share.[1] Instead, the king made a lump sum request to provincial authorities and let them decide how to raise it. Lords and priests continued to collect their rents and their tithes, which were not overly resented because the beneficiaries lived close by and provided the population with tangible protection, justice and religious services. In the sixteenth and seventeenth centuries, dignitaries of some French provinces, the *Pays d'Etats*, like those of all the major components of the Habsburg states, still met annually to consent to royal taxes and controlled the levy themselves. These lands usually paid a lower share than the regions under direct fiscal rule, but the inhabitants paid additional money to provincial institutions, and so the net advantage of autonomy was modest.[2]

The amount to be paid by each province and its chief sub-districts (dioceses in Languedoc, for example) was arrived at by guesswork and informed by the money paid in previous years. The provincial authorities allocated a sum to be paid by each community, the amount of which bore *collectively* on the inhabitants. This meant that if one person or group was excused payment for any reason, the money would have to be paid by the others. Parish officials assembled every year to establish the amount of direct taxes (the *taille*, principally) to be assessed on each hearth (a unit of habitation), and designated an official to go quarterly from door to door to collect it. In much of Europe, detailed landholding registers (*livres terriers* in France, or the *estimi* in Italy) enabled the authorities to establish a rough hierarchy of taxpayers, with the proviso that the poorest households paid no tax at all. The most docile inhabitants paid the most, while those who braved the local authorities and raised a ruckus often succeeded in obtaining a reduction. Legal proceedings to compel irate taxpayers to pay the full amount demanded of them entailed their own costs. The amount collected was then forwarded to local receivers, who sent it on to provincial treasurers. Should the community not succeed in levying the assessed amount, the communal officials were personally liable to debtors' prison, or worse, companies of light horse would be billeted upon the jurisdiction until the desperate inhabitants borrowed the sum from someone solvent. Collecting direct taxes entailed costs that were not negligible; *tax farmers* typically kept back 5% of the levy to cover management costs. Royal taxes had to be paid in coin. This detail is more than incidentally important, for large swaths of the medieval economy lay outside the realm of monetary exchange. Tithes paid to the church were paid in kind, in sheaths of grain or baskets of grapes, while many feudal dues were paid similarly in service, corvées or commodities. Householders had to meet the king's demands by entering the commercial economy with objects and services for sale, even in paltry amounts. This compelled families to perform paid occupations or else to sell even minute quantities of produce in village markets in order to accumulate coins.

In the interest of tightening royal control, French kings from the time of Henri IV phased out most of the regional estates and confided tax collection to district bodies called Elections, whose venal office-holders, the *élus*, assessed each village and town's direct taxes. Like military officers, tax officials purchased the right to collect taxes, and received a modest salary equivalent to 4 or 5% of what they paid. These officials also needed to pay a caution for good behaviour upon taking up their office, and promised to respect the tax privileges of communities and social groups. Privilege, in itself, was not a contested concept, since almost every group enjoyed a set of distinct immunities and exemptions. Privileges constituted the strongly-defended 'rights' and 'liberties' of each group making up the commonwealth, and kings customarily swore to uphold them at the outset of each reign. Soon after the diffusion of the *élus* to most of France, the Crown flanked these officials with non-venal commissioners, the *provincial intendants*, who supervised the smooth functioning of all the levels of regional government. They corresponded daily with Paris to alert the king and his ministers of ongoing problems and negotiations surrounding their resolution. These functionaries had a very limited staff and their coercive force consisted of a single company of soldiers in each of the 30-odd *généralités* (whose average population numbered over half a million people). Until the later seventeenth century, these intendants had a primarily supervisory function.[3]

Direct taxation, assessed against the relative wealth in real estate of each 'hearth', increased only with the pace of inflation over the sixteenth century. The age of Henri IV after the Wars of Religion was regarded with nostalgia by later generations. Total royal revenues in the 1520s were 10 million *livres tournois* (hereafter l.t.), which rose to 30 million in the tormented 1580s. Henri IV might have collected that amount with the restoration of peace, but sixteenth-century inflation multiplied prices by four or five. It was Cardinal Richelieu who, in anticipation of entering the Thirty Years' War against the Habsburg dynasty, tripled the real weight of royal taxation in the latter part of the reign of Louis XIII. The number of venal office holders increased prodigiously, many of whom could designate their successor by paying the Crown a substantial fee called the Paulette (1604). The revenues from the taille alone rose from 24 million l.t. in 1630 to 54 million in 1648, before falling in the aftermath to 35 million with the onset of peace after 1659.[4] The original taille was supplemented by similar direct taxes with different names that were assessed on the same criteria. Since all were assessed on real estate, they penalized landowners most of all. The principal difficulty of finance ministers was to extract money from prosperous social groups otherwise exempt. The French clergy consented to tax itself (and thereby control the whole process of assessment and collection) and offered a 'free gift' to the King (the *Don Gratuit*) worth 3–4 million l.t., which was a modest share of that order's considerable wealth. The king, who designated bishops to vacant sees, also conferred on himself the right to collect the prelates' revenues during the time the position remained unfilled, a policy that led to strife with the Pope, who laid claim to the same income. During wartime, many dioceses might remain without bishops for years on end.

Following the disastrous harvest of 1693 and the resultant famine of 1694 during the War of the League of Augsburg, Louis XIV and his ministers devised a head tax, called the Capitation, in 1695, to which everyone but the king was liable, whatever their status or order. Initially, this was assessed according to 22 social categories, but when the tax was restored at the onset of the War of the Spanish Succession in 1701, its amount was simply based on a proportion of the taille. This was not enough to cover expenditures when the next crisis came, following the Great Winter of 1709–1710. Louis XIV introduced a *dixième* (tenth) on all profits and revenues. That tax was suppressed following the end of the war in 1717, but restored for the War of the Polish Succession from 1733 to 1736. These new impositions made it clear that both nobles and ecclesiastics should be subject to some measure of royal taxation, but privileged bodies retained some advantages, nevertheless. Wealthy social groups were encouraged to pay a large initial lump sum (an *abonnement*) and thereby not be required to pay every year. In 1710, the clergy paid 24 million l.t. to exonerate itself from the capitation for many years.[5] By the end of Louis XIV's reign in 1715, direct taxation brought in 70 million l.t., of 110 million total revenues. Hincker claims that total fiscal revenues were in the order of 180 million *livres*, of which 120 million derived from direct taxes. Notwithstanding these very large sums, France's 20 million inhabitants were not overtaxed by contemporary standards. Hincker considers that it required about ten days' work for a family to pay its taxes in the eighteenth century, 3–5% of its income, down from perhaps ten per cent under Cardinal Richelieu during the Thirty Years' War. This was the equivalent of the cost of a cow, or the yield from half a hectare of land.[6] Remember, however, that on top of royal taxes they still paid money to the seigneur and to the Church.

Just like today, indirect taxes placed on the consumption of commodities (called *excise* in England) occasionally matched direct taxes, as in 1683 when they brought in 66 million l.t. In France (and elsewhere) the salt tax, or *gabelle*, provided about ten per cent of all revenues. People were compelled to purchase a minimum amount of salt every year, and to fetch it from royal storehouses near the salt pans or the mines where the substance was extracted. The cost of taxed salt varied wildly from one jurisdiction to another, and, as a result, it fostered an enormous smuggling industry. Additional consumption taxes, or *aides*, were levied on alcoholic beverages consumed in taverns, but, as the century progressed, they were added to all manner of goods, from metal objects to paper, oil and soap. Status objects, such as coaches and wigs, were perfect targets, as were playing cards, liquor and tobacco, whose consumption rose steadily. In some places, hefty taxes were levied on windows, doors and chimneys, which were easy for local authorities to document and which served as proxies for the standard of living. The crown introduced a tax on legal documents via stamped paper (a document without the stamp possessed no legal value), which bore on everyone who consumed legal services and notarized documents. Even the clergy was compelled to purchase stamped paper on which to record baptisms, marriages and burials. The privileged orders were gouged as much as possible in this way, since they were less liable to direct taxation.

These indirect taxes were leased to businessmen called *farmers*, who bid for the collection rights. Tax farming saw financiers advance large lump sums to the Crown at regular intervals, while assuming the troublesome task of collecting small sums on a daily basis. There was some risk for themselves, for, in crisis years, people would curtail their consumption and tax receipts would fall. These financiers possessed specialized knowledge of consumption patterns for a host of commodities, which they deployed to their benefit over the duration of the lease. In France, about fifty tax farms existed in 1650; the minister Colbert, when he reordered the kingdom's finances in the 1660s, amalgamated them into five large farms with jurisdiction over northern France. Concentration diminished the opportunities for corruption and sped up collection. In 1726, the remaining farms were united into a single General Farm, managed by barely 100 families, who employed armies of men and flotillas of boats to crack down on smuggling. They had sweeping powers of search and inspection over nobles and clergy, military officers and soldiers, even warships. Tax farmers did not rely on their own personal assets, and, in order to guarantee their solvency, they sold 'shares' in their activities to some 30,000 people who tended to belong to the upper classes.[7]

Kings since the medieval era raised money from the *royal domain*, or jurisdiction. To some extent this was real estate, such as the royal forests leased to businessmen, who derived their income from the lumber. Kings possessed the eminent property rights over the subsoil, by which they claimed a percentage (typically a fifth) of extracted products. The domain included any right that accrued to the status and prerogatives of kingship. It was admitted that tariffs on imported goods belonged to royal jurisdiction, but these were levied on exports, too. Tolls were levied on goods entering the kingdom and its principal cities, where a collector armed with a thick book of tariffs greeted every cart and laden animal. Over time, the frontiers moved, but the collectors remained at their post, creating a series of internal tax borders. Another revenue stemming from the royal domain was the sale of letters of legitimation (of bastards), or letters of naturalization for immigrants, which conferred on them the legal rights of subjects. Fines owed to tribunals could constitute considerable revenues, as well as the confiscated property of criminals. No European monarch neglected to raise money from the sale of letters of nobility, which was unpopular with existing nobles, who resented the newcomers. King François I created on average only six new nobles annually in the early sixteenth century. Louis XIV adopted this on quite another scale: during the 1690s he was purported to have printed up 1,000 of these, sold at 6,000 *livres* apiece.[8]

In addition to regular, legal taxation, the Crown could reap enormous windfall revenues during wartime. Occupied enemy territories were pressed hard for contributions, such as the 23 million l.t. collected by Marshal Villars from Germany after routing the Imperial army in 1707.[9] Guy Rowlands estimates that contributions paid 10–12% of total army expenditure during the War of the Spanish Succession.[10] Privateers were obligated to deliver a fifth of their prizes to the Crown in exchange for their letters of marque. In 1709 alone, the privateers of Saint Malo, in Brittany, brought home prizes worth 30 million l.t., staving off a royal default.[11] It is not clear from the literature how these huge sums entered royal accountancy, and we do know that successful generals like Villars skimmed a portion of these funds for their personal benefit, which was tolerated as long as they were successful. Diversion of military funds by senior officers was a common practice in all armies. The transfer of public funds from London and from the paymaster resident in Amsterdam, Benjamin Sweet to the British army in Flanders, passed through several hands. Cash raised at Amsterdam, in Frankfurt and other large towns of the theatre was subject to manipulation of the rates of exchange. General William Cadogan, Marlborough's Chief of Staff, Marlborough's secretary, Adam de Cardonnel, and William Bridges, member of the Board of Ordnance, enriched themselves by deals with financiers. Quartermaster-General Cadogan 'executed' peasants (that is, extorted money from them) for his personal profit. Great sums passed through Marlborough's own hands, but we do not know how much was spent on public service.[12]

As invasive and imaginative as these taxes were, they were still no match for expenditures of the state during a major war. French royal taxation brought in perhaps 120 million l.t. in 1700, but annual expenses in wartime were often double that amount. Colbert limited the crown's expenses to about 100 million l.t. in 1680, about 810 tonnes of pure silver, but the great wars pushed them higher. French royal annual expenditure after 1700 averaged about 200 million l.t., equal to 1,400 tonnes of pure silver in 1714.[13] Recruiting troops and supplying them with weapons and food was the chief expenditure. Moving money entailed considerable costs, too, which historians have only recently explored. Moving cash from one receiver to another was done by paper assignations, but bankers did not always accept them at face value. Tax officials and farmers did not usually pay the promised sums on the specified day: they were entitled to lend out the crown's money in the short term for their private profit and held on to the cash collected as long as possible. Tax officers, and even the personnel going door to door to collect small sums, were encouraged to make money from their functions.

At the centre of the French system, there was no single minister responsible for both revenue and expenditures; the modern concept of a budget lay far in the future. For most of the War of the Spanish Succession, the minister, or *Contrôleur-Général des Finances*, Michel Chamillart, was simultaneously minister of war, with an impossibly heavy workload. His ministry was too short-staffed to undertake proper auditing and to follow the expenditures in detail. Double-entry book-keeping, still unusual outside mercantile circles, was not introduced into government accountancy procedures until 1716. Transferring money to other countries and converting it to local currency was hugely expensive, and fighting in distant theatres such as Spain, Germany and Italy entailed a premium. The cost of moving money from 1703 to 1706 cost the French Crown from 40–60 million l.t., and foreign bankers, who amassed the appropriate coins, charged 20–30% in fees. The Lyon bankers who served as intermediaries could not cope with the demands for money arriving from every direction and suffered a crash in 1706.[14] French difficulties should not be overstated, for the kingdom gradually adapted to the strain and recovered lost ground in 1712.

The predicament of the French Crown was by no means original, or even the most complicated – it was merely the largest. Imperial finances were famously complex and confused, in part because the regional bureaucracy tended to direct incoming revenues to local purposes instead of passing them on to Vienna. German Habsburg taxation was famously inefficient under Emperor Leopold I, as it tried to cope with an army that grew six times over between 1660 and 1710. During the first 20 years of his reign, the military budget oscillated between three and four million florins, a small fraction of the French revenues, and most of it was spent along the Ottoman frontier in Hungary. Under the weight of the Ottoman invasion in 1683, these expenditures were ramped up considerably. By 1685, military expenditures touched 12 million florins, and 23 million in 1695, when the empire was mobilized both against the Turks and the French. After the peace of Karlowitz in 1699, expenditures were curtailed to 14 million florins, but rose anew after 1701 to meet the Spanish Succession crisis.[15] Taxes had to be increased to meet the expenditures, but, in the Empire, this meant negotiating with multiple regional estates in Austria and Bohemia, who controlled collection and record-keeping. The pious Habsburg rulers were unwilling to tax the Church or the nobility. The German rulers were very slow to reduce local autonomy, such that royal officials never directly supervised tax collection before the mid-eighteenth century. Emperor Leopold himself was averse to any serious reform, and few tax delinquents were punished harshly. The tax revenues of the various Estates in the German and Bohemian lands covered less than half the military expenditure in 1693, less than a third of it in 1695 and barely a quarter in 1705.[16] Hungary submitted to moderate taxation only after the Turkish threat receded in the 1690s. By dint of great efforts, total Imperial revenue climbed from 4.3 million florins in 1661 to 16.5 million in

1699, still considerably less than expenditures. The Empire also received money from its Catholic allies. The Papacy and the Order of Malta provided almost a million florins annually in the 1680s. These ceased when the war with France began, but Imperial troops began to extract enormous sums from unwilling Italian states on the pretext of paying for winter quarters to 'protect' them. Italian princes and republics without armies of their own were subjected to demands of cash worth millions of florins during the 1690s. If they failed to comply, soldiers seized money, grain and livestock worth much more. During the War of the Spanish Succession, contribution levies were so heavy and harshly applied in conquered Bavaria and occupied Italy that it led to years of violence.[17] Emperor Joseph I (1705–1711) made attempts to streamline the bureaucracy and introduced more advanced methods of book-keeping. In the aftermath of the War of the Spanish Succession, and following the example of Savoy, the German Habsburg regime compiled an innovative *cadastre*, a great surveying project mapping and assessing the tax potential of every plot of land and building in the realm, beginning in Milan in 1718. A bureaucratic revolution on its own, the cadastre required decades to bring to fruition. In the meantime, Imperial debt ballooned, from 22 million florins in 1700 and 49 million in 1711 to 70 million in 1718 at the close of the Turkish war. Deficit spending was a definite stimulus to the regions producing commodities for the army, particularly around Vienna and in Bohemia.[18]

Bourbon Spain was a better example of fiscal rectitude, revamping the shambolic finances of the previous Habsburg dynasty in just a few short years. Almost immediately after the accession of Philip V to the throne, the financial controller, Jean Orry, took charge of finding the money to defend the great empire. Revenues were barely 10 million escudos in 1703. The principal problem was that the king's power to raise taxes varied dramatically from one region to another, as the component kingdoms of the Crown of Aragon (Aragon proper, Catalonia, Valencia and Sardinia) enjoyed rights of consent (*fueros*) that made it difficult to raise money there. Castile, with some support from Naples in Italy (until its conquest by the Habsburg army in 1707) carried most of the burden of wartime taxation. The king raised from Castile a variety of revenues, beginning with a direct tax, the *servicio*, consented to by the parliament, or Cortès, of the kingdom. The king could raise money from Church lands, as well as the usual array of regalian rights such as customs duties. Castile benefited from the providential arrival of the Indies fleet, bringing considerable liquidity in silver, but this was irregular, less than one flotilla a year. The king claimed a fifth of the treasure – the *quinta* – as his share. We should not imagine that Spain's power was based on American treasure. The Indies typically provided 10–20% of Castile's revenues, and a smaller proportion of Spain's, and even less if we add the Low Countries and the Italian possessions.[19]

Jean Orry possessed a background in both army provisioning and high finance, thereby acquiring expertise in money-changing, and he was considered to be an exceptionally careful book-keeper. He had acquired all the skills of merchants and financiers, and knew how they operated and employed money.

With his team of French and Spanish assistants, in 1701 he set about marshalling resources from Castile with a focus on army financing in Madrid and the provinces. Like most states, there existed not one central treasury, but a multiplicity of offices receiving funds and making expenditures that it was urgent to consolidate. A workaholic obsessed with detail, like his model, Colbert, Orry concentrated revenue into fewer hands, amalgamated tax farms and lengthened their leases to encourage moneyed men to invest in them.[20] Orry examined all the bills for payment himself, and refused to release funds without first knowing their destination. The crux of the problem was that the Habsburg state was governed by committees or councils. The Bourbon monarchy empowered a handful of ministers who were close collaborators of the king. He removed the reality of power from a dozen ministerial councils or committees and concentrated decision making among the king's leading secretaries who, together with the French ambassador, formed an inner cabinet. By 1705, he introduced French-style army intendants who relayed orders arriving from Madrid, but he also encouraged local communities to raise and equip troops on their own initiative. Military victories in 1707 emboldened Philip V to confiscate the properties of pro-Habsburg aristocrats on a grand scale, and to impose Castilian taxes on Aragon and Valencia.[21] The king then created a network of French-style provincial intendants, the great majority of whom were native Castilians, to collect information and administer Madrid's policies in a similar manner everywhere.[22] As a result, Philip V more than doubled his tax revenues during a long and arduous period of civil war and foreign military intervention. Spanish revenues stabilized at about 20 million escudos after 1720.

No state was as successful as the Dutch United Provinces in mobilizing money to fight long wars on an unprecedented scale; however, each of the seven provinces considered itself to be a sovereign entity. There was no unified Dutch tax system, for each province acted separately and resisted standardization. Even the monetary system was completely decentralized, with 14 official mints in the Republic, and some 800 foreign coins officially permitted in 1600. Under William III of Orange, there was some unification of mints in 1686.[23] Dutch provinces each contributed a quota to the treasury of the States-General, while the latter raised additional revenue from the largely Catholic Generality Lands along the southern periphery of the Republic. An ongoing point of contention was that the Province of Holland by itself paid 58.6% of the tax revenues in 1658, thereby taking a commanding role in foreign policy. Holland's economy was so precociously commercialized and urban that raising money in direct taxes from rural real estate was not considered the best method to raise large sums from the population. Indirect consumer taxes were considered more expedient and politically acceptable in a heavily urbanized economy. Holland, in particular, levied excise taxes on almost everything, tripling or quadrupling the base cost of most items. Taxes on basic foodstuffs and consumer items impacted the poor more than the rich, who were relatively favoured, but, as elsewhere, vices and luxuries, such as tobacco, liquors and silk, were particularly milked by politicians. These excises were then farmed out to the highest bidder for fairly short periods. There were few exemptions to these taxes, which were designed to hit the entire population, like the grain milling tax, or the one on beer. There were taxes on stamped paper and death duties. Holland's farmed taxes were 4.3 million gulden in 1608, but 8.8 million in 1645, largely because of the increase in trade. After the French invasion of 1672, just about all of those taxes were increased again, which tripled the previous real rate. If taxes were equal to the income of seven working days in 1510, it required 20 days' work to acquit one's taxes by 1700, before the ruinously expensive War of the Spanish Succession. This was twice the tax burden of a subject of the king of France.[24]

The English Crown was also held to be a model of fiscal rectitude, but this was not true for any Stuart king, who sought financial expedients in order to govern without having to request money from Parliament. England went through early fiscal centralization at the end of the Middle Ages, making tax rates uniform across the kingdom. Only the colonies enjoyed tax-free status. Before 1688, total public expenditure rarely exceeded 2 million pounds sterling. In the last two decades of the Stuart kings, the Crown phased out tax farming entirely and hired 2,500 excise tax collectors who became expert at assessing public consumption. Their aim was to make revenue collection as efficient and centrally controlled as possible. The Customs tax farm was cancelled in 1671, the excise farm ended in 1683, and the hearth tax farm was transferred to public officials in 1684. Both revenue and expenditure were supervised by a single Treasury Board. From his rising revenues, and without requiring the assent of Parliament, James II was able to establish a sizeable standing army in England and Ireland and a powerful fleet. This was, in fact, an ambitious political programme aimed at overturning the result of the English Civil War.

James' overthrow by William of Orange led to a fateful pact between the stern and ambitious ruler of the Dutch Republic and the English Parliament, which consented to raise taxes to fight France in exchange for frequent sessions and a right to review *in public* all royal expenditures. The Crown did not acquire this expertise immediately, and the excise administration fell into disarray in the 1690s, but gradually improved thereafter. The development of taxes and trade spurred a growing interest in statistical information, reflected in the works of a generation of 'political arithmeticians', whose calculations guide modern historians. By the early 1690s, annual tax revenue was 3.6 million pounds, about double the amount under James II. By the War of the Spanish Succession, public expenditure increased to 15 million pounds in 1710, far beyond the increase in revenues.[25] This vastly increased tax flow maintained an army of 80 battalions and a navy far superior in numbers to its adversary, 60 ships of the line and 120 smaller vessels. The 2.25 million pounds Britain spent on its navy was equal to four per cent of GNP, while, at its peak, the total military expenditure was equal to about 10–15% of national income. Taxes (which were inferior to expenditure) amounted to nine per cent of GNP in 1712. Englishmen, like the Dutch, paid about double the taxes as the subjects of the French king. About a quarter of the expenditure went towards foreign subsidies and continental mercenaries. The figures are, no doubt, inflated, but, in 1710, Britain paid for 139,000 troops (largely Germans), 105,000 foreign troops (again, mostly German) in British pay, and 48,000 sailors and marines, mostly natives of the United Kingdom.[26]

War and public debt

State expenditures in wartime far surpassed tax revenues, which meant that the difference would have to be made up by borrowing. The earliest successful practitioners of deficit financing were the merchant republics of Italy, and Venice in particular. Medieval states periodically compelled moneyed men and institutions to lend their wealth to the city during emergencies, but coercive measures proved inadequate in the long run. The Venetian patriciate sought to raise money on the open market, granting lenders titles on the mint, which could circulate as paper money and which paid an annual interest of six per cent exempt from any taxes. This made them attractive investments in an era without inflation. At the end of the Candia War in 1670, the Venetian public debt stood at eight times annual tax revenue, and servicing the debt (paying the interest on its bonds) absorbed over half of income. Still, the likelihood of repayment by the stable Venetian regime attracted foreign investors as well as local lenders. The Genoese made up most of the 30% of foreign investors on the Venetian bond market. In 1672, the bonds were consolidated and the interest was reduced to three per cent, but they still looked attractive to investors. By 1679, the republic's budget was balanced again.[27] We must keep in mind that much of Europe, and Italy in particular, underwent a long period of deflation between 1630 and 1730, and economic growth rarely surpassed one or two per cent annually. Interest payments of 3–4% served the function of conserving accumulated wealth without risk.

Princes made their first important entry into financial markets in the 1520s in the context of the Wars of Italy; Charles V borrowed money in Antwerp in 1522, while François I emitted bonds on the Hotel de Ville in Paris the following year. The Pope launched the first Monti, or convertible bearer bonds, in Rome in 1526, to finance his share of the same wars.[28] States began to sell offices to solvent eligible candidates in the same period, whereby the government promised to pay interest on the price of the office in the form of an annual salary of about four per cent. The regular payment of interest was not always observed, and neither was the transferability of bonds and offices always respected, but too many obstacles to their recovery would depress public confidence and make it more expensive to borrow later. At first, the *public sphere* was not an abstraction: people lending money to the Crown and living off the interest tended to live in the capital city and constituted an audible and visible presence there. In the seventeenth century, agricultural rents were declining, commerce was anything but flourishing and only taxes were increasing. Government bonds looked like a secure investment.

During the Thirty Years' War, the French Crown every year spent about 30% more than it raised in taxes. Financiers would not lend their money without some kind of collateral, so governments organized their borrowing around three techniques. One was to confer the control of the tax administration on the lenders, who would reimburse themselves; this signified alienating the tax revenue for a fixed term. In France, there were 2,723 such loans from 1596 to 1653, worth 641 million l.t. This technique was also the standard feature of Habsburg finance in Spain, to the benefit of Genoese financiers in particular. The second technique was to emit rents or bonds that would in practice never be redeemed (although that possibility always existed). The state raised money also from the sale of office, especially those which conferred nobility on socially ambitious purchasers. The lenders did not own all the money they advanced; they borrowed most of it from a network of backers who received a share of the profits. Kings were not ideal borrowers, for they were tempted to declare partial bankruptcy, or delayed payments, or manipulated the currency such that they paid out less silver than they had received. Monarchies such as France and Spain periodically 'restructured' their debt by transforming a mass of short-term certificates into long-term rents at lower rates of interest. The Dutch United Provinces did this as well, in 1648 and in 1655, in order to make their debt more manageable. French kings repudiated part of their debts in 1598 at the end of the Wars of Religion, in 1648 at the onset of the Fronde, and again in 1661 when Louis XIV took the reins of power. Kings might review their debts and 'verify' them, that is, decide that specific engagements were made under duress, and then arbitrarily reduce the rate of interest or cancel the debt entirely. French local communities groaned under the weight of debts accumulated over half a century. The Crown authorized them to increase their local taxes in order to reduce these. In Aquitaine in 1663, creditors of the city of Agen were summoned to present their bills to the provincial intendant for 'verification'. He would either cut them off or reduce the interest rate. More than half the creditors were convents, monasteries and other religious bodies flush with Counter-Reformation cash. Reducing indebtedness in this way enabled municipalities to pay their royal taxes more easily.[29] Colbert supervised a partial repudiation of France's royal debt by this means between 1661 and 1665, and reduced the payment of interest by about one fifth. (Today, this practice, which still continues, is called a 'haircut'.)

Despite all these dangers, people continued to lend money to kings and republics, in the relative absence of more attractive secure investments, at rates of interest that continued to fall over the long term. The legal rate of interest in France was five per cent in the later seventeenth century, although most short-term borrowing operated at interest rates of about seven per cent. When the state was too deeply in debt to be able to service it adequately, the king and his ministers had to select the beneficiaries of what little cash was available, often in exchange for new loans. Those with high social status were reimbursed or had their interest paid before the others. The nobles and officials in Paris and leading commercial centres such as Lyon were deeply integrated in the financial system.

After the escalation of the Dutch war in 1674, France invited foreign investment too, such that the Genoese invested heavily in French bonds at five per cent, which they considered attractive. The French credit system functioned without major difficulty until 1700. Under Colbert, it cost only eight million l.t. to service the restructured debt, but the war of the League of Augsburg pushed this up to 35 million l.t. in 1698, equal to about a third of state revenues. The first bonds were payable to the name indicated on the certificate, which restricted its transferability, but, as in Holland (where a secondary market for debt certificates developed after 1670), the rents were increasingly transferable to third parties. The minimum cost of bonds fell and thousands of smallholders invested in state debt, too, or inherited certificates. After the death of Louis XIV, an inquest revealed that some 164,000 people received interest payments from the Crown, concentrated disproportionately in the capital city.[30]

The War of the Spanish Succession subjected the system to unprecedented strain, although the Crown paid most of the interest it owed until 1710. France paid for its own vast army and fleet, and carried much of the Spanish burden in addition. The war cost 66% more than the League of Augsburg, and borrowing costs exploded. It required 60 million l.t. to service the debt in 1708, before the economic collapse of the following year. The French public debt stood at only 240 million l.t. at the death of Colbert in 1683 (about 2.5 times tax revenues) but it spiralled out of control after 1704, the year of the first military defeats, when it could borrow only at 8–10% interest. The crown emitted an ever larger number of paper certificates designed to be accepted by its creditors, beginning with traditional letters of exchange, cleared in large part in Lyon, the kingdom's capital of international finance. Specie was scarce: there was a limited stock of coin in the kingdom, equal to about 500 million l.t., and the taxation process tended to drain it towards the capital city, starving the provinces for cash. The Crown tried to create a cash substitute for people depositing silver at the mint, or Mint Bills, but these paper certificates depreciated quickly – meaning that private individuals would not accept them at full value. Army officers in particular were paid with paper money, which depressed their real income considerably.[31]

Starting in 1709, when Louis XIV resolved to continue fighting in order to defend the rights of his grandson, the new finance minister, Nicolas Desmaretz, adopted a whole series of expedients to prevent complete financial meltdown. Increased taxation provoked a flurry of local revolts after 1706, but not on the same scale as under the cardinals Richelieu and Mazarin, nor did they attract the sympathy of social elites.[32] Naturalized subjects, financiers and aspiring nobles were subject to forced loans during this period. With military expenditure in the later years of the war running over 200 million l.t. annually, Desmaretz was forced to alienate tax revenue for several years in advance. In 1709, the Crown was compelled to manipulate the money of account, by reducing the silver content of the *livre tournois* from 8 grams to 5.5. By these financial expedients, Desmaretz saved the kingdom from complete collapse and paid most of the interest due in a timely fashion. The rents paid ran at 6.3–7%, although some 'haircuts' were inflicted on selected creditors who lacked political influence. People still continued to purchase royal offices in exchange for a return of five per cent, although they might have to wait for payment. The largest lenders, like the Protestant banker, Samuel Bernard, were simply too big to fail, as the Crown feared to alienate not just that single individual, but a host of international financiers in his network. At the death of Louis XIV, the French public debt stood upwards of 1.5 billion l.t., about ten times annual revenue, but the debt service cost was less than under Cardinals Richelieu and Mazarin in the 1640s.[33] The most critical period was over. There was no sign of a turning point in French financing in 1715, because the political tensions were much lower then than in 1648 or 1788. With the conversion of short-term loans to long-term bonds at the end of the war in 1713–1715, servicing the debt fell to a manageable 40 million l.t. In Paris, these certificates were increasingly passed around like paper money.

French methods were followed in Spain too, where state debt came to be considered to be a safe investment, even if the interest rate was modest. At the end of the War of the Spanish Succession, Philip V owed only 11 million escudos in long-term debt, which he was able to reduce by a third or half in the aftermath of the war. In 1727, he was able to reduce the interest rate from five per cent to a mere three per cent (equal to Holland), and the cost of servicing the debt declined by three-quarters. With the Italian war against Austria in 1734–1735 and the onset of colonial war with Britain in 1739, the Spanish debt rose to about 49–50 million escudos, which was a modest 2.5 times annual tax revenue, serviced at three per cent interest. Kings of Spain in the sixteenth and seventeenth century were borrowers from hell, but Philip, Orry and his successors restored credit confidence completely.[34]

The Dutch Republic was awash in capital seeking a safe haven after 1650, when the international economic climate soured. Until the creation of the Bank of England in 1694, the Dutch had the most effective borrowing machine anywhere. Bonds were issued by the States-General, by each of the seven provinces, by the major cities and by the boards of Admiralty (which collected customs duties). Unfortunately, the debt figures in the published literature in English and French are partial (often only considering the province of Holland) and are incompatible from one author to another. Maarten Prak fixes Holland's debt in 1648 at 125 million gulden, with interest rates of only four per cent. Following the disastrous French invasion of 1672 and years of emergency borrowing, the province's debt stood at 300 million in 1678, with the interest owing on it to the bondholders absorbing about 60% of taxes.[35] In the 1690s, debt service still absorbed 60% of Holland's tax revenue. The States-General began to borrow more heavily in its own name, owing 14 million gulden in 1650 and 19 million in 1700. The Republic fought the War of the Spanish Succession largely on credit. After 1710, it became impossible to float new loans, and Holland turned to lotteries to find money just to pay the interest on the debt. After 1715, the Public Treasury of the Union had to suspend payments for nine months. The combined debt of the Province of Holland and of the States-General ran close to 400 million gulden in 1714, equal to twenty years' tax revenue.[36]. Nevertheless, interest rates fell to three per cent because there was still a lot of private money looking for safe investment in a period of relative economic stagnation.[37]

Dutch coins were no longer manipulated after the 1590s, which, along with the Spanish silver piece of eight (ancestor to the dollar) and the Venetian zecchino, made them internationally desirable. Bills of exchange and cashiers' certificates became common, and became payable to the bearer after 1663, which increased the money supply.[38] The Bank of Amsterdam, founded in 1609 (modelled on the Rialto bank of Venice), was set up to cash these bills. All the major merchants possessed accounts with the bank, for an average amount of 3,500 gulden. While the bank did not offer credit, Amsterdam traders could cash their bills almost anywhere in the world. By the 1690s, the wars began to draw much of this capital into the Republic's coffers, but into English finance, too. After the War of the Spanish Succession, excessive Dutch debt motivated people with money to diversify their investments by purchasing foreign securities, including those of the old enemy, France. The Dutch elite also began to invest more heavily in land and in conspicuous consumption.

The English example is also noteworthy, but not because of greater financial rectitude. England ceased to be a significant military power in Europe for 250 years after the end of the Hundred Years' War in 1453. There was no need to develop a system of heavy borrowing, and, as a result of its limited credit facilities, the kingdom declared bankruptcy at the onset of the Third Dutch War in 1672.[39] The public debt was still negligible in 1688 and taxes were modest by continental standards. King William's war (1689–1697) imposed an unprecedented financial burden on the kingdom, and, in addition to implementing a host of new taxes, the public debt ballooned to 16.7 million pounds sterling in 1698, equivalent to four years' tax income. Parliament had not anticipated a long war, and preferred short-term borrowing at interest rates of 8.3% to finance it. The borrowing system almost collapsed in the 1690s due to mismanagement, and the financially exhausted kingdom proceeded to manipulate its coinage in 1696–1697.[40]

With the onset of the War of the Spanish Succession in 1702, the Lord Treasurer, Sidney Godolphin, worked with the Bank of England and the London financial community to borrow large sums at longer terms. Military expenditures consistently outpaced tax revenues by about 30%, as in France; however, the victories against Louis XIV between 1704 and 1708 maintained the enthusiasm of lenders, who were paid about 6.3% interest. Merchants and bankers were keen to invest in state securities, but better so if they could exchange their bonds easily. After 1708, the military context darkened, the war became unpopular, and annuities sold for nine per cent. In order to attract more money, the Crown introduced lotteries from Italy, which fed off the rise of gambling. The national debt rose to 40 million pounds in 1714, equal to about three years' revenue, which absorbed 2.4 million to service the debt, a mere 20% of revenues. At war's end in 1714, the Crown restructured this debt and converted short-term obligations into long-term rents at lower rates of interest. English financial arrangements largely copied Dutch ones, just as Dutch financiers organized the Bank of England in 1694 and invested Dutch capital into it. The Dutch could still lend more cheaply and attracted borrowers from far and wide; English financial primacy emerged only later in the century.

Conclusion: melting the debt

At the end of the War of the Spanish Succession in 1714, all the belligerents had accumulated a public debt of unprecedented dimensions (Table 13.1). How they coped with this burden in the post-war era is an interesting problem. During the war, the French Crown passed a multitude of contracts with financiers, who made a profit from collecting taxes, from lending money at interest, and from manipulating the coinage itself and exchanging it for profit. Behind these *traitants*, (482 individuals) was a veritable army of 30,000 employees, collectors, accountants and guards. Interest payments on most of the loans hovered between 5–7.14 per cent. Acting as intermediaries in the sale of offices, financiers might earn 20–26% profit if they knew their business and worked at maximum efficiency, but they incurred some risk. Only a handful of these men earned really large amounts of over half a million *livres*, and not all of them made a profit. The crown needed these people, and provincial intendants leaned on them to open their purses. Once the war was over, however, the French regency government felt strong enough to take back as much as half the financiers' profits. This was accomplished in 1716, as in 1661, by creating a Chamber of Justice, which reviewed all the contracts and the payments to date, and levied a tax of 20 million l.t. on the financiers.[41]

During the war, paper instruments were increasingly used to supplement the lack of coins. In France, after the war, there was a government-sponsored effort to convert bonds (which paid modest interests but were stable) into equities, which could rise in value if the market was favourable. The public was led to believe that with the return of peace, commerce would rebound and the

Table 13.1 Revenues and debts of belligerents in 1714

	Revenues, currency	Revenues, silver	Debt in currency	Debt in silver	Per capita debt, silver
Britain	14,000,000 pounds sterling	1,685 tonnes	40,000,000 pounds sterling	5,055 tonnes	0.63 kg
Netherlands	24,000,000 gulden	240 tonnes	400,000,000 gulden	4,000 tonnes	2.1 kg
France	200,000,000 l.t.	1,400 tonnes	1,200,000,000 l.t.	9,000 tonnes	0.43 kg
Spain	20,000,000 escudos	1,000 tonnes	40,000,000 escudos	2,000 tonnes	0.25 kg

government-backed companies would reap enormous profits, pay dividends and make them rich. In May 1716, John Law, a Scottish professional gambler, secured a charter for a Banque Générale that would issue bank notes and offer the usual services of moving money around (giro). The Regent, Philippe d'Orléans, backed it by depositing a million l.t. into it. In October of the same year, French tax farmers could make payments to the treasury in banknotes, and soon after, other people were allowed to pay their taxes with this paper. The assets soared over the next two years, when it became the Banque Royale with branch offices outside Paris. The next step was to take over the moribund *Compagnie d'Occident* (Mississippi) and turn it into a joint-stock company, selling shares for 500 *livres* apiece. People could purchase shares by exchanging government bonds for them. Law then took over the *Compagnie d'Orient* and merged it with the other, forming a mercantilist *Compagnie des Indes.* Law proposed to convert the entire national debt of 1.2 billion l.t. into company shares. These ventures looked increasingly attractive to the public, and soon people who had never invested in stocks before rushed to acquire these assets. Law announced a 12% dividend on the company stocks, several times the yield of royal annuities. Hundreds of thousands of new shares were printed, whose price climbed to 10,000 l.t., 20 times the level of 1716. The bank, on the collateral of the company, issued paper notes to the value of 2.5 billion *livres,* almost five times the amount of metallic currency in the kingdom. In the enthusiasm for quick and easy profit, money poured into France from Holland to take advantage of rising values. By the winter of 1720, Law attempted to demonetize precious metals entirely, by calling for all payments above 100 l.t. to be made with paper notes. But the *Compagnie des Indes* could not hope to meet the expectations of investors, and the price of company shares started to stagnate over the winter, until people would no longer accept paper certificates as currency. The whole system crashed in May 1720 and the Banque was dissolved. It had reduced the Crown's debt by about a third in the interval.[42] Not content with this, the Regency established a new board in 1721–1722, the Visa, to liquidate additional notes and to reduce the servicing costs of the debt to a manageable 40 million l.t., equal to about a quarter of tax revenues.[43]

A similar experiment took place across the channel. The British Tory government under Horace Walpole created a mercantilist venture, the *South Sea Company,* in 1711, in expectation of peace with Spain and the resumption of colonial commerce. Government annuities could be exchanged for stock in the company, as in France. In January 1720, Parliament was notified that the entire British national debt of 30 million pounds would be taken over by the company, and 300,000 shares of 100 pounds each were offered to the public. Alongside a crowd of first-time investors in Britain, money from Holland and France poured in to snap up these shares as their value rose from 100 pounds sterling at the initial offering to 950 pounds in early July. As in Paris, the most experienced traders perceived the bubble and exited the market in time. In August, the bubble burst, with financial losses to the public of unprecedented dimensions.[44]

In all the major powers, what restored financial health was almost a quarter-century of (relative) peace and a quickening of commerce at the end of the Little Ice Age around 1730. Because the French Revolution of 1789 was precipitated by a crisis in royal debt, many people imagine that such a momentous event must have been looming on the horizon for a very long time. In fact, this is not true; France fought two major wars without undue strain before 1750, without increasing its taxes significantly, knowing that this would trigger widespread unrest. Relative to its neighbours, French subjects carried a moderate fiscal burden for most of the eighteenth century. During the period covered by this book, the Dutch Republic underwent a prodigious rise in prosperity and had a military impact far out of proportion to its population of fewer than two million inhabitants. But starting in 1700, gravity reasserted its hold and the United Provinces entered a long period of pronounced decline.

Notes

1   James B Collins, 1988: 2–7.
2   François Hincker, 1971: 19.
3   William Beik, 1985: 105–16.
4   Gauthier Aubert, 2015: 46.
5   Guy Rowlands, 2012: 62.
6   Hincker, 1971: 41.
7   Hincker, 1971: 29–33.
8   Pierre Goubert, 1969: 148–9.
9   Charles W Ingrao, 1979: 61.
10 Guy Rowlands, 2017.
11 Françoise Bayard, 1996.
12 Stewart Stansfield, 2016: 85–110.
13 Bayard, 1996.
14 Rowlands, 2012.
15 Jean Bérenger1975, 2 vols.
16 Ingrao, 1979: 4–12; Michael Hochedlinger, 2003: 34–8.
17 Hochedlinger, 2003: 179.
18 Antonio di Vittorio, 1982.
19 Henry Kamen, 1993.
20 Anne Dubet, 2009.
21 Christopher Storrs, 2016; Joachim Albareda Salvadò, 2010: 113.
22 Didier Ozanam, 1995.
23 Pit Dehing & Marjolein 't Hart, 1997.
24 't Hart, Jonker & van Zanden, 2010: 7, 80; Jan de Vries & Adriaan van der Woude, 1997: 120.
25 John Brewer, 1989: 34–65.
26 Brewer, 1989: 49.
27 Luciano Pezzolo, 1995.
28 Katia Béguin, 2012: 11.
29 Francis Loirette, 1998: 143–66.
30 Béguin, 2012: 352.
31 Rowlands, 2012: 205.
32 Aubert, 2015: 60.
33 Rowlands, 2012: 236.

34 Storrs, 2016: 115–22.
35 Maarten Prak, 2005: 75–84; Jonathan Israel, 1995: 986;
36 Wantje Fritschy & Réné van der Voort, 2010.
37 J. Aalbers, 1977.
38 Peter Spufford, 1995.
39 P.G.M. Dickson, 1967: 40.
40 Dickson, 1967: 56.
41 Joël Félix, 2015.
42 Niall Ferguson, 2001: 312–16.
43 Béguin, 2012: 207.
44 Ferguson, 2001: 316; Dickson, 1967: 154.

Conclusion
Eighteenth-century continuity

Technological stasis

In a general manner, armies fought in 1810 largely as they did in 1710. Once flintlock fusils with bayonets replaced pikes in the decade after 1700, small-arms technology barely evolved for over a century. European armies gradually improved their firing performance by introducing pre-packaged cartridges containing musket balls.[1] Well-drilled troops could unleash volleys between two and three times a minute – at first. The French commander of the Low Countries army in 1745, Maurice de Saxe, made salvo fire the regulation method, like the English and the Prussians, but this had only modest impact on the outcome of battles, for the effect of musketry has been exaggerated. Until the 1740s, all European armies moved from column to line using processional methods, which took hours to effect.[2] Instead of perfecting firing lines, Saxe developed the method of brisk attacks deploying smallish columns of men only eight deep, and well spaced to reduce casualties.[3] The cartridge for reloading cannon became more widespread in the 1730s and 1740s. Howitzers made their appearance in North European armies after 1700, although they were not embraced by the French until 1746.[4] All armies attempted to reduce the weight of their guns, but the available solutions of shortening the barrel and reducing the thickness of the metal resulted in less accurate fire and more rapid overheating. Small cannon towed behind raiding parties to increase the effectiveness of small war multiplied after 1740.[5]

Erik Lund emphasizes that war was fought with a particular economy of knowledge. Larger armies required more staff officers, whose task was to prevent confusion on marches.[6] Armies cut back their reliance on private teamsters, and in the Imperial army, transport became a corps of its own, consisting of ten per cent of army strength in 1740 and 15–20% of the total budget.[7] The capacity to support large armies in the field was similarly enhanced by gradually increasing investment in navigable canals and river navigation. Highways suitable for large numbers of wheeled vehicles made constant progress over the eighteenth century, but these were concentrated in the most developed regions. Napoleonic operations characterized by autonomous army corps moving quickly along parallel highways could not have functioned a hundred years previously save in localized theatres. A quickening of commerce and a gradually warming climate, together with the introduction of new sources of food – maize, rice and potatoes – increased the population and provided extra food for armies, too. Other phenomena unfolded slowly in the background: better milling for grain, better fodder (alfalfa) for large animals, more resistant horses, bigger wagons. This was not a military, or even an agricultural, revolution, but the cumulative effect increased the efficiency of large armies.[8]

Finally, military thinking seemed immobile because the generals of the War of the Spanish Succession aged in the saddle. Prince Eugene of Savoy, who served as chief minister to Emperor Charles VI in Vienna, jealously blocked the rise of newcomers through the ranks. By 1733 and the next major war, Imperial armies were poorly led by a geriatric senior command.[9] The Hofkriegsrat, whose 38 members were more civilian than military, made no gains in efficiency. The Imperial army was a polyglot army that still did not reflect the large number of ethnic groups in the empire. Eugene adopted a policy of discouraging subjects of certain nationalities from enlisting: French-speakers (Walloons and Lorrainers, for example), Italians, Swiss, Poles and Hungarians, he considered of doubtful loyalty. Croats and Serbs were confined largely to grenzer units along the southern frontier. The Habsburg army remained largely German and Czech. Its demeanour was more casual than the Prussian army of King Frederick William I.[10] Similarly, in France, elderly heroes remained ensconced in the high command until they died in 1734; Villars died of old age while campaigning in Lombardy, and a cannonball decapitated Berwick at the siege of Philippsburg.

Eighteenth-century war unfolded according to predictable routines – if not rituals – that contrasted with the ferocity of the Thirty Years' War or the religious wars that preceded them. This was what the French call *la guerre en dentelles*, in which officers and men dressed in smart uniforms *à la mode* and generals campaigned in lace-festooned sleeves and cravats. In the tournament model of European great power politics, today's enemy could be tomorrow's ally. In peacetime, the aristocratic officer class travelled as never before, acquiring a more French-speaking cosmopolitan outlook in the process. War could still be fought with episodes of cruelty, but large armies manoeuvred with increasing concern not to disturb the population or deprive civilians of their food, their livestock and transport. The distinction between full-time soldiers and unarmed civilians sharpened over time. When armed civilians harassed armies and resisted invading armies to defend their prince – as in Piedmont in the 1740s, generals reacted harshly with fire and firing squads. Conventions developed between armies to respect the frailty of enemy sick and wounded, and there was distinct progress in the development of field hospitals in the eighteenth century.[11]

Overturning Utrecht

King Philip V ascended the throne of the Spanish empire, still largely intact since the time of Philip III, and he resented his grandfather's willingness to concede the

Low Countries, Lombardy, the kingdom of Naples, Sicily and Sardinia, as well as tiny Gibraltar and the island of Minorca, to the Coalition powers at Utrecht in 1713 and 1714. His second marriage, to Elisabetta Farnese of Parma in 1714, flanked him with a strong-willed queen (Philip was subject to long bouts of depression) who intended to recover territories in Italy for her own sons. The queen rid herself of Jean Orry and French influence, preferring the hedonistic Cardinal Alberoni (a Parman subject and a remarkable man) and a coterie of Italians and 'Belgians' who occupied high positions at court.[12] Alberoni scaled back the army of 100,000 men in 1714 to a standing force of 60,000 troops, half of which was garrisoned on the restive provinces of the Crown of Aragon.[13] Alberoni also oversaw the rapid creation of a Spanish navy (often warships the Dutch could no longer afford to maintain). In 1718, an amphibious force reconquered Austrian Sardinia in mere weeks, while the Imperial army was fighting the Ottomans in the Balkans. Shortly after, a fleet of 30 warships escorted an army of 30,000 men and 100 siege guns to Sicily, whose Piedmontese regime quickly collapsed, not least because the population welcomed the return of the Spaniards.[14] This assault on the Treaty of Utrecht so soon after the War of the Spanish Succession could not be tolerated by the great powers. A British fleet destroyed most of the Spanish warships off Sicily in 1718, while a French army invaded the Basque country. The combined onslaught forced Philip to relinquish his conquests in January 1719, and to dismiss Alberoni as his chief minister, but he prepared for the next opportunity unchastened.

The Spanish navy almost immediately re-emerged with the construction of important shipyards in El Ferrol (for the Atlantic fleet), Cartagena (base of the Mediterranean galleys) and Cadiz, whose ships escorted the precious silver convoys bringing the equivalent of 10–20% of Spanish state revenues. Another naval arsenal at Havana produced almost a third of Spanish ships. These vessels numbered about 45 ships of the line and 15 frigates, typically smaller than British men-o'-war but they were not intended to challenge the Royal Navy in fleet engagements.[15] Behind the shipyards were royal foundries casting guns and ships' hardware, and manufactures of cables and sails, on the model of Colbert sixty years previously.[16] Royal administrators were not shy about soliciting the aid of private contractors, either.[17] Italian ministers made way for Spaniards, of whom Jose Patiño was the most important. A French-style system of naval conscription produced seamen, and Spain developed a corps of about 500 naval officers of diverse background. By the early 1730s, the navy had restored the Spanish threat to the Barbary Corsair states of North Africa. French influence was discernible in the fashioning of the Spanish army in the decades after the end of the War of the Spanish Succession. Provincial intendants and army commissaires supervised private contractors who provided the troops with food and uniforms. Royal foundries in Cantabria (Asturias and the Basque country) and Catalonia provided 20,000 muskets annually in the early 1720s. In 1734, 33 militia regiments were created to serve as a pool of reservists and to guard the coasts. By the 1740s, they were being sent to field armies in a combat role, usually against their will.[18] Of the regular battalions, up to a third of them comprised foreign troops, largely the ubiquitous Germans.[19]

A new occasion for war with the victors of Utrecht emerged in 1733 over the succession to the Polish throne; Louis XV's father-in-law, Stanislaus Leszczynski, was elected king by the Diet following the death of Augustus the Strong, in the face of Russian and Imperial opposition. Philip V and Queen Elisabetta Farnese sent an amphibious army of 34,000 men to the Ligurian and Tuscan coast, along with 16-year-old Prince Carlos, heir to the duchies of Parma and Tuscany. The troops marched south at a leisurely pace to lay siege to Naples early in 1734, to the applause of the populace. The undermanned Austrian army retired to Puglia hoping for seaborne reinforcements, but it was defeated and largely captured at Bitonto. A new Spanish fleet reoccupied Sicily before the summer was over. Prince Carlos was installed as King of Naples under the watchful supervision of his mother, and his father awarded him the nucleus of a standing army.[20] More Spanish troops marched across Languedoc and Provence to join French and Sardinian (Piedmontese, in fact) troops in Lombardy. The Bourbon and Savoyard armies ejected the Imperials from northern Italy in several hard-fought battles in 1734, with Spain and Sardinia both claiming sovereignty over Milan.

French armies invaded the Rhineland to compel the Habsburgs to an advantageous peace, but they refrained from attacking the Austrian Low Countries to avoid giving Britain and the Netherlands a pretext to intervene. Imperial armies and their Reichs Contingent reinforcements were very numerous but gave a poor performance against the French in the field. Peace was quickly agreed in 1735, recognizing King Stanislas's ejection from Poland but according him Lorraine in exchange, which reverted to the French Crown upon his death in 1766. In Tuscany, the Medici dynasty, upon its extinction (in 1737), passed to Duke François Etienne of Lorraine, husband of Maria Theresa, the emperor's eldest daughter. Prince Carlos of Spain obtained recognition as King of Naples and Sicily and set about creating a viable Bourbon kingdom there.

A final aspect of the revision of the Treaty of Utrecht was Spain's intention to recover control of its colonial trade from Britain, which had finally surpassed the Netherlands as the principal maritime power. The Asiento Treaty, providing the Spanish Caribbean with African slaves, turned out to be a disappointment, with only half the annual quota of 5,000 being effectively delivered. The legal trade was intended to be a pretext for large-scale British smuggling in the Spanish Main, but the Spanish navy and an energetic coastguard quickly curtailed its scale. Meanwhile, French merchants moved to Cadiz and quickly dominated the community of foreign merchants trading legitimately with the Spanish empire.[21] French manufactures – and Spanish manufactures too, particularly in Catalonia – were expanding considerably during the period, with sizeable merchant navies to support them. Commercial interests in London and other British ports pressured Parliament to declare war against Spain in order to capture Bourbon colonies.[22] England's declaration of war in 1739 did not deliver the expected benefits, however. Spanish warships proved numerous enough to evade British blockades and to reinforce colonial garrisons in time. A British amphibious operation against Cartagena (in modern Columbia) resulted in the deaths of 20,000 men from disease and combat, perhaps the country's biggest naval failure before Gallipoli.[23] Spanish privateers (and French ships sailing under Spanish colours) unleashed themselves on British seaborne trade and made a rich haul of prizes. Britain constituted Europe's leading seapower by a large margin, but Spain proved to be surprisingly resilient.

The Habsburg succession in Germany

A new problem loomed on the horizon in the 1730s: Habsburg Emperor Charles VI had no son or nephew to ascend the Imperial throne at his death, and there was no legal precedent for a female monarch of Bohemia and Hungary. Therefore, he pushed the claim that his territories should pass intact to his young daughter, Maria Theresa, and her husband François of Lorraine – Grand Duke of Tuscany after 1737. The problem had loomed from 1720, and the solution was to create a treaty, the *Pragmatic Sanction*, to which all the component parts of the Habsburg lands would adhere. The Imperial Diet consented to observe the document in 1732, but with several important holdouts, like Bavaria, Saxony and the Palatinate. Next, the Pragmatic Sanction was presented to European states. Britain consented to it after Austria dismantled a fledgling colonial trading company based at Ostend on the North Sea coast across from London. France, under the careful guidance of the elderly Cardinal Fleury, accepted the Pragmatic Sanction in 1738, for refusing the treaty meant full-scale war with the Habsburg dynasty. Cardinal Fleury hoped to keep France out of any impending conflict over the issue, but, at the court of Versailles, a growing party around the Marshal Belle-Isle thought the moment propitious to dismember France's traditional Habsburg rival.

The Austrian failure against the Ottomans was added proof that the Habsburg empire deserved to disappear. An improvised campaign in Hungary in 1737 made no progress against the Turks, and, following a defeat at Banja Luka in Bosnia, generals were dismissed for timidity or incompetence. The following year's campaign also obtained no advantages. Not all the troops were available for service in Hungary: some 40,000 troops were held back in Italy over fears of new initiatives by Spain and France. The 1739 campaign saw Imperial troops disgrace themselves: after a short advance into Serbia, they were repulsed by the Ottomans in a field battle at Grocka in July, with heavy loss. Seized with strategic panic, Imperial troops withdrew from northern Serbia across the Sava river and the Ottomans captured strongly fortified Belgrade. A hasty peace relinquished all the gains of 1718 in Serbia and Wallachia. In the aftermath of the war, Habsburg troops declined by about half their regulation strength to 80,000 men, spread across not only Central Europe, but also Milan and the Low Countries.

Upon the death of Emperor Charles VI on 20 October 1740, young King Frederick II of Prussia, whose father had adhered to the Pragmatic Sanction, mobilized his army and marched into the rich province of Silesia with almost no opposition. Maria Theresa sent a force to eject the Prussians in April 1741 but Frederick's army routed it at Möllwitz, thereby confirming everyone's low opinion of Habsburg military potential. The Elector Charles Albert of Bavaria was the closest male successor to Charles VI and he had never consented to the Pragmatic Sanction. In the course of 1741, Bavaria, Saxony and Prussia established an offensive alliance to seize various Habsburg provinces, while France assisted the Bavarians in expectation of occupying the Low Countries. Two French field armies of 80,000 men marched deep into Central Europe, one to occupy Vienna and another army of observation dispatched to Westphalia in order to dissuade the Netherlands and Hanover/Britain from interfering. Not having the strength to advance on Vienna, the Franco–Bavarian force marched north into Bohemia and occupied Prague instead. By the end of 1741, Maria Theresa had lost her two most important provinces by revenue: Bohemia and Silesia. In desperation, she travelled to Buda and appealed to the chivalry of her Hungarian magnate subjects. In exchange for solid benefits, these consented to raise an army of 100,000 men from the kingdom, although the number effectively levied was less than half of that.[24] At the end of the campaigning season, Frederick II ceased hostilities in Silesia and, by abandoning his allies, enabled the beleaguered empress to concentrate all her strength elsewhere.

The assembled Imperial Diet at Frankfurt declared Charles-Albert of the Bavarian Wittelsbach dynasty to be the legitimate emperor on 24 January 1742, and he was crowned as Charles VII on 12 February. But already 'Austrian' armies unfurled over Bavaria itself, cutting off the French in Bohemia. Meanwhile, Spain joined the rush for Habsburg territory by marching an army through southern France with the intention of conquering Milan. Another Spanish and Neapolitan army marched north from Central Italy to deprive Imperial forces of vital supplies and reinforcements. Maria Theresa responded by forging a pact with Piedmont/Sardinia that awarded King Charles-Emmanuel III part of Lombardy. Prussia withdrew completely from the war against the Habsburgs in June 1742.

In 1743, both France and Britain entered the war on a formal basis, and King George II in person took command of a British and North German army that pushed the French force south. The Franco–Bavarian army in Prague dwindled and withdrew from Habsburg territories during the winter. After a poorly disciplined French army was defeated by the Anglo–Germans at Dettingen, Bourbon troops were withdrawn to the west bank of the Rhine. The British army of this period numbered about 70,000 men, half the size as in the time of Marlborough, but more emphasis was placed on the navy and the still fruitless fight against Spain. A British fleet imposed a blockade on the northwest coast of Italy and Provence, but a combined Franco–Spanish fleet forced it to withdraw during the winter of 1744. The French navy also prepared to land the Stuart claimant to the throne of the United Kingdom, but the ships were dispersed during a storm. A French field army of 87,000 men, accompanied by King Louis XV in person, occupied several fortresses in western Flanders in the face of an Anglo–Dutch–Imperial coalition. Once Habsburg forces were fully engaged against the French, Frederick of Prussia invaded Bohemia and occupied Prague with little effort.

The year 1745 saw fresh opportunities for the anti-Habsburg alliance, attacking from the east, west and south simultaneously. In Italy, Philip V and his son, Charles of Naples, combined no fewer than 50,000 troops alongside the French and a new ally, the Republic of Genoa. This last was going to be ceded to Savoy by Maria Theresa and its anxious rulers joined France and Spain for their preservation. An imposing Gallispan army marched north from the Riviera and routed the Piedmontese on the Tanaro river. Elisabetta Farnese commanded her Spanish general to march on Milan and on Parma, which was effected easily enough. French troops laid siege to Piedmontese forces and so operated apart from their ally. In the Low Countries, an even larger French army than the precedent, accompanied by the king, invested the town of Tournai and the covering army of 45,000 men, then repulsed the Pragmatic army of 60,000 at Fontenoy in May. (The French field commander, Marshal Maurice de Saxe, was the Lutheran bastard son of King Augustus of Poland; his talented adjoint, the Comte de Lowendal was the bastard of the King of Denmark.) The French occupied most of Flanders in the aftermath of the battle. During the summer, a French flotilla succeeded in depositing the Stuart pretender, Prince Charles, in Scotland, and he raised that kingdom in revolt. British and German troops hurriedly withdrew from the continent to quell the rebellion, which occurred at Culloden on 27 April 1746.

Emperor Charles VII died in Munich early in 1745 and his son, Maximilian, refused to be considered as a candidate. The Imperial Diet now elected François Etienne of Lorraine, Grand Duke of Tuscany to the Imperial throne alongside Maria Theresa. Frederick II decided to withdraw from the war a second time in order to consolidate his grasp on Silesia. This freed Habsburg troops for the Italian theatre, and these, together with the Piedmontese, encircled the Gallispan army at Piacenza. The French commander, Maillebois, fought his way out of the trap but was forced to evacuate northern Italy as far as the Alps of Provence. King Philip of Spain died at that juncture and his son, Ferdinand VI, suspended active hostilities without demobilizing his armies. Imperial troops would have pressed further into coastal Provence with the support of the British fleet, but occupied Genoa rebelled and ejected its German garrison. French troops, and eventually Spanish units, too, arrived in small vessels to stiffen the resistance and to worry the Austrian army from the rear. Fighting in the Alps entailed its own difficulties for both sides. Every passage from France to the north Italian plain was dominated by mountains for 200 kilometres, and troops could only move on narrow tracks. No more than seven or eight thousand men could move from one camp to another in a single day. Close to 10,000 Piedmontese mountain peasants harassed the Gallispan supply lines without pause, and the soldiers replied with great harshness against them.[25] The well-entrenched Piedmontese army also easily repulsed a French direct assault on the mountain pass at Fenestrelle.

France placed its greatest effort in the Low Countries where Marshal de Saxe led a field army of unprecedented size, 180,000 men, twice as large as the so-called Pragmatic army of British, Dutch, Imperial and Reichs Contingent forces.

This huge force advanced across what remained of the Austrian Netherlands, capturing Antwerp, Brussels and Namur. On 11 October, the French commander attacked the coalition army at Rocoux, just outside Liège, with 150,000 men, probably the largest field army in a single engagement in European history to date. The event followed the classic pattern of battles: a preliminary bombardment lasting one hour, a French attack by small columns using bayonets, the Allies waiting until the last moment to fire, and then inflicting casualties on the French from canister fire. Pragmatic infantry soon gave way under the weight of the attack and it abandoned its guns and its stores.[26]

Operations in 1747 saw Marshal de Saxe press northwards into the Dutch Republic in order to break up the coalition. He won a new victory at Laufeld, near Antwerp, on 2 July against the British, Dutch and German troops and, in the aftermath, the Comte de Lowendal besieged and took by storm the strongest Dutch fortress, Bergen-op-Zoom, at the end of two months. At the beginning of the campaign season of 1748, Marshal de Saxe laid siege to Maastricht in April, which surrendered the following month. By that time, all the belligerents had had enough and suspended hostilities, signing the peace at Aachen later that year. Despite being present at Fontenoy, Louis XV was not an authentic 'roi de guerre'. The first French king to conquer most of the Low Countries, he was happy, even in the face of outraged public opinion, to end the war without increasing French territory. Maria Theresa emerged from the war with her throne secure, but with the loss of Silesia. Resolved not to accept the loss, she began immediately to revamp the empire's tax system and to improve her military preparedness in view of recovering the lost province. Britain made no progress against Spain, and had to return to France its sole conquest in the Americas, the island fortress of Louisbourg. Bourbon overseas commerce made another leap forward, and their military presence intensified in the Mississippi, Ohio and Great Lakes watersheds, as well as in southeast India. The European tournament, in its fierce pageantry, was, therefore, set to continue.

Notes

1 Laurent Vergez, 2016: 92.
2 Brent Nosworthy, 1990: 67.
3 Vergez, 2016: 102.
4 Frédéric Naulet, 2002: 135; Clément Oury, 2011: 47.
5 Fadi el-Hage, 2017: 107.
6 Erik A Lund, 1999: 144.
7 Lund, 1999: 108.
8 Lund, 1999: 67.
9 Michael Hochedlinger, 2003: 235.
10 Christopher Duffy, 1977: 12, 66; Karl Roider, 1972: 20.
11 Vergez, 2016: 101, 119.
12 Jean-François Labourdette, 2001: 317.
13 Christopher Storrs, 2016: 20.
14 Labourdette, 2001: 349.
15 Storrs, 2016: 67, 103–107.

16 Labourdette, 2001: 484.
17 Rafael Torres Sánchez, 2016.
18 Storrs, 2016: 32.
19 Francisco Andujar Castillo, 1991: 74.
20 Gregory Hanlon, 1998b: 322.
21 François Crouzet, 2012/3.
22 John Brewer, 1989: 168.
23 Labourdette, 2001: 491.
24 El-Hage, 2017: 34.
25 Spenser Wilkinson, 1927: 3, 163, 256.
26 Vergez, 2016: 200.

Glossary

Akinji Unpaid light cavalry of the Ottoman army. They raided enemy territory seeking captives and booty both in time of war and of peace. Able akinji horsemen could hope to receive a timar, or else a position in a janissary corps. They could also police their home district under the authority of the local sanjak bey, or pasha.

Army intendant A civilian official holding a temporary commission from the crown in order to distribute justice, to manage the funds and to arrange the supply of an army in wartime. He was not under the authority of the commanding general and corresponded frequently with the Crown and its ministers.

Arrière-ban French noblemen owed the king personal service in his armies, armed, outfitted and providing a horse at their own expense, serving for free for a period of several months. These inexperienced and usually reluctant warriors were rarely called up after the sixteenth century.

Asiento A contract between a private entrepreneur (or a consortium thereof) and the king of Spain for the purpose of providing provisions, ships or slaves over a set term, for the entire kingdom or for a single place.

Bagno A holding pen, typically in port cities, for captives awaiting their ransom. Galley convicts and slaves could be sheltered there for years at a time.

Bastion An angular projection from the wall, typically no higher than the wall itself, which served as a platform for artillery defending a fortification. Bastions were designed to fire into the ditch, and to eliminate dead ground where the enemy could take shelter.

Cadastre A public register containing a description and the dimensions of each plot of land or building in a local community, from the eighteenth century containing a surveyor's map numbering each separate parcel. With each passage of property to another individual, the document had to be emended. The cadastre was the basis of direct taxation.

Casemates A bomb-resistant sheltered compartment underneath a wall or a bastion, sometimes with narrow embrasures for guns or muskets. Men and equipment could be lodged there in security.

Chevauchée A medieval style of warfare in which an army dominated by knights and mounted retainers wreaks as much damage as possible over a wide swath of the enemy's country, burning farms and villages, seizing livestock, taking captives for ransom. Sieges and battles were not an important part of these operations.

Circle (Kreise) Ten permanent administrative subdivisions of the Holy Roman Empire that coordinated collection of money for war, recruitment of troops and their provisioning in the field.

Citadel A fort built at the edge of a city wall whose principal purpose was to control the community with a small garrison. Enhanced citadels were typically the strongest part of a fortress, where the commander had his lodgings, and stored food and ammunition.

Condottiere A military entrepreneur who specialized in raising professional soldiers quickly and leading them on campaign. The 'condotta' was a recruiting contract conceded to these men by an Italian city-state or principality from the fourteenth to the sixteenth century.

Contributions Money and/or provisions levied forcibly by armies from civilians. Instead of indiscriminate looting, officers negotiated the amounts and the payment schedule with local authorities in order to retain better discipline and avoid violence.

Cordon sanitaire A buffer zone guarded by soldiers to prevent the arrival of people stricken with contagious diseases such as the plague. These checkpoints allowed passage of food into infected areas, but prohibited the movement of people, livestock or merchandise in the other direction. Highly effective in the elimination of the plague from Western and Central Europe in the seventeenth and eighteenth centuries, given that there was no cure for the disease once it broke out.

Corvée A work detail undertaken as part of the obligations of serfs towards their lords, or as a kind of non-monetary tax devoted to the upkeep of roads and other public infrastructure. Usually undertaken for one or two weeks by heads of households in rotation.

Cossacks Former Russian or Ukrainian serfs who established farms and fortified villages on the perilous frontier with the Ottoman Empire and the Tatar raiders in the present-day Ukraine. Most adhered to a loose confederation under shifting leadership. These enrolled in a militia (comprising mostly infantry) for local defence, and for raiding Moslem territories. They were quickly hired as effective auxiliary forces by the Kingdom of Poland, the Muscovite state and (briefly) the Ottoman Empire.

Countermarch Since muskets took time to reload, the countermarch tactic arrayed the men six to ten (or more) rows deep, with each row advancing together, firing in unison, and then proceeding to the back of the line to recharge their piece. This prevented confusion and assured a certain regularity of musket fire from the unit.

Counterscarp The area on the edge of the moat across from the walls of a fortress contained a ledge for forward defence by infantry, who might also place small mortars there to launch bombs into the trenches of the advancing sappers. They also served as staging areas for sorties. Only once the counterscarp was carried by the attackers could they post cannon to fire at the bastions and the ravelins or place mines underneath them.

Devshirme A tax on Christian households subject to the Ottoman sultan (principally in the Balkans) where adolescent boys were levied for the sultan's service, converted to Islam and then trained as janissary soldiers or civil servants. Technically slaves, the janissary soldiers were paid and could rise to the highest positions in the empire.

Dienstgeld A retainer payment to experienced military commanders in time of peace to keep them in readiness for mobilization for war. They would usually have private stocks of weaponry and large stables of horses to maintain. They were frequent fixtures at the court in various capacities.

Dragoons Highly mobile infantry mounted on smaller, cheaper horses who could serve as second-rate cavalry. Fast-moving dragoon regiments were ideal skirmishers with polyvalent capabilities.

Étapes Like the organization of the modern Tour de France, an étape was a place where small contingents of troops on the march would find lodgings and food ready for them on the day they required it. They required these facilities for every day of their travel.

Fortifications 'à la huguenotte' Medieval walls could be buttressed with earthen bastions, ravelins and other outworks in a short period of months. They did not require expensive building materials, and could be raised using corvée labour.

Forward panic A universal instinctive behaviour, a form of fear, which consists of pursuing a fleeing enemy and killing them before they can rally. The urge to kill the adversary is much greater then, compared to fighting them face-to-face.

Gabelle These were taxes placed on objects of consumption. The most important in many countries was the salt gabelle, where one could control the acquisition of minimum amounts of the product for each locality. In addition to the minimum purchase for people and animals, one could buy additional amounts from designated vendors who possessed a licence. The variation in cost from one jurisdiction to another resulted in vast rings of people selling salt from unauthorized locations.

Galeass Originally a galley wide enough and high enough to carry cargo, Venice repurposed these to carry cannon firing from the sides and hundreds of soldiers. Slow, expensive in manpower but manoeuvrable in calm weather, these warships possessed many times the firepower of a typical galley. Ottoman galeasses were called 'mahones'.

Gallispan With the accession of the Bourbon King Philip V to the thrones of Spain, French and Spanish armies operated combined contingents in Iberia and Italy. Gallispan was the term designating Franco–Spanish forces.

Gendarmes These originated as heavily armoured aristocratic cavalry companies in government pay, although each gendarme was followed by a handful of retainers and volunteers. The expectation of high pay, the requirement of an expensive charger, and the cost of full body armour limited their numbers to just a few companies after the late sixteenth century.

Ghazis   Warriors who fight to extend the influence of Islam against infidels and non-Moslems. No permanent peace could be established with unbelievers, and ghazis raided their territories even if formal peace had been signed.

Grands (les)   These consisted of about 70 senior aristocratic houses, connected to each other through marriage and kinship, who dominated the French court in the sixteenth and first half of the seventeenth centuries. Each one might hold sway over large districts of the provinces.

Grenadiers   An elite assault unit derived from Venetian troops at the siege of Candia. Originally specialized in throwing bombs into enemy trenches, they came to constitute sections of every regiment or even battalions and regiments detailed for especially dangerous tasks.

Grenzers   Border militias created along the southern frontier of the kingdom of Hungary. In exchange for the absence of serfdom, access to cultivated land, religious toleration of Orthodox clergy and low taxation, these farmer–soldiers (Croatian if Catholic, Serbian if Orthodox) skirmished against Ottoman raiders and made forays of their own into Bosnia and Ottoman Serbia. They fought in loose order, and were unreliable as regular infantry in line of battle.

Haiduks   Broadly defined, haiduks were irregular infantry raised by Magyar lords from their fiefs to defend their castles and to skirmish with Ottoman invaders. Some, however, were refugees from Ottoman territories who were resettled, like the grenzers in frontier villages of eastern Hungary, free of serfdom, in exchange for military service.

Hofkriegsrat   This Imperial War Council, a bureaucratic committee, located in Vienna after 1612, consisted of several dozen courtiers, both civilians and military. Their task was to oversee the processes of recruitment, selection and promotion of officers, provisioning of troops in the field and military procurement.

Hussars (Hungary)   Feudal lords raised contingents of light cavalry in addition to haiduk infantry that would skirmish with the Ottoman invader. They fought in loose order and were not effective against tight formations of cavalry. Polish hussars, on the other hand, were armoured heavy cavalry designed for battlefield deployment.

Insurrectio   The Polish and medieval Hungarian kings were kept tightly in check by powerful feudal lords, the magnates. The response to enemy threats was to declare a general mobilization of vassals led by their lords in the field. In addition, nobles in the two kingdoms enjoyed a legal right of armed rebellion against royal abuse of power. Leopold I removed this from the Hungarian constitution in 1682, but such rebellions continued until 1711.

Janissaries   Technically slave-soldiers of the sultan, they were levied as adolescents from Christian populations, primarily in the Balkans, converted to Islam and dispatched to Istanbul for training as professional soldiers. A large contingent of them resided in the capital, where they constituted a turbulent pressure group capable of overthrowing both sultans and viziers.

Landesknecht   Like the Swiss mercenaries on whom they were modelled, these were professional infantry who followed German princes in the field on multiple theatres in the sixteenth century. Conscious of their value to their employers, the rank and file had considerable influence over their working conditions and the application of military justice.

Letters of marque   A government licence conceded to privateers authorizing them to capture enemy ships and crews. The letters specified which banners were off limits to them and what percentage of the prizes would revert back to the government. A single letter might serve for multiple ships operating in concert.

Maison du Roi   Infantry and cavalry troops attached to the jurisdiction of the French court, instead of the army, designed to guard the royal household and to take part in its ceremonies. Given their proximity to the monarch, these were elite regiments with numerous aristocrats even among the rank and file, destined to become officers in other regiments. Precursor of the Napoleonic Imperial Guard, the household troops served actively on campaign.

Malcontents (kuruç)   Irregular bands of infantry and cavalry following their noble leaders into rebellion against the Habsburg sovereigns, Leopold I (1655–1705) and Joseph I (1705–1711). Pressed by German regular forces, they would withdraw across the Ottoman and Polish frontiers.

Matchlock   Early firing mechanisms for muskets were often too fragile for use on campaign. The matchlock was the most reliable of these: it entailed attaching a wick (burning at both ends) to the lock, which was lowered to the priming pan when pulling on the trigger. They were not substituted on a large scale by the quicker-firing flintlock until 1700.

Military frontier (Habsburg)   A particular jurisdiction along the eastern border of Habsburg Hungary, then the southern border with the Ottoman along the River Sava, in which the population enjoyed freedom from Magyar and Croat feudalism, a measure of religious toleration for Orthodox clergy and low taxation. The farmer–militia population served in village-based militia companies under their own leaders.

Munitionnaire   These were private businessmen who specialized in supplying armies. They differed from ordinary merchants in two important ways. They needed to accumulate very large amounts of a few products and then transport them over long distances quickly. Second, they might face long delays of payment by a cash-strapped government, and so needed access to credit.

Ordre du Tableau   In order to facilitate the continued rise of experienced officers to higher ranks, and to downplay the influence of senior commanders and dignitaries of the realm, Louvois and Louis XIV established a chart indicating at what point each officer was due for promotion. Undistinguished soldiers could be held back, while those showing great promise could be fast-tracked, but regularity of promotion was the principal aim.

Palanka fort   Makeshift forts constructed of logs and reinforced earthworks strong enough to withstand limited artillery bombardments multiplied on both sides of the Ottoman–Habsburg frontier in the sixteenth century. They constituted command and surveillance strongpoints and served as a base for raiders. They were not built to sustain long bombardment from heavy cannon.

Parallels (Vauban)   A method of digging a sap that economized on labour and which afforded greater protection to the trench crews. Each parallel was dug wide enough to advance cannon and mortars forward and to protect them with infantry parties.

Parasympathetic backlash   A universal instinctive reaction whereby men who survive a dangerous military operation lose heart and abandon security measures. Until they recover, they will not be capable of new efforts.

Pioneers   Term designating work parties building earthworks and bridges, clearing or blocking roads, under the direction of an officer or an engineer. They might be drawn from the regular soldiers, or from the militia, or might include civilian volunteers working for pay.

Pragmatic Sanction   A document modifying the constitutions of the Habsburg hereditary states (Austrian lands, Bohemia, Hungary, Naples and the Low Countries) in order to admit smooth succession of rule to a female candidate, in the absence of a male. Signed by officials from each of those subject territories, most other European powers added their signatures in exchange for various advantages. Frederick II of Prussia, whose father signed the document, repudiated the treaty in 1740 and triggered the War of the Austrian Succession.

Pré carré (Vauban)   A defensive strategy that organized the frontier behind a fairly straight line of interlocking fortresses. It more clearly demarcated the border with the enemy at the same time.

Provincial intendants   French non-venal officials held commissions sending them to a province for several years, with the task of supervising the smooth functioning of the royal administration so as to facilitate the levy of taxes. They corresponded daily with the central government and identified political problems as they emerged. By the early 1700s, similar officials were established in Spain and in Piedmont–Sardinia.

Ravelin   A triangular free-standing structure placed in the ditch of a fortress, usually between two bastions so as to block the ability of guns to hit those parts of the fortification. Cannon could be placed in them in order to slow the advance of enemy sappers. Ravelins were open to the rear, enabling musketeers in the main fortress to fire on enemy soldiers occupying it.

Reichs contingents   The Holy Roman Empire was subdivided into ten different circles containing larger and smaller states. These consented to levy troops and money for collective defence under their own officers. The regiments generally fought under the direction of Imperial generals, but large states might finance their own standing armies.

Renegades   A renegade was someone who renounced God for personal advantage. The term was applied to Christians who converted to Islam freely in order to serve the Ottomans. This gave the Ottoman Empire a direct conduit to European technology.

Royal domain Not just composed of real estate, the domain was made up of all the prerogatives of a prince and recognized his right to monetize access to these resources. In addition to rights over public forests and to underground minerals, tolls and tariffs, the domain included pardons, legitimization of bastards, naturalization of foreign-born subjects, conferral of nobility and titles.

Sea beggars (Gueux) Initially, these were Protestant refugees fleeing Spanish repression of the Dutch Revolt in 1567–1568. From their refuges they harassed Spanish and neutral shipping and launched pinprick attacks on the occupied Netherlands. Foreign ships and men (like French Huguenots) soon constituted a large portion of them.

Ship of the line A purpose-built warship (unsuitable for commerce) large enough to be able to take its place in the line of battle with other similar ships. A huge investment in naval capital (each one carried more cannon than a large fortress) they carried large fighting crews of seamen and soldiers.

Sipahi Armoured cavalry of the Ottoman empire, the cost of whose horses and weapons was usually supported by a revenue-bearing timar. They fought in loose order, frequently changing horses when the animals tired, and were expert in mounted archery, like other Asian cavalry.

Sortie A surprise attack on the besieger's trenches by parties of troops defending a fortress. If successful, they could spike the cannon and fill in part of the works, thereby delaying the progress of a siege.

Spanish Road A series of interconnected roads passing over the Italian Alps and crossing Switzerland, Savoy, Franche-Comté, the Rhineland and Lorraine to reach Luxembourg and the Spanish Low Countries. Spanish troops and provisions raised or equipped in Lombardy regularly reinforced the Spanish Army of Flanders.

Stadtholder Originally the military governor of each province in the Netherlands, this dignitary enjoyed command over local troops. During the Dutch revolt against Spain, five of the seven rebel provinces endowed William of Orange and his heirs with this office. The power and prestige accruing to the office made leaders of the House of Orange the uncrowned kings of the Dutch Republic.

Taille A direct tax levied on each hearth, or household, assessed by local authorities on the value of its real estate, which was specified in a large register. Aristocratic and ecclesiastic landowners were not usually subject to this tax, and poor people with no land were not liable to it either.

Tatars Descendants of the Turkic and Mongol Golden Horde that dominated medieval Russia and the steppes of the Ukraine, they settled in and around the Crimean Peninsula where they practised a limited agriculture. Tatar leaders recognized the suzerainty of the Ottoman sultan and served his armies in a mercenary capacity. Tatar raids deep into Eastern Europe took as many as two million slaves from the sixteenth to the eighteenth century, who were mostly shipped to Istanbul.

Tax farming   In a period before government bureaucrats could assess the wealth of each household, the right to collect taxes was leased to individuals or a consortium of businessmen who advanced large sums of money at regular intervals to the state, and then recouped their outlay (and a profit, too) by collecting taxes door to door. A "farm" was a lease, usually obtained in a competitive bidding process. The lease usually covered several years, for harvest failures or war might reduce everyone's revenues in the short term.

Tercios   Originally, these constituted permanent formations of professional Spanish or Italian infantry comprising ten or fifteen companies, led by a mestre de camp or a colonel holding a commission from the Crown. The long duration of standing infantry companies was a novelty in the sixteenth century and enabled them to build a large nucleus of veterans.

Timar   A revenue-bearing local jurisdiction created by the Ottoman sultans in Anatolia, Greece and the Balkans destined to pay the costs of a mounted sipahi and a couple of retainers or subalternate soldiers. Sipahis lost their timar if they could not serve personally on campaign (or send a son or close relative in their stead), and they were rarely held for long periods of time.

Union of Arms   This policy of the Spanish chief minister, or valido, Count Duke of Olivares (1623–1642), established an annual quota of men and money from each of the constituent territories of the Spanish empire in Europe, thereby spreading the weight of war more equally. The policy was resisted by force of arms in regions with long traditions of self-government and consensual taxation, such as Catalonia, Portugal and Sicily.

Venal office-holding   It was discovered in the early sixteenth century that wealthy people would pay money to the government for the privilege of holding government office, particularly if they could sell the position when they retired or bequeath it to their heirs. They received a small portion of that sum (three or four per cent) in the guise of a salary. In wartime, the French Crown often created hundreds of judicial offices at a time for the principal purpose of acquiring money. The same principle was extended to captains and colonels in the army.

Venice Arsenal   Arsenals were developed to build ships and to outfit them with everything they needed. They contained not only shipyards, but rope-making and sail-making workshops and foundries, and warehouses to stock them. (Ships returning to port were 'disarmed' and the hulls were housed in sheds to protect them from the elements.) The Venice Arsenal covered a large district of the city and, in the sixteenth century, employed as many as 5,000 workers, making it Europe's largest 'factory' by far.

References

J. Aalbers, 'Holland's financial problems (1713–1733) and the wars against Louis XIV', *Britain and the Netherlands vol. 6: War and Society*, AD Duke & CA Tawse, eds, The Hague, the Netherlands, 1977, 79–93.

Gabor Agoston, 'Empire and warfare in east-central Europe, 1550–1750: the Ottoman–Habsburg rivalry and military transformations', *European Warfare 1350–1750*, F. Tallett & DJB Trim, eds, Cambridge, UK: Cambridge University Press, 2010, 110–34.

Gabor Agoston, 'Firearms and military adaptation: the Ottomans and the European military revolution', *Journal of World History*, 25, 2014, 85–124.

Gabor Agoston, 'La frontière militaire ottomane en Hongrie', *Histoire, Economie et Société*, 2015 3, 36–53.

Virginia Aksan, *Ottoman Wars 1700–1870: An Empire Besieged* (London, UK, 2007).

Joachim Albareda Salvadò, *La Guerra de Sucesión de España (1700–1714)* (Barcelona, Spain, 2010).

J Alcalà Zamora y Queipo de Llano, 'Razon de estado y geoestrategia en la politica italiana de Carlos II: Florencia y los Presidios 1677–1681', *Boletin de la Real Academia de la Historia*, 173, 1976, 297–358.

R.C. Anderson, *Naval Wars in the Levant, 1559–1853* (Princeton, NJ, 1952).

Louis André, *Michel Le Tellier et l'organisation de l'armée monarchique* (Paris, France, 1906).

Francisco Andujar Castillo, *Los Militares en la España del siglo XVIII: Un estudio social* (Granada, Spain, 1991).

Charles Ardant Du Picq, *Etudes sur le combat: Combat antique et combat moderne* (Paris, France, 2004 1904 edn).

Maurizio Arfaioli, *The Black Bands of Giovanni: Infantry and Diplomacy during the Italian Wars (1526–1528)* (Pisa, Italy, 2005).

Philip Argenti, *The Occupation of Chios by the Venetians (1694)* (London, UK, 1935).

Ronald G Asch, 'Wo der soldat hinkoembt, da ist alles sein: Military violence and atrocities in the Thirty Years' War re-examined', *German History*, 18, 2000, 291–309.

Tommaso Astarita, Aspetti dell'organizzazione militare del regno di Napoli alla fine del Viceregno spagnolo, Tesi di laurea, Università degli Studi di Napoli, 1982–83.

Gautier Aubert, *Révoltes et répressions dans la France moderne* (Paris, France, 2015).

Alain Ayats, 'Armées et santé en Roussillon au cours de la guerre de Hollande (1672–1678)', *Cadre de vie, équipement, santé dans les sociétés méditerranéennes*, JM Goger & N Marty, eds, Perpignan, France, 2006, 119–35.

Maurice Aymard, 'Chiourmes et galères dans la seconde moitié du XVIe siècle', *Il Mediterraneo nella seconda metà del '500 alla luce di Lepanto*, G Benzoni ed., Florence, 1974, 71–94.

Paul Azan, *Un tacticien du XVIIe siècle* (Paris, France, 1904).

Fulvio Babudieri, 'Gli Uscocchi. Loro formazione e loro attività a terra ed in mare', *Le Genti del Mare Mediterraneo*, Rosalba Ragosta, ed., Naples, 1981, 445–98.

Zoltan Peter Bagi, *Stories of the Long Turkish War* (Beau Bassin, Mauritius, 2018).

Zoltan Peter Bagi, 'The life of soldiers during the Long Turkish War (1593–1606)', *Hungarian Historical Review*, 4, 2015, 384–417.

Roberto Barazzutti, 'La guerre de course hollandaise sous Louis XIV: essai de quantification', *Revue Historique de Dunkerque et du Littoral*, 37, 2004, 269–80.

Thomas M Barker, *Double Eagle and Crescent: Vienna's Second Turkish Siege and its Historical Setting* (Albany, NY, 1967).

Thomas Barker, *The Military Intellectual and Battle: Raimondo Montecuccoli and the Thirty Years' War* (Albany, NY, 1975).

Thomas M Barker, 'Ottavio Piccolomini (1599–1659): a fair historical judgment?' *Army, Aristocracy, Monarchy: Essays on War, Society and Government in Austria 1618–1780*, Boulder, CO, 1982, 61–111.

Karen Barkey, *Bandits and Bureaucrats: The Ottoman Route to State Centralization* (Ithaca, NY, 1997).

Martin Barros, Nicole Salat & Thierry Sarmant, *Vauban: L'intelligence du territoire* (Paris, France, 2006).

Gabor Barta, 'The first period of the Transylvanian Principality 1526–1606, *History of Transylvania vol.1: From the Beginnings to 1606*, Laszlo Makkai & Andras Mocsy, eds, New York, 2002, 593–770.

Reinhard Baumann, *I Lanzichenecchi: la loro storia e cultura dal tardo medioevo alla Guerra dei Trent'anni* (Turin, 1996).

Douglas Clark Baxter, *Servants of the Sword: French Intendants of the Army 1630–1670* (Urbana, IL, 1976).

Françoise Bayard, 'Un instrument de l'absolutisme et ses limites: les finances de l'Etat classique', *L'Etat Classique: Regards sur la pensée politique de la France dans le second XVIIe siècle*, H Méchoulan & Joël Cornette, eds, Paris, France, 1996, 201–19.

Jean-Pierre Antoine Bazy, *Etat militaire de la monarchie espagnole sous le règne de Philippe IV* (Poitiers, France, 1864).

Katia Béguin, *Financer la guerre au XVIIe siècle: la dette publique et les rentiers de l'absolutisme* (Seyssel, France, 2012).

William Beik, *Absolutism and Society in Seventeenth-Century France: State Power and Provincial Aristocracy in Languedoc* (Cambridge, UK, 1985).

Bartolomé Bennassar & Lucile Bennassar, *Les Chrétiens d'Allah: L'histoire extraordinaire des rénégats, XVIe–XVIIe siècles* (Paris, France, 1989).

Martyn Bennett, *The Civil Wars Experienced: Britain and Ireland 1638–1661* (London, UK, 2000).

Yves-Marie Bercé, *Histoire des Croquants: Etude des soulèvements populaires au XVIIe siècle dans le Sud-Ouest de la France*, 2 vols. (Paris, France, 1974).

Jean Bérenger, *Finances et Absolutisme autrichien dans la seconde moitié du XVIIe siècle* (Paris, France, 1975).

Jean Bérenger, *Turenne* (Paris, France, 1987).

Jean Bérenger, 'La collaboration militaire austro-espagnole aux XVIe–XVIIe siècles', *L'Espagne et ses guerres: De la fin de la Reconquête aux guerres d'Indépendance*, Annie Molinié & Alexandra Merle, eds, Paris, France, 2004, 11–33.

Jean Bérenger, *Léopold Ier (1640–1705): Fondateur de la puissance autrichienne* (Paris, France, 2004).

Jean Bérenger, 'Les commandes d'armes de Léopold (1657–1705) pour l'armée impériale', *Armes et cultures de guerre en Europe centrale, XVe–XIXe siècle; Cahiers d'Etudes et de Recherches du Musée de l'Armée* n. 6, 2005–2006, 155–81.

Ilya Berkovich, *Motivation in War: The Experience of Common Soldiers in Old-Regime Europe* (Cambridge, UK, 2017).

Carlo Bitossi, 'Il Piccolo sempre succombe al grande: La Repubblica di Genova tra Francia e Spagna, 1684–1685', *Il Bombardamento di Genova nel 1684*, Genoa, Italy, 1988, 39–69.

Jeremy Black, *War in European History 1494–1660* (Washington, DC, 2006).

Jeremy Black, *War in the World: A Comparative History* (Basingstoke, UK, 2011).

Salvatore Bono, *Corsari nel Mediterraneo: Cristiani e musulmani fra guerra, schiavitù e commercio* (Milan, Italy, 1993).

Boris Bouget, 'D'une guerre à l'autre: le double retard de l'infanterie française, un handicap limité (1688–1715)', *Les Dernières guerres de Louis XIV 1688–1715*, H Drévillon, B Fonck & J-P Cénat, eds, Rennes, France, 2017, 143–56.

C.W. Bracewell, 'Uskoks in Venetian Dalmatia before the Venetian-Ottoman War of 1714–1718', *East-Central European Society and War in the Pre-Revolutionary Eighteenth Century*, GE Rothenberg, BK Kiraly & PF Sugar, eds, Boulder, CO, 1982, 431–47.

Philippe Bragard, 'La 'trace italienne': Réflexion sur une expression infondée', *La Genèse du système bastionné en Europe 1500–1550*, Nicolas Faucherre, Pieter Martens & Hugues Paucot, eds, Aix-Marseille, France, 2014, 49–52.

John Brewer, *The Sinews of Power: War, Money and the English State 1688–1783* (New York, 1989).

Peter Brightwell, 'The Spanish system and the twelve years' truce', *English Historical Review*, 89, 1974, 270–92.

Peter Brightwell, 'Spain and Bohemia: the decision to intervene, 1619', *European Studies Review*, 12, 1982, 117–41.

Gian Paolo Brizzi, *La formazione della classe dirigente nel Sei-Settecento: I seminaria nobilium nell'Italia centro-settentrionale* (Bologna, Italy, 1976).

Vladimir Brnardic, *Imperial Armies of the Thirty Years' War (2): Cavalry* (Oxford, UK, 2010).

Emmanuel de Broglie, *Catinat: L'homme et la vie (1637–1712)* (Paris, France 1902).

Jaap R Bruijn, 'Dutch privateering during the second and third Anglo-Dutch wars', *The Low Countries History Yearbook*, I Schoffer, ed, The Hague, Netherlands, 1978, 79–93.

Jaap Bruijn, 'William III and his two navies', *Notes and Records of the Royal Society of London*, 43, 1989, 117–32.

Jaap Bruijn, *The Dutch Navy in the Seventeenth And Eighteenth Centuries* (St John's, Newfoundland, 2011).

Giampiero Brunelli, *Soldati del Papa: Politica militare e nobiltà nello Stato della Chiesa, 1560–1644* (Rome, Italy, 2003).

Serge Brunet, 'Les milices dans la France du Midi au début des guerres de Religion (vers 1559–1564)', *Les Milices dans la première modernité*, Serge Brunet & José Javier Ruiz Ibàñez, eds, Rennes, 2015, 63–116.

Richard Brzezinski, *Lützen 1632: Climax of the Thirty Years' War* (Oxford, UK, 2001).

David Buisseret, *Ingénieurs et fortifications avant Vauban: L'organisation d'un service royal XVIe–XVIIe siècles* (Paris, France, 2002).

Antonio Calabria, *The Cost of Empire: The Finances of the Kingdom of Naples in the Time of Spanish Rule* (New York, 1991).

Niccoló Capponi, *Victory of the West: the Great Christian–Muslim Clash at the Battle of Lepanto* (Cambridge, MA, 2006).

Charles Carlton, *Going to the Wars: The Experience of the British Civil Wars, 1638–1651* (London, UK, 1992).

Charles Carlton, *This Seat of Mars: War and the British Isles 1485–1746* (New Haven, CT, 2011).

Stuart Carroll, 'The peace in the feud in sixteenth and seventeenth-century France', *Past and Present*, 178, 2003, 74–115.

F. L. Carsten, *Princes and Parliaments in Germany, from the Fifteenth to the Eighteenth Century* (Oxford, 1959).

Michel Cassan, *Le Temps des Guerres de Religion: le cas du Limousin (vers 1530 – vers 1630)* (Paris, France, 1996).

Jean-Philippe Cénat, 'Le ravage du Palatinat: politique de destruction, stratégie de cabinet et propagande au début de la guerre de la Ligue d'Augsbourg', *Revue Historique*, 307, 633, 2005, 97–132.

Jean-Philippe Cénat, *Louvois: le double de Louis XIV* (Paris, France, 2015).

Jean-Philippe Cénat, 'La direction de la guerre de Louis XIII à Louis XIV', *Combattre et gouverner: Dynamique de l'histoire militaire de l'époque moderne (XVIIe et XVIIIe siècles)*, B Fonck & N Genet-Rouffiac, eds, Rennes, France, 2015, 249–59.

Giovanni Cerino Badone, *Potenza di Fuoco: Eserciti, tattica e tecnologia nelle guerre europee dal Rinascimento all'Età della Ragione* (Milan, Italy, 2013).

Robert Chaboche, 'Les soldats de la guerre de Trente Ans, une tentative d'approche', *Revue d'Histoire Moderne et Contemporaine*, 20, 1973, 10–24.

Jean Chagniot, 'Mobilité sociale et l'armée (vers 1660 – vers 1760)', *XVIIe siècle*, 31, 1979, 37–49.

Jean Chagniot 'Ethique et pratique de la "profession des armes" chez les officiers français au XVIIe siècle', *Guerre et Pouvoir en Europe au XVIIe siècle*, Paris, France, 1991, 79–93.

Jean Chagniot, *Guerre et Société à l'époque moderne* (Paris, 2001).

Olivier Chaline, *La bataille de la Montagne Blanche (8 novembre 1620). Un mystique chez les guerriers* (Paris, France, 1999).

Olivier Chaline, 'La marine de Louis XIV fut-elle adaptée à ses objectifs?', *Revue Historique des Armées*, 263, 2011 40–52.

Olivier Chaline, *Les Armées du Roi: le grand chantier XVIIe–XVIIIe siècles* (Paris, 2016).

Frédéric Chauviré, 'Le problème de l'allure dans les charges de cavalerie du XVIe au XVIIIe siècle', *Revue Historique des Armées*, 249, 2007, 16–27.

Frédéric Chauviré, *Histoire de la Cavalerie* (Paris, 2013).

Frédéric Chauviré, 'Le bras droit des armées: le rôle de la cavalerie dans les dernières guerres de Louis XIV', *Les Dernières guerres de Louis XIV 1688–1715*, H Drévillon, B Fonck & J-P Cénat, eds, Rennes, France, 2017, 175–90.

John Childs, *The Army of Charles II* (London, UK, 1976).

John Childs, *The Nine Years' War and the British Army 1688–1697: The Operations in the Low Countries* (Manchester, UK, 1991).

John Childs, 'The laws of war in seventeenth-century Europe and their application to the Jacobite War in Ireland, 1688–1691', *Age of Atrocity: Violence and Political Conflict in Early Modern Ireland*, D Edwards, P Lenihan & C Tait, eds, Dublin, Ireland, 2007, 283–300.

John Childs, 'Surrender and the laws of war in Western Europe ca. 1660–1783', *How Fighting Ends: A History of Surrender*, H Afflerbach & H Strachan, eds, Oxford, UK, 2012, 153–68.

Renzo Chiovelli, 'Ingegneri ed opera militari nella prima Guerra di Castro', *La dimensione europea dei Farnese: Bulletin de l'Institut Historique Belge de Rome*, 63, 1993, 155–92.

Jack Alden Clarke, *Huguenot Warrior: The Life and Times of Henri de Rohan 1579–1638* (The Hague, Netherlands, 1966).

James B Collins, *Fiscal Limits of Absolutism: Direct Taxation in Early Seventeenth-century France* (Berkeley, CA, 1988).

Ennio Concina, *Le Trionfanti et invittissime armate venete: le milizie della Serenissima del 16 al 18 secolo* (Venice, 1971).

Ennio Concina, 'Sostener in vigore le cose del Mare: Arsenali, Vascelli, Cannoni', *Venezia e la difesa del Levante, da Lepanto a Candia 1570–1670*, Venice, Italy, 1986, 47–58.

Jean-Marie Constant, *Les Français pendant les Guerres de Religion* (Paris, France, 2002).

Jose Contreras Gay, 'Aportacion al studio de los sistemas de reclutamiento militar en la España moderna', *Anuario de Historia Contemporanea*, 8, 1981, 7–45.

José Contreras Gay, 'El siglo XVII y su importancia en el cambio de los sistemas de reclutamiento', *Studia Historica, Historia Moderna*, 14, 1996, 141–54.

Joël Cornette, *Le roi de guerre: Essai sur la souveraineté dans la France du Grand Siècle* (Paris, France, 2000).

André Corvisier, *Louvois* (Paris, France, 1983).

Dragos Cosmescu, *Venetian Fortifications in the Mediterranean* (Jefferson, NC, 2015).

Edward J Coss, *All for the King's Shilling: The British Soldier under Wellington 1808–1814* (Norman, OK, 2010).

Marco Costa, *Psicologia militare: elementi di psicologia per gli appartenenti alle forze armate* (Milan, Italy, 2003).

Ovidiu Cristea, 'The friend of my friend and the enemy of my enemy: Romanian participation in Ottoman campaigns', *The European Tributary States of the Ottoman Empire in the 16th and 17th Centuries*, G Karman & L Kuncevic, eds, Leiden, the Netherlands, 2013, 253–74.

John Jeremiah Cronin and Padraig Lenihan, 'Wars of Religion 1641–1691', *The Cambridge History of Ireland, vol. II 1550–1730*, J. Ohlmeyer, ed., Cambridge, UK, 2017, 246–70.

Louis Crocq, *Les Traumatismes psychiques de guerre* (Paris, France, 1999).

François Crouzet, 'La rivalité commerciale franco-anglaise dans l'empire espagnol, 1713–1789', *Histoire: Economie et Société*, 31, 2012/3, 19–29.

C.G. Cruickshank, *Elizabeth's Army*, 2nd edn (Oxford, UK, 1966).

Fra Bartolomeo Dal Pozzo, *Historia della Sacra Religione militare di S. Giovanni gerosolimitano, detta di Malta* (Verona, Italy, 1703).

Geza David, 'Ottoman armies and warfare 1453–1603', *The Ottoman Empire as a World Power 1453–1603: The Cambridge History of Turkey vol.2*, Suraiya Faroqhi and Kate Fleet, eds, Cambridge, 2013, 276–319.

Brian Davies, *Warfare, State and Society on the Black Sea Steppe 1500–1700* (London, UK, 2007).

Norman Davies, *God's Playground: A History of Poland, vol. 1: The Origins to 1795* (New York, 1982).

Robert C Davis, *Christian Slaves, Muslim Masters: White Slavery in the Mediterranean, the Barbary Coast and Italy, 1500–1800* (Basingstoke, UK, 2003).

Claudio De Consoli, *Al soldo del duca: L'amministrazione delle armate sabaude (1560–1630)* (Turin, Italy, 1999).

Pit Dehing & Marjolein 't Hart, 'Linking the fortunes: currency and banking 1550–1800', *A Financial History of the Netherlands*, Marjolein 't Hart, Joost Jonker & Jan Luiten van Zanden, eds, Cambridge, UK, 1997, 37–63.

Paul Delsalle, François Pernot, Marie-France Romand, 'Peut-on connaitre la vie quotidienne des soldats?', *Hommes d'armes et gens de guerre du Moyen Age au XVIIe siècle: Franche Comté de Bourgogne et comté de Montbéliard*, A Preneel & Paul Delsalle, eds, Besançon, France, 2007, 183–200.

Catherine Denys, 'Quelques réflexions sur la régulation de la violence de guerre dans les Pays-Bas méridionaux aux XVIIe et XVIIIe siècles', *Les ressources des faibles: Neutralités, sauvegardes, accommodements en temps de guerre (XVIe–XVIIIe siècles)*, JF Chanet & C Windler, eds, Rennes, France, 2009, 205–19.

Catherine Desos, 'Les ingénieurs du roi de France auprès de la couronne d'Espagne, 1704–1715', *Vegueta: Anuario de la Facultad de Geografía y Historia*, 16, Las Palmas, Gran Canaria, 2016, 67–92.

Michel Devèze, *L'Espagne de Philippe IV (1621–1665)* (Paris, France, 1971, vol. 2) 493–500.

P.G.M. Dickson, *The Financial Revolution in England: A Study in the Development of Public Credit 1688–1756* (London, UK, 1967).

Antonio Dominguez Ortiz, 'España ante la Paz de los Pireneos', *Crisis y Decadencia de la España de los Austrias*, Barcelona, Spain, 1969, 157–93.

Antonio Dominguez Ortiz, 'La crise intérieure de la monarchie des Habsbourgs espagnols sous Charles II', *The Peace of Nijmegen 1676–1678/79: La Paix de Nimègue*, Amsterdam, the Netherlands, 1980, 157–68.

Barbara Donagan, *War in England 1642–1649* (Oxford, UK, 2008).

Peter Drake, *Amiable Renegade: Memoirs of Captain Peter Drake (1671–1753)* (Stanford, CA, 1960).

Hervé Drévillon, *L'Impôt du Sang: le métier des armes sous Louis XIV* (Paris, France, 2005).

Hervé Drévillon, 'La guerre à l'époque moderne: histoire d'une histoire', *Combattre et gouverner: dynamiques de l'histoire militaire de l'époque moderne*, Bertrand Fonck & Nathalie Genet-Rouffiac, eds, Rennes, France, 2015, 19–33.

Anne Dubet, *Jean Orry et la réforme du gouvernement de l'Espagne (1701–1714)* (Clermont-Ferrand, France, 2009).

Christopher Duffy, *Fire and Stone: The Science of Fortress Warfare 1660–1860* (Newton Abbot, UK, 1975).

Christopher Duffy, *The Army of Maria Theresa: The Armed Forces of Imperial Austria 1740–1780* (New York, 1977).

Christopher Duffy, *Siege Warfare: The Fortress in the Early Modern World 1494–1660* (London, UK, 1979).

Hugh Dunthorne, *Britain and the Dutch Revolt 1560–1700* (Cambridge, UK, 2018).

Peter Earle, *Corsairs of Malta and Barbary* (London, UK, 1970).

Stephen Ede-Barrett, *The Army of James II 1685–1688: The Birth of the British Army* (Solihull, UK, 2017).

J.H. Elliott, *Richelieu and Olivares* (Cambridge, UK, 1984).

J.H. Elliott, 'Managing decline: Olivares and the Grand Strategy of Imperial Spain', *Grand Strategies in War and Peace*, Paul Kennedy, ed., New Haven, CT, 1991, 87–104.

Réné Emmanuelli, *Gênes et l'Espagne dans la guerre de Corse (1559–1569)* (Paris, 1963).

Peter Engerisser & Pavel Hrnčirik, *Nördlingen 1634: Die Schlacht bei Nördlingen: Wendepunkt des Dreissigjahringen Kriegs* (Weissenstadt, Germany, 2009).

Lars Ericson, 'The Swedish army and navy during the Thirty Years' War: from a national to a multi-national force', *1648: War and Peace in Europe*, K Bussmann & H Schilling, eds, Munster/Osnabruck, Germany, 1998, vol. 1, 301–07.

Joël Félix, 'Profits, malversations, restitutions: Les bénéfices des financiers durant la Guerre de la Ligue d'Augsbourg et la taxe de Chamillart', *Revue Historique*, 317, 676, 2015, 831–73.

Niall Ferguson, *The Cash Nexus: Money and Power in the Modern World* (New York, 2001).

Felipe Fernandez-Armesto, *The Spanish Armada: The Experience of War in 1588* (Oxford, UK, 1988).

Giuliano Ferretti, 'La politique italienne de la France et le duché de Savoie au temps de Richelieu', *Dix-septième siècle*, 1 262, 2014, 7–20.

Caroline Finkel, *The Administration of Warfare: The Ottoman Military Campaigns in Hungary 1593–1606*, (Vienna, Austria, 1988).

Michael Flinn, *The European Demographic System 1500–1820* (Baltimore, MD, 1981).

Pal Fodor, 'Making a living on the frontiers: Volunteers in the 16th century Ottoman army', *Ottomans, Hungarians and Habsburgs in Central Europe: The Military Confines in the Era of Ottoman Conquest*, Geza David and Pal Fodor, eds, Leiden, the Netherlands, 2000, 229–63.

Pal Fodor, 'Maltese pirates, Ottoman captives and French traders in the early 17th-century Mediterranean', *Ransom Slavery along the Ottoman Borders (early 15th–early 18th Centuries)*, G David & P Fodor, eds, Leiden, the Netherlands, 2007, 221–37.

Bertrand Fonck, *Le maréchal de Luxembourg et le commandement des armées sous Louis XIV* (Seyssel, France, 2014).

Bertrand Fonck & George Satterfield, 'The essence of war: French armies and small war in the Low Countries (1672–1697)', *Small Wars and Insurgencies*, 25, 2014, 767–83.

Bertrand Fonck, 'Cartographie, direction de la guerre et commandement des armées sous Louis XIV', *Combattre et gouverner: Dynamiques de l'histoire militaire de l'époque moderne (XVIIe–XVIIIe siècles)*, Bertrand Fonck & Nathalie Genet-Rouffiac, eds, Rennes, France, 2015, 143–56.

Michel Fontenay, 'La place de la course dans l'économie portuaire: l'exemple de Malte et des ports barbaresques', *Annales: Economies, Sociétés, Civilisations*, 1988, 1321–47.

Michel Fontenay, 'Chiourmes turques au XVIIe siècle', *Le Genti del Mare mediterraneo*, Rosalba Ragosta, ed., Naples, Italy, 1981, vol. 2, 877–903.

Jean-Louis Fournel et Jean-Claude Zancarini, *Les Guerres d'Italie: Des batailles pour l'Europe (1494–1559)* (Paris, 2003).

David Francis, *The First Peninsular War 1702–1713* (New York, 1975).

Wantje Fritschy & Réné van der Voort, 'From fragmentation to unification: public finance 1700–1914', *A Financial History of the Netherlands*, Marjolein 't Hart, Joost Jonker Jan Luiten van Zanden, eds, Cambridge, UK, 2010, 64–94.

Stéphane Gaber, *La Lorraine meurtrie*, 2nd edn (Nancy, France, 1991).

Stéphane Gal, *Lesdiguières: Prince des Alpes et connétable de France* (Grenoble, France, 2007).

Giuseppe Galasso, *Napoli Spagnola dopo Masaniello: Politica, cultura, società* (Florence, Italy, 1982).

Gianni Galliani, 'Il Bombardamento come atto militare: alcuni interrogative e considerazioni', *Il Bombardamento di Genova nel 1684*, Genoa, Italy, 1984, 95–107.

Martial Gantelet, 'Réguler la guerre aux frontières des Pays-Bas espagnols: la naissance empirique du droit des gens (Metz 1635–1659)', *Les ressources des faibles: Neutralités, sauvegardes, accommodements en temps de guerre (XVIe–XVIIIe siècles)*, JF Chanet & C Windler, eds, Rennes, France, 2009, 221–40.

Janine Garrisson, *L'Edit de Nantes et sa révocation: Histoire d'une intolérance* (Paris, France, 1985).

Janine Garrisson-Estèbe, *Protestants du Midi 1559–1598* (Toulouse, France, 1980).

Stephane Genêt, 'Espions d'armée et renseignement opérationnel (1740–1763)', *Combattre et gouverner: Dynamiques de l'histoire militaire de l'époque moderne (XVIIe–XVIIIe siècles)*, B Fonck & Nathalie Genet-Rouffiac, eds, Rennes, France, 2015, 157–67.

Nathalie Genet-Rouffiac, 'L'administration de la guerre et le 'vol des oies sauvages': mise en place et administration des régiments jacobites irlandais (1688–1697)', *Combattre et gouverner: Dynamiques de l'histoire militaire de l'époque moderne (XVIIe–XVIIIe siècles)*, B Fonck & Nathalie Genet-Rouffiac, eds, Rennes, France, 2015, 171–87.

Ian Gentles, *The English Revolution and the Wars in the Three Kingdoms 1638–1652* (Harlow, UK, 2007).

Thierry Giappiconi, *De l'épopée vénitienne aux Révolutions corses: engagements militaires et combats politiques insulaires (XVe–XVIIIe siècles)* (Ajaccio, France, 2018).

Jan Glete, 'War, entrepreneurship, and the fiscal-military state', *European Warfare, 1350–1750*, Frank Tallett & DJB Trim, eds, Cambridge, UK, 2010, 300–21.

Fernando Gonzalez de Leon, *The Road to Rocroi: Class, Culture and Command in the Spanish Army of Flanders 1567–1659* (Boston, MA, 2009).

Geoffrey Goodwin, *The Janissaries* (London, UK, 1997).

Luis Gorrochategui Santos, *The English Armada: The Greatest Naval Disaster in English History* (London, UK, 2018).

Molly Greene, *Catholic Pirates and Greek Merchants: A Maritime History of the Mediterranean* (Princeton, NJ, 2010).

Mark Greengrass, 'The anatomy of a religious riot in Toulouse in May 1562', *Journal of Ecclesiastical History*, 34, 1983, 367–91.

Mark Greengrass, 'The later wars of Religion in the French Midi', *The European Crisis of the 1590s*, Peter Clark, ed., London, UK, 1985, 106–34.

Paddy Griffith, *Forward into Battle: Fighting Tactics from Waterloo to the Near Future* (Novato, CA, 1991).

Dave Grossman, *On Killing: The Psychological Cost of Learning to Kill in War and Society* (Boston, MA, 1995).

Dave Grossman, *On Combat: The Psychology and Physiology of Deadly Conflict in War and in Peace* (Mascoutah, IL, 2004).

Anja Grothe & Bettina Jungklaus, 'Archaeological and anthropological examinations of a mass grave from the 1636 battle at Wittstock: a preliminary report', *Limping Together through the Ages: Joint Afflictions and Bone Infections*, G Grupe, G McGlynn & J Peters, eds, Rahden Westfalen, Germany, 2008, 127–35.

Pierre Goubert, *L'Ancien Régime: vol.1: La Société* (Paris, France, 1969).

Alain Guéry, 'Les comptes de la mort vague après la guerre. Pertes de guerre et conjoncture du phénomène guerre', *Histoire et Mesure*, 6, 1991, 289–312.

John Francis Guilmartin, *Gunpowder and Galleys: Changing Technology and Mediterranean Warfare at Sea in the Sixteenth Century* (Cambridge, UK, 1974).

John F Guilmartin, 'Ideology and conflict: the wars of the Ottoman Empire', *Journal of Interdisciplinary History*, 18, 1988, 721–47.

Giuseppe Gullino, 'Tradimento e ragion di stato nella caduta di Candia', *Venezia e la difesa del Levante*, Maddalena Redolfi & Palazzo Ducale, eds, Venice, Italy, 1986, 146–83.

Emrah Safa Gurkan, 'The centre and the frontier: Ottoman cooperation with the North African corsairs in the sixteenth century', *Turkish Historical Review*, 1, 2010, 125–63.

Emrah Safa Gurkan, 'My money or your life: the Habsburg hunt for Uluc Ali', *Studia Historica, Historia Moderna*, 26, 2014, 121–45.

William P Guthrie, *The Later Thirty Years' War: From the Battle of Wittstock to the Treaty of Westphalia* (Westport, CT, 2003).

Myron Gutmann, 'Putting crises in perspective: the impact of war on civilian populations in the seventeenth century', *Annales de Démographie Historique*, 1977, 1977, 101–28.

Myron P Gutmann, *War and Rural Life in the Early Modern Low Countries* (Princeton, NJ, 1980).

Myron P Gutmann, *Toward the Modern Economy: Early Industry in Europe 1500–1800* (Philadelphia, PA, 1988).

Bertrand Haan, 'L'Amitié, norme des relations entre princes: Philippe II et la France des guerres de religion', *Normes et Transgressions dans l'Europe de la première modernité*, F Piat, L Braguier-Gouverneur, eds, Rennes, France, 2013, 133–42.

Fadi el-Hage, 'Le duc de Vendôme en Italie (1702–1706)', *Les dernières guerres de Louis XIV 1688–1715*, H Drévillon, B Fonck & J-P Cénat, eds, Rennes, France, 2017, 191–203.

Fadi el-Hage, *La Guerre de Succession d'Autriche (1741–1748): Louis XV et le déclin de la France* (Paris, France, 2017).

J.R. Hale, 'The end of Florentine liberty: the Fortezza da Basso', *Florentine Studies: Politics and Society in Renaissance Florence*, Nicolai Rubinstein, ed., London, UK, 1968, 501–32.

J.R. Hale, 'From peacetime establishment to fighting machine: the Venetian army and the War of Cyprus and Lepanto', *Il Mediterraneo nella seconda metà del '500 alla luce di Lepanto*, Gino Benzoni, ed., Florence, Italy, 1974, 163–84.

John R Hale, *War and Society in Renaissance Europe 1450–1620* (Baltimore, MD, 1986).

Bert Hall, *Weapons and Warfare in Renaissance Europe: Gunpowder, Technology and Tactics* (Baltimore, MD, 1997).

Philippe Hamon, 'For whom the bell tolls: rural engagement during the French wars of religion: the case of Brittany', *Journal of Historical Sociology*, 28, 2015, 11–25.

Philippe Hamon, 'La défaite ou le chaos: Les paysans bas-bretons à la bataille pendant les guerres de la Ligue sous le regard du chanoine Moreau', *La Bataille: Du fait d'armes au combat idéologique, XIe–XIXe siècle*, A. Boltanski, Y Lagadec & F Mercier, eds, Rennes, France, 2015, 143–56.

Gregory Hanlon, 'The Venetian Epic 1600-1718', *The Twilight of a Military Tradition: Italian Aristocrats and European Conflicts, 1560–1800*, London, UK, 1998a, 143–78.

Gregory Hanlon, *The Twilight of a Military Tradition: Italian Aristocrats and European Conflicts, 1560–1800* (London, UK, 1998b).

Gregory Hanlon, 'The decline of violence in the West: from cultural to post-cultural history', *The English Historical Review*, 128, 531, 2013, 367–400.

Gregory Hanlon, *The Hero of Italy: Odoardo Farnese, Duke of Parma, His Soldiers and His Subjects in the Thirty Years' War* (Oxford, UK, 2014).

Gregory Hanlon, *Italy 1636: Cemetery of Armies* (Oxford, UK, 2016).

Gregory Hanlon, Destruction and reconstruction in the duchy of Parma during the Thirty Years' War, *Storia Economica*, 19, 2016, 249–78.

Marjolein 't Hart, Joost Jonker, & Jan Luiten van Zanden, eds, *A Financial History of the Netherlands* (Cambridge, UK, 2010).

Marjolein 't Hart, *The Dutch Wars of Independence: Warfare and Commerce in the Netherlands 1570–1680* (Oxford, UK, 2014).

Ragnhild Hatton, *George I Elector and King* (London, UK,, 1978).

Dionysios Hatzopoulos, *La Dernière guerre entre la République de Venise et l'Empire ottoman (1714–1718)* (Montreal, Canada, 1999).

Klara Hegyi, 'The Ottoman network of fortresses in Hungary', *Ottomans, Hungarians and Habsburgs in Central Europe: The Military Confines in the Era of Ottoman Conquest*, G David & P Fodor, eds, Leiden, the Netherlands, 2000, 163–93.

Tryntje Helfferich & Paul Sonnino, 'Civilians in the Thirty Years' War', *Daily Lives of Civilians in Wartime Europe, 1618–1900*, Linda S Frey & Marsha L Frey, eds, Westport, CT, 2007, 23–58.

Laurent Henninger, *Rocroi, 1643* (Paris, France, 1993).

Charles van den Heuvel, 'Bartolomeo Campi successor to Francesco Paciotto. A different method of designing citadels: Groningen and Flushing', *Architetti e ingegneri militari italiani all'estero dal XV al XVIII secolo*, Livorno, 1994, 153–67.

Henning Hillmann & Christina Gathmann, 'Overseas trade and the decline of privateering', *Journal of Economic History*, 71, 2011, 730–61.

François Hincker, *Les Français devant l'impôt sous l'Ancien régime* (Paris, France, 1971).

Michael Hochedlinger, *Austria's Wars of Emergence, 1683–1797* (London, UK, 2003).

Philip Hoffman, *Why did Europe Conquer the World?* (Princeton, NJ, 2015).

Max P Holt, *The French Wars of Religion 1562–1629* (Cambridge, UK, 1995).

Quentin Hughes, *Fortress: Architecture and Military History in Malta* (London, 1969).

Alain Hugon, 'Des Habsbourg aux Bourbons: le combat espagnol pour la conservation de l'hégémonie européenne', *Bulletin de la Société d'Histoire Moderne et Contemporaine*, 3–4, 2000, 34–55.

Alain Hugon, *Naples insurgée 1647–1648: de l'événement à la mémoire* (Rennes, France, 2011).

Ronald Hutton & Wylie Reeves, 'Sieges and fortifications', *The Civil Wars: A Military History of England, Scotland and Ireland 1638–1660*, John Kenyon, Jane Ohlmeyer & John Morrill, eds, Oxford, UK, 1998, 195–233.

Charles W Ingrao, *In Quest and Crisis: Emperor Joseph I and the Habsburg Monarchy* (West Lafayette, IN, 1979).

Jonathan Israel, *The Dutch Republic: Its Rise, Greatness and Fall* (Oxford, UK, 1995).

Jonathan I Israel, 'Olivares, the Cardinal-Infante and Spain's strategy in the Low Countries (1635–1642): the road to Rocroi', *Spain, Europe and the Atlantic World: Essays in Honour of John H. Elliott*, Cambridge, UK, 1995, 267–95.

Maria Ivanics, 'Enslavement, slave labour and the treatment of captives in the Crimean Khanate', *Ransom Slavery along the Ottoman Borders (early 15th–early 18th Centuries)*, Geza David & Pal Fodor, eds, Leiden, the Netherlands, 2007, 193–219.

Maria Ivanics, 'The military cooperation of the Crimean Khanate with the Ottoman Empire in the 16th and 17th centuries', *The European Tributary States of the Ottoman Empire in the Sixteenth and Seventeenth Centuries*, G Karman & Lovro Kuncevic, eds, Leiden, the Netherlands, 2013, 275–99.

Alan James, *The Navy and Government in Early Modern France* (Woodbridge, UK, 2004).

Peter January & Michael Knapton, 'The demands made on Venetian Terraferma society for defence in the early seventeenth century', *Ateneo Veneto: Rivista di Scienze, Lettere ed Arti*, 194, 2007, 25–115.

Antonio Jimenez Estrella, 'Pavie (1525) et Rocroi (1643): Impact politique et idéologique de deux batailles contre 'el francés', *La Bataille: Du fait d'armes au combat idéologique, XIe–XIXe siècle*, Franck Mercier, Yann Lagadec & Ariane Boltanski, eds, Rennes, France, 2015, 157–70.

James R Jones, *The Anglo-Dutch Wars of the Seventeenth Century* (London, UK, 1996).

Jerome Kagan, *Galen's Prophecy: Temperament in Human Nature* (New York, 1994).

Henry Kamen, *The War of Succession in Spain, 1700–1715* (London, UK, 1969).

Henry Kamen, *Spain in the Later Seventeenth Century 1665–1700* (London, UK, 1980).

Henry Kamen, 'España en la Europa de Luis XIV', *Historia de España Menendez Pidal, t. 28, La Transicion del Siglo XVII al XVIII*, Pere Molas Ribalta, ed., Madrid, Spain, 1993, 205–98.

Henry Kamen, *Spain 1469–1714: A Society of Conflict* (London, UK, 2005).

John Keegan, *The Face of Battle* (Harmondsworth, UK, 1976).

John Keegan, 'Towards a theory of combat motivation', *A Time to Kill*, P Addison & A Calder, eds, London, UK, 1997, 3–11.

Josef Kelenik, 'The military revolution in Hungary', *Ottomans, Hungarians and Habsburgs in Central Europe: The Military Confines in the Era of Ottoman Conquest*, Geza David & Pal Fodor, eds, Leiden, the Netherlands, 2000, 117–59.

Özgür Kolçak, 'The composition, tactics and strategy of the Ottoman field army at Zrinyi-Ujvar and St. Gotthard (1663–1664)', *La bataille de Saint-Gotthard et la paix de Vasvar: Expansion ottomane – coopération européenne*, Ferenc Toth ed., Budapest, 2017, 73–92.

Klara Kovacs, 'The construction of bastioned fortresses in 16th-century Transylvania', *Studies in the History of Early Modern Transylvania*, G Kovacs Kiss, ed., Highland Lakes, NJ, 2011, 359–95.

Peter Krenn, 'Test-firing selected 16th–18th century weapons', *Military Illustrated Past and Present*, 33, February 1991, 34–38.

Bernhard Kroener, 'Conditions de vie et origine sociale du personnel militaire subalterne au cours de la Guerre de Trente Ans', *Francia*, 15, 1987, 321–50.

Bernhard Kroener, 'Le maraudeur: à propos des groupes marginaux de la société militaire au début de l'époque moderne', *Nouveaux regards sur la guerre de Trente Ans*, Vincennes, France, 1998, 167–79.

Bernhard Kroener, 'The soldiers are very poor, bare, naked, exhausted': The living conditions and organizational structure of military society during the Thirty Years' War', *1648: War and Peace in Europe*, K Bussmann & H Schilling, eds, Munster/Osnabruck, Germany, 1998, 285–91.

A.N. Kurat, 'The reign of Mehmed IV 1648–1687', *A History of the Ottoman Empire to 1730*, MA Cook, ed., Cambridge, UK, 1976 157–77.

A.N. Kurat & J.S. Bromley, 'The retreat of the Turks, 1683–1730', *A History of the Ottoman Empire to 1730*, MA Cook, ed., Cambridge, UK, 1976, 178–220.

Sieur de La Colonie, *Mémoires de Monsieur de La Colonie, maréchal de camp des armées de l'Electeur de Bavière*, Anne-Marie Cocula, ed. (Paris, France, 1992).

Jean-François Labourdette, *Philippe V, Réformateur de l'Espagne* (Paris, France, 2001).

Emile Laloy, *La Révolte de Messine, l'expédition de Sicile et la politique française en Italie (1674–1678)* (Paris, France, 1929) 2 vols.

Nicolas Le Roux, *Les Guerres de Religion 1559–1629* (Paris, France, 2009).

Wayne Lee, *Waging War. Conflict, Culture and Innovation in World History* (Oxford, UK, 2016).

Benjamin Lellouch, 'Puissance et justice retenue du sultan ottoman: les massacres sur les fronts iranien et égyptien', *Le Massacre, objet d'histoire*, David El Kenz, ed., Paris, France, 2005, 171–82.

Padraig Lenihan, 'War and population 1649–1652', *Irish Economic and Social History*, 24, 1997, 1–21.

Padraig Lenihan, 'Unhappy campers: Dundalk (1689) and after', *Journal of Conflict Archaeology*, 2007, 196–216.

Padraig Lenihan, 'Namur citadel 1695: a case study in Allied siege tactics', *War in History*, 19, 2011, 282–303.

Padraig Lenihan, *Fluxes, Fevers and Fighting Men: War and Disease in Ancien Régime Europe 1648–1789* (Warwick, UK, 2019).

Jean-Denis Lepage, *Vauban and the French military under Louis XIV: An Illustrated History of Fortification and Strategies* (Jefferson, NC, 2010).

Gérard Lesage, *Denain (1712): Louis XIV sauve sa mise* (Paris, France, 1992).

Michel Lesure, *Lépante: crise de l'empire ottoman* (Paris, France, 1972).

Francis Loirette, *L'Etat et la region: L'Aquitaine au XVIIe siècle: centralisation monarchique, politique régionale et tensions sociales* (Bordeaux, France, 1998).

Sabina Loriga, *Soldats: Un laboratoire disciplinaire: l'armée piémontaise au XVIIIe siècle* (Paris, France, 1991).

Gérard Louis, *La Guerre de Dix Ans, 1634–1644* (Besançon, France, 1998).

Erik A Lund, *War for the Every Day: Generals, Knowledge and Warfare in Early Modern Europe 1680–1740* (Westport, CT, 1999).

John Lynn, 'How war fed war: the tax of violence and contributions during the Grand Siècle', *Journal of Modern History*, 65, 1993, 286–310.

John Lynn, 'Recalculating French army growth during the Grand Siècle, 1610–1715', *French Historical Studies*, 18, 1994, 881–906.

John A Lynn, *Giant of the Grand Siècle: The French Army 1610–1715* (Cambridge, UK, 1997).

John A Lynn, *The Wars of Louis XIV 1667–1714* (London, UK, 1999).

John A Lynn, *Women, Armies and Warfare in Early Modern Europe* (Cambridge, UK, 2008).

John A Lynn, 'Honourable surrender in early modern European history 1500–1789', *How Fighting Ends: A History of Surrender*, H Afflerbach & H Strachan, eds, Oxford, UK, 2012, 99–110.

Davide Maffi, 'Il Potere delle armi: la monarchia spagnola e i suoi eserciti (1635–1700): Una revisitazione del mito della decadenza', *Rivista Storica Italiana*, 118, 2006, 394–445.

Davide Maffi, *Il Baluardo della Corona: Guerra, esercito, finanze e società nella Lombardia Seicentesca (1630–1660)* (Florence, Italy, 2007).

Davide Maffi, *La Cittadella in Armi: Esercito, società e finanza nella Lombardia di Carlo II 1660–1700* (Milan, Italy, 2010).

Noel Malcolm, *Bosnia: A Short History* (Basingstoke, UK, 1994).

Dorothée Malfoy-Noël, *L'Epreuve de la bataille (1700–1714)* (Montpellier, France, 2007).

Michael Mallett & John Hale, *The Military Organization of a Renaissance State* (Cambridge, UK, 1984).

Michael Mallett and Christine Shaw, *The Italian Wars: 1494–1559: War, State and Society in Early Modern Europe* (London, UK, 2012).

Golo Mann, *Wallenstein: His Life Narrated* (New York, 1976).

Roger Manning, *An Apprenticeship in Arms: The Origins of the British Army* (Oxford, UK, 2006).

Robert Mantran, 'La Navigation vénitienne et ses concurrentes en Mediterranée orientale aux XVIIe et XVIIIe siècles', *Mediterraneo e Oceano indiano*, Manlio Cortelazzo, ed., Florence, 1970, 375–91.

Lionel Marquis, *Les Soldats de Louis XIV* (Versailles, France, 2015).

Luigi Ferdinando Marsigli, *L'Etat militaire de l'Empire ottoman*, (Amsterdam, the Netherlands, 1732).

Pieter Martens, 'La Puissance de l'artillerie de Charles Quint au milieu du XVIe siècle: Le siège de Thérouanne en 1553', *Artillerie et fortification 1200–1600*, N. Faucherre, N. Prouteau, E. de Crouy-Chanel, eds, Rennes, 2011, 119–42.

Philippe Martin, *Une guerre de Trente Ans en Lorraine 1631–1661* (Metz, France, 2002).

Lauro Martines, *Furies: War in Europe 1450–1700* (New York, 2013).

Bernard Masson, 'Un aspect de la discipline dans les armées de Louis XIII: la lutte contre la désertion du soldat 1635–1643', *Revue Historique des Armées*, 162, 1986, 12–23.

Vaclav Matoušek, 'Building a model of a field fortification of the Thirty Years' War near Olbramov (Czech Republic)', *Journal of Conflict Archaeology*, 2005, 114–32.

Roy L McCullough, *Coercion, Conversion and Counterinsurgency in Louis XIV's France* (Leiden, the Netherlands, 2007).

Derek McKay, *The Great Elector* (Harlow, UK, 2001).

William H. McNeill, *Keeping Together in Time: Dance and Drill in Human History* (Cambridge, MA, 1995).

John A Mears, 'The influence of the Turkish Wars in Hungary on the military theories of Count Raimondo Montecuccoli', *Asia and the West: Encounters and Exchanges in the Age of Explorations*, C Pullapilly & E Van Kley, eds, n.p. Columbia, MD, 1986, 129–45.

Jean Meuvret, 'Louis XIV et l'Italie', *XVIIe siècle*, 46–47 1960, 84–102.

William Miller, *Essays on the Latin Orient* (Cambridge, UK, 1921).

Luciana Miotto, 'Francesco Maria della Rovere et les nouvelles fortifications de Pesaro', *Les Guerres d'Italie: histoire, pratiques, représentations*, D. Boillet & M. F. Piéjus, eds, Paris, France, 2002, 179–90.

Ruth Mohrmann, 'Everyday life in war and peace', *1648: War and Peace in Europe*, K Bussmann & H Schilling, eds, Munster/Osnabruck, Germany, 1998, 319–28.

Charles Monchicourt, *L'Expédition espagnole de 1560 contre l'Ile de Djerba* (Paris, France, 1913).

Raimondo Montecuccoli, *Mémoires de Montecuculi, généralissime des troupes de l'Empereur, divisé en trois livres* (Amsterdam, the Netherlands, 1752).

J.A. de Moor, 'Experience and experiment: some reflections upon the military developments in 16th and 17th-century Western Europe', *Exercise of Arms: Warfare in the Netherlands 1568–1648*, Marco van der Hoeven, ed., Leiden, the Netherlands, 1997, 17–32.

Paolo Morachiello, 'Candia: I baluardi del Regno', *Venezia e la difesa del Levante, da Lepanto a Candia 1570–1670*, M Redolfi, ed., Venice, Italy, 1986, 133–43.

Geoff Mortimer, 'Individual experience and perception of the Thirty Years' War in eyewitness personal accounts', *German History*, 20, 2002, 141–60.

Geoff Mortimer, 'War by contract, credit and contribution: the Thirty Years' War', *Early Modern Military History 1450–1815*, G. Mortimer, ed., Basingstoke, UK, 2004, 101–17.

Geoff Mortimer, *Wallenstein: The Enigma of the Thirty Years' War* (Basingstoke, UK, 2010).

Rory Muir, *Tactics and the Experience of Battle in the Age of Napoleon* (New Haven, CT, 1998).

Steve Murdoch, Kathrin Zickermann & Adam Marks, 'The battle of Wittstock 1636', *Northern Studies*, 43, 2012, 71–109.

Rhoads Murphey, *Ottoman Warfare 1500–1700* (London, UK, 1999).

Michel Nassiet, 'La noblesse à l'époque moderne: une démilitarisation ?', *Enquêtes et Documents*, 25, 1998, 91–104.

Frédéric Naulet, *L'Artillerie française (1665–1765): Naissance d'une arme* (Paris, France, 2002).

David Nicolle, *Ottoman Fortifications, 1300–1710* (Oxford, 2010).

Olaf van Nimwegen, *The Dutch Army and the Military Revolutions 1588–1688* (Woodbridge, UK, 2010).

Brent Nosworthy, *The Anatomy of Victory: Battle Tactics 1689–1763* (New York, 1990).

Jean Nouzille, *Le Prince Eugène de Savoie et le sud-est européen (1683–1736)* (Paris, France, 2012).

Hugo O'Donnell, Duque de Estrada, 'El reposo del ejercito: Estudio del campamento temporal del tiempo de los Austrias', *Guerra y Sociedad en la Monarquia Hispanica: Politica, Estrategia y cultura en la Europa Moderna (1500–1700)*, E Garcia Hernan & Davide Maffi, eds, Madrid, 2006, 381–99.

Brian Hugh St. John O'Neil, *Castles and Cannon: A Study of Early Artillery Fortifications in England* (Oxford, UK, 1960).

Jane Ohlmeyer, 'The Civil Wars in Ireland', *The Civil Wars: A military history of England, Scotland and Ireland 1638–1660*, John Kenyon, Jane Ohlmeyer & John Morrill, eds, Oxford, UK, 1998, 73–102.

Francisco Felipe Olesa Muñido, *La Organizacion naval de los estados mediterraneos y en especial de España durante los siglos XVI y XVII* (Madrid, 1968).

Giulio Ongaro, *Peasants and Soldiers: The Management of the Venetian Military Structure in the Mainland Dominion between the 16th and 17th Centuries* (London, UK, 2017).

Robert Oresko, 'The house of Savoy in search for a royal crown in the seventeenth century', *Royal and Republican Sovereignty in Early Modern Europe: Essays in Memory of Ragnhild Hatton*, Robert Oresko, GC Gibbs & HM Scott, eds, Cambridge, UK, 1997, 272–350.

Jamel Ostwald, 'The decisive battle of Ramillies 1706: prerequisites for decisiveness in early modern warfare', *Journal of Military History*, 64, 2000, 649–77.

Jamel Ostwald, *Vauban under Siege: Engineering Efficiency and Martial Vigor in the War of the Spanish Succession* (Leiden, the Netherlands, 2007).

Jamel Ostwald, 'Louis XIV aimait-il trop la bataille?', *Les dernières guerres de Louis XIV 1688–1715*, H Drévillon, B Fonck & JP Cénat, eds, Rennes, 2017, 99–120.

Clément Oury, Les défaites françaises de la guerre de Succession d'Espagne, 1704–1708, Thèse de Doctorat, (Université de Paris IV-Sorbonne, 2011).

Clément Oury, 'L'efficacité du fer et du feu dans les batailles de la guerre de Succession d'Espagne', *Combattre et Gouverner: Dynamiques de l'histoire militaire de l'époque moderne (XVIIe–XVIIIe siècle)*, B Fonck & N Genet-Rouffiac, eds, Rennes, France, 2015, 37–51.

Clément Oury, 'Au coeur de la bataille: l'expérience des combats de la guerre de Succession d'Espagne', *Les dernières guerres de Louis XIV 1688–1715*, H Drévillon, B Fonck & J-P Cénat, eds, Rennes, France, 2017, 121–41.

Quentin Outram, 'The demographic impact of early modern warfare', *Social Science History*, 26, 2002, 245–72.

Didier Ozanam, 'La restauration de l'Etat espagnol au début du règne de Philippe V (1700–1724): le problème des hommes', *Philippe V d'Espagne et l'Art de son temps*, S Osorio-Robin, ed., Sceaux, France, 1995, 79–90.

Geza Palffy, 'Ransom slavery along the Ottoman-Hungarian frontier in the 16th and 17th centuries', *Ransom Slavery along the Ottoman Borders (Early 15th–Early 18th Centuries)*, Geza David & Pal Fodor, eds, Leiden, the Netherlands, 2007, 35–83.

Geza Palffy, *The Kingdom of Hungary and the Habsburg Monarchy in the Sixteenth Century* (Boulder, CO, 2009).

Geoffrey Parker, *The Army of Flanders and the Spanish Road 1567–1659: The Logistics of Spanish Victory and Defeat in the Low Countries' Wars* (Cambridge, UK, 1972).

Geoffrey Parker, *The Dutch Revolt* (Harmondsworth, UK, 1977).

Geoffrey Parker, *The Thirty Years' War* (London, UK, 1984).

Geoffrey Parker, 'The etiquette of atrocity: the laws of war in early modern Europe', *Empire, War and Faith in Early Modern Europe*, Harmondsworth, UK, 2002, 143–68.

David Parrott, 'Strategy and tactics in the Thirty Years' War: the 'military revolution' revisited', *Militargeschichtliche Mitteilungen*, 38/2, 1985, 7–25.

David Parrott, 'French military organization in the 1630s: the failure of Richelieu's ministry', *Seventeenth Century French Studies*, 9, 1987, 151–67.

David Parrott, 'Richelieu, the Grands and the French army', *Richelieu and his Age*, J Bergin & L Brockliss, eds, Oxford, UK, 1992, 137–73.

David Parrott, 'The role of fortifications in the defence of states: the Farnese and the security of Parma and Piacenza', *I Farnese: Corti, Guerra e nobiltà in Antico Regime*, A. Bilotto, P. Del Negro, C. Mozzarelli, eds, Rome, 1997, 509–60.

David Parrott, *Richelieu's Army: War, Government and Society in France, 1624 to 1642* (Cambridge, UK, 2001).

David Parrott, 'Cultures of combat in the Ancien Régime: Linear warfare, noble values and entrepreneurship', *International History Review*, 27, 2005, 518–33.

David Parrott, 'The utility of fortifications in early modern Europe: Italian princes and their citadels', *War in History*, 7, 2007, 127–53.

David Parrott, *The Business of War: Military Enterprise and Military Revolution in Early Modern Europe* (Cambridge, UK, 2012).

David Parrott, 'The military enterpriser in the Thirty Years' War', *War, Entrepreneurs and the State in Europe and the Mediterranean 1300–1800*, Jeff Fynn-Paul, ed., Leiden, the Netherlands, 2014, 63–86.

James M Paton, *The Venetians in Athens 1687–1688, from the Istoria of Cristoforo Ivanovich* (Cambridge, MA, 1940).

Radu Paun, 'Enemies within: Networks of influence and the military revolts against the Ottoman power (Moldavia and Wallachia, 16th-17th centuries)', *The European Tributary States of the Ottoman Empire in the Sixteenth and Seventeenth Centuries*, G Karman & L Kuncevic, eds, Leiden, the Netherlands, 2013, 209–49.

Marco Pellegrini, *Le Guerre d'Italia* (Bologna, Italy, 2009).

Simon Pepper & Nicholas Adams, *Firearms and Fortifications: Military Architecture and Siege Warfare in 16th Century Siena* (Chicago, IL, 1986).

Simon Pepper, 'Castles and cannon in the Naples campaign of 1494–1495', *The French Descent into Renaissance Italy 1494–1495: Antecedents and Effects*, D. Abulafia, ed., Aldershot, UK, 1995, 263–91.

Simon Pepper, 'Aspects of operational art: communications, cannon and small war', *European Warfare 1350–1750*, F Tallett, ed., Cambridge, UK, 2000, 181–202.

Geza Perjés, 'Army provisioning, logistics and strategy in the second half of the seventeenth century', *Acta Historica Academiae Scientiarum Hungaricae*, 16, 1970, 1–51.

Angelo Pernice, 'Un episodio del valore toscano nelle guerre di Valacchia alla fine del secolo XVI', *Archivio Storico Italiano*, 1925, 249–97.

Jean-Christian Petitfils, *Louis XIII* (Paris, France, 2008).

Luciano Pezzolo, 'Aspetti della struttura militare veneziana in Levante fra Cinque e Seicento', *Venezia e la difesa del Levante, da Lepanto a Candia 1570–1670*, Maddalena Redolfi & Palazzo Ducale, eds, Venice, Italy, 1986, 86–96.

Luciano Pezzolo, 'Elogio della rendita: Sul debito pubblico degli Stati italiani nel Cinque e Seicento', *Rivista di Storia Economica*, 12, 1995, 283–328.

Sandrine Picaud, 'La 'guerre de partis' au XVIIe siècle en Europe', *Stratégique*, 88, 2007, 101–46.

Sandrine Picaud-Monnerat, *La Petite Guerre au XVIIIe siècle* (Paris, France, 2010).

Paola Piccoli & Simona Pruno, *Il Castello e le mura di Novara: Storia e progetti per una città fortezza tra il XVI e il XVII secolo* (Novara, Italy 2010).

Martha Pollak, *Turin 1564–1680: Urban Design, Military Culture and the Creation of the Absolutist Capital* (Chicago, IL, 1991).

Olivier Poncet, 'Rentes sur l'Hotel de Ville', *Dictionnaire de l'Ancien regime*, L. Bély, ed., Paris, France, 1996, 1079–81.

Luca Antonio Porzio, *The Soldier's Vademecum* (London, UK, 1747).

David Potter, *Renaissance France at War: Armies, Culture and Society c. 1480–1560* (London, 2008).

Maarten Prak, *The Dutch Republic in the Seventeenth Century* (Cambridge, UK, 2005).

Carlo Promis, *Biografie di Ingegneri militari italiani dal secolo XV alla metà del XVIII, 2 vols., Miscellanea di Storia Italiana t. 14* (Turin, Italy, 1874).

Réné Quatrefages, 'Un professionnel militaire: L'infante du Tercio', *L'Homme de guerre au XVIe siècle*, Gabriel-André Pérouse, André Thierry & André Tournon, eds, Saint-Etienne, France, 1992, 191–204.

Jean Quéniart, *La Révocation de l'Edit de Nantes: Protestants et catholiques français de 1598 à 1685* (Paris, France, 1985).

Evgeni Radushev, 'Peasant Janissaries?', *Journal of Social History*, 42, 2008, 447–67.

Charles Rahlenbeck, *Gilles de Haes* (Ghent, Belgium, 1854).

Richard Rapp, 'The unmaking of the Mediterranean trade hegemony: international trade rivalry and the commercial revolution', *Journal of Economic History*, 35, 1975, 499–525.

Fritz Redlich, *De Praeda Militari: Looting and Booty 1500–1815* (Wiesbaden, Germany, 1956).

Fritz Redlich, *The German Military Enterpriser and his Work Force: A Study in European Economic and Social History* (Wiesbaden, Germany, 1964).

Luis A. Ribot Garcia, 'Les types d'armée en Espagne au début des temps modernes', *Guerre et concurrence entre les Etats européens du XIVe au XVIIIe siècle*, P. Contamine, ed., Paris, France, 1998, 43–81.

Keith Roberts, *Matchlock Musketeer 1588–1688* (Oxford, UK, 2002).

NA Roberts, JW Brown, B Hammett & PDF Kingston, 'A detailed study of the effectiveness and capabilities of 18th-century musketry on the battlefield', *Journal of Conflict Archaeology*, 4, 2008, 1–21.

Gavin Robinson, 'Equine battering rams? A reassessment of cavalry charges in the English Civil War', *Journal of Military History*, 75, 2011, 719–31.

Daniel Roche *La Culture des apparences. Une histoire du vêtement (XVIIe–XVIIIe siècle)* (Paris, France, 2007).

N.A.M. Rodger, *The Command of the Ocean* (New York, 2004).

Antonio José Rodriguez Hernandez, 'El Ejercito que heredó Felipe V: su numero y su composición humana', *La Sucesión de la Monarquia Hispanica, 1665–1725:*

Biografías relevantes y procesos complejos, José Manuel de Bernardo Ares, ed., Madrid, Spain, 2009, 265–96.

Karl Roider, *The Reluctant Ally: Austria's policy in the Austro-Turkish War, 1737–1739* (Baton Rouge, LA, 1972).

Guy Rowlands, *The Dynastic State and the Army under Louis XIV: Royal Service and Private Interest 1661–1701* (Cambridge, UK, 2002).

Guy Rowlands, *The Financial Decline of a Great Power: War, Influence and Money in Louis XIV's France* (Oxford, UK, 2012).

Guy Rowlands, 'Les armées de Louis XIV comme sociétés de cour', *Combattre et gouverner: Dynamiques de l'histoire militaire de l'époque moderne (XVIIe–XVIIIe siècles)*, Bertrand Fonck & Nathalie Genet-Rouffiac, eds, Rennes, France, 2015, 281–96.

Guy Rowlands, 'Géostratégie et poids de la guerre à la fin du règne de Louis XIV', *Combattre et gouverner: Dynamique de l'histoire militaire de l'époque moderne (XVIIe–XVIIIe siècles)*, B Fonck & N Genet-Rouffiac, eds, Rennes, France, 2017, 261–66.

François Royal, 'Les quartiers d'hiver des armées: pause et continuité dans la guerre. L'exemple de l'armée de Flandre entre les campagnes de 1711 et 1712', *Combattre et gouverner: Dynamiques de l'histoire militaire de l'époque moderne (XVIIe–XVIIIe siècles)*, Bertrand Fonck & Natalie Genet-Rouffiac, eds, Rennes, France, 2015, 75–89.

François Royal, 'A l'aube de la campagne: l'impact du quartier d'hiver dans la campagne de Flandre de 1712', *Les Dernières guerres de Louis XIV 1688–1715*, H Drévillon, B Fonck & J-P Cénat, eds, Rennes, France, 2017, 205–26.

Fernando Sanchez-Marcos, 'The struggle for freedom in Catalonia and in Portugal', *1648: War and Peace in Europe*, K Bussmann & H Schilling, eds, Munster/Osnabruck, Germany, 1998, vol. 1, 207–13.

Brian Sandberg, 'The magazine of all their pillaging: Armies as sites of second-hand exchanges during the French Wars of Religion', *Alternative Exchanges: Second-hand Circulations from the 16th Century to the Present*, L Fontaine, ed., New York, 2008, 76–96.

Brian Sandberg, *Warrior Pursuits: Noble Culture and Civil Conflict in Early Modern France* (Baltimore, MD, 2010).

Tommaso Sandonnini, *Il Generale Raimondo Monteuccoli e la sua famiglia* (Modena, Italy, 1913).

F Sassi, 'Le campagne di Dalmazia durante la guerra di Candia (1645–1658)', *Nuovo Archivio Veneto*, 19–20, 1936–1937, 211–50, 21–22, 1937–1938, 60–100.

George Satterfield, *Princes, Posts and Partisans: The Army of Louis XIV and Partisan Warfare in the Netherlands 1673–1678* (Leiden, the Netherlands, 2003).

Jean-Frédéric Schaub, 'La crise hispanique de 1640: le modèle des 'révolutions périphériques' en question', *Annales: Histoire, Sciences sociales*, 49, 1994, 218–40.

Christoph Seidler, 'Mass grave begins revealing soldiers' secrets', *Der Spiegel Online*, 27 April 2012.

Kenneth Setton, *The Papacy and the Levant (1204–1571): vol. IV, The Sixteenth Century from Julius III to Pius V* (Philadelphia, PA, 1984).

Idan Sherer, *Warriors for a Living: The Experience of the Spanish Infantry in the Italian Wars 1494–1559* (Leiden, the Netherlands, 2017).

Louis Sicking, 'Naval warfare in Europe c.1330–c.1680', *European Warfare 1350–1750*, Frank Tallett ed., Cambridge, UK, 2010, 236–63.

Louis Sicking, 'Selling and buying protection. Dutch war fleets at the service of Venice (1617–1667)', *Studi Veneziani*, 67, 2013, 89–106.

Louis Sicking, 'Islands, pirates, privateers and the Ottoman Empire in the early modern Mediterranean', *Seapower, Technology and Trade: Studies in Turkish Maritime History*, Dejanirah Couto, Feza Emergun, Maria Pia Pedani, eds, Istanbul, 2014, 239–52.

Gianvittorio Signorotto, 'Il marchese di Caracena al Governo di Milano (1648–1656)', *Cheiron*, 17–18, 1993, 135–81.

B.J. Slot, *Archipelagus Turbatus: Les Cyclades entre colonisation latine et occupation ottomane, c.1500–1718*, 2 vols. (Leiden, the Netherlands, 1982).

Carla Sodini, *L'Ercole Tirreno: Guerra e dinastia medicea nella prima metà del '600* (Florence, Italy, 2001).

Violet Soen, 'Reconquista and reconciliation in the Dutch Revolt: the campaign of Governor-General Alexander Farnese (1578–1592)', *Journal of Early Modern History*, 16, 2012, 1–22.

Pierre-Jean Souriac, *Une Guerre civile: Affrontements religieux et militaires dans le Midi Toulousain (1562–1596)* (Seyssel, France, 2008).

Giorgio Spini, 'Introduzione', *Architettura e politica da Cosimo I a Ferdinando I*, G. Spini, ed., Florence, Italy, 1976, 9–77.

Laurence Spring, *The First British Army 1624–1628: The Army of the Duke of Buckingham* (Solihull, UK, 2016).

Laurence Spring, *The Bavarian Army during the Thirty Years' War: The Backbone of the Catholic League* (Solihull, UK, 2017).

Peter Spufford, 'Access to credit and capital in the commercial centres of Europe', *A Miracle Mirrored: The Dutch Republic in European Perspective*, K Davids & Jan Lucassen, eds, Cambridge, UK, 1995, 303–337.

Stewart Stansfield, *Early Modern Systems of Command: Queen Anne's Generals, Staff Officers and the Direction of Allied Warfare in the Low Countries and Germany 1702–1711* (Solihull, UK, 2016).

John M Stapleton, 'The Dual Monarchy in Practice: Anglo-Dutch Alliance and War in the Spanish Netherlands 1689–1697', *Redefining William III: The Impact of the King-Statholder in International Context*, Esther Mijers & David Onnekink, ed., Aldershot, UK, 2007, 69–90.

John M Stapleton, 'Marlborough, the allies and the campaigns in the Low Countries 1702–1706', *Marlborough, Soldier and Diplomat*, John Hattendorf, Augustus Veenendaal & Rolof van Hövel Tot Westerflier, eds, Rotterdam, the Netherlands, 2012, 145–71.

Mark L. Stein, *Guarding the Frontier: Ottoman Border Forts and Garrisons in Europe* (London, UK, 2007).

Christopher Storrs, 'Health, sickness and medical services in Spain's armed forces c. 1665–1700', *Medical History*, 50, 2006, 325–50.

Christopher Storrs, 'Imperial authority and the levy of contributions in 'Reichsitalien' in the Nine Years War (1690–1696)', *L'Impero e l'Italia nella prima età moderna*, M Schnettger & M Verga, eds, Bologna, Italy, 2006, 241–73.

Christopher Storrs, *The Spanish Resurgence 1713–1748* (New Haven, CT, 2016).

John Stoye, *The Siege of Vienna* (London, UK, 1964).

Robert Stradling, *Europe and the Decline of Spain: A Study of the Spanish System, 1580–1720* (London, UK, 1981).

Robert Stradling, *The Armada of Flanders. Spanish Maritime Policy and European War, 1568–1668* (Cambridge, UK, 1992).

Erik Swart, 'From 'Landsknecht' to 'soldier': the low German foot soldiers of the Low Countries in the second half of the 16th century', *International Review of Social History*, 51, 2006, 75–92.

Erik Swart, 'Qualifications, knowledge and courage: Dutch military engineers c. 1550–c. 1660', *Military Engineers and the Development of the Early Modern European State*, BP Lenman, ed., Dundee, Scotland, 2013, 47–70.

Geoffrey Symcox, *Victor Amadeus II: Absolutism in the Savoyard State 1675–1730* (Berkeley, CA, 1983).

Janos Szabo, 'Splendid isolation? The military cooperation of the principality of Transylvania with the Ottoman Empire (1571–1688) in the mirror of the Hungarian Historiography's dilemmas', *The European Tributary States of the Ottoman Empire in the 16th and 17th Centuries*, G Karman & L Kuncevic, eds, Leiden, the Netherlands, 2013, 301–339.

Frank Tallett, *War and Society in Early Modern Europe* (London, UK, 1992).

Angelo Tamborra, 'Dopo Lepanto: lo spostamento della lotta anti-Turca sul fronte terrestre', *Il Mediterraneo nella seconda metà del '500 alla luce di Lepanto*, Gino Benzoni, ed., Florence, 1974, 371–91.

Evliya Tchélébi, *La Guerre des Turcs: récits de batailles (extraits du 'Livre de voyages)*, translation and introduction Faruk Bilici (Arles, France, 2000).

Osmân de Temechvar, *Prisonnier des Infidèles: un soldat ottoman dans l'Empire des Habsbourg*, translation & introduction Frédéric Hitzel (Arles, France, 1998).

Alberto Tenenti, *Piracy and the Decline of Venice 1580–1615* (London, 1967).

Charles Terlinden, *Le Pape Clément IX et la guerre de Candie, 1667–1669, d'après les archives sécrètes du Saint-Siège* (Louvain, Belgium, 1904).

John Thiebault, 'The demography of the Thirty Years' War re-visited: Gunther Franz and his critics', *German History*, 15, 1997, 1–21.

Andrea Thiele, 'The Prince as military entrepreneur? Why smaller Saxon territories sent 'Holländische Regimenter' to the Dutch Republic', *War, Entrepreneurs and the State in Europe and the Mediterranean 1300–1800*, Jeff Fynn-Paul, ed., Leiden, the Netherlands, 2014, 170–92.

I.A.A. Thompson, *War and Government in Habsburg Spain 1560–1620* (London, UK, 1976).

I.A.A. Thompson, 'El soldado del Imperio: una aproximacion al perfil del recluta español en el Siglo de Oro', *Manuscrits* 21, 2003, 17–38.

Rafael Torres Sánchez, *Military Entrepreneurs and the Spanish Contractor State in the Eighteenth Century* (Oxford, UK, 2016).

Ferenc Toth, *Saint-Gotthard 1664: Une bataille européenne* (Limoges, France, 2007).

James D Tracy, *Emperor Charles V, Impresario of War: Campaign Strategy, International Finance and Domestic Politics* (Cambridge, UK, 2002).

James D Tracy, 'The road to Szigetvar: Ferdinand I's defense of the Hungarian border, 1548–1566', *Austrian History Yearbook*, 44, 2013, 17–36.

James D Tracy, 'The Habsburg monarchy in conflict with the Ottoman Empire 1527–1593: a clash of civilizations', *Austrian History Yearbook*, 46, 2015, 1–26.

James D Tracy, *Balkan Wars: Habsburg Croatia, Ottoman Bosnia and Venetian Dalmatia, 1499–1617* (Lanham, MD, 2016).

Giuseppe Tricoli, *Un periodo del governo spagnolo di Sicilia nella relazione del Viceré Uzeda (1687–1696)* (Palermo, Italy, 1980).

Allan A. Tulchin, 'Massacres during the French wars of religion', *Past and Present*, 214 supplement 7, 2012, 100–26.

Otto Ulbricht, 'The experience of violence during the Thirty Years' War: a look at the civilian victims', *Power, Violence and Mass Death in Pre-modern and Modern Times*, J Canning, H Lehmann & J Winter, eds, Burlington, VT, 2004, 97–129.

Mesut Uyar & Edward J Erickson, *A Military History of the Ottomans, from Osman to Ataturk* (Santa Barbara, CA, 2009).

Apostolos Vacalopoulos, *The Greek Nation 1453–1669: The Cultural and Economic Background of Modern Greek Society* (New Brunswick, NJ, 1976).

Ivo Van Loo, 'For freedom and fortune: the rise of Dutch privateering in the first half of the Dutch Revolt', *Exercise of Arms: Warfare in the Netherlands 1568–1648*, Marco Van der Hoeven, ed., Leiden, the Netherlands, 1997, 173–95.

James A Vann, *The Making of a State: Wurttemburg 1593–1793* (Ithaca, NY, 1984).

Gilles Veinstein, 'L'empire dans sa grandeur', *Histoire de l'Empire ottoman*, Robert Mantran, ed., Paris, 1989, 159–226.

Gilles Veinstein, 'On the Ottoman Janissaries (fourteenth–nineteenth centuries)' *Fighting for a Living: A Comparative History of Military Labour 1500–2000*, Erik-Jan Zurcher, ed., Amsterdam, 2013, 115–35.

Michel Vergé-Franceschi, *Colbert: La politique du bon sens* (Paris, France, 2003).

Laurent Vergez, *Rocoux 1746: Bataille et combats pendant la guerre en dentelles* (Le Coudray-Macouard, France, 2016).

Hélène Vérin, *La Gloire des ingénieurs: L'intelligence technique du XVIe au XVIIIe siècle* (Paris, France, 1993).

Antonio di Vittorio, 'Un caso di correlazione tra guerre, spese militari e cambiamenti economici: le guerre asburgiche della prima metà del XVIII secolo e le loro ripercussioni sulla finanza e l'economia dell 'Impero', *Nuova Rivista Storica*, 66, 1982, 59–81.

Paul Vo-Ha, *Rendre les Armes: Le sort des vaincus XVIe–XVIIIe siècles* (Seyssel, France, 2017).

Hans Vogel, 'Arms production and exports in the Dutch Republic, 1600–1650', *Exercise of Arms: Warfare in the Netherlands, 1568–1648*, Marco van der Hoeven, ed., Leiden, the Netherlands, 1997, 197–210.

Jan de Vries & Adriaan van der Woude, *The First Modern Economy: Success, Failure and Perseverance of the Dutch Economy 1500–1815* (Cambridge, UK, 1997).

Wayne S. Vucinich, 'Prince-Bishop Danilo and his place in Montenegro's History', *East-Central European Society and War in the Pre-Revolutionary Eighteenth Century*, G.E. Rotheberg, B.K. Kiraly & P.F. Sugar, eds, Boulder, CO, 1982, 271–99.

Malcolm Wanklyn, *Decisive Battles of the English Civil Wars: Myth and Reality* (Barnsley, UK, 2006).

Hermann Weber, 'La stratégie de la terre brulée: le cas du Palatinat en 1689', *La Vendée dans l'Histoire: Actes du Colloque*, Alain Gérard & Thierry Heckmann, eds, Paris, 1994, 193–208.

Joachim Whaley, *Germany and the Holy Roman Empire: vol. 1, From Maximilian I to the Peace of Westphalia 1493–1648* (Oxford, UK, 2012).

Andrew Wheatcroft, *The Enemy at the Gate: Habsburgs, Ottomans and the Battle for Europe* (New York, 2008).

Spenser Wilkinson, *The Defence of Piedmont, 1742–1748* (Oxford, UK, 1927).

Phillip Williams, *Empire and Holy War in the Mediterranean: The Galley and Maritime Conflict between the Habsburg and Ottoman Empires* (London, UK, 2014).

Peter H Wilson, *German Armies; War and German Politics 1648–1806* (London, UK, 1998).

Peter H Wilson, *From Reich to Revolution: German History 1558–1806* (Basingstoke, UK, 2004).

Peter H Wilson, *The Thirty Years War: Europe's Tragedy* (Cambridge, MA, 2010).

Michael Wolfe, 'Walled towns during the French Wars of Religion', *City Walls: The Urban Enceinte in Global Perspective*, James D Tracy, ed., Cambridge, UK, 2000, 317–48.

James Wood, 'The impact of the wars of religion: a view of France in 1581', *Sixteenth Century Journal*, 15, 1984, 131–68.

Marvin Zuckerman, *Sensation-seeking and Risky Behavior* (Washington, DC, 2007).

H.L. Zwitzer, 'The Eighty Years War', *Exercise of Arms: Warfare in the Netherlands 1568–1648*, Marco Van der Hoeven, ed., Leiden, the Netherlands, 1997, 33–55.

Index